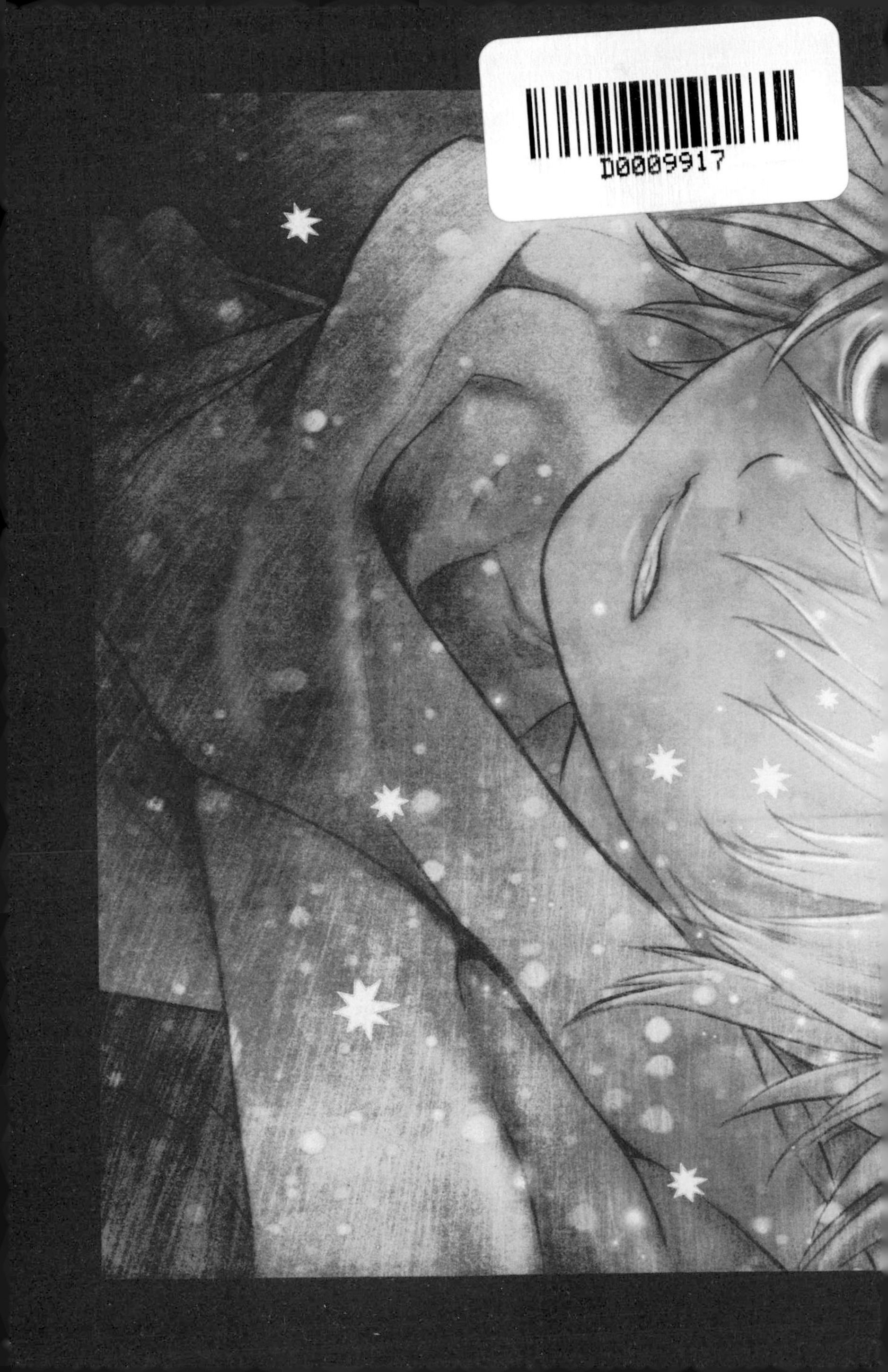

TEGAMI BACHI
LETTER · BEE

Volume 11

SHONEN JUMP Manga Edition

Story and Art by Hiroyuki Asada

English Adaptation/Rich Amtower
Translation/JN Productions
Touch-up & Lettering/Annaliese Christman
Design/Amy Martin
Editor/Shaenon K. Garrity

Printed in Canada

Published by VIZ Media, LLC
P.O. Box 77010
San Francisco, CA 94107

10 9 8 7 6 5 4 3 2 1
First printing, November 2012

RATED T FOR TEEN

PARENTAL ADVISORY
TEGAMI BACHI is rated T for Teen and is recommended for ages 13 and up. This volume contains fantasy violence and tobacco use.
ratings.viz.com

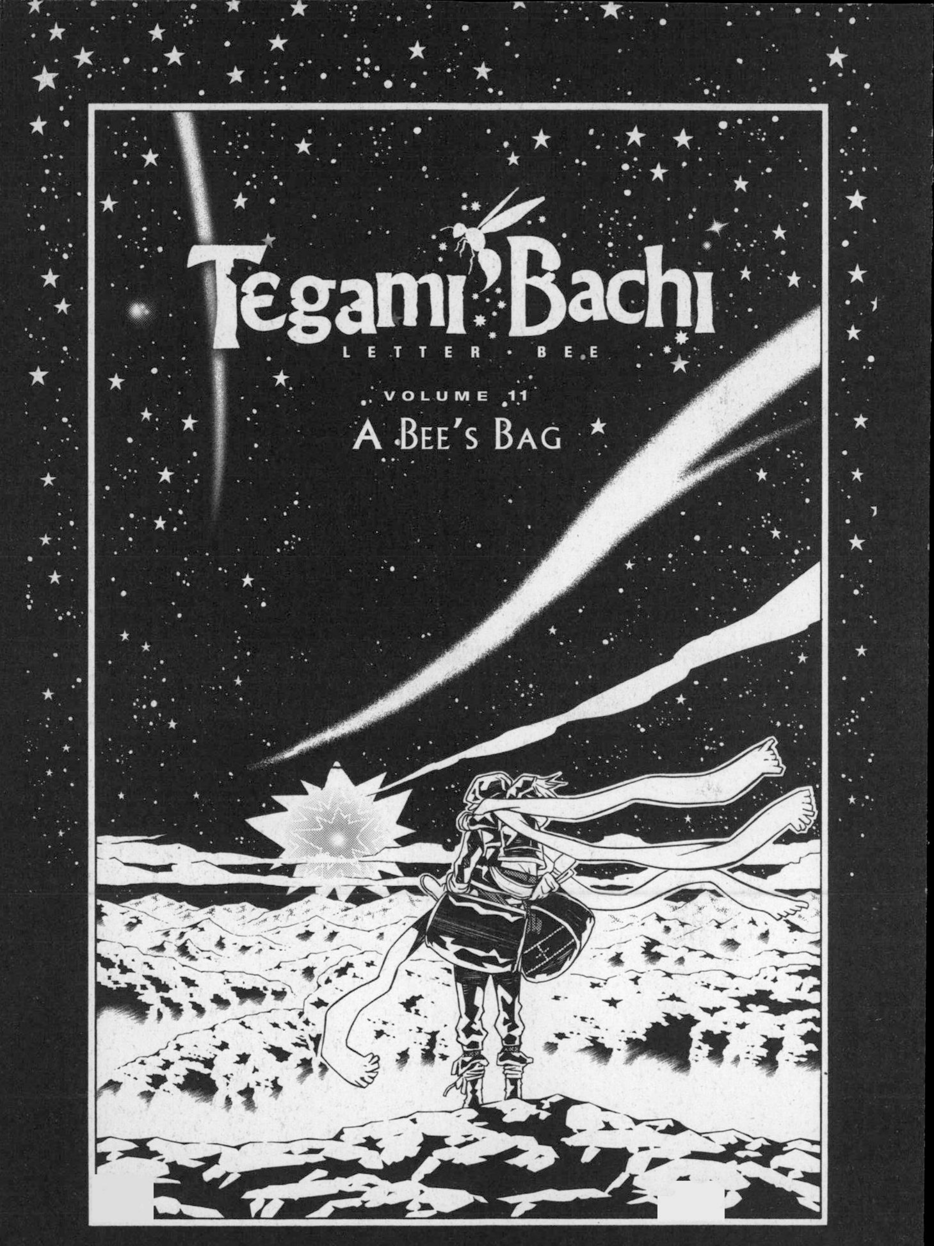
Tegami Bachi
LETTER · BEE
VOLUME 11
A Bee's Bag

This is a country known as Amberground, where night never ends.

Its capital, Akatsuki, is illuminated by a man-made sun. The farther one strays from the capital, the weaker the light. The Yuusari region is cast in twilight; the Yodaka region survives only on pale moonlight.

Letter Bee Gauche Suede and young Lag Seeing meet in the Yodaka region— a postal worker and the "letter" he must deliver. In their short time together, they form a fast friendship, but when the journey ends, each departs down his own path. Gauche longs to become Head Bee, while Lag himself wants to be a Letter Bee, like Gauche.

In time, Lag becomes a Letter Bee. He learns that Gauche has lost his *heart* and become a marauder named Noir, working for the rebel organization Reverse. After many adventures, Lag returns with the unconscious Gauche, throwing the Beehive into an uproar.

Two inspectors from the Capital, Garrard and Valentine, are sent to investigate. They fire Director Largo Lloyd and put Lag and Assistant Director Aria Link to work at the Dead Letter Office, processing "undeliverable" letters. In the course of their deliveries, Lag and Aria learn more about a mysterious accident in the past involving the man-made sun.

Meanwhile, Gauche has awakened, but whether he has truly regained his *heart* remains to be seen...

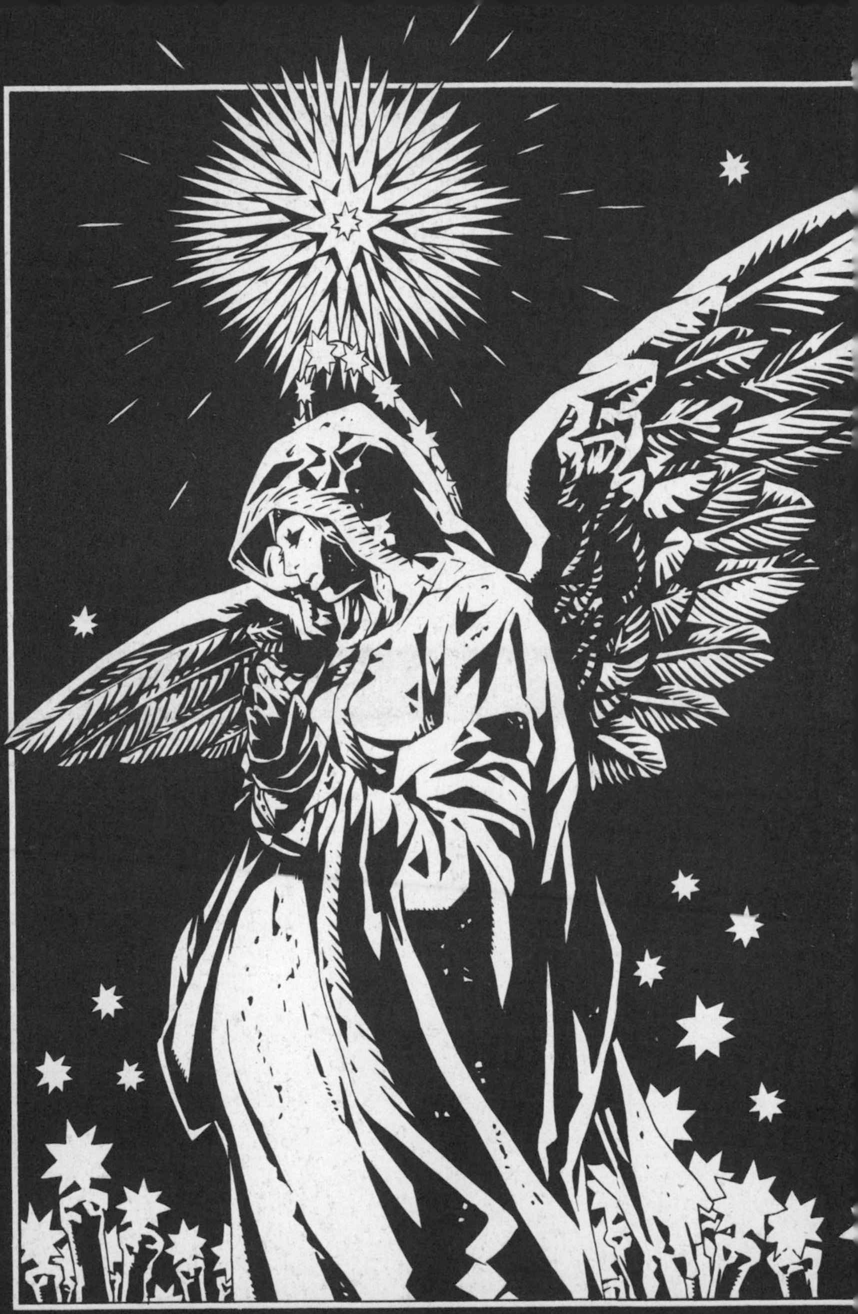

List of Characters

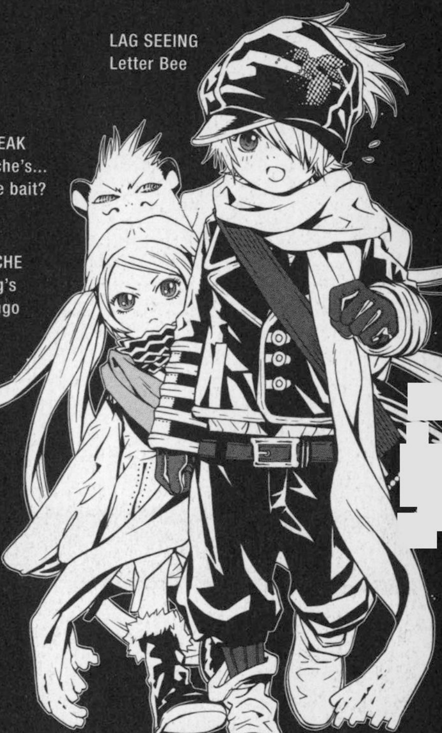

LAG SEEING
Letter Bee

STEAK
Niche's... live bait?

NICHE
Lag's Dingo

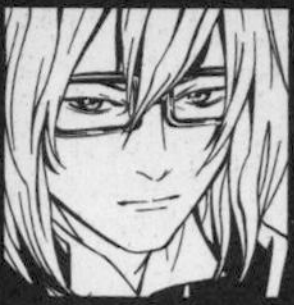

LARGO LLOYD
Beehive Director

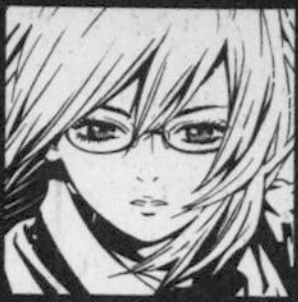

ARIA LINK
Beehive Assistant Director

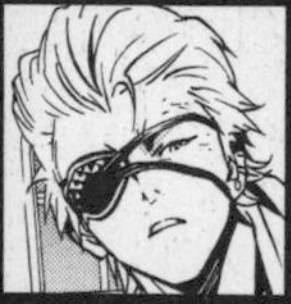

DR. THUNDERLAND, JR.
Member of the AG Biological Science Advisory Board, Third Division and head doctor at the Beehive

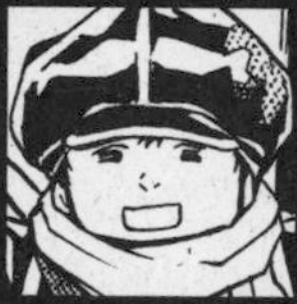

CONNOR KLUFF
Letter Bee

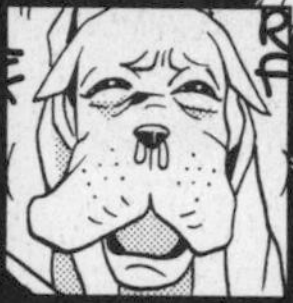

GUS
Connor's Dingo

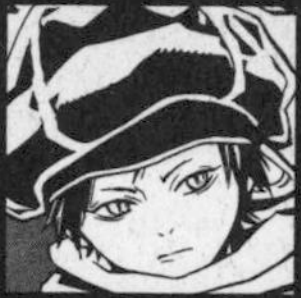

ZAZIE
Letter Bee

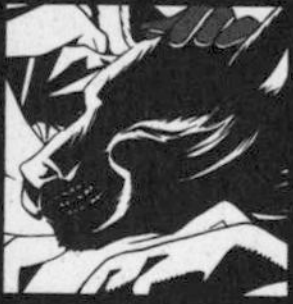

WASIOLKA
Zazie's Dingo

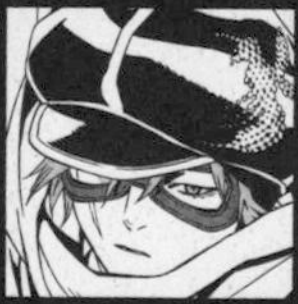

JIGGY PEPPER
Express Delivery Letter Bee

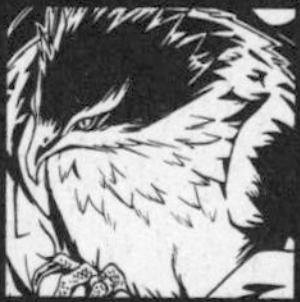

HARRY
Jiggy's Dingo

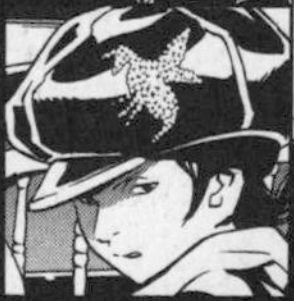

MOC SULLIVAN
Letter Bee

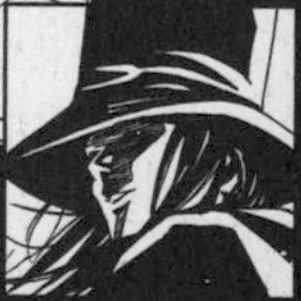

THE MAN WHO COULD NOT BECOME SPIRIT
The ringleader of Reverse

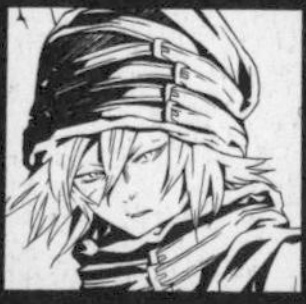

NOIR (FORMERLY GAUCHE SUEDE)
Marauder for Reverse and an ex–Letter Bee

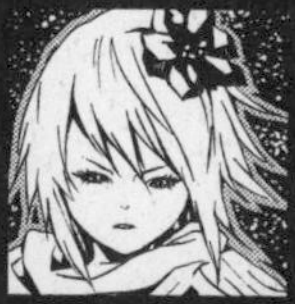

RODA
Noir's Dingo

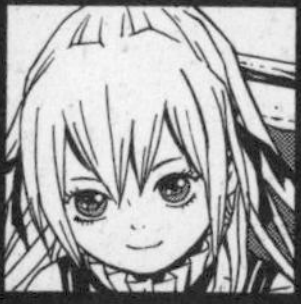

SYLVETTE SUEDE
Gauche's Sister

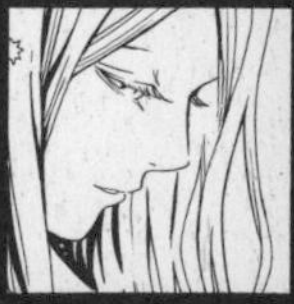

ANNE SEEING
Lag's Mother (Missing)

Tegami Bachi

LETTER · BEE

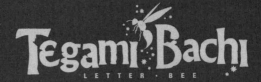

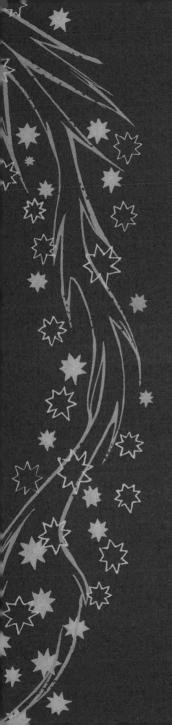

VOLUME 11

A Bee's Bag

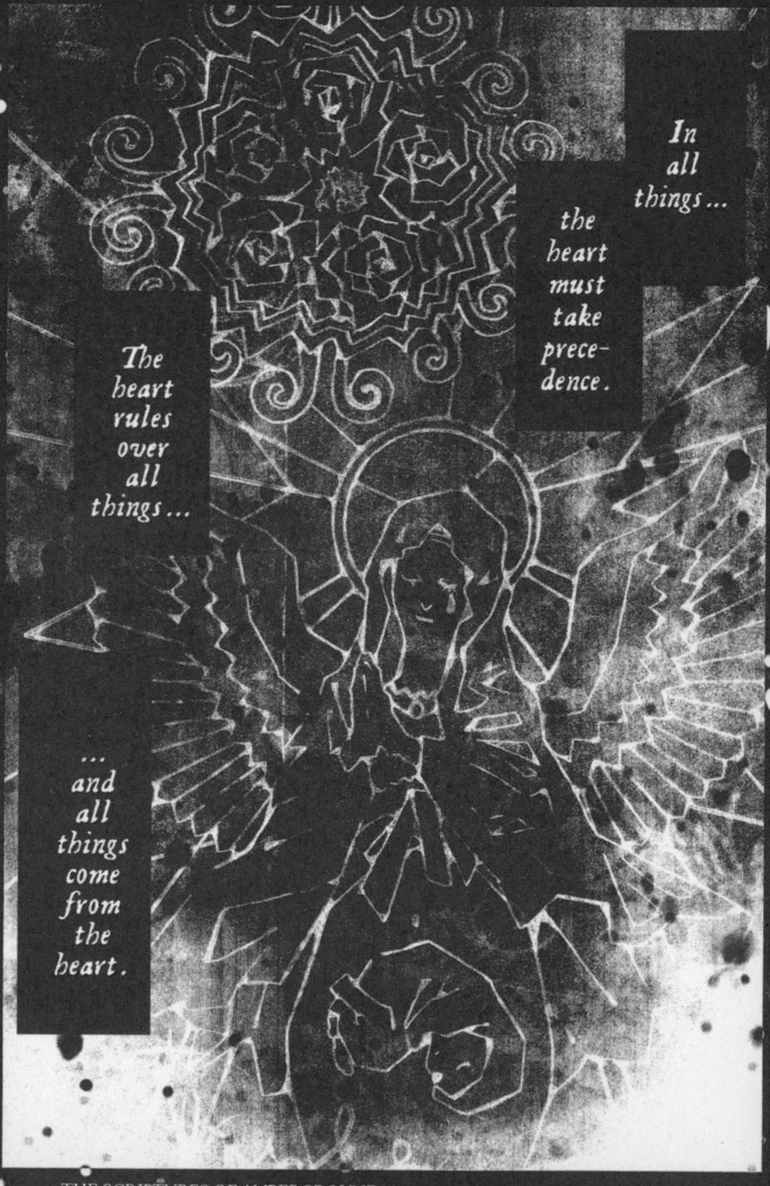
In all things...
the heart must take precedence.
The heart rules over all things...
... and all things come from the heart.

–THE SCRIPTURES OF AMBERGROUND, 1st verse

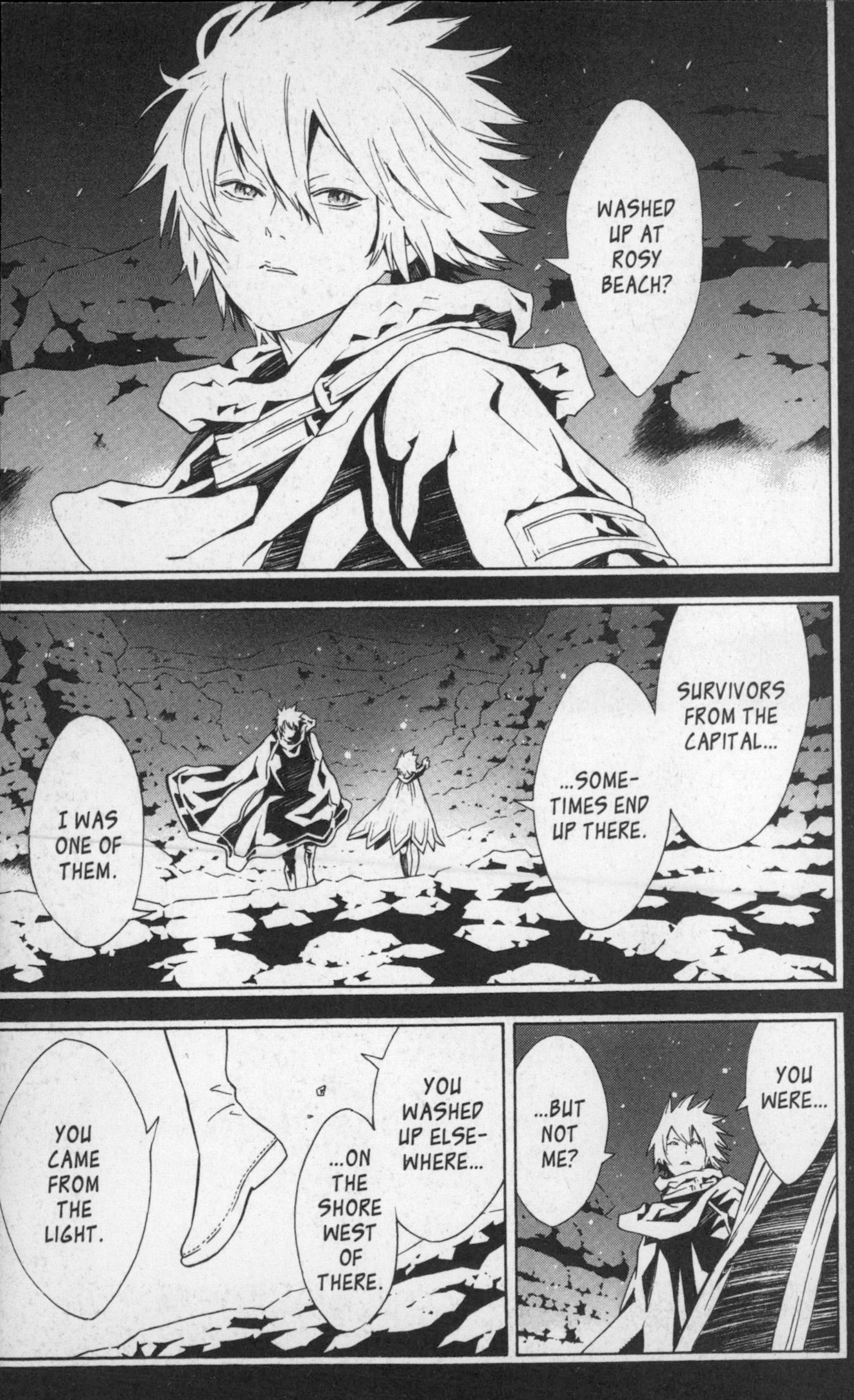
WASHED UP AT ROSY BEACH?
SURVIVORS FROM THE CAPITAL...
...SOME-TIMES END UP THERE.
I WAS ONE OF THEM.
YOU WERE...
...BUT NOT ME?
YOU WASHED UP ELSE-WHERE...
...ON THE SHORE WEST OF THERE.
YOU CAME FROM THE LIGHT.

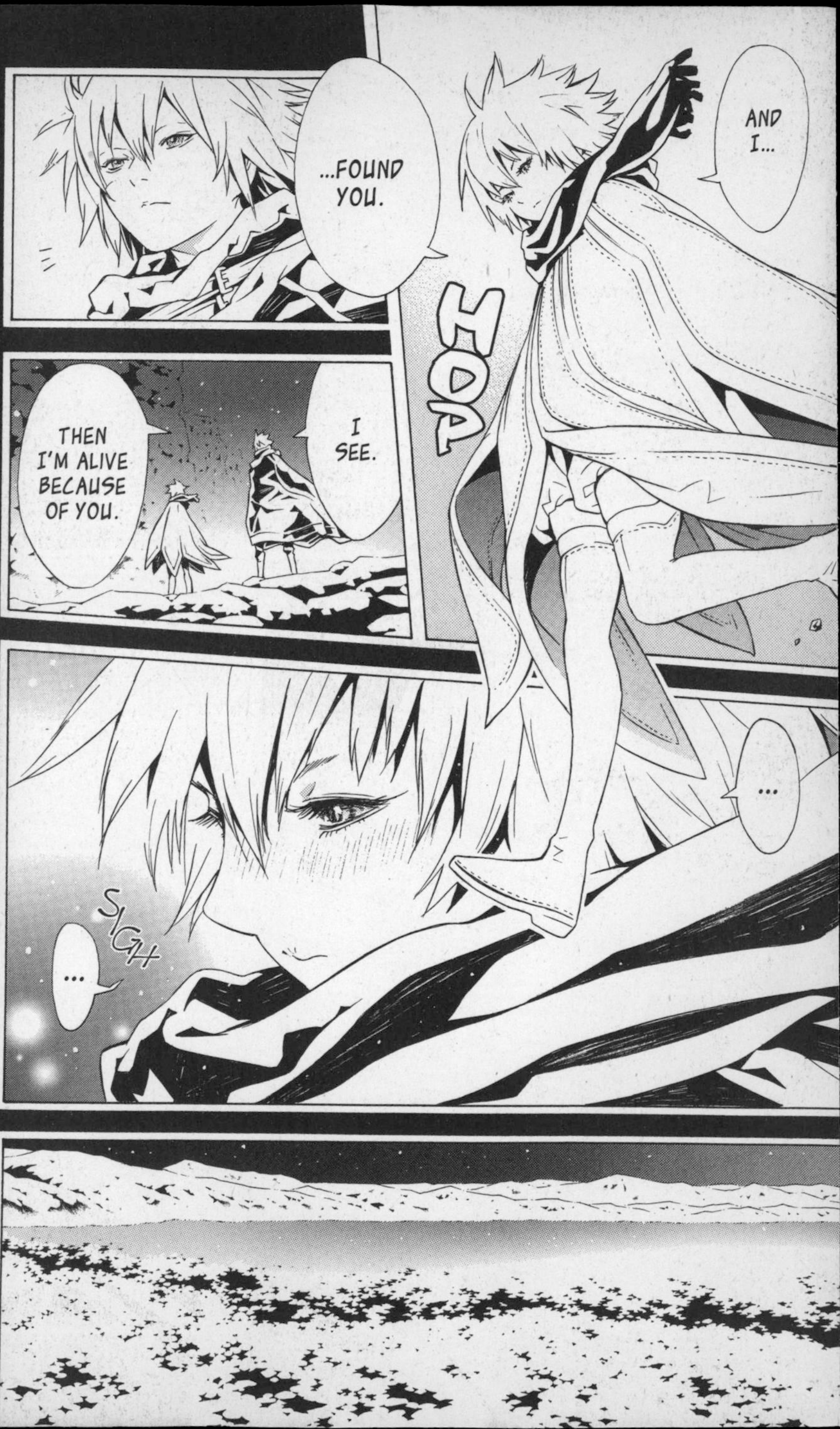
AND I...
HOP
...FOUND YOU.
I SEE.
THEN I'M ALIVE BECAUSE OF YOU.
...
SIGH
...

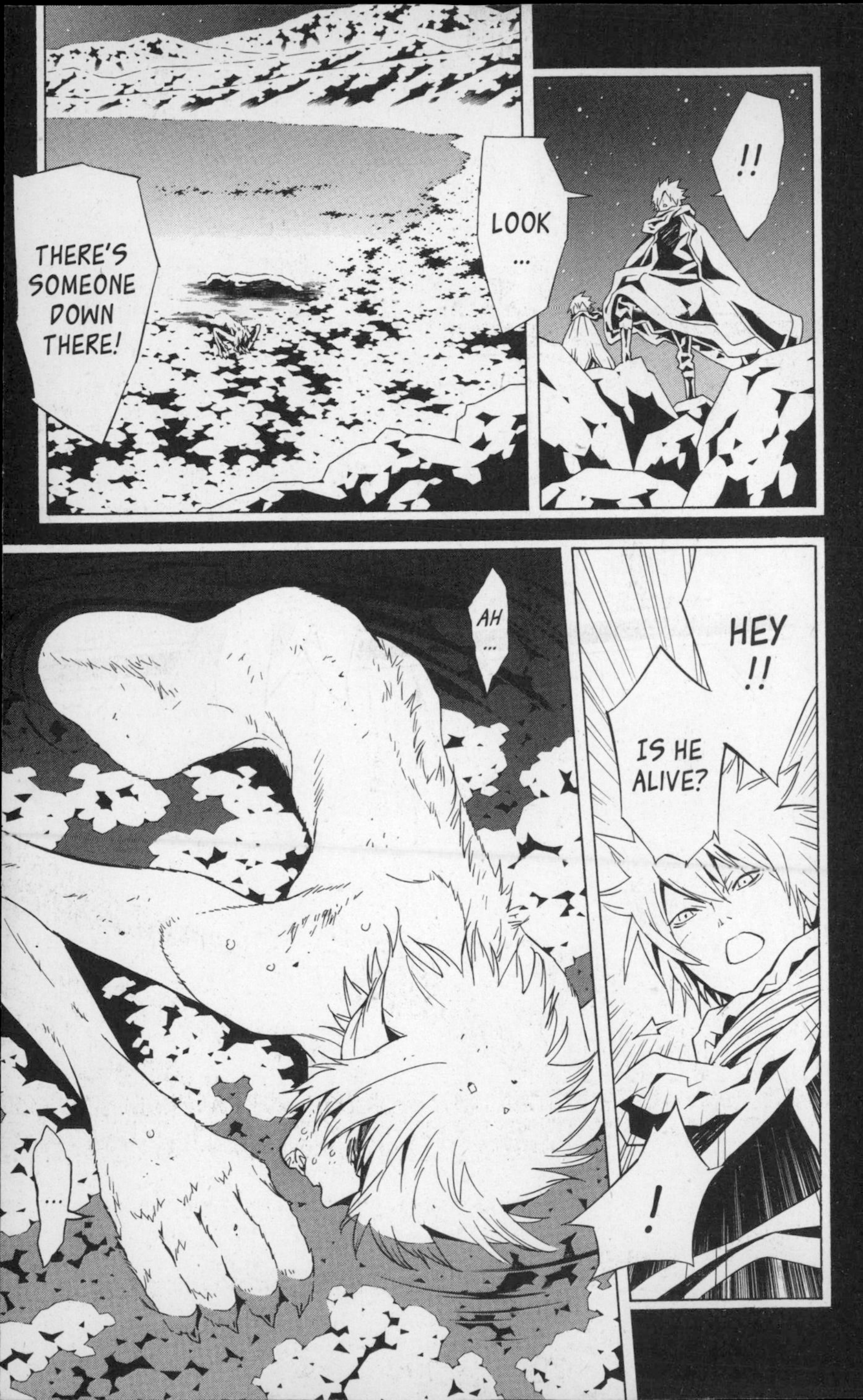
!!
LOOK ...
THERE'S SOMEONE DOWN THERE!
HEY !!
IS HE ALIVE?
AH ...
!
...

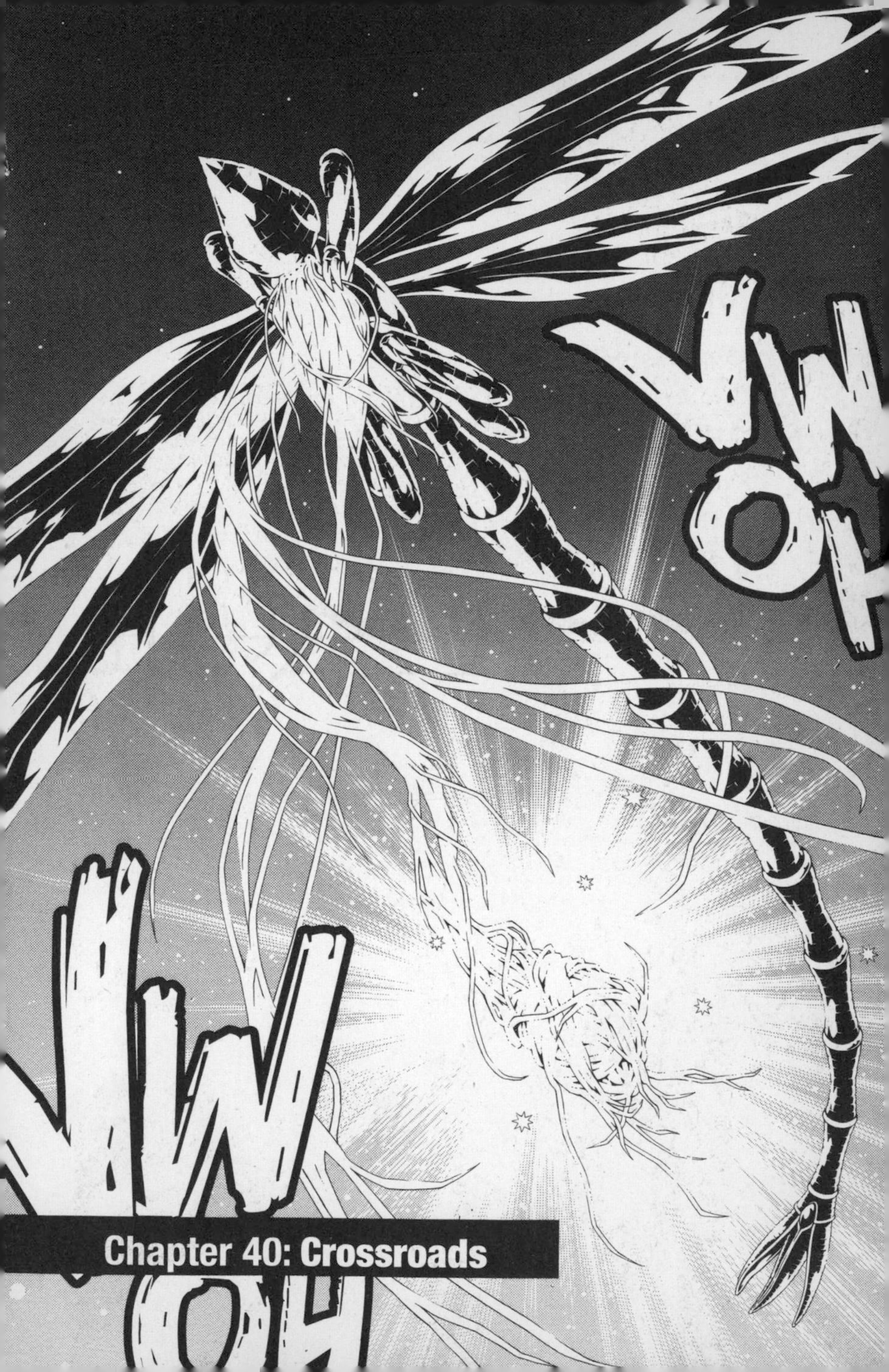
VWOH
VWOH

Chapter 40: Crossroads

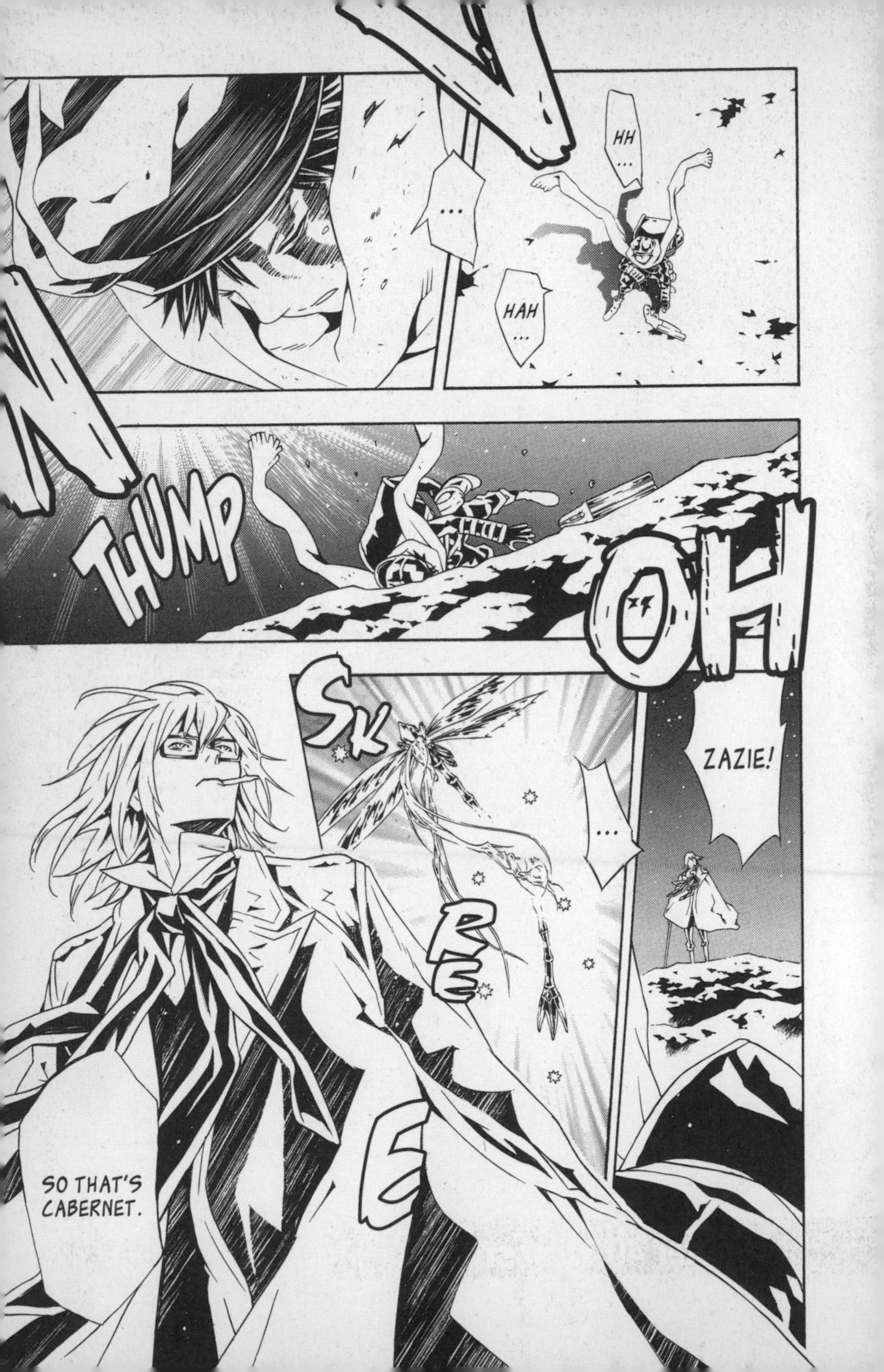
HH ...
HAH ...
...
THUMP
OH
ZAZIE!
...
SKREE
SO THAT'S CABERNET.

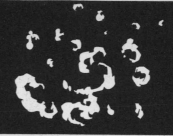

...IT WAS PITCH BLACK.

WHEN I CAME TO...

SPL ASH

KOFF

KOFF

ACH!

SHK

SSS

HAAAH

HAAAH

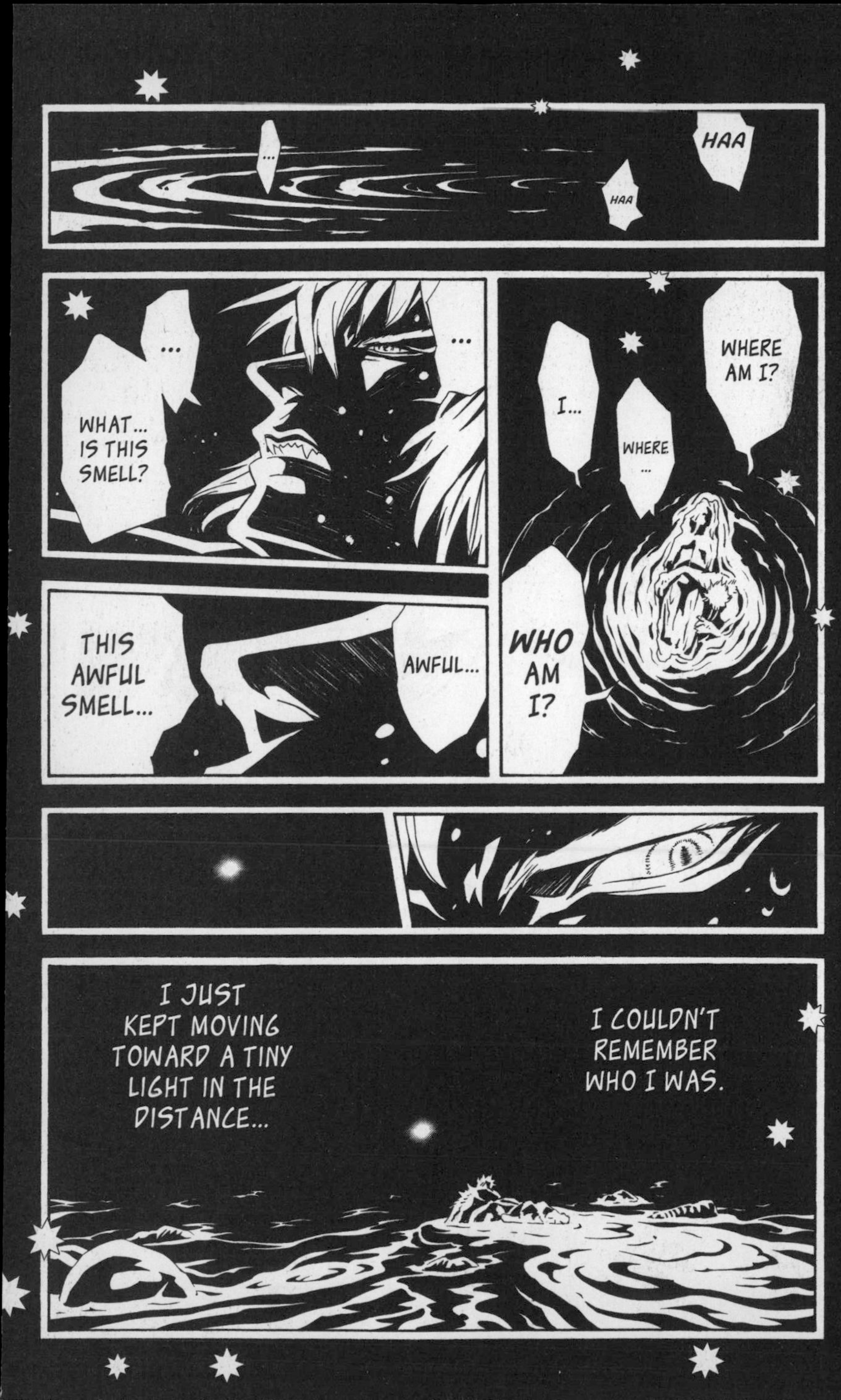
...
HAA
HAA
...
...
WHAT... IS THIS SMELL?
WHERE AM I?
I...
WHERE ...
AWFUL...
THIS AWFUL SMELL...
WHO AM I?
I COULDN'T REMEMBER WHO I WAS.
I JUST KEPT MOVING TOWARD A TINY LIGHT IN THE DISTANCE...

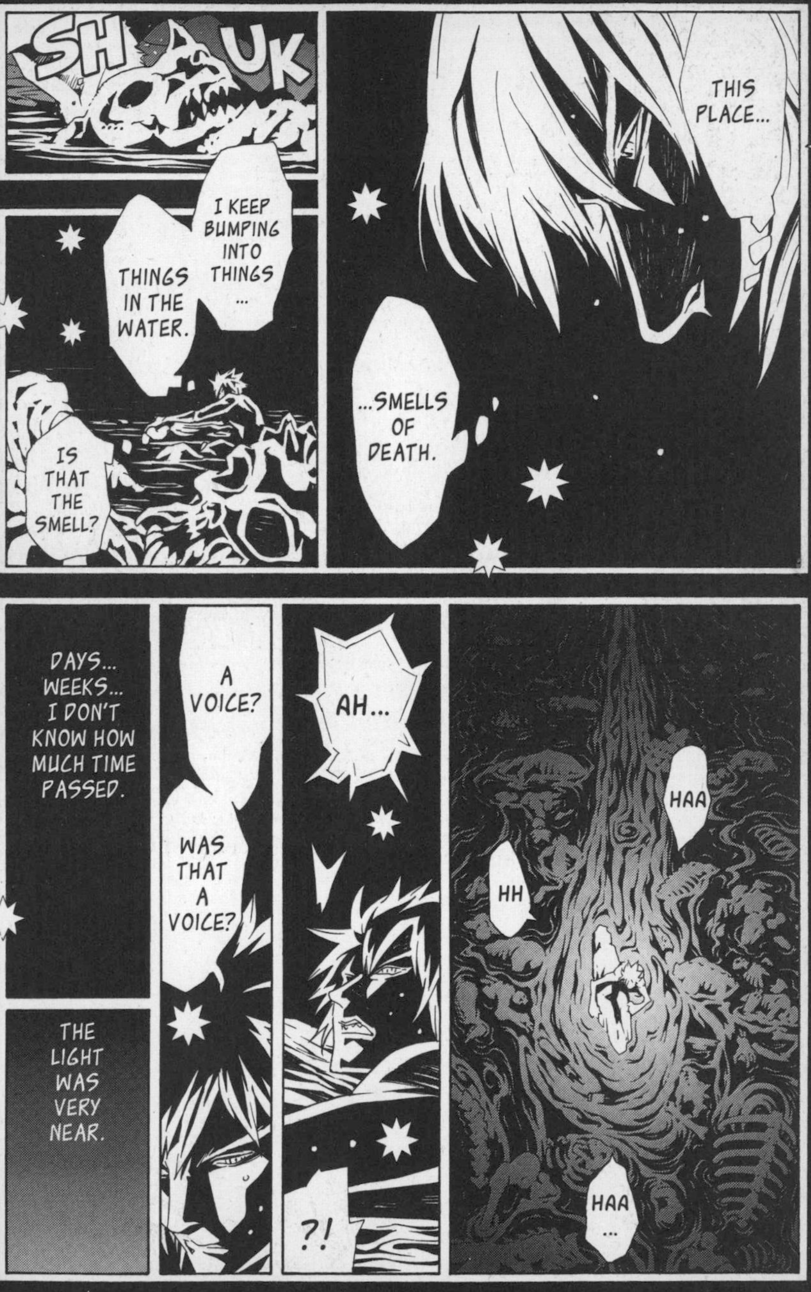
THIS PLACE...
...SMELLS OF DEATH.
SHUK
I KEEP BUMPING INTO THINGS...
THINGS IN THE WATER.
IS THAT THE SMELL?
HAA
HH
HAA...
AH...
?!
A VOICE?
WAS THAT A VOICE?
DAYS... WEEKS... I DON'T KNOW HOW MUCH TIME PASSED.
THE LIGHT WAS VERY NEAR.

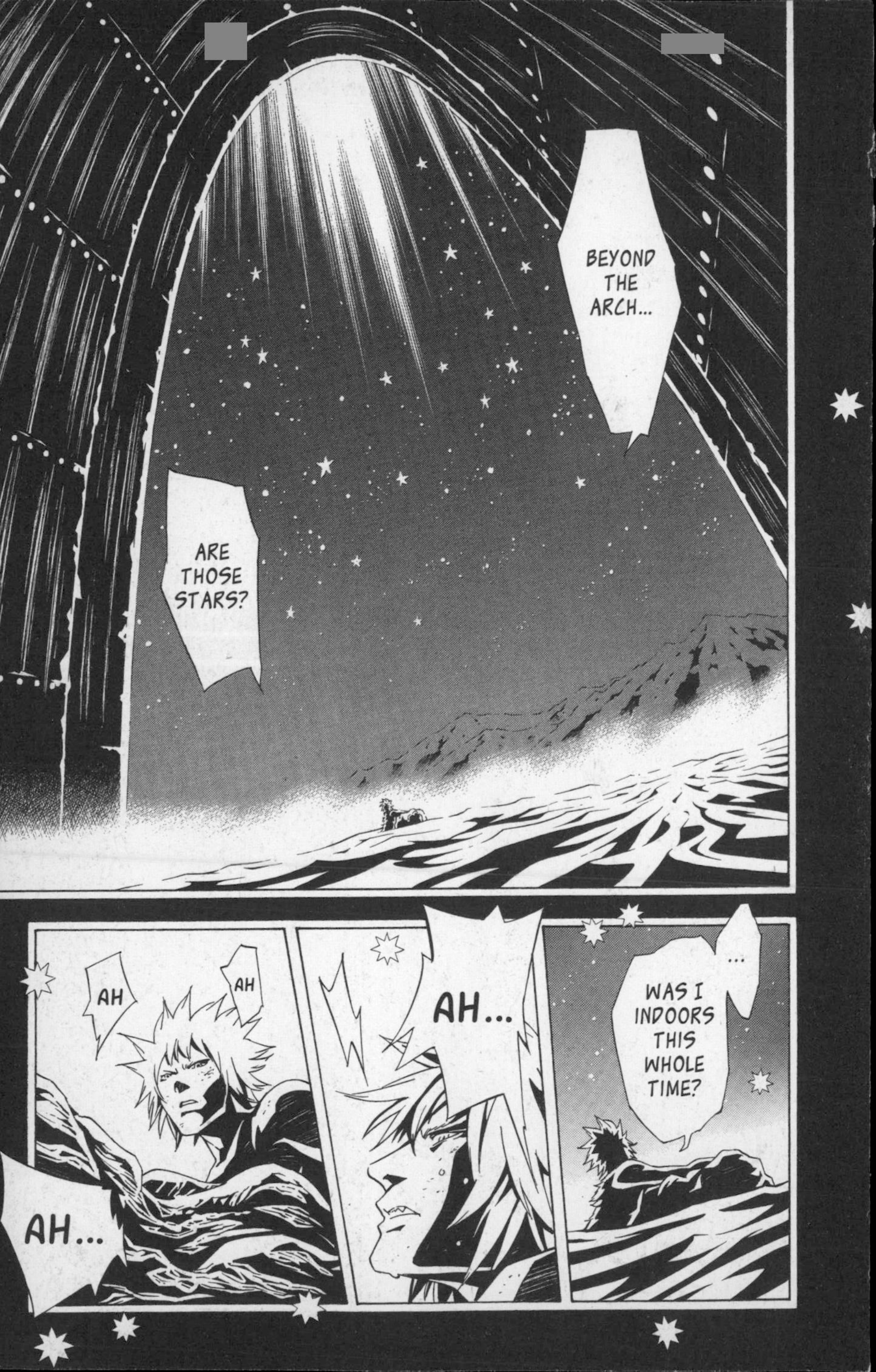
BEYOND THE ARCH...
ARE THOSE STARS?
...
WAS I INDOORS THIS WHOLE TIME?
AH...
AH
AH
AH...

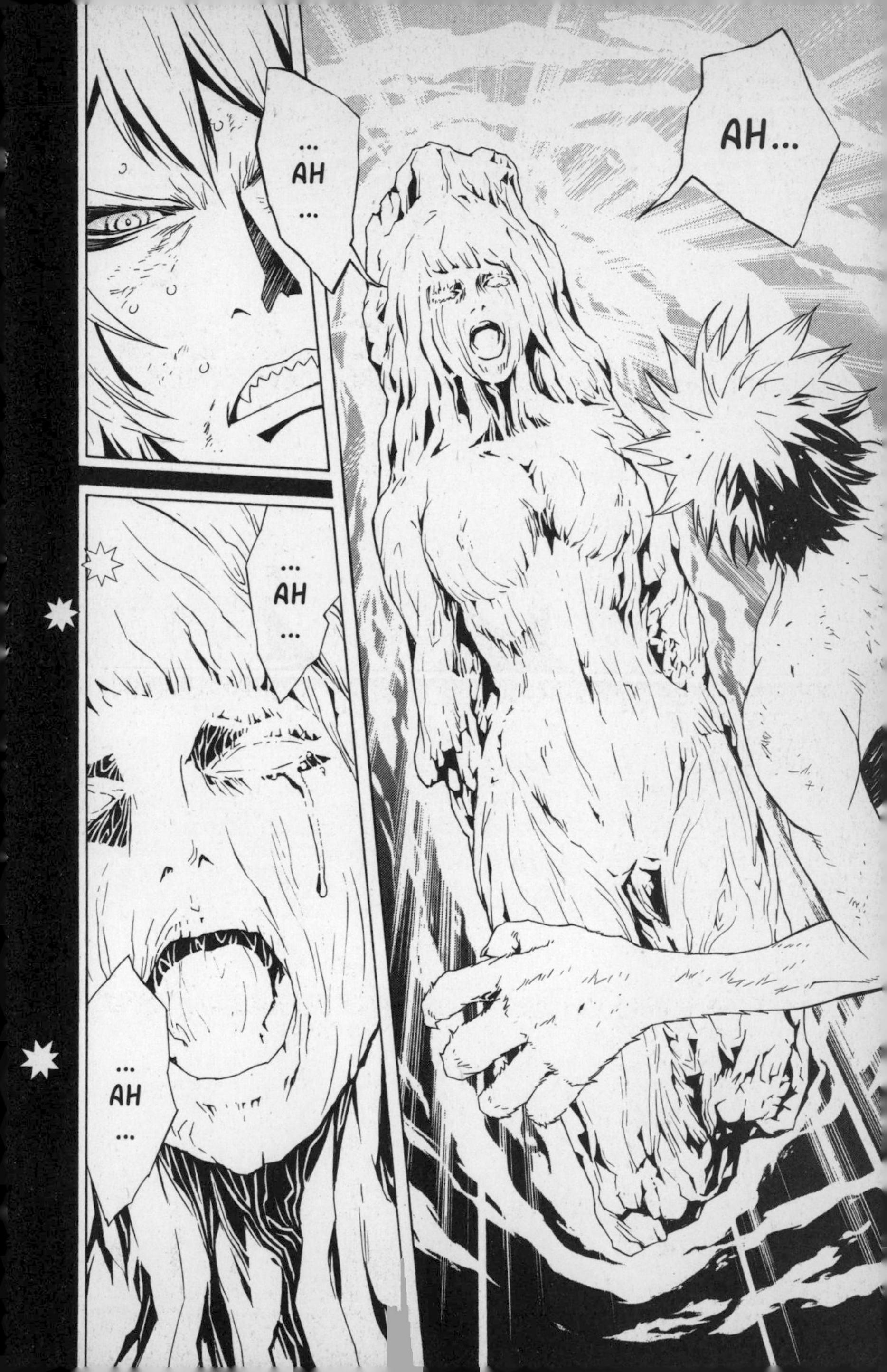
AH...
...AH...
...AH...
...AH...

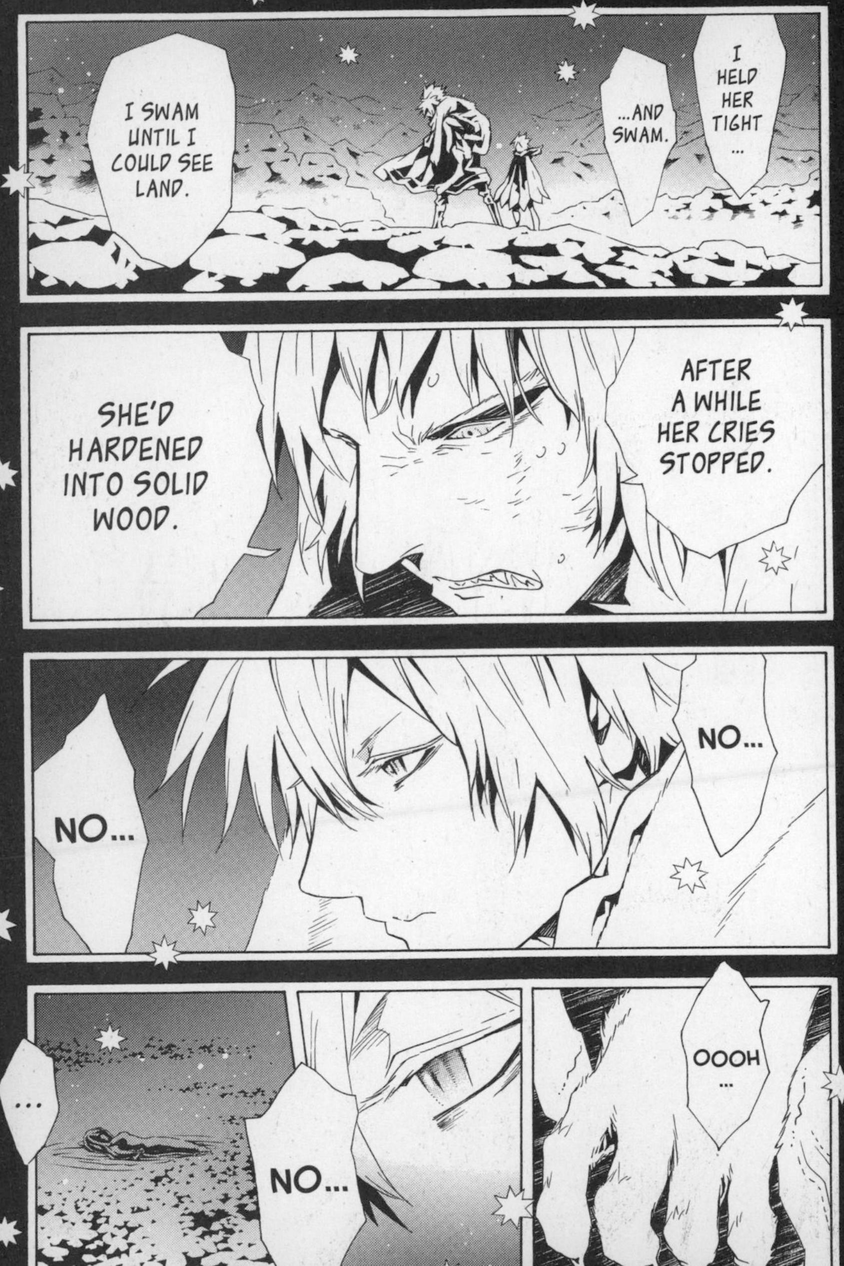
I HELD HER TIGHT ...
...AND SWAM.
I SWAM UNTIL I COULD SEE LAND.
AFTER A WHILE HER CRIES STOPPED.
SHE'D HARDENED INTO SOLID WOOD.
NO...
NO...
OOOH ...
NO...
...

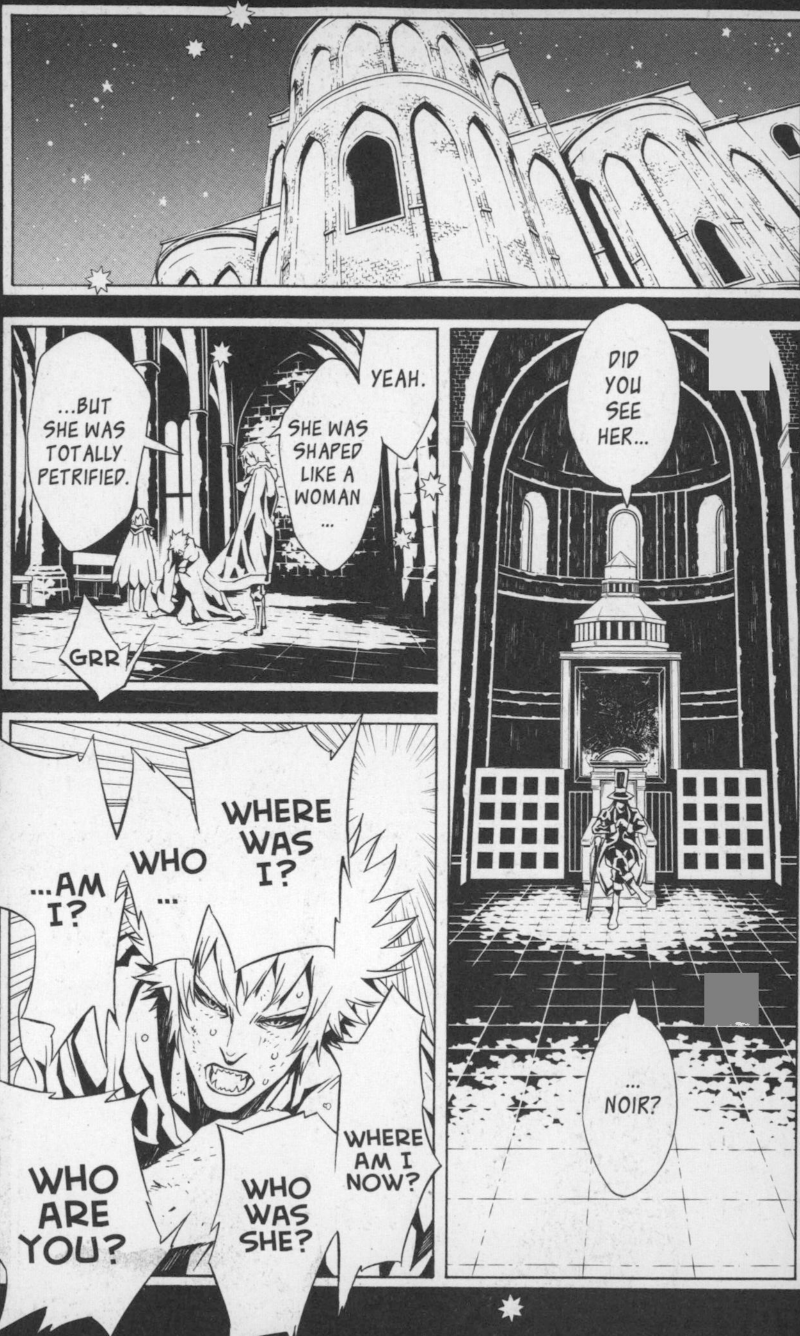
DID YOU SEE HER...
... NOIR?
YEAH.
SHE WAS SHAPED LIKE A WOMAN ...
...BUT SHE WAS TOTALLY PETRIFIED.
GRR
WHERE WAS I?
WHO ...
...AM I?
WHERE AM I NOW?
WHO WAS SHE?
WHO ARE YOU?

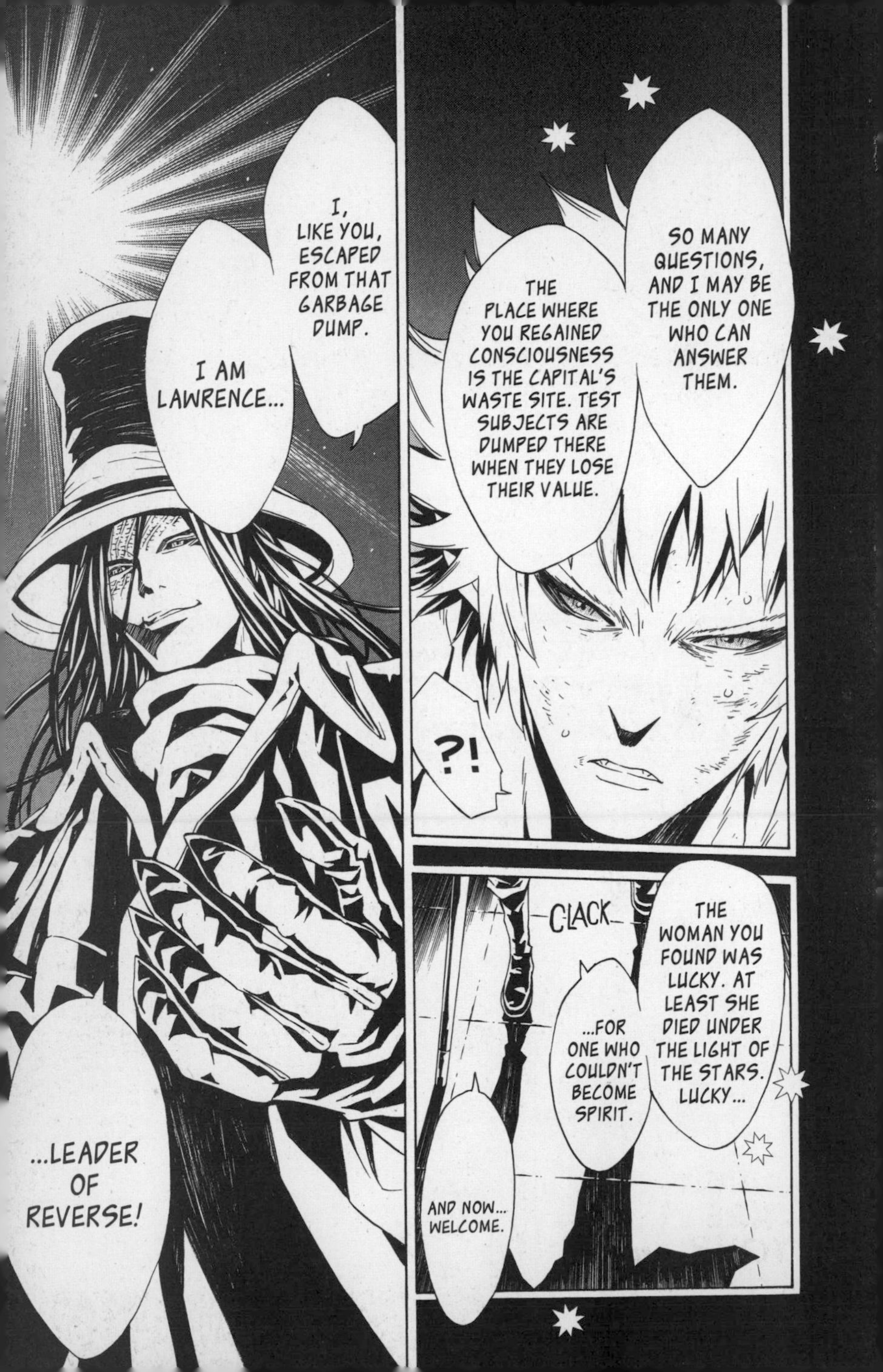
SO MANY QUESTIONS, AND I MAY BE THE ONLY ONE WHO CAN ANSWER THEM.
THE PLACE WHERE YOU REGAINED CONSCIOUSNESS IS THE CAPITAL'S WASTE SITE. TEST SUBJECTS ARE DUMPED THERE WHEN THEY LOSE THEIR VALUE.
?!
CLACK
THE WOMAN YOU FOUND WAS LUCKY. AT LEAST SHE DIED UNDER THE LIGHT OF THE STARS. LUCKY...
...FOR ONE WHO COULDN'T BECOME SPIRIT.
AND NOW... WELCOME.
I, LIKE YOU, ESCAPED FROM THAT GARBAGE DUMP.
I AM LAWRENCE...
...LEADER OF REVERSE!

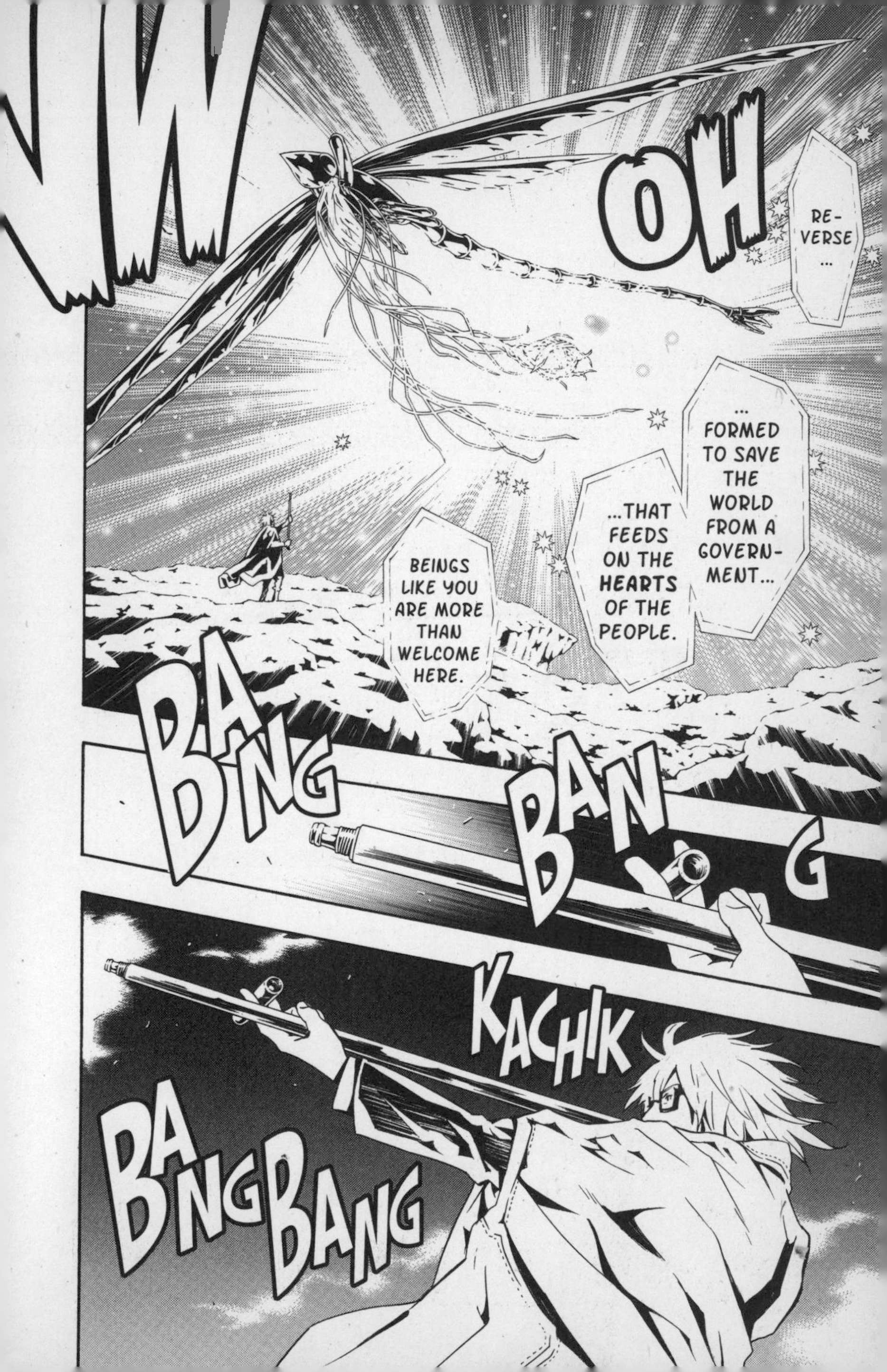

VWOOOH
RE-VERSE ...
... FORMED TO SAVE THE WORLD FROM A GOVERN-MENT...
...THAT FEEDS ON THE HEARTS OF THE PEOPLE.
BEINGS LIKE YOU ARE MORE THAN WELCOME HERE.
BANG
BANG
KACHIK
BANG BANG

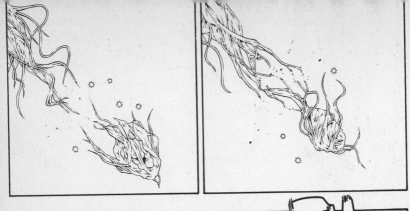

NICE LANDING!

THUP

THAT SOUND...

BRUM

BRUM BRUM

BRUM

EH?

ZAZIE IS SO YOUNG.

TOO YOUNG TO BEAR THE BURDEN OF THE KILL...

GRUFFLE PFF

GROWF PFF

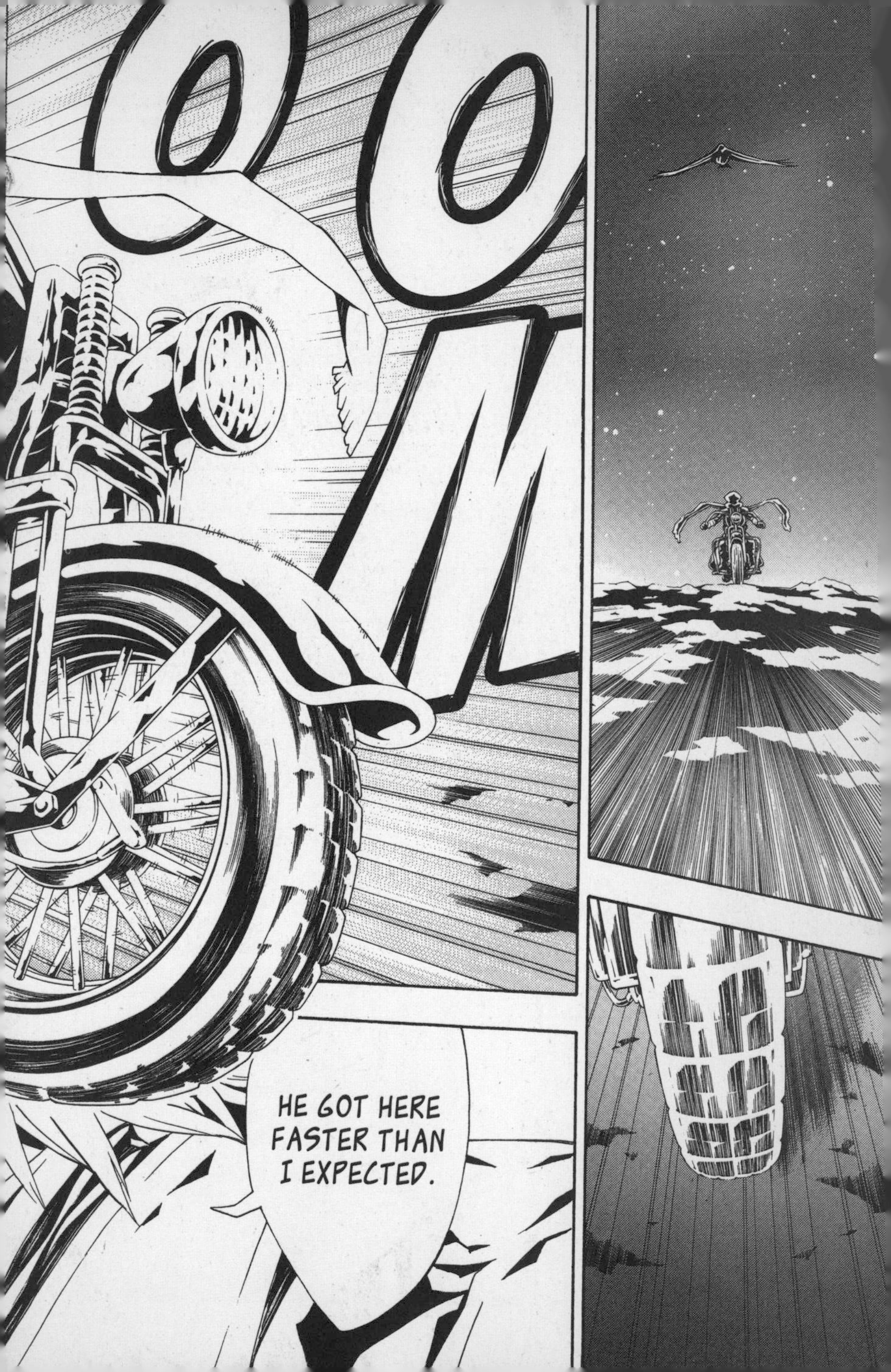
HE GOT HERE FASTER THAN I EXPECTED.

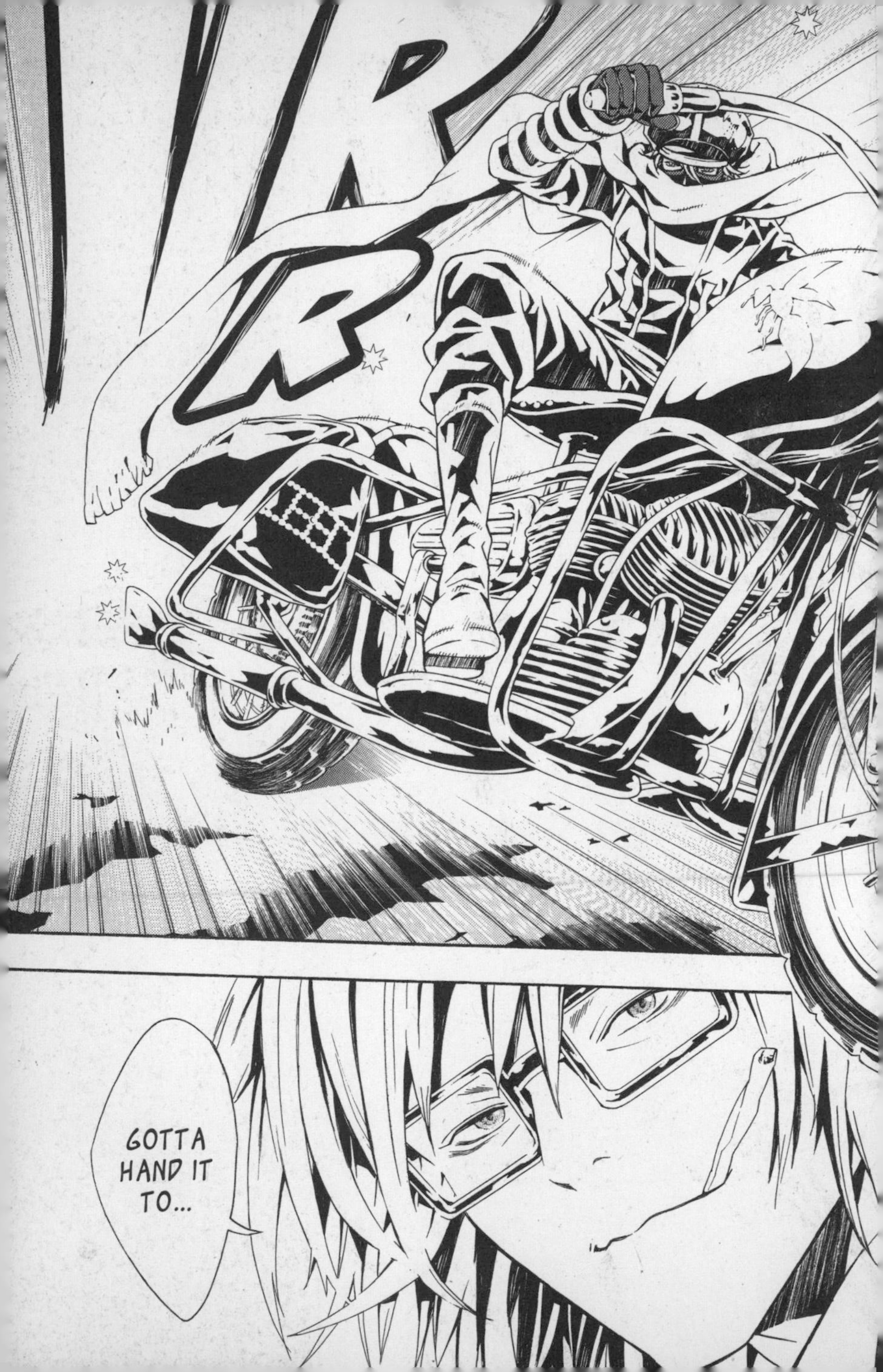
GOTTA HAND IT TO...

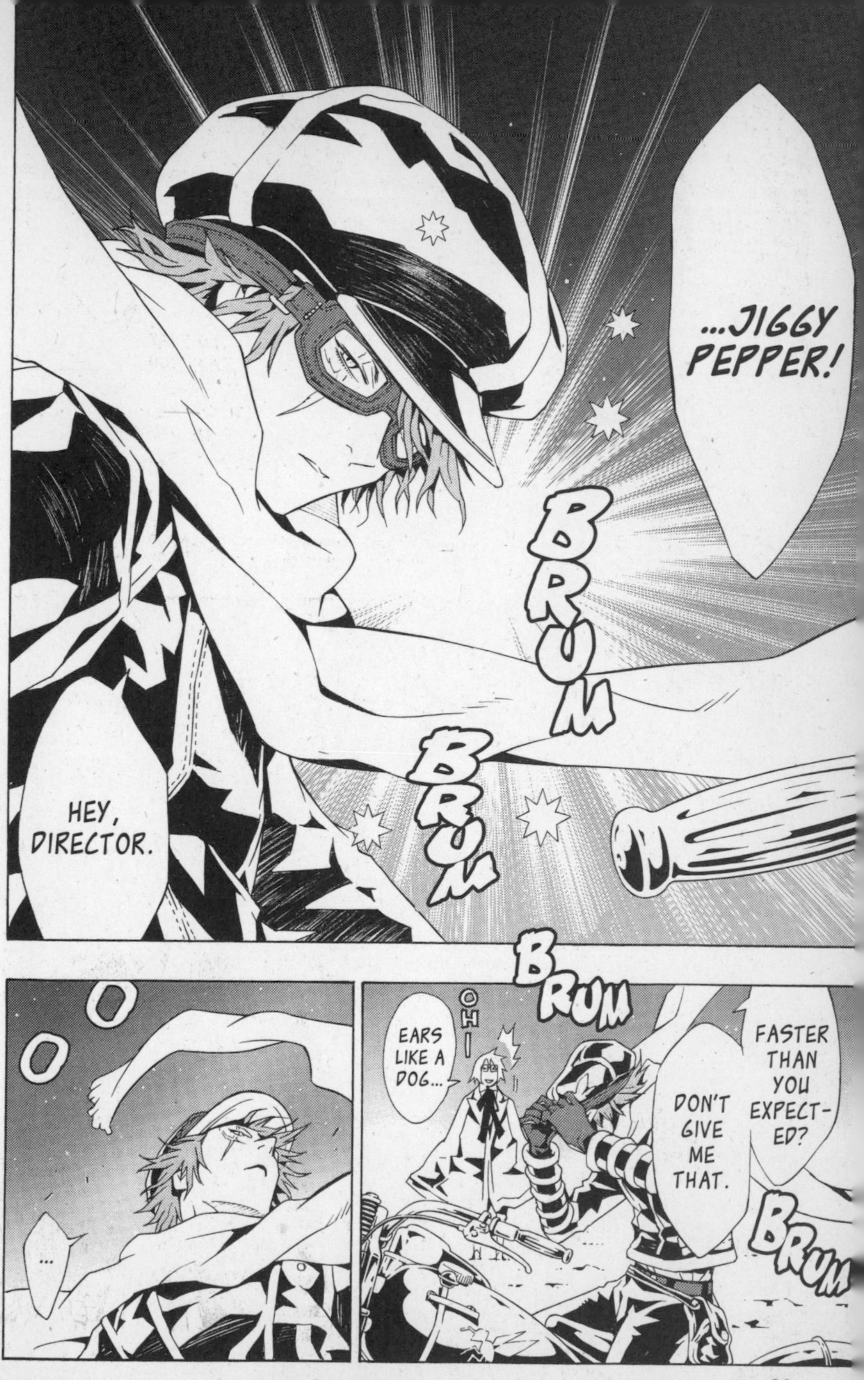
...JIGGY PEPPER!
BRUM
BRUM
HEY, DIRECTOR.
BRUM
FASTER THAN YOU EXPECTED?
DON'T GIVE ME THAT.
BRUM
OH!
EARS LIKE A DOG...
...

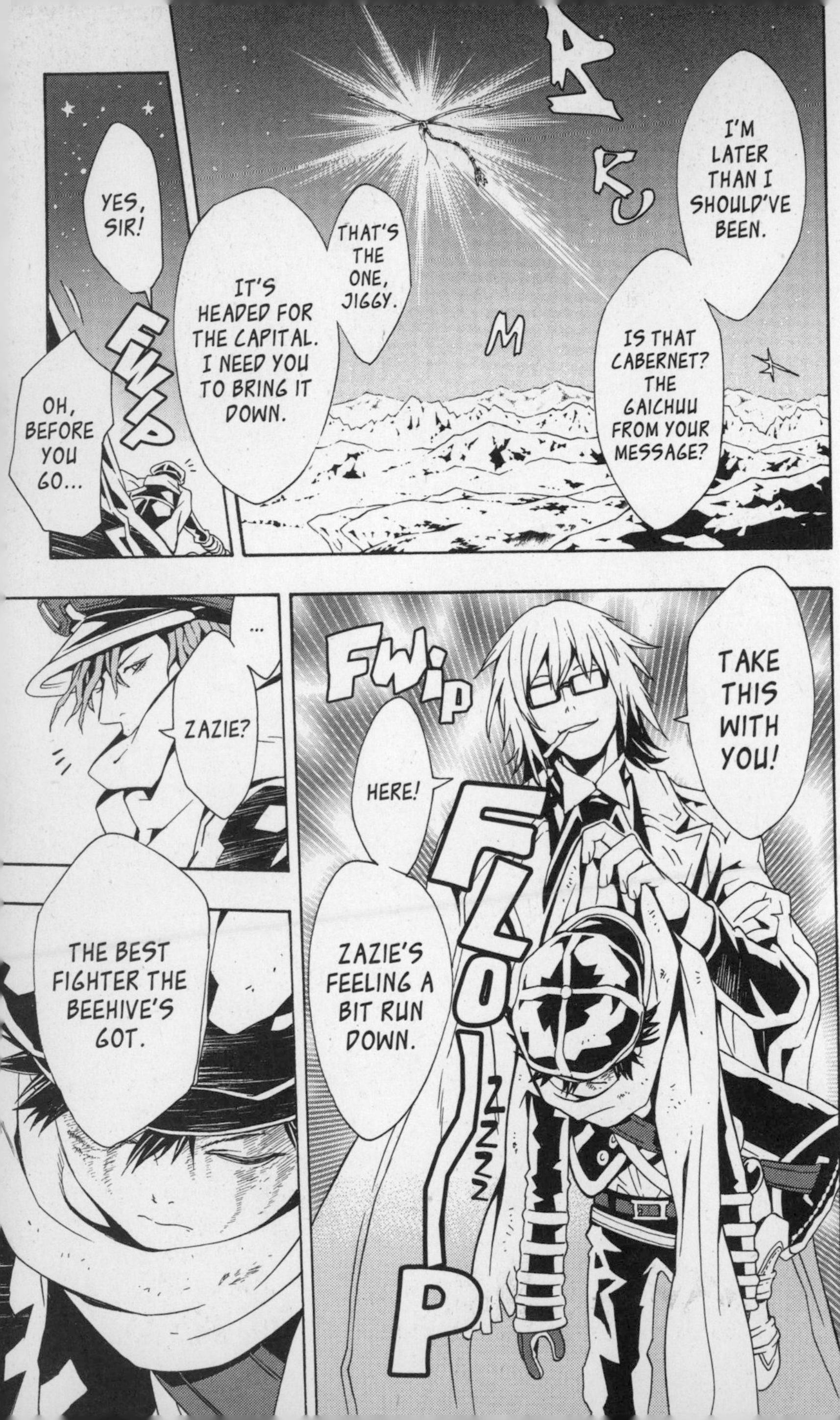
I'M LATER THAN I SHOULD'VE BEEN.
IS THAT CABERNET? THE GAICHUU FROM YOUR MESSAGE?
THAT'S THE ONE, JIGGY.
IT'S HEADED FOR THE CAPITAL. I NEED YOU TO BRING IT DOWN.
YES, SIR!
FWIP
OH, BEFORE YOU GO...
TAKE THIS WITH YOU!
FWIP
HERE!
...
ZAZIE?
FLOP
ZZZZ
ZAZIE'S FEELING A BIT RUN DOWN.
THE BEST FIGHTER THE BEEHIVE'S GOT.

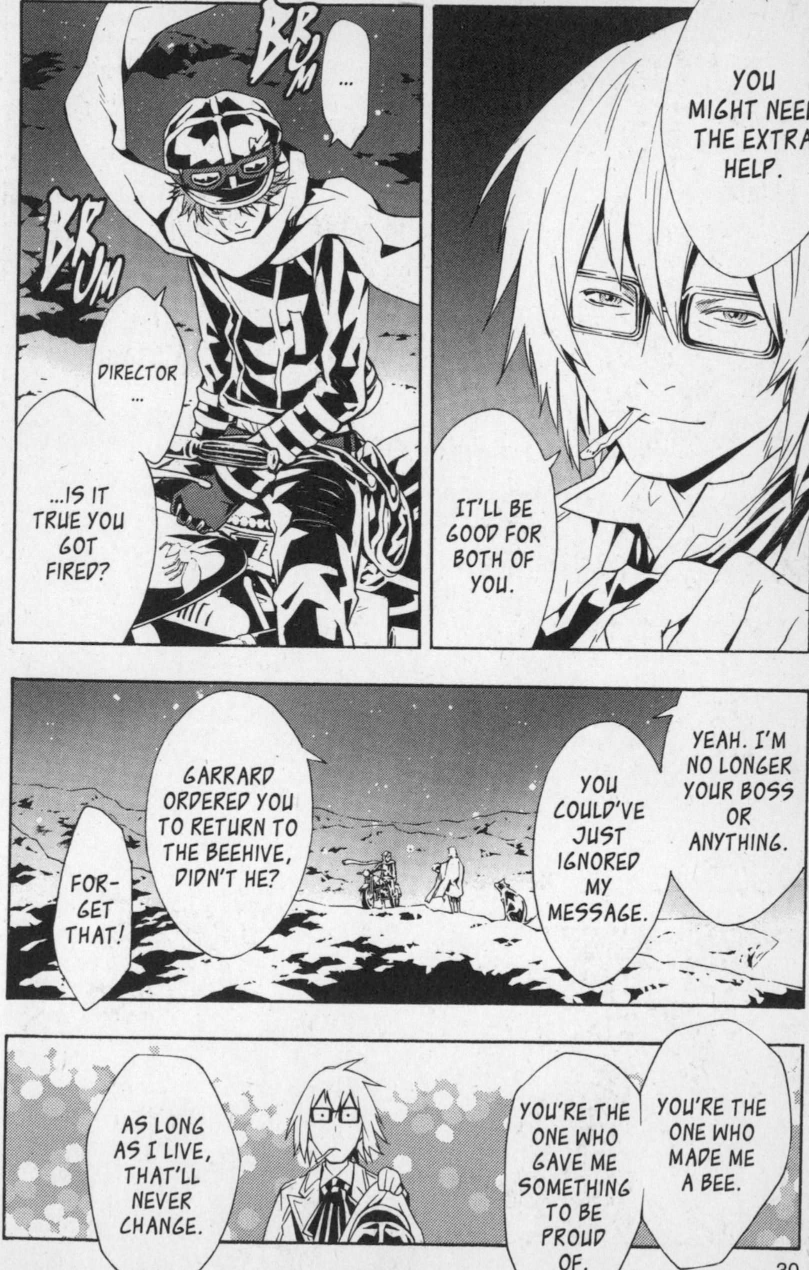
YOU MIGHT NEED THE EXTRA HELP.
IT'LL BE GOOD FOR BOTH OF YOU.
BRUM
...
BRUM
DIRECTOR ...
...IS IT TRUE YOU GOT FIRED?
YEAH. I'M NO LONGER YOUR BOSS OR ANYTHING.
YOU COULD'VE JUST IGNORED MY MESSAGE.
GARRARD ORDERED YOU TO RETURN TO THE BEEHIVE, DIDN'T HE?
FOR-GET THAT!
YOU'RE THE ONE WHO MADE ME A BEE.
YOU'RE THE ONE WHO GAVE ME SOMETHING TO BE PROUD OF.
AS LONG AS I LIVE, THAT'LL NEVER CHANGE.

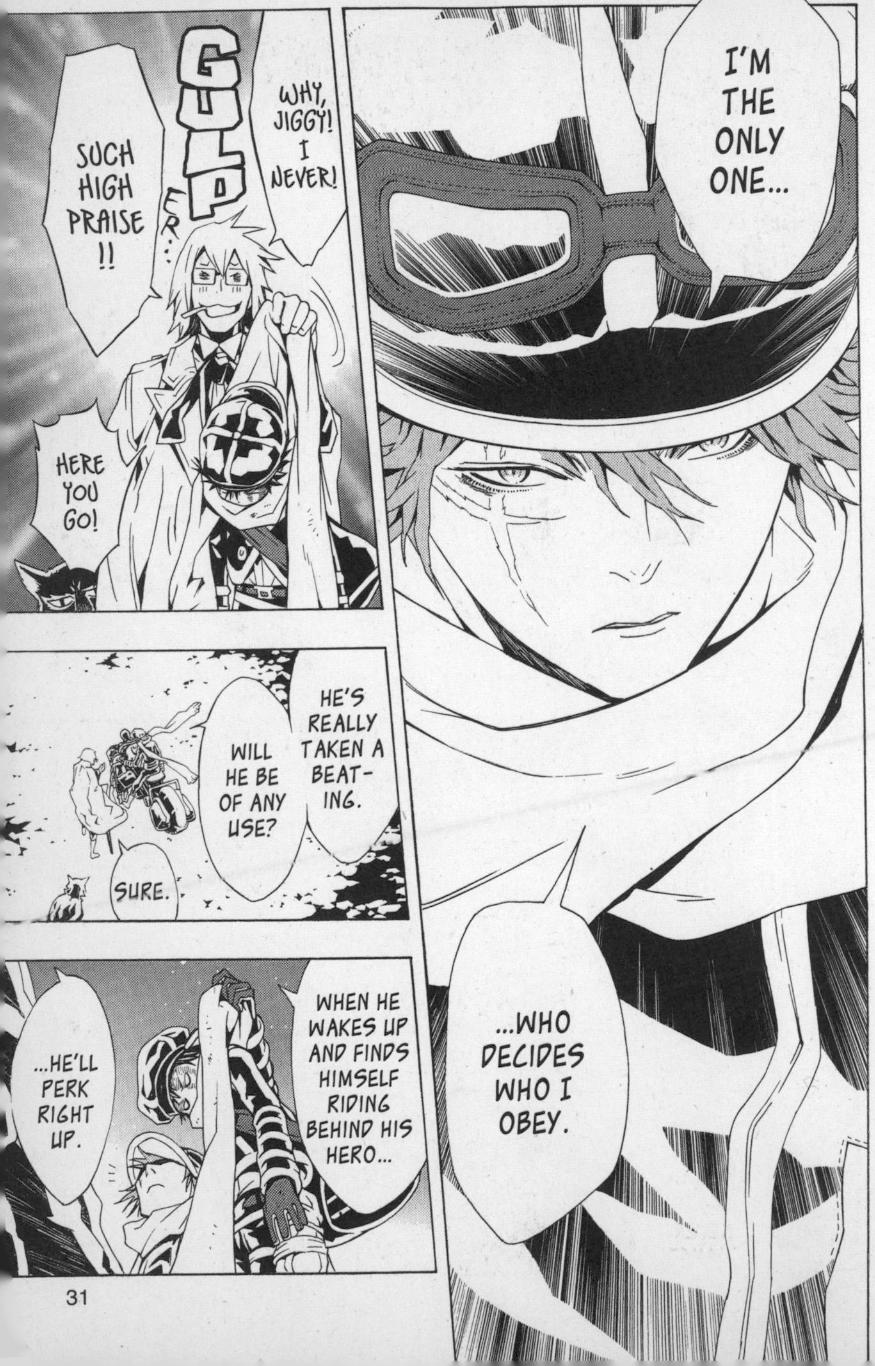
I'M THE ONLY ONE...
...WHO DECIDES WHO I OBEY.
WHY, JIGGY! I NEVER!
GULP
ER...
SUCH HIGH PRAISE!!
HERE YOU GO!
HE'S REALLY TAKEN A BEAT-ING.
WILL HE BE OF ANY USE?
SURE.
WHEN HE WAKES UP AND FINDS HIMSELF RIDING BEHIND HIS HERO...
...HE'LL PERK RIGHT UP.

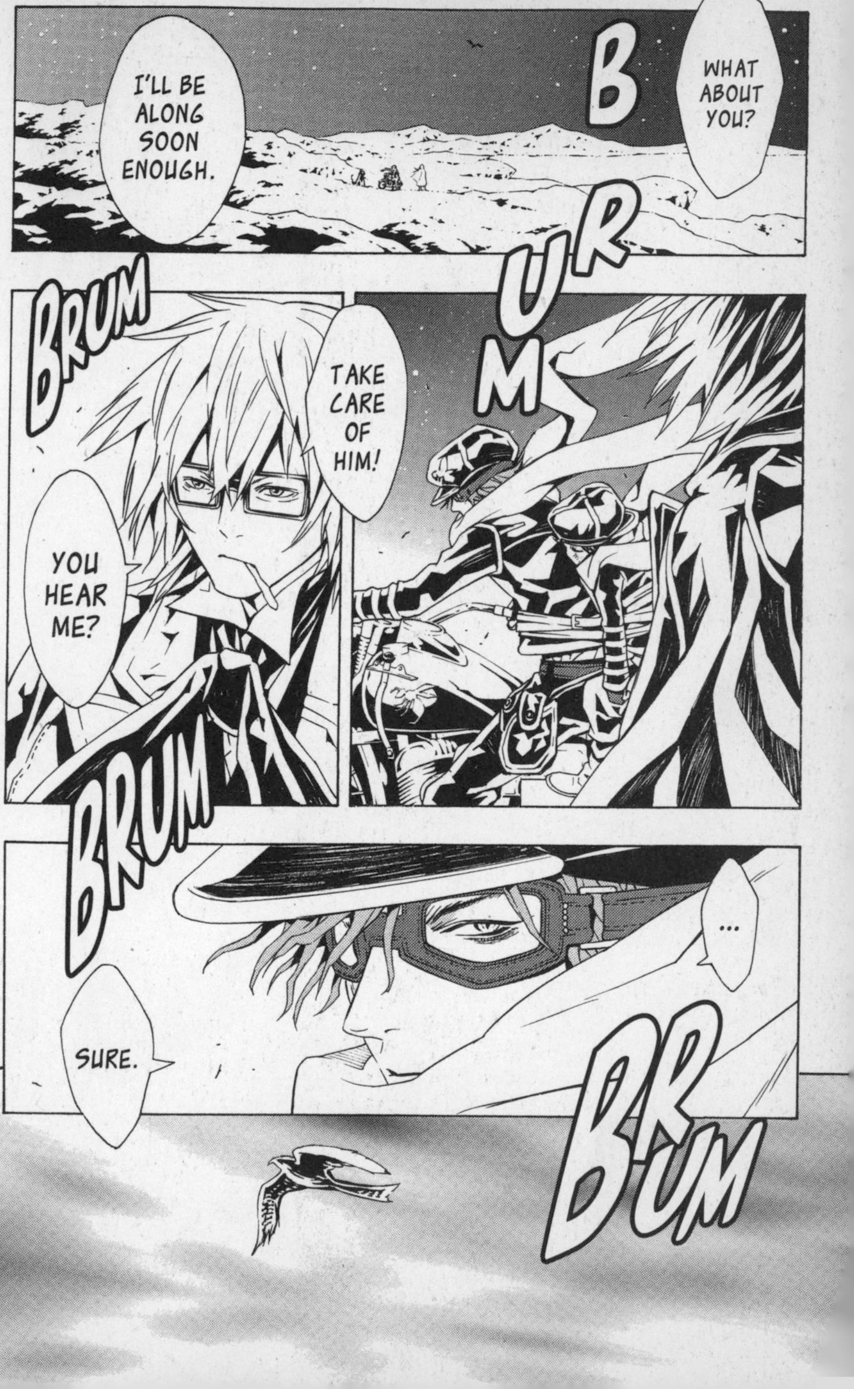
WHAT ABOUT YOU?
I'LL BE ALONG SOON ENOUGH.
B
UR
M
BRUM
TAKE CARE OF HIM!
YOU HEAR ME?
BRUM
...
SURE.
BR
UM

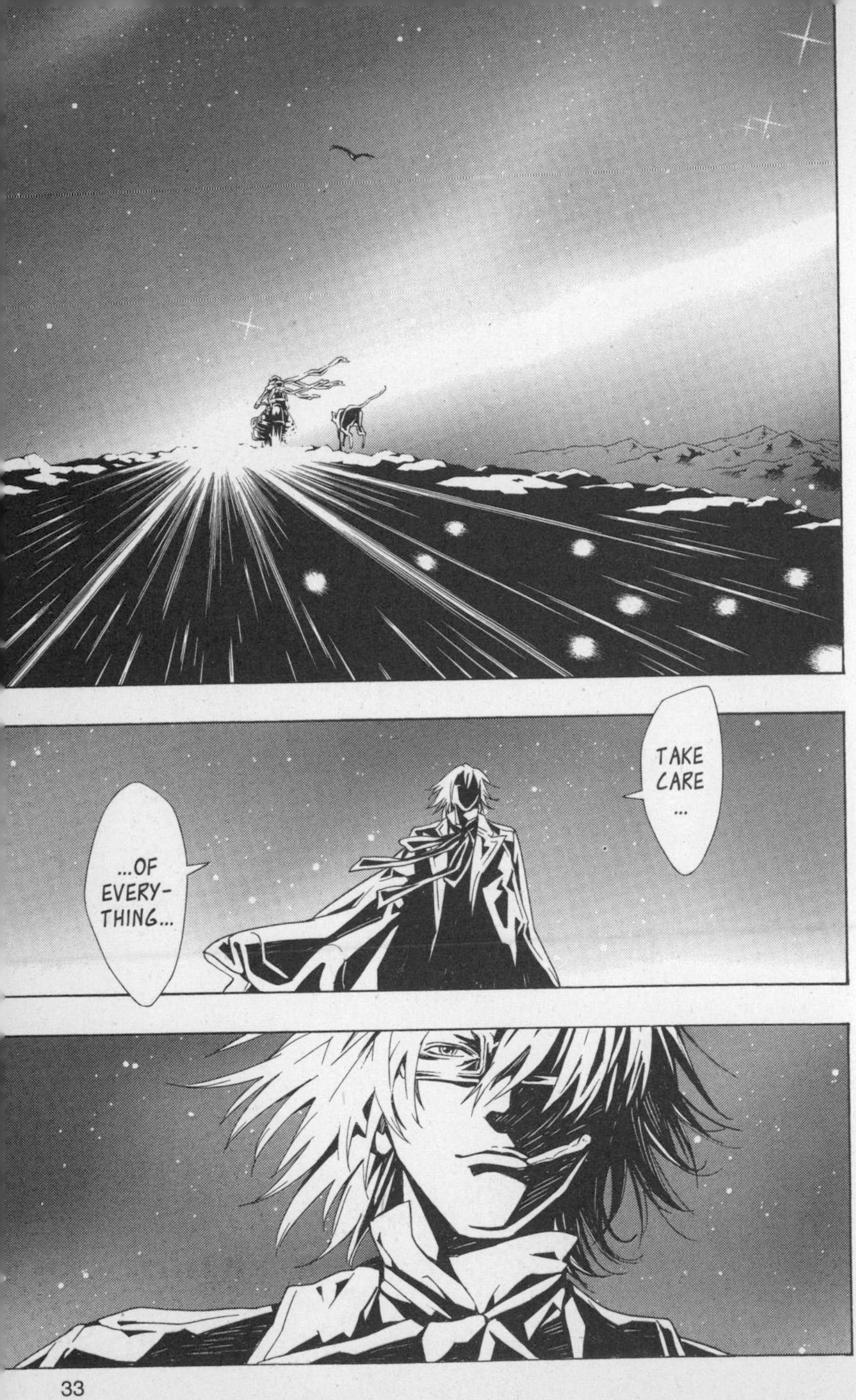
TAKE CARE ...
...OF EVERY-THING...

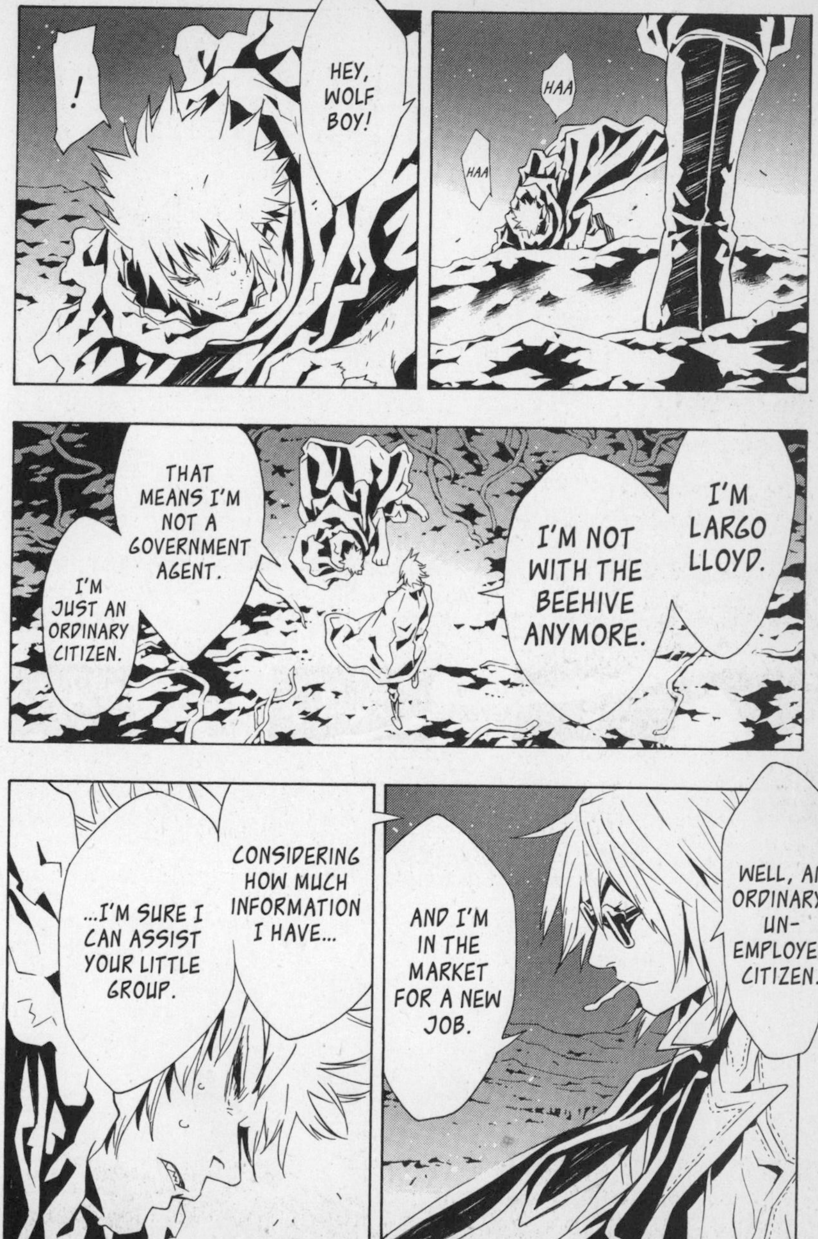
HAA
HAA
HEY, WOLF BOY!
!
I'M LARGO LLOYD.
I'M NOT WITH THE BEEHIVE ANYMORE.
THAT MEANS I'M NOT A GOVERNMENT AGENT.
I'M JUST AN ORDINARY CITIZEN.
WELL, AN ORDINARY, UN-EMPLOYED CITIZEN.
AND I'M IN THE MARKET FOR A NEW JOB.
CONSIDERING HOW MUCH INFORMATION I HAVE...
...I'M SURE I CAN ASSIST YOUR LITTLE GROUP.

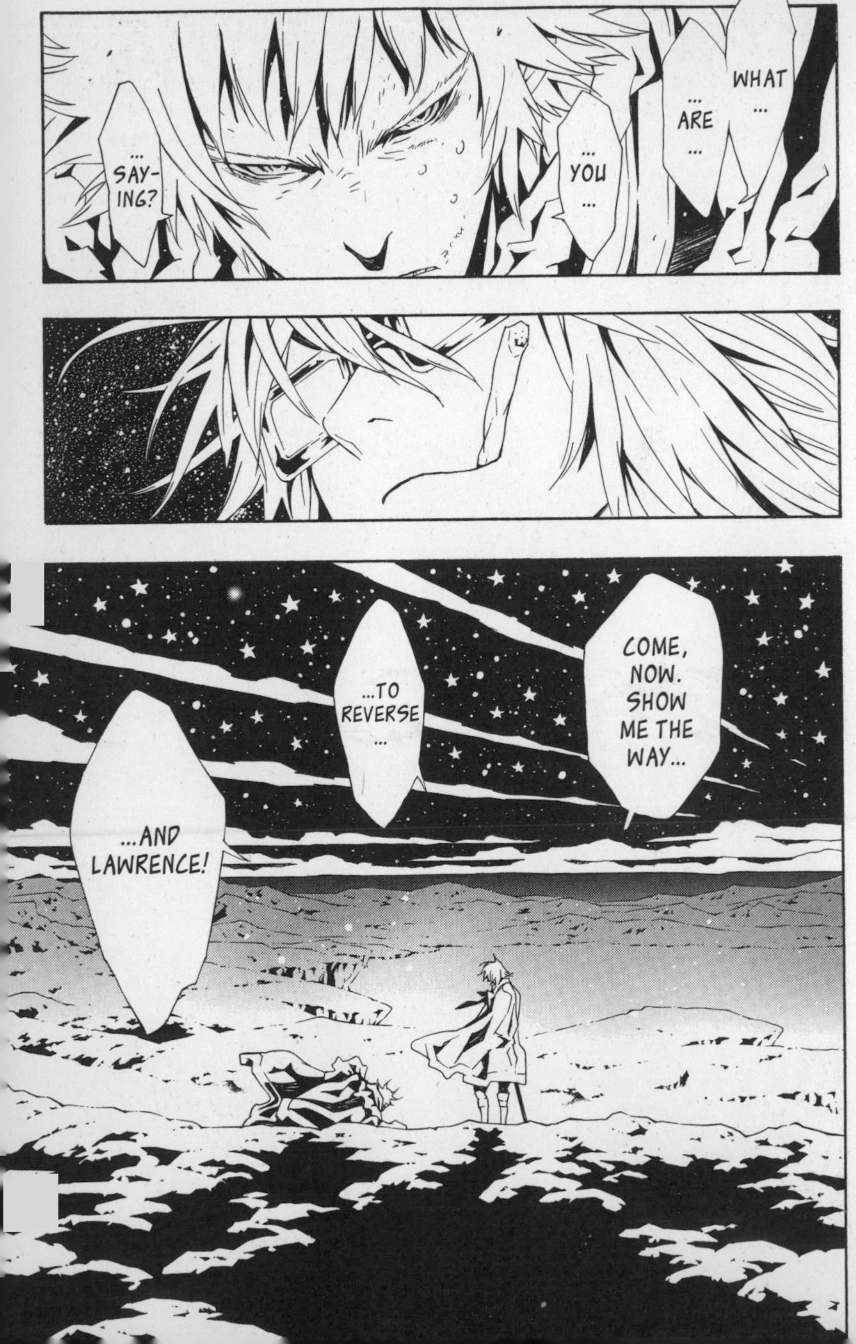
WHAT ...
... ARE ...
... YOU ...
... SAY-ING?
COME, NOW. SHOW ME THE WAY...
...TO REVERSE ...
...AND LAWRENCE!

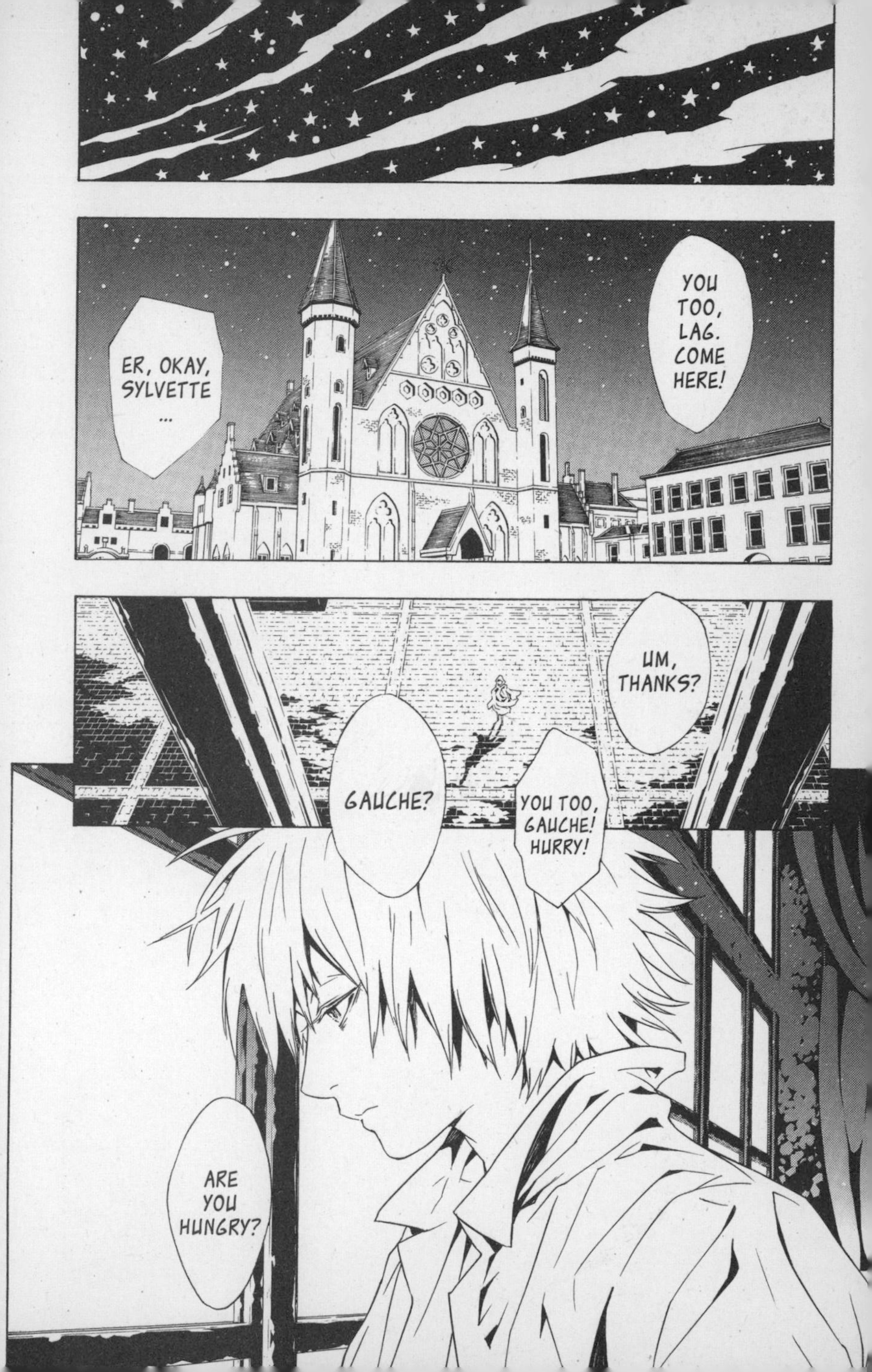
YOU TOO, LAG. COME HERE!
ER, OKAY, SYLVETTE ...
UM, THANKS?
YOU TOO, GAUCHE! HURRY!
GAUCHE?
ARE YOU HUNGRY?

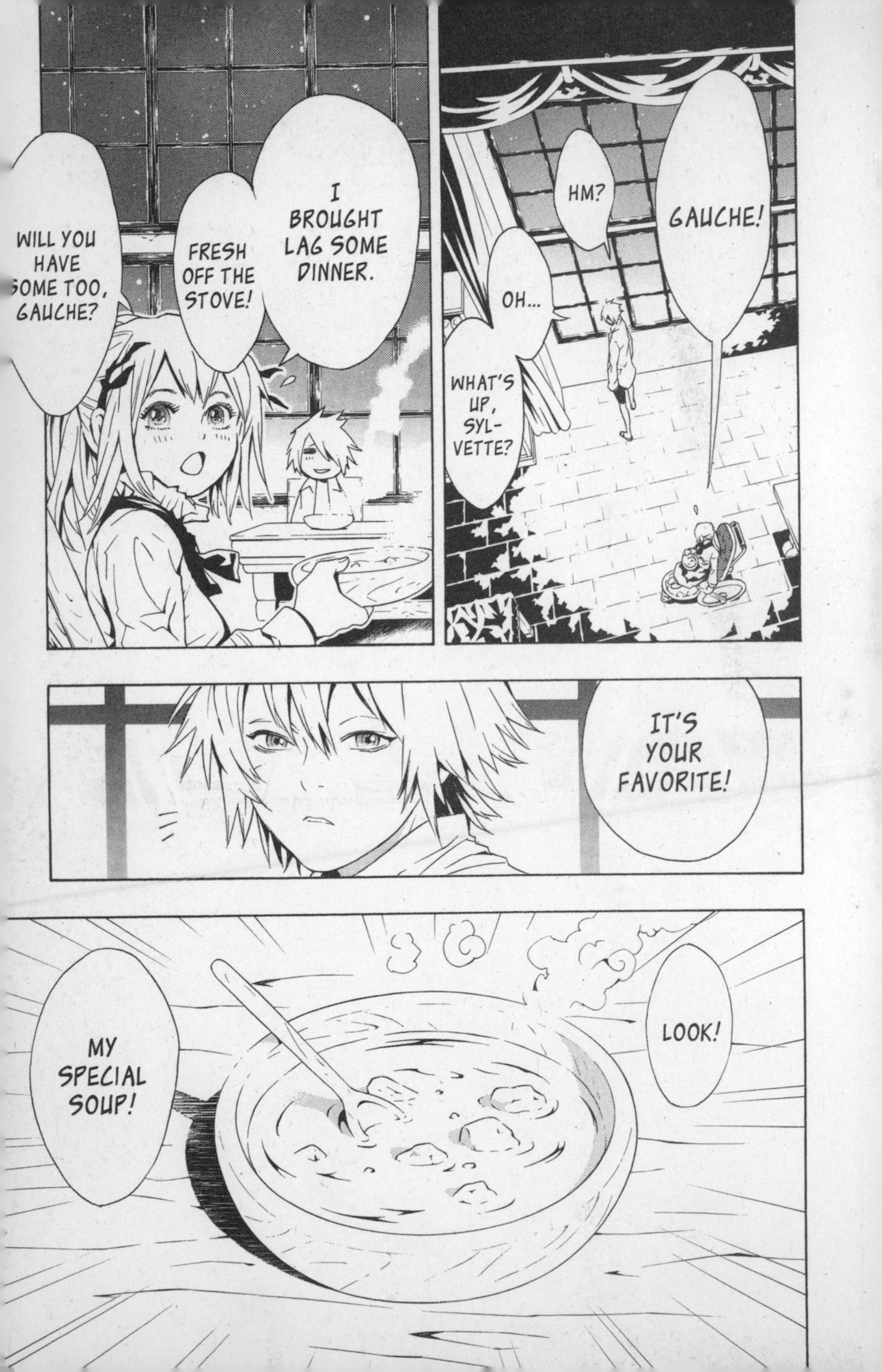
GAUCHE!
HM?
OH...
WHAT'S UP, SYLVETTE?
I BROUGHT LAG SOME DINNER.
FRESH OFF THE STOVE!
WILL YOU HAVE SOME TOO, GAUCHE?
IT'S YOUR FAVORITE!
LOOK!
MY SPECIAL SOUP!

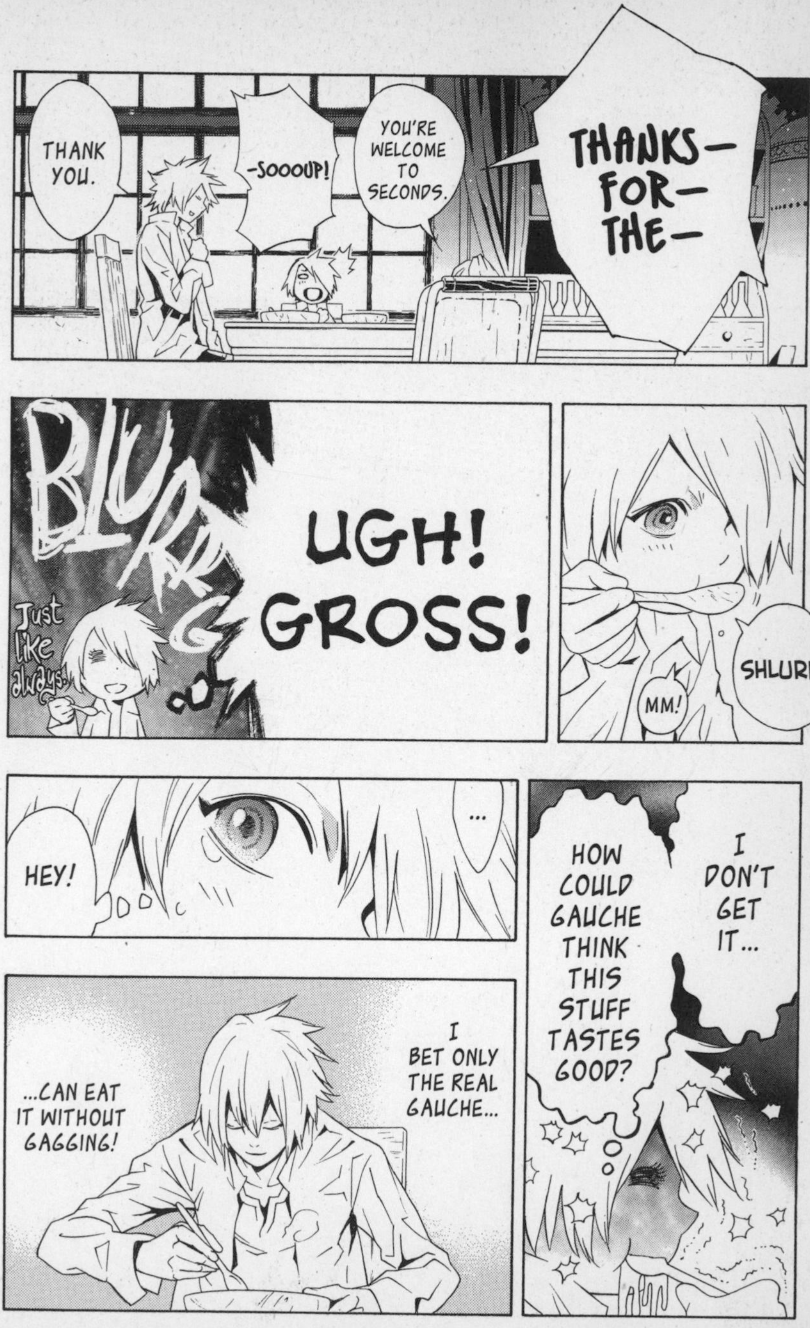
THANKS— FOR— THE—
YOU'RE WELCOME TO SECONDS.
-SOOOUP!
THANK YOU.
SHLURP
MM!
UGH! GROSS!
BLURG
Just like always!
I DON'T GET IT...
HOW COULD GAUCHE THINK THIS STUFF TASTES GOOD?
...
HEY!
I BET ONLY THE REAL GAUCHE...
...CAN EAT IT WITHOUT GAGGING!

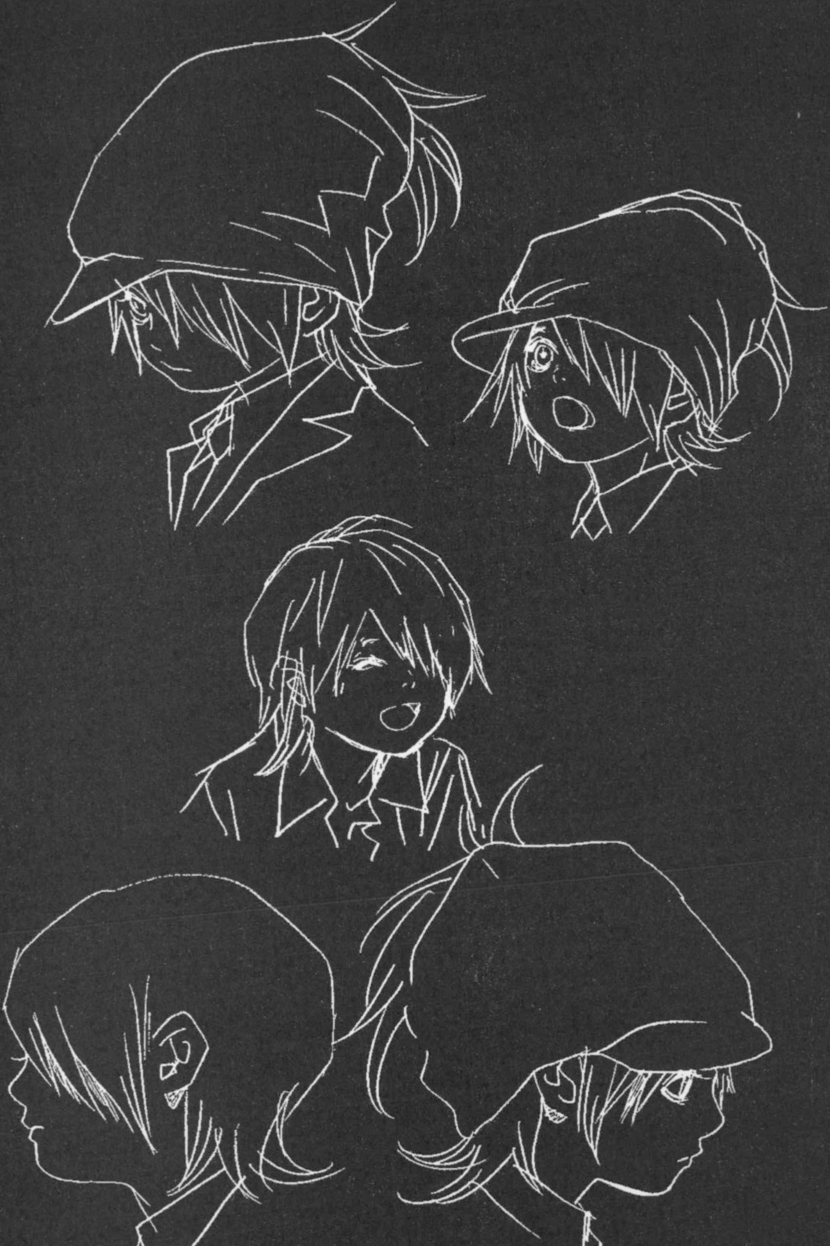

Rough sketches of Lag drawn before *Tegami Bachi* was published.

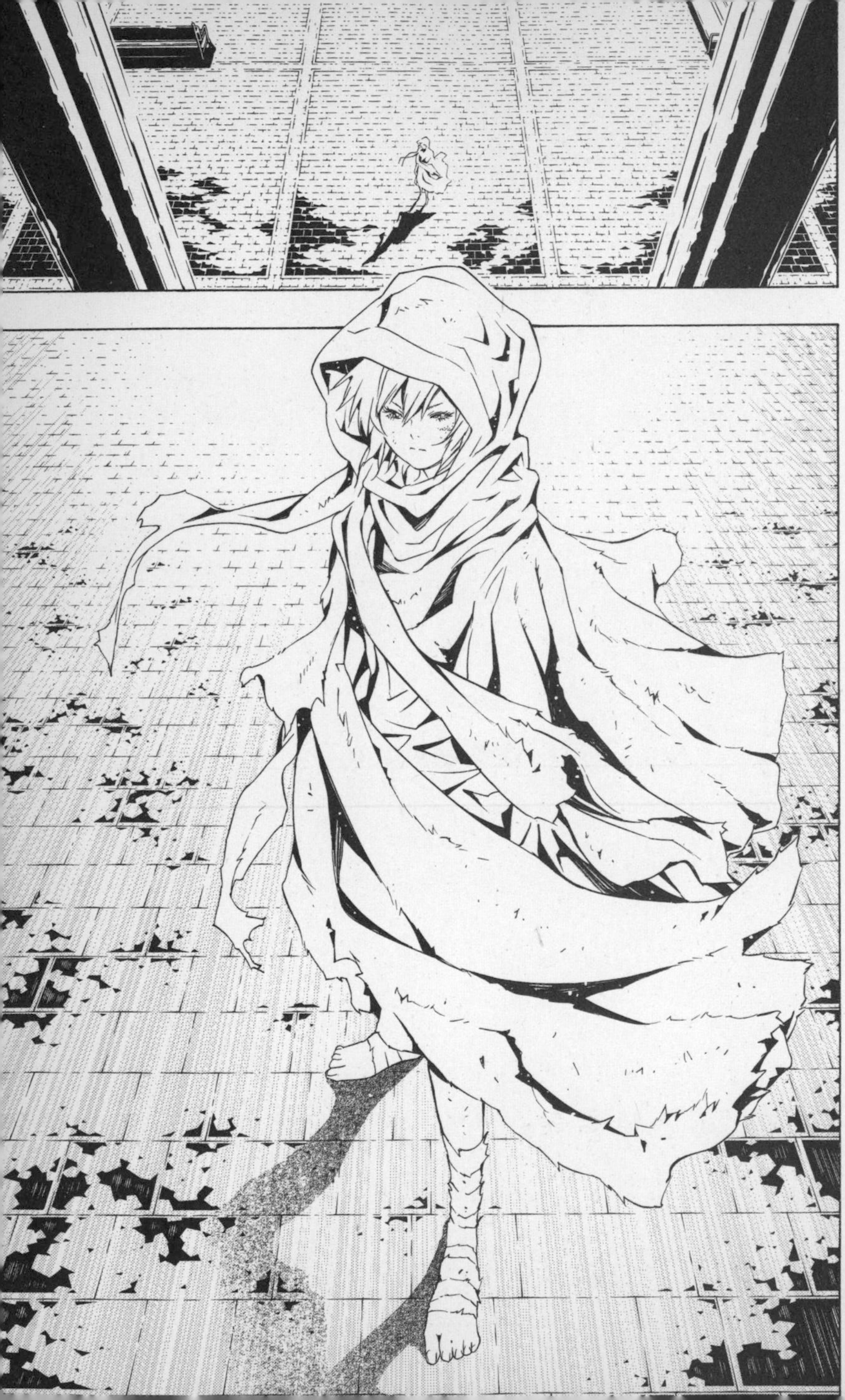

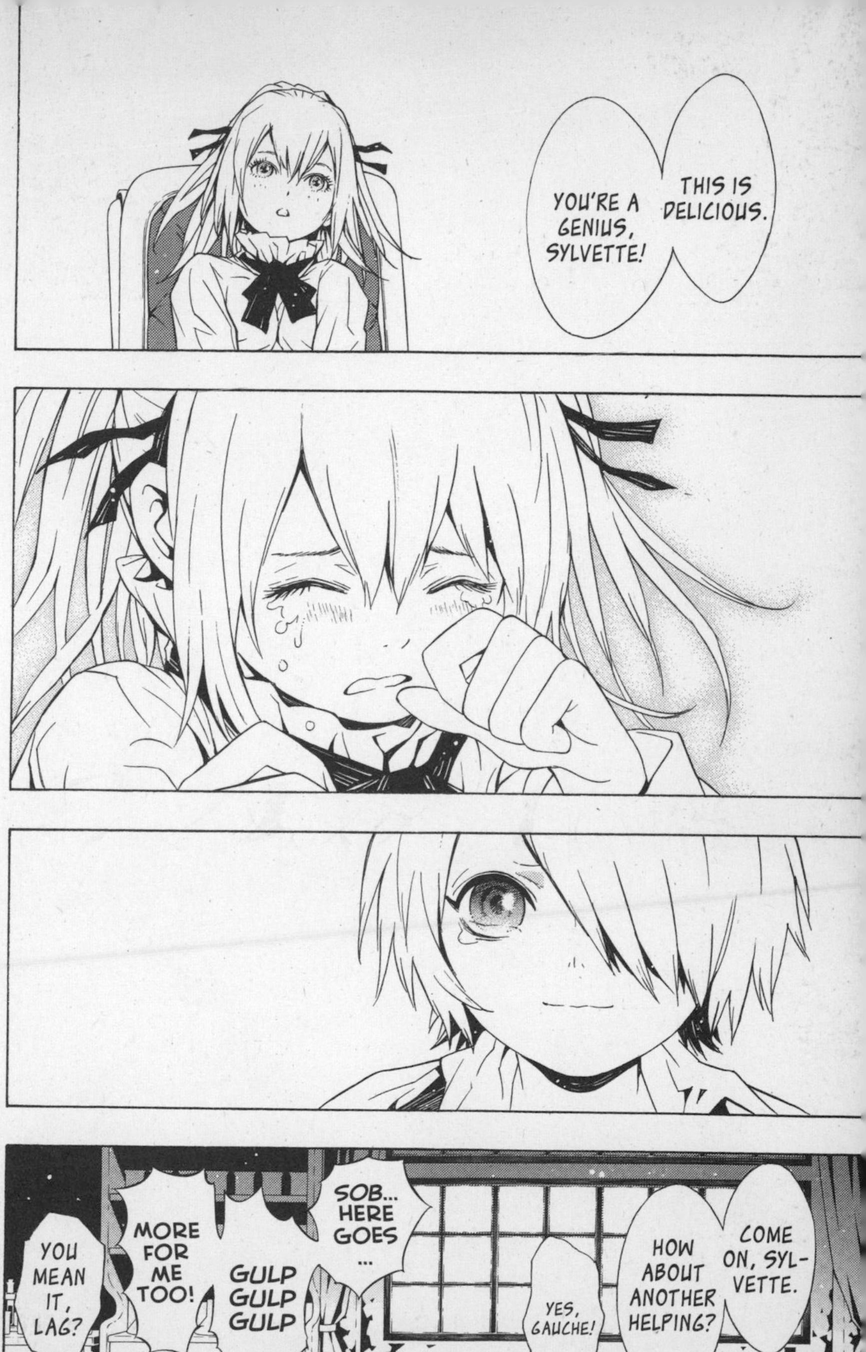
THIS IS DELICIOUS.
YOU'RE A GENIUS, SYLVETTE!
COME ON, SYLVETTE.
HOW ABOUT ANOTHER HELPING?
YES, GAUCHE!
SOB... HERE GOES ...
GULP GULP GULP
MORE FOR ME TOO!
YOU MEAN IT, LAG?

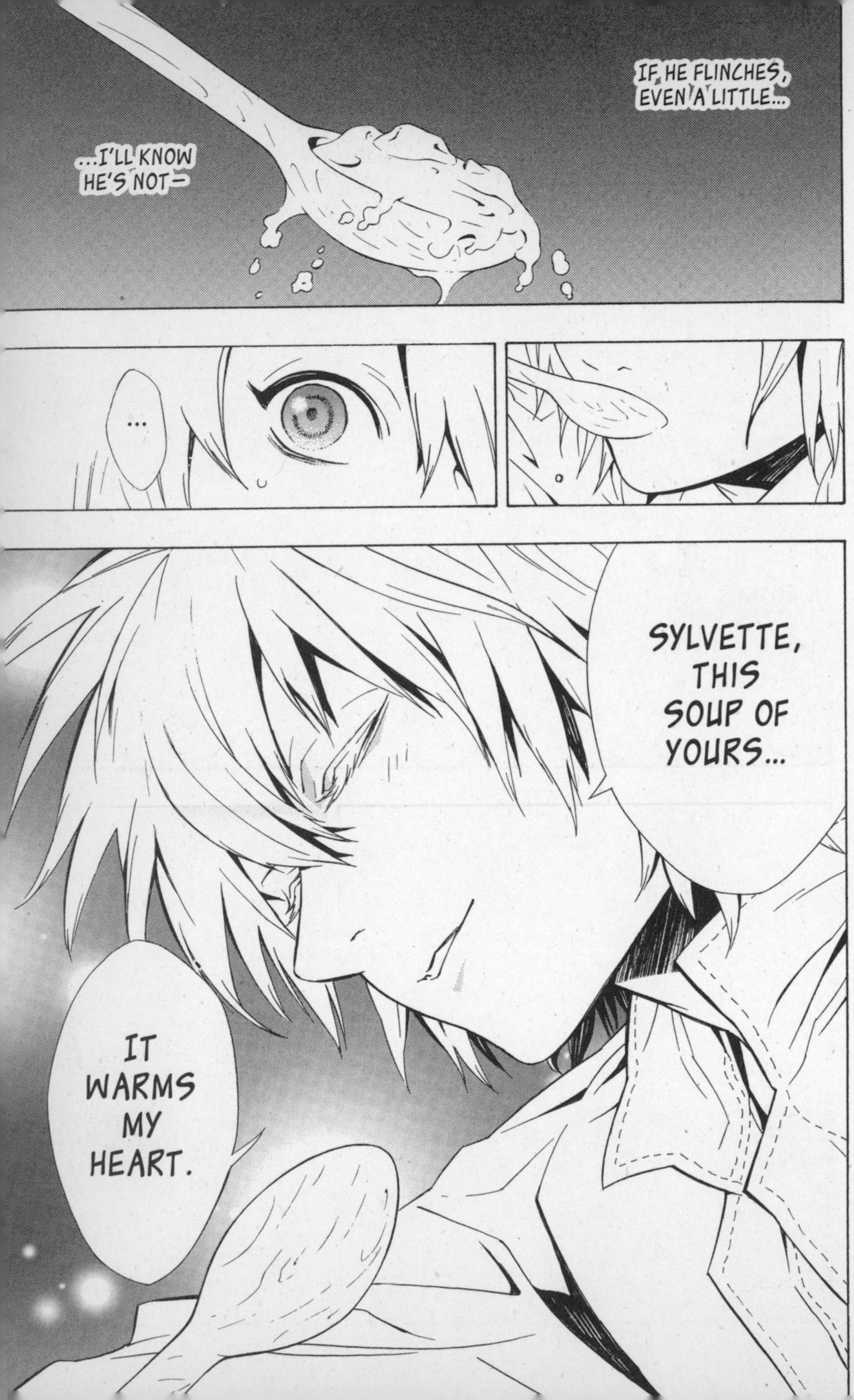
IF HE FLINCHES, EVEN A LITTLE...
...I'LL KNOW HE'S NOT—
...
SYLVETTE, THIS SOUP OF YOURS...
IT WARMS MY HEART.

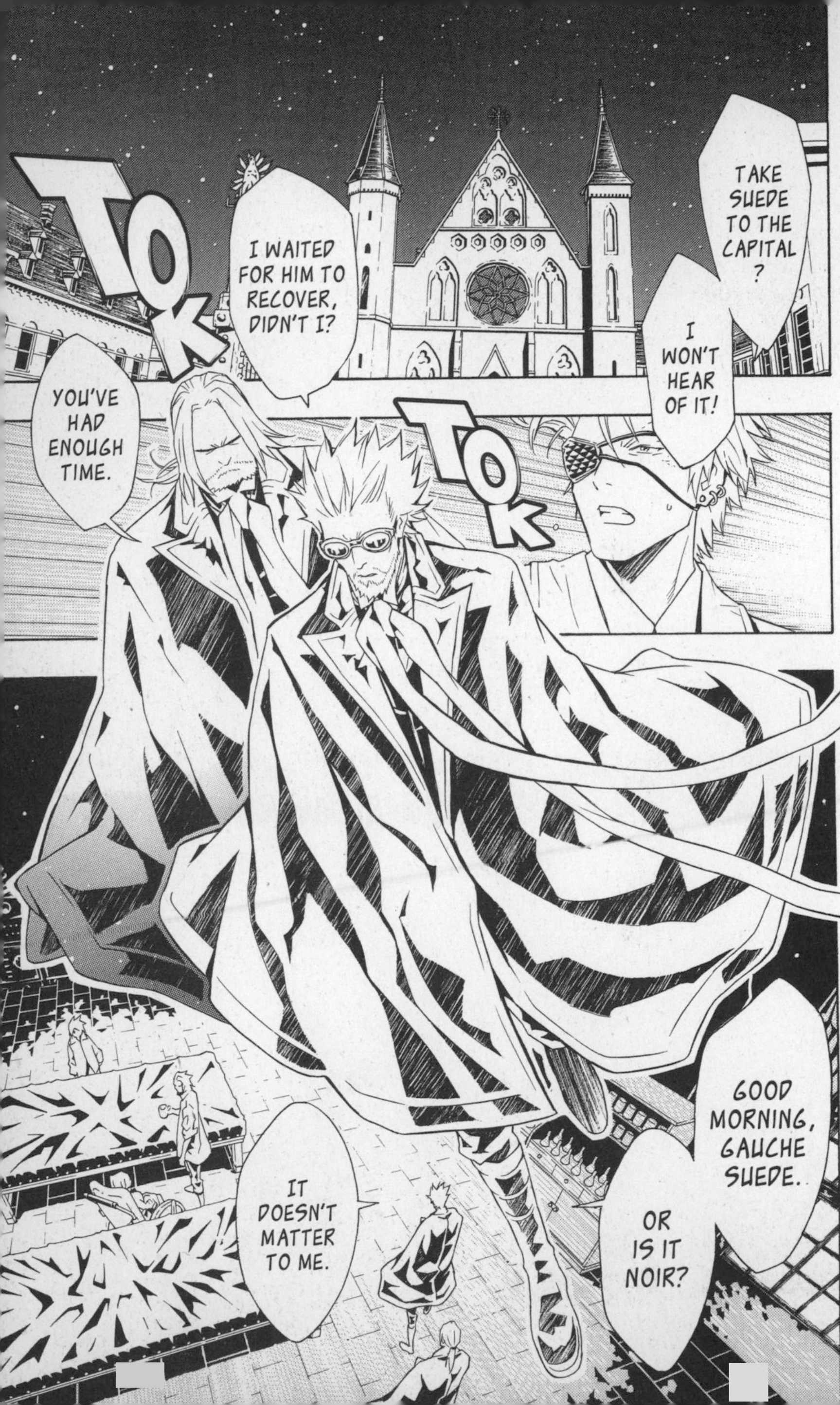
TAKE SUEDE TO THE CAPITAL?
TOK
I WAITED FOR HIM TO RECOVER, DIDN'T I?
YOU'VE HAD ENOUGH TIME.
I WON'T HEAR OF IT!
TOK
GOOD MORNING, GAUCHE SUEDE.
OR IS IT NOIR?
IT DOESN'T MATTER TO ME.

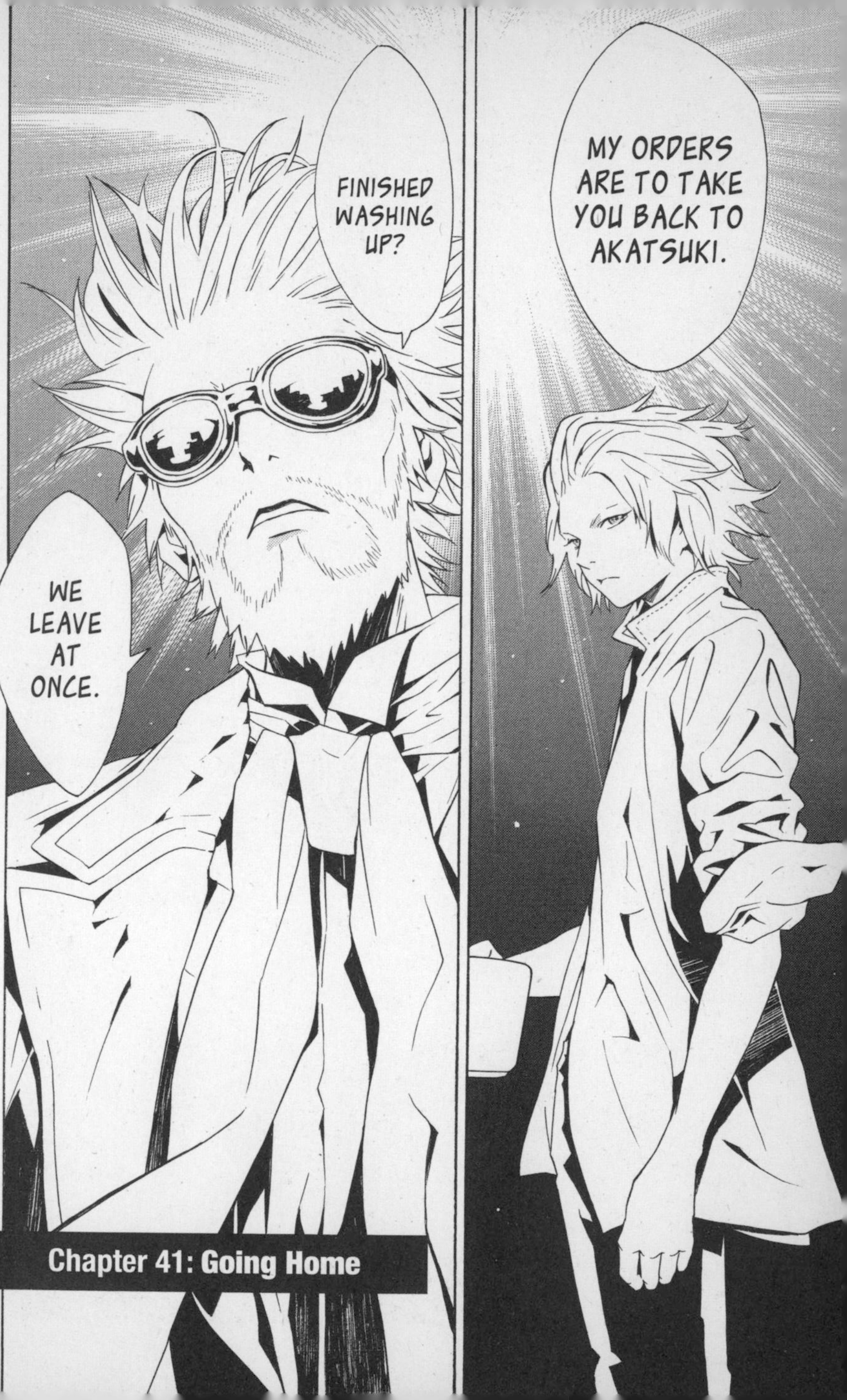
MY ORDERS ARE TO TAKE YOU BACK TO AKATSUKI.
FINISHED WASHING UP?
WE LEAVE AT ONCE.

Chapter 41: Going Home

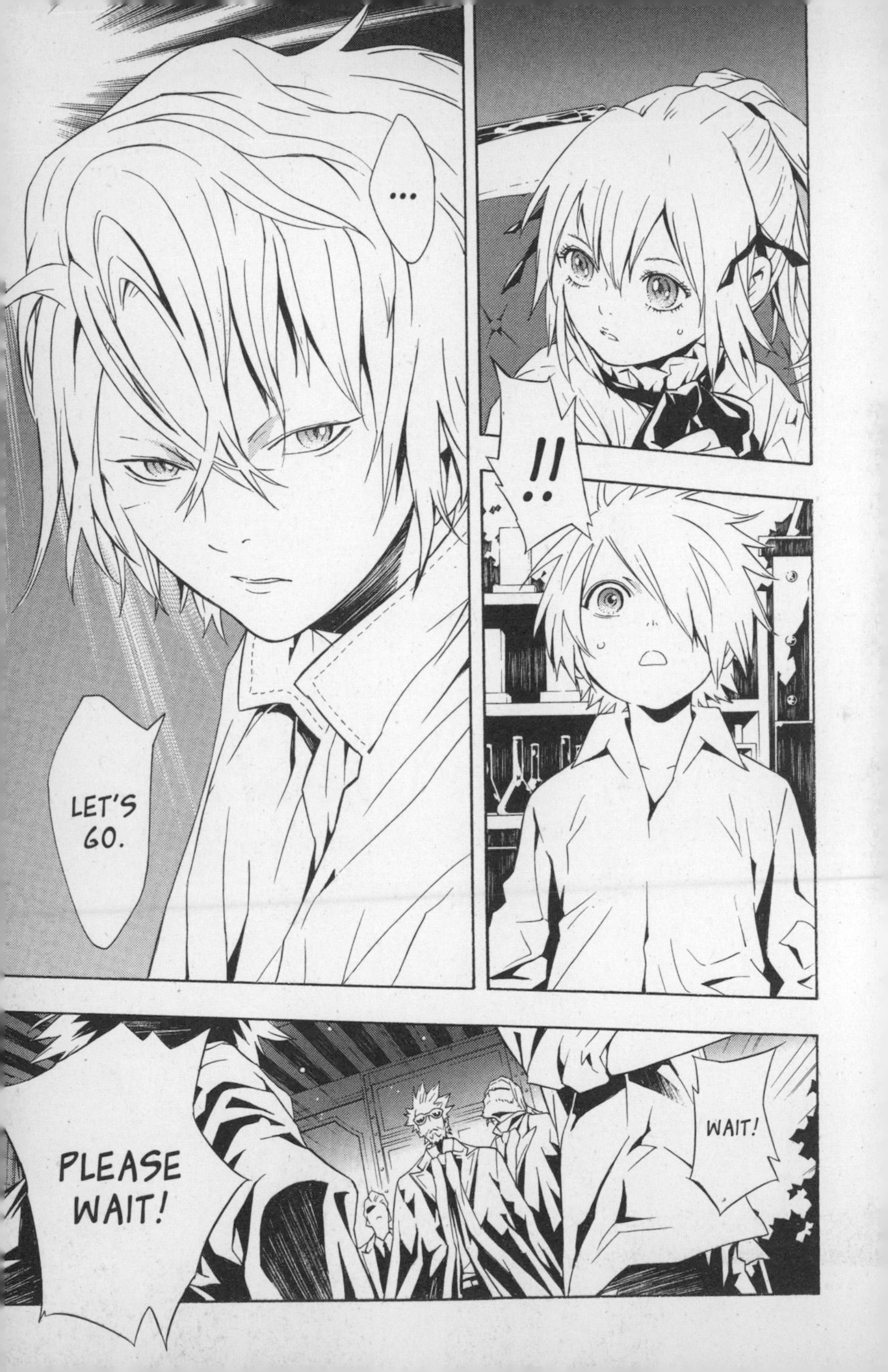

!!
...
LET'S GO.
WAIT!
PLEASE WAIT!

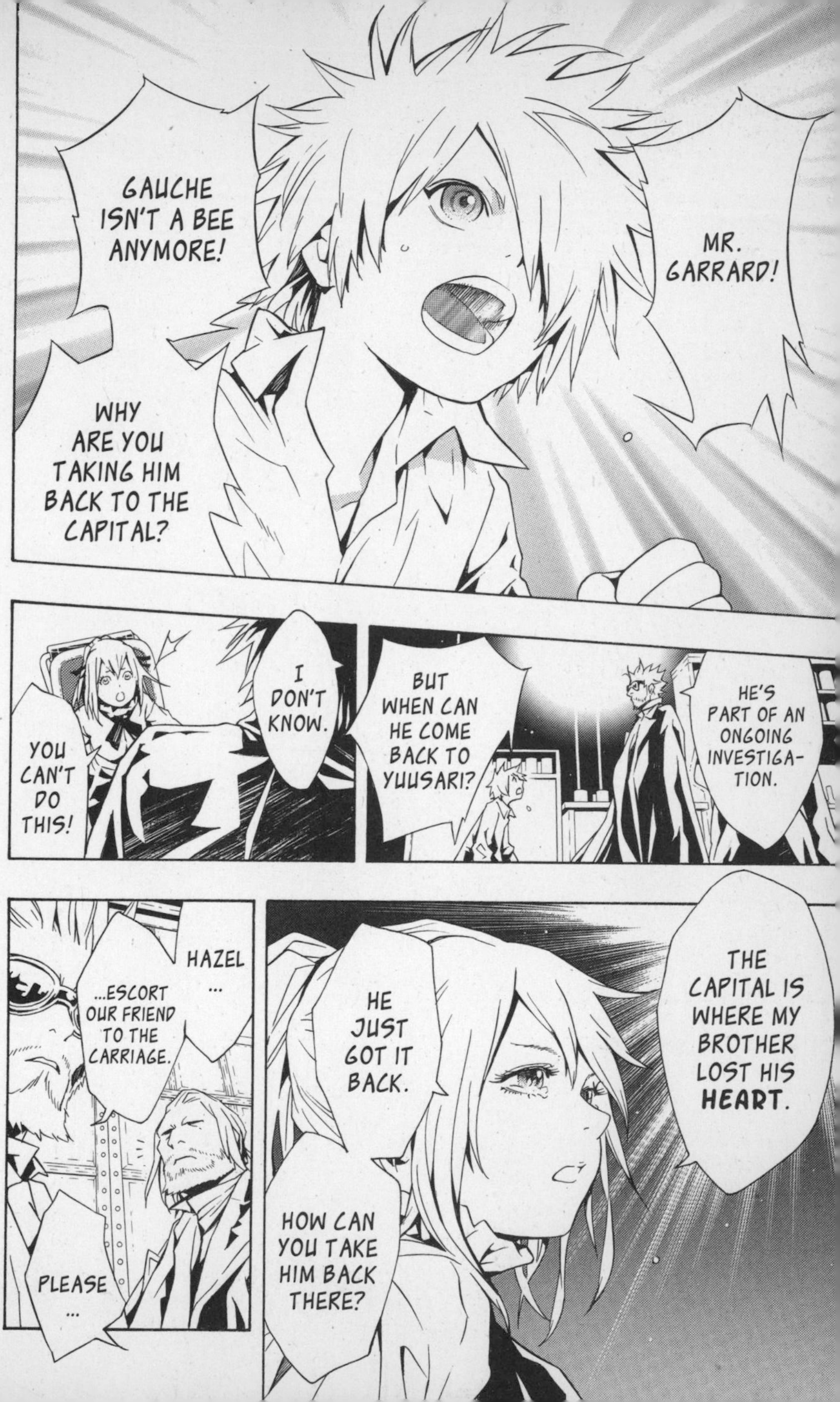
MR. GARRARD!
GAUCHE ISN'T A BEE ANYMORE!
WHY ARE YOU TAKING HIM BACK TO THE CAPITAL?
HE'S PART OF AN ONGOING INVESTIGA-TION.
BUT WHEN CAN HE COME BACK TO YUUSARI?
I DON'T KNOW.
YOU CAN'T DO THIS!
THE CAPITAL IS WHERE MY BROTHER LOST HIS **HEART**.
HE JUST GOT IT BACK.
HOW CAN YOU TAKE HIM BACK THERE?
HAZEL...
...ESCORT OUR FRIEND TO THE CARRIAGE.
PLEASE...

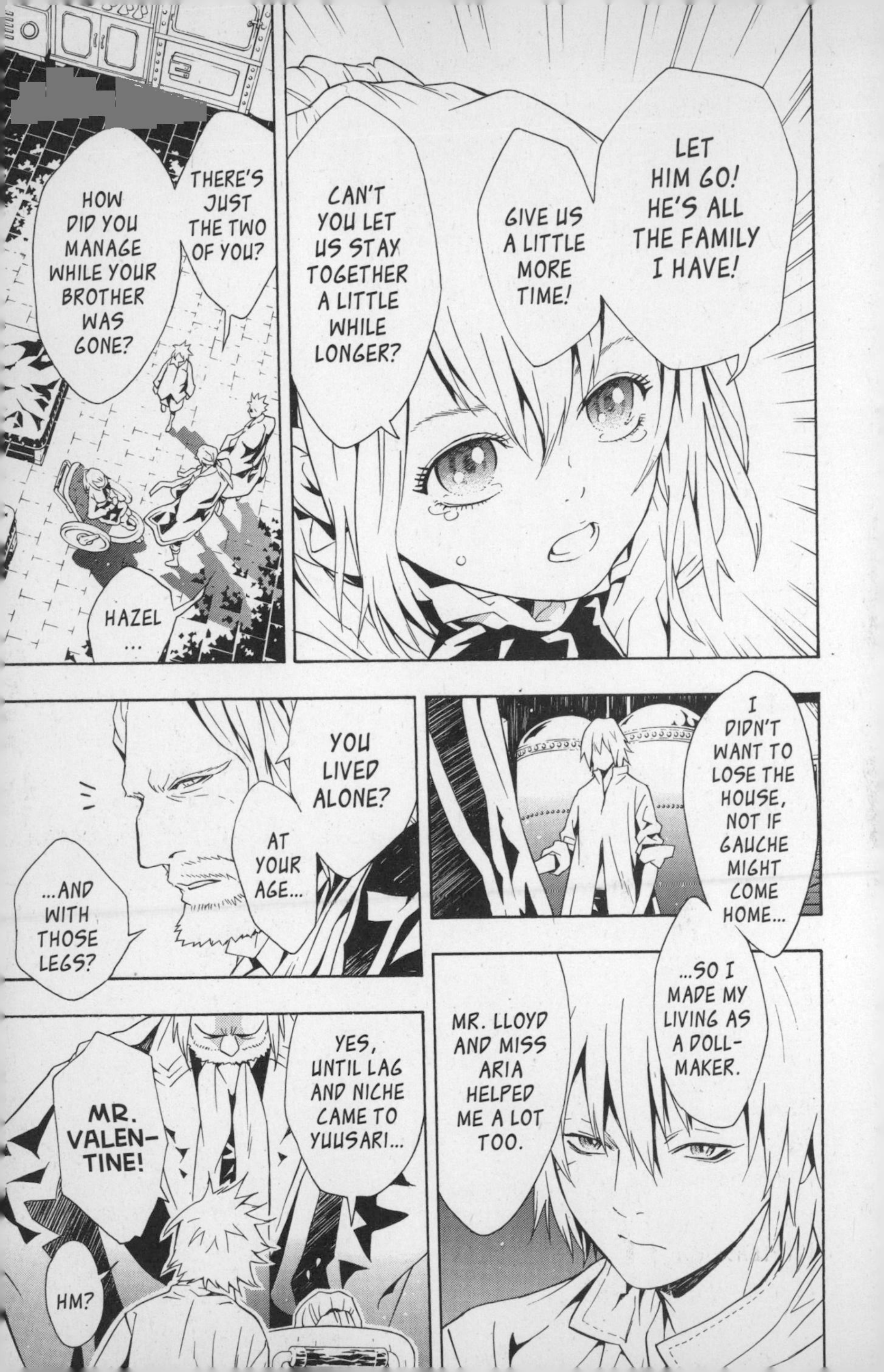
LET HIM GO! HE'S ALL THE FAMILY I HAVE!
GIVE US A LITTLE MORE TIME!
CAN'T YOU LET US STAY TOGETHER A LITTLE WHILE LONGER?
THERE'S JUST THE TWO OF YOU?
HOW DID YOU MANAGE WHILE YOUR BROTHER WAS GONE?
HAZEL...
I DIDN'T WANT TO LOSE THE HOUSE, NOT IF GAUCHE MIGHT COME HOME...
YOU LIVED ALONE?
AT YOUR AGE...
...AND WITH THOSE LEGS?
...SO I MADE MY LIVING AS A DOLL-MAKER.
MR. LLOYD AND MISS ARIA HELPED ME A LOT TOO.
YES, UNTIL LAG AND NICHE CAME TO YUUSARI...
MR. VALENTINE!
HM?

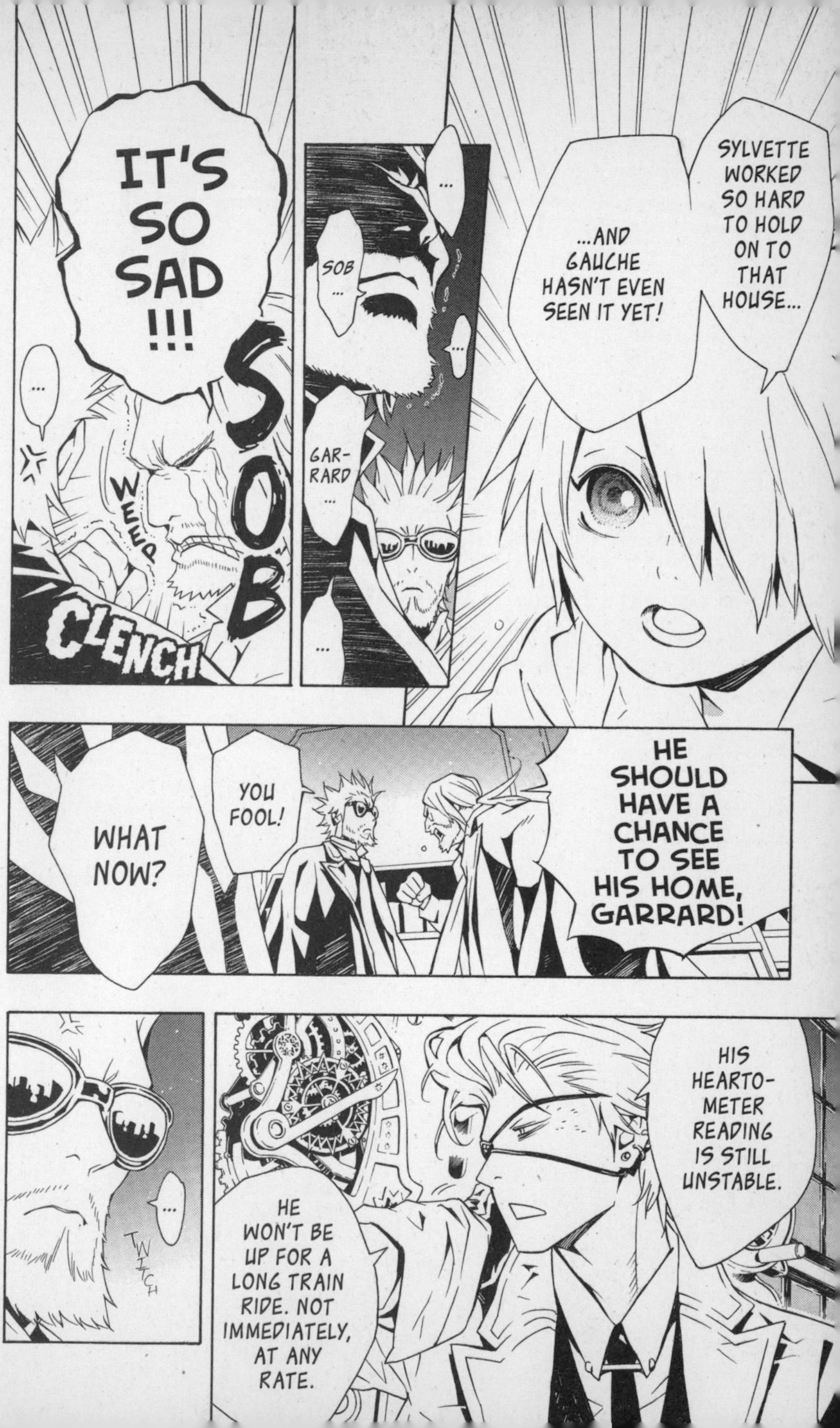
SYLVETTE WORKED SO HARD TO HOLD ON TO THAT HOUSE...
...AND GAUCHE HASN'T EVEN SEEN IT YET!
...
SOB ...
...
GAR-RARD ...
...
IT'S SO SAD !!!
SOB
WEEP
CLENCH
...
HE SHOULD HAVE A CHANCE TO SEE HIS HOME, GARRARD!
YOU FOOL!
WHAT NOW?
HIS HEARTO-METER READING IS STILL UNSTABLE.
HE WON'T BE UP FOR A LONG TRAIN RIDE. NOT IMMEDIATELY, AT ANY RATE.
...
TWITCH

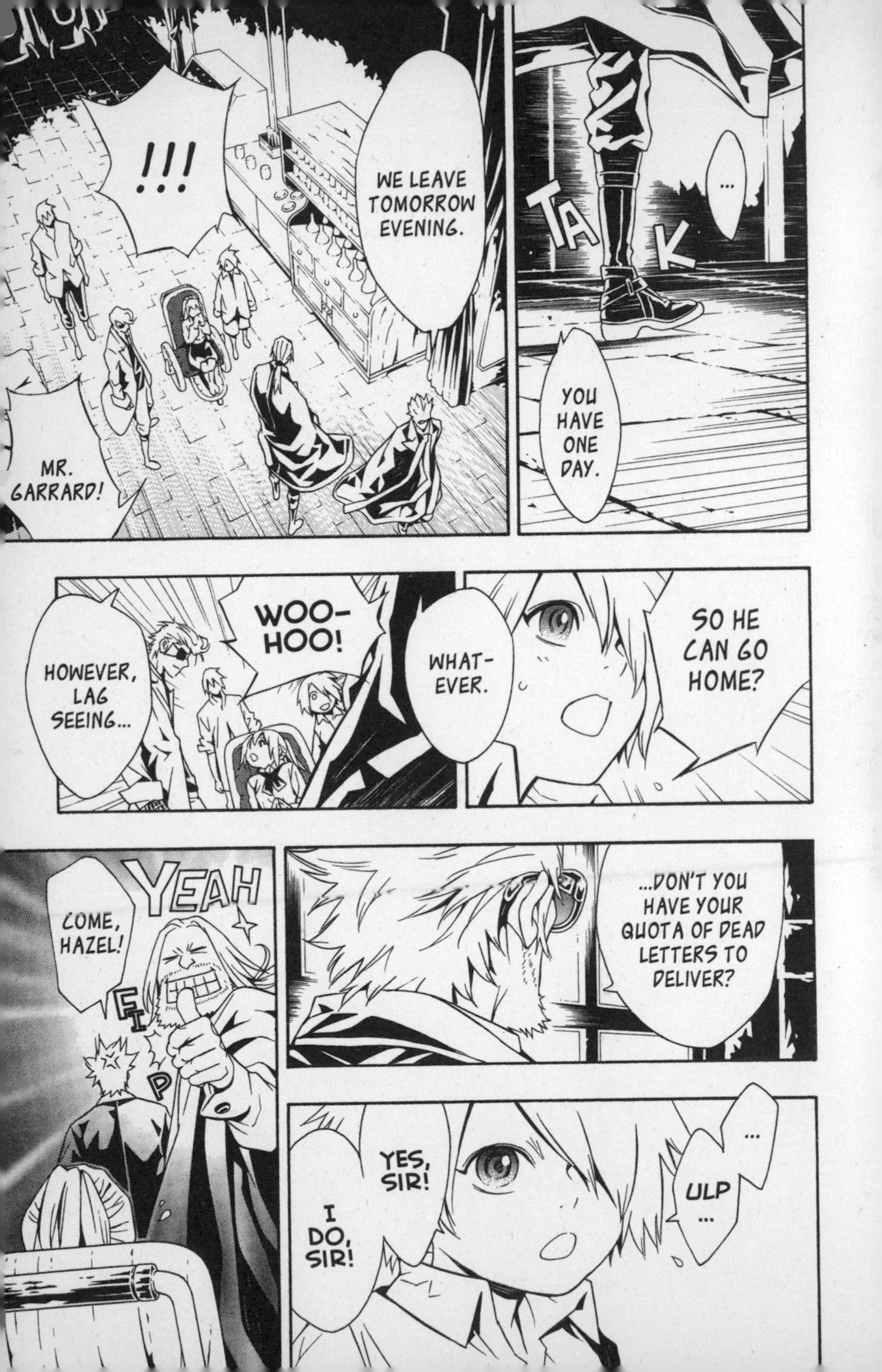
...
TAK
YOU HAVE ONE DAY.
WE LEAVE TOMORROW EVENING.
!!!
MR. GARRARD!
SO HE CAN GO HOME?
WHAT-EVER.
WOO-HOO!
HOWEVER, LAG SEEING...
...DON'T YOU HAVE YOUR QUOTA OF DEAD LETTERS TO DELIVER?
...
ULP...
YES, SIR!
I DO, SIR!
YEAH
COME, HAZEL!
FLIP

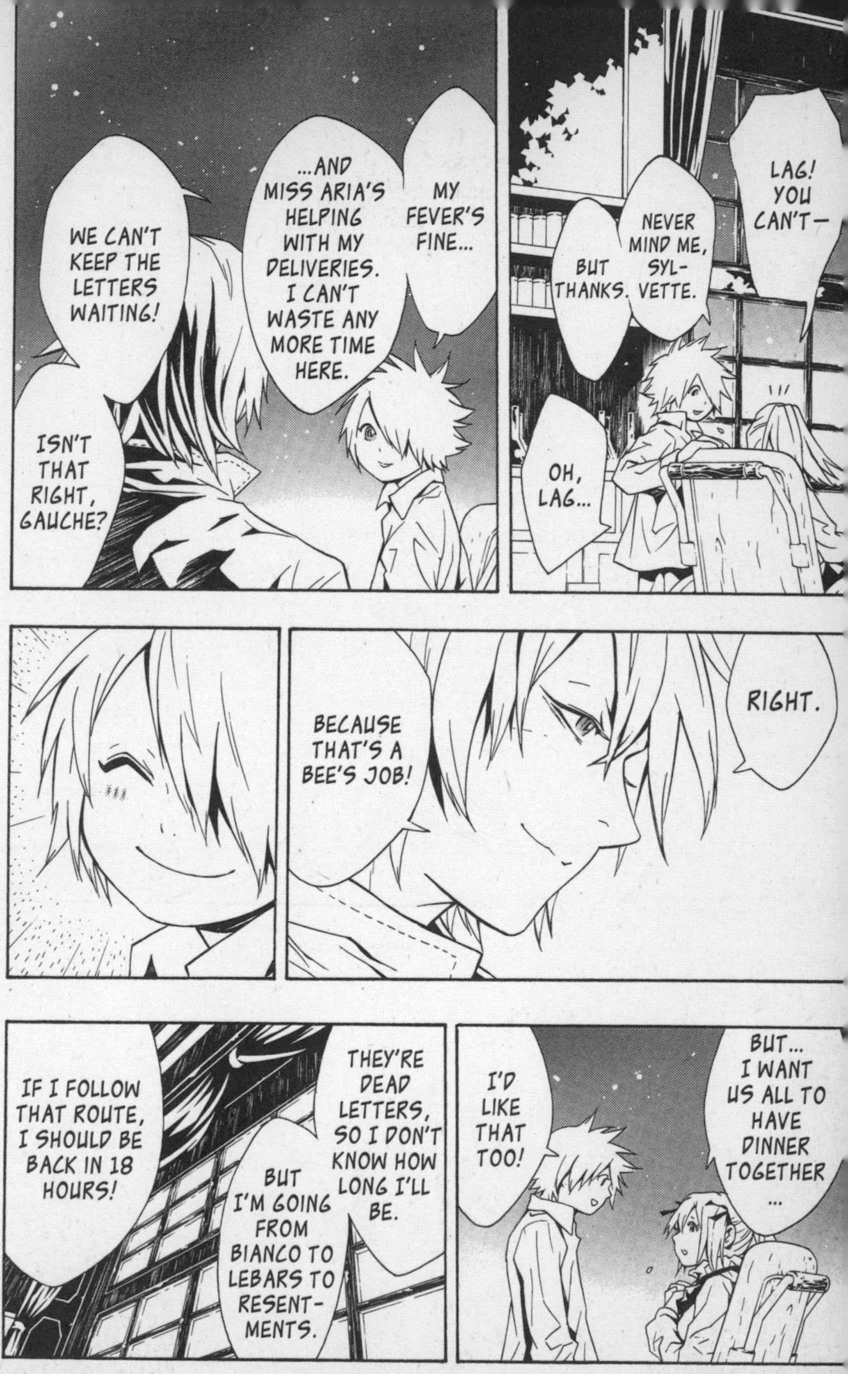
LAG! YOU CAN'T—
NEVER MIND ME, SYLVETTE.
BUT THANKS.
OH, LAG...
MY FEVER'S FINE...
...AND MISS ARIA'S HELPING WITH MY DELIVERIES. I CAN'T WASTE ANY MORE TIME HERE.
WE CAN'T KEEP THE LETTERS WAITING!
ISN'T THAT RIGHT, GAUCHE?
RIGHT.
BECAUSE THAT'S A BEE'S JOB!
BUT... I WANT US ALL TO HAVE DINNER TOGETHER ...
I'D LIKE THAT TOO!
THEY'RE DEAD LETTERS, SO I DON'T KNOW HOW LONG I'LL BE.
BUT I'M GOING FROM BIANCO TO LEBARS TO RESENTMENTS.
IF I FOLLOW THAT ROUTE, I SHOULD BE BACK IN 18 HOURS!

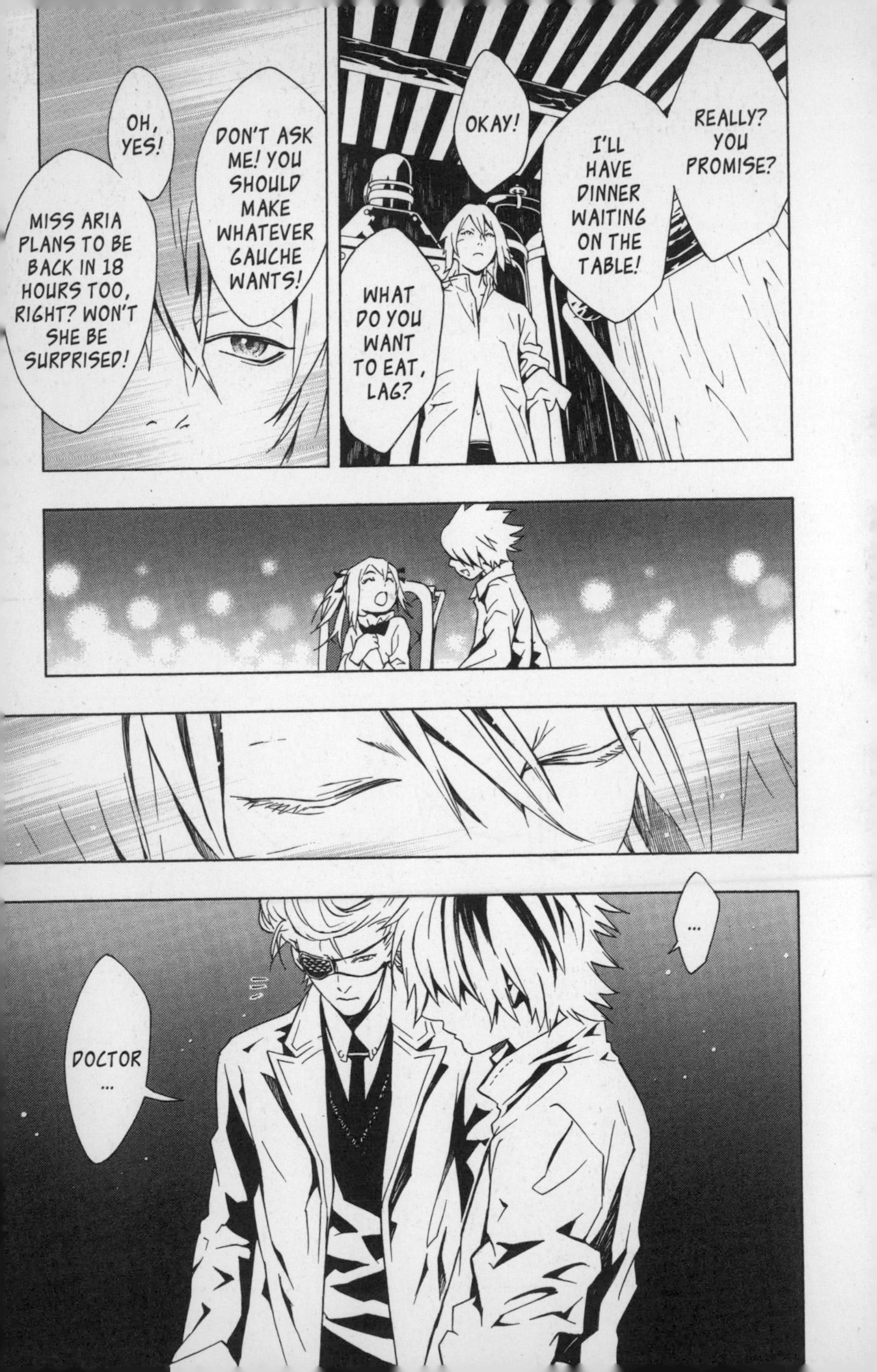
REALLY? YOU PROMISE?
I'LL HAVE DINNER WAITING ON THE TABLE!
OKAY!
WHAT DO YOU WANT TO EAT, LAG?
DON'T ASK ME! YOU SHOULD MAKE WHATEVER GAUCHE WANTS!
OH, YES!
MISS ARIA PLANS TO BE BACK IN 18 HOURS TOO, RIGHT? WON'T SHE BE SURPRISED!
...
DOCTOR ...

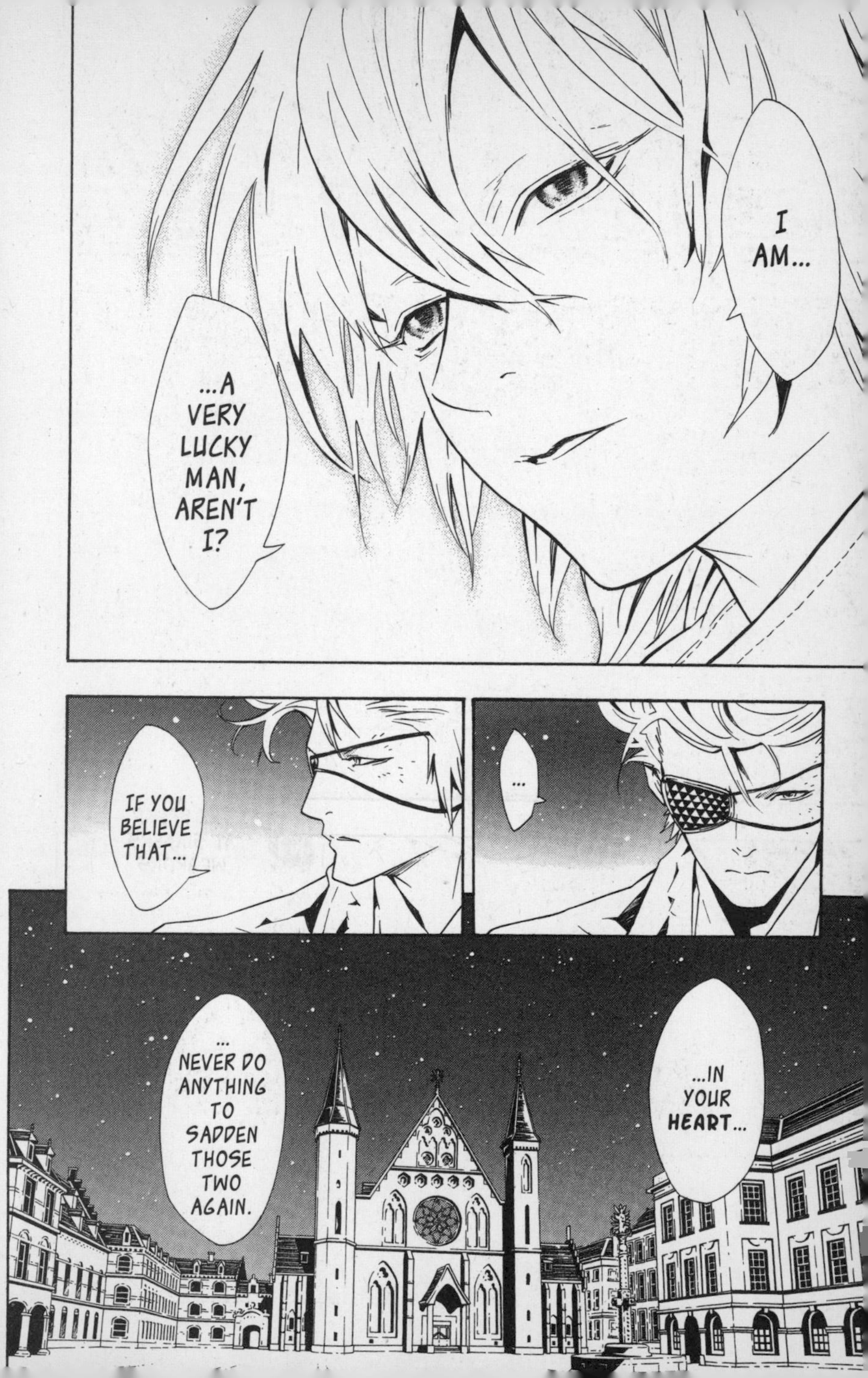
I AM...
...A VERY LUCKY MAN, AREN'T I?
...
IF YOU BELIEVE THAT...
...IN YOUR HEART...
... NEVER DO ANYTHING TO SADDEN THOSE TWO AGAIN.

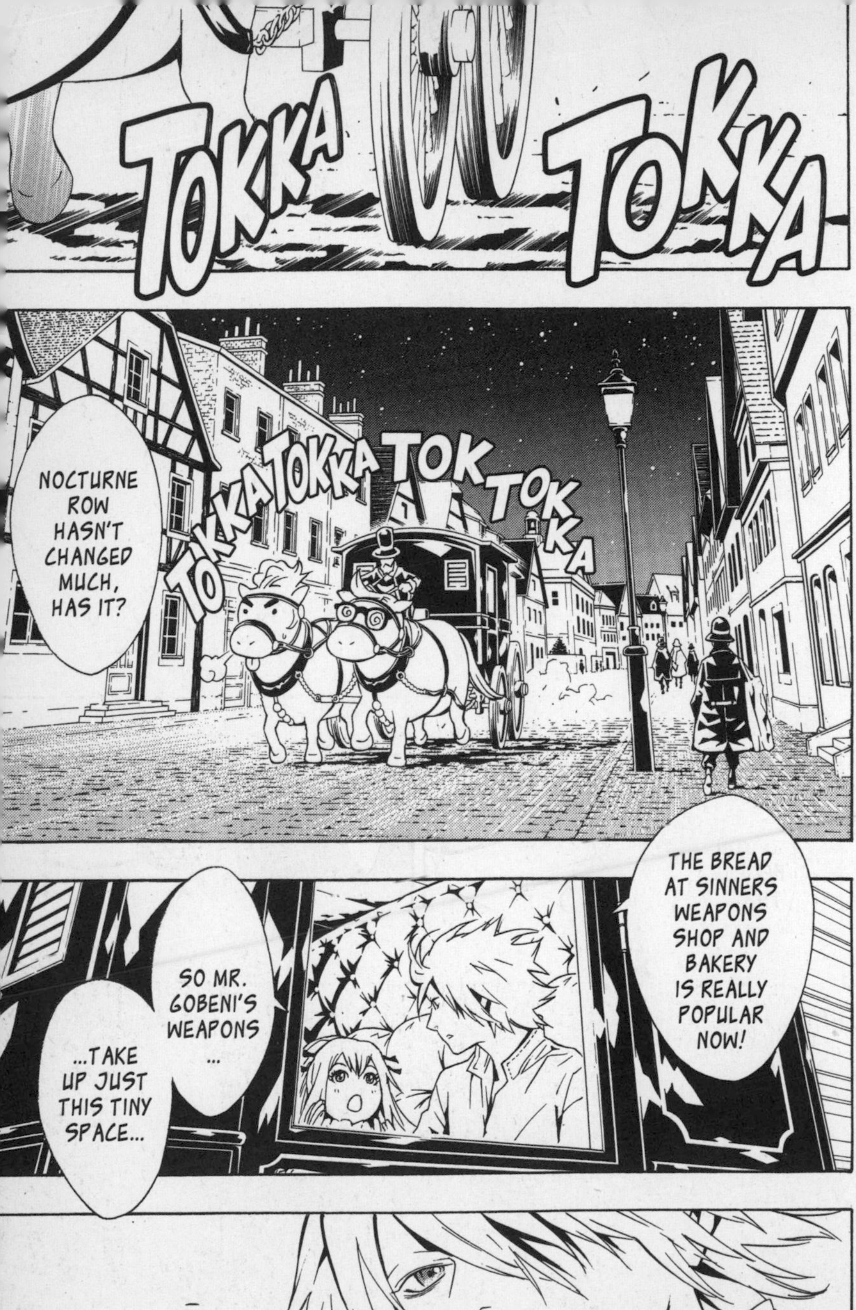
TOKKA
TOKKA
TOKKA TOKKA TOK
TOKKA
NOCTURNE ROW HASN'T CHANGED MUCH, HAS IT?
THE BREAD AT SINNERS WEAPONS SHOP AND BAKERY IS REALLY POPULAR NOW!
SO MR. GOBENI'S WEAPONS ...
...TAKE UP JUST THIS TINY SPACE...

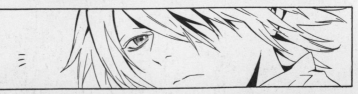

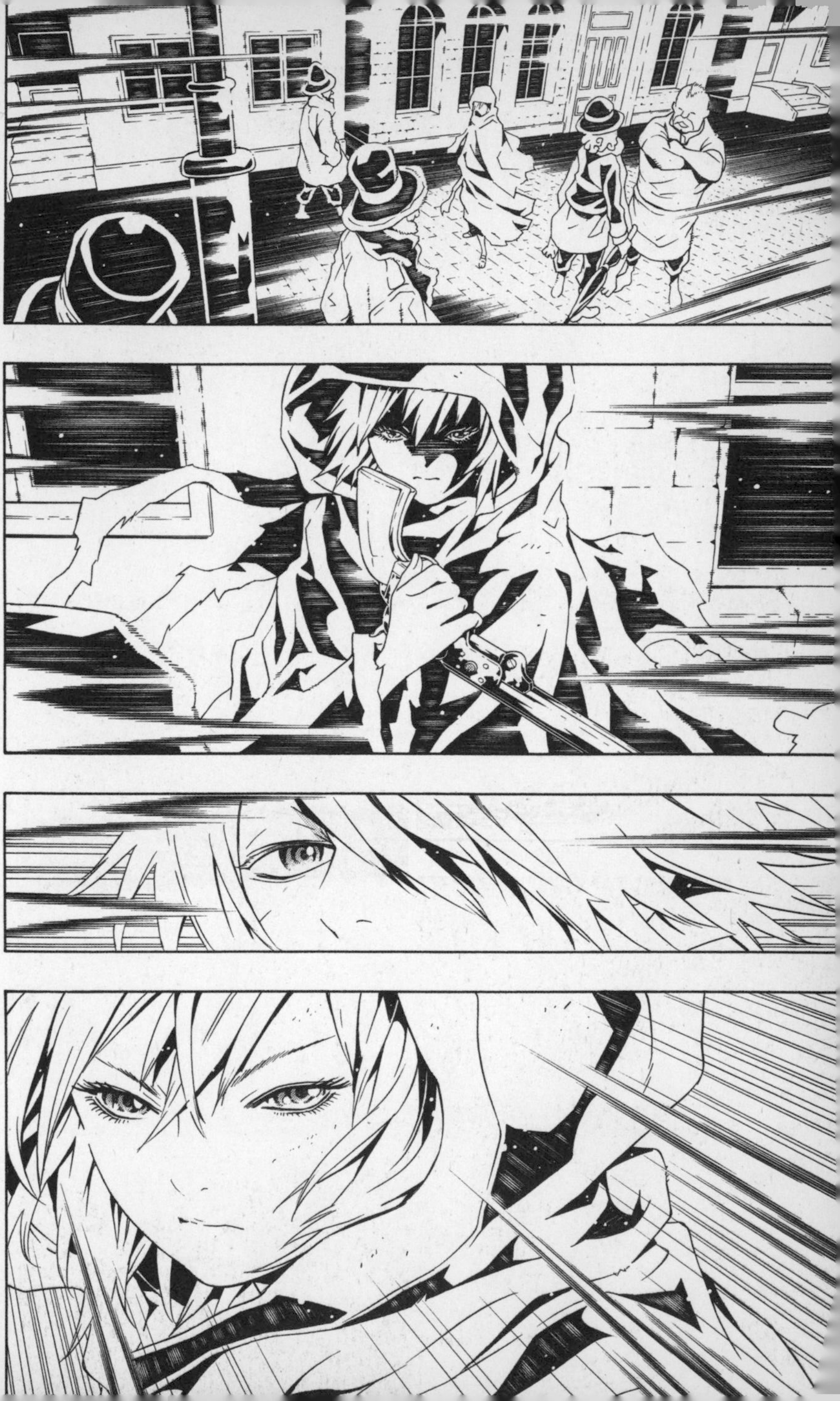

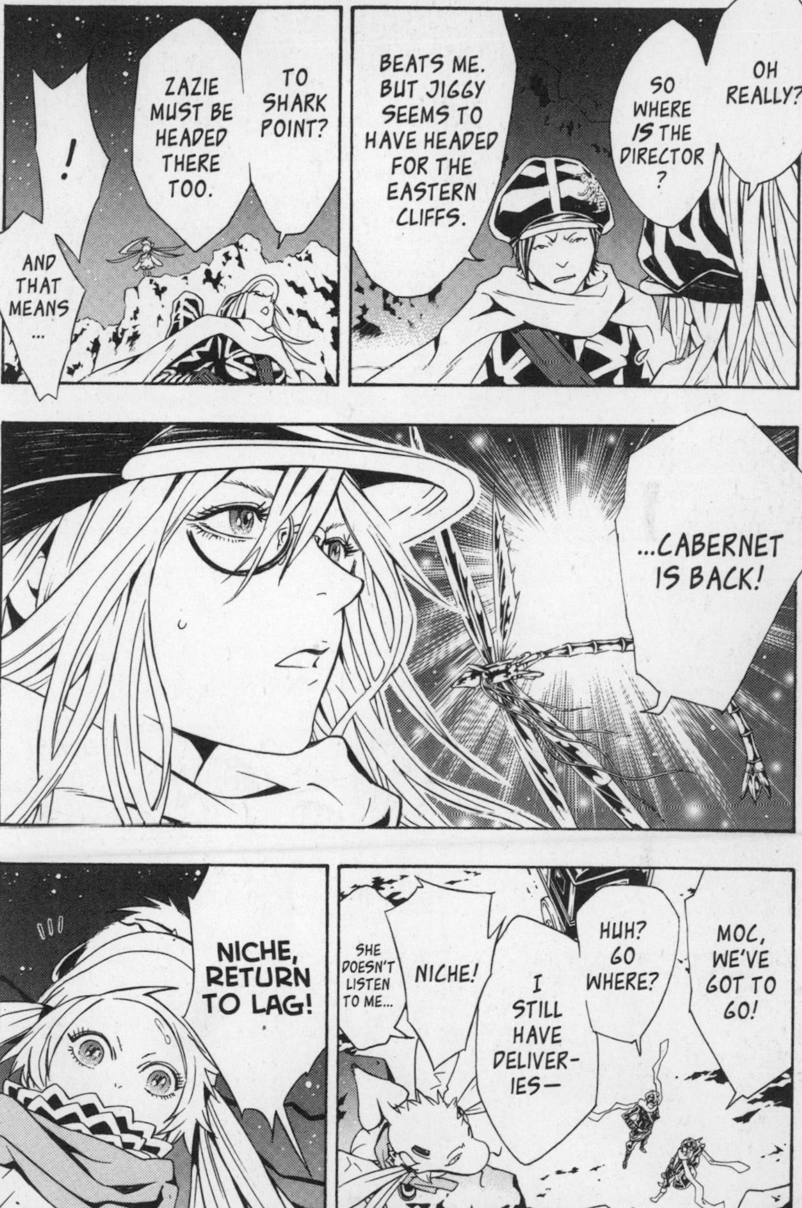
OH REALLY?
SO WHERE IS THE DIRECTOR?
BEATS ME. BUT JIGGY SEEMS TO HAVE HEADED FOR THE EASTERN CLIFFS.
TO SHARK POINT?
ZAZIE MUST BE HEADED THERE TOO.
!
AND THAT MEANS ...
...CABERNET IS BACK!
MOC, WE'VE GOT TO GO!
HUH? GO WHERE?
I STILL HAVE DELIVER-IES—
NICHE!
SHE DOESN'T LISTEN TO ME...
NICHE, RETURN TO LAG!

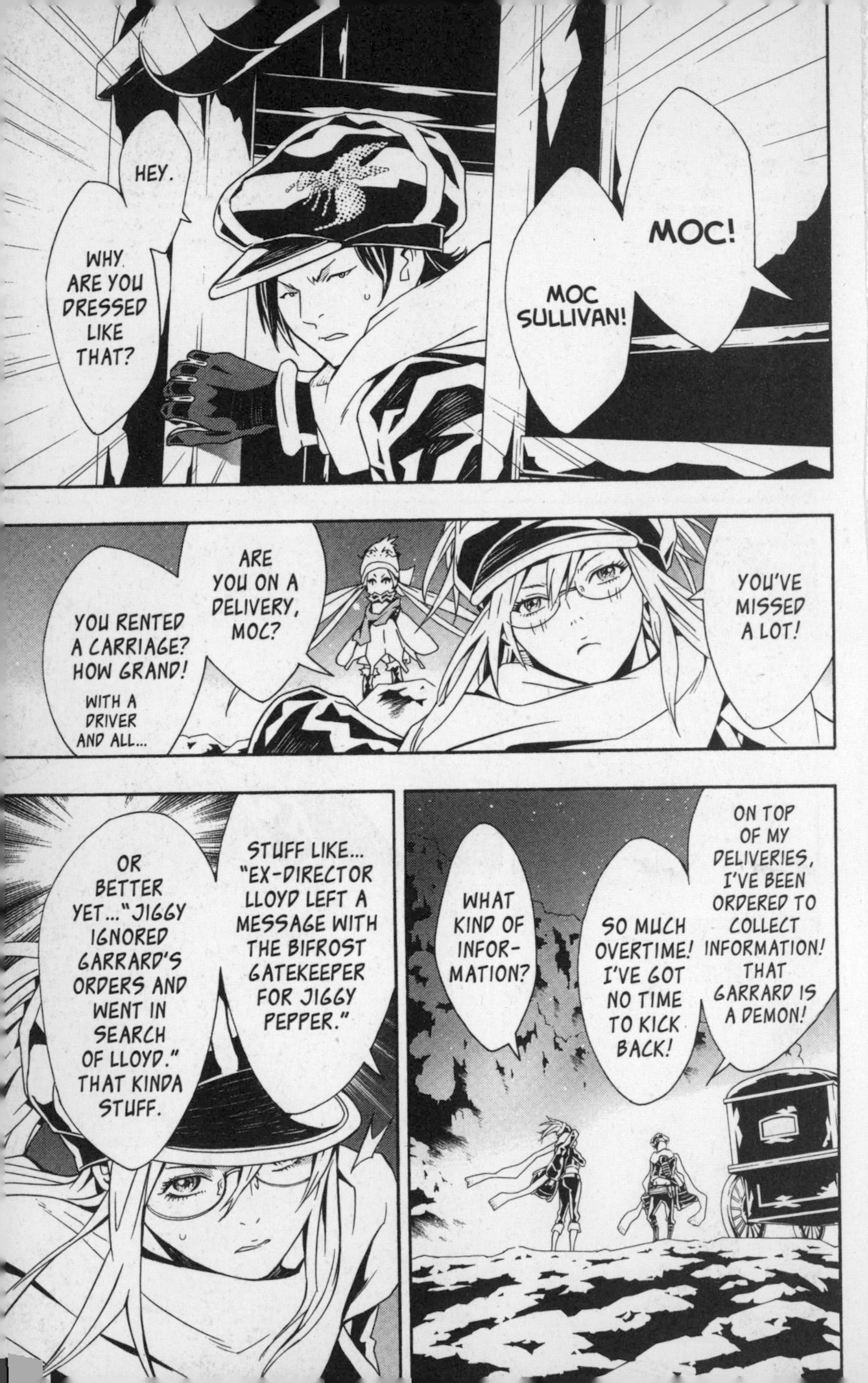
MOC!
MOC SULLIVAN!
HEY.
WHY ARE YOU DRESSED LIKE THAT?
YOU'VE MISSED A LOT!
ARE YOU ON A DELIVERY, MOC?
YOU RENTED A CARRIAGE? HOW GRAND!
WITH A DRIVER AND ALL...
ON TOP OF MY DELIVERIES, I'VE BEEN ORDERED TO COLLECT INFORMATION! THAT GARRARD IS A DEMON!
SO MUCH OVERTIME! I'VE GOT NO TIME TO KICK BACK!
WHAT KIND OF INFOR-MATION?
STUFF LIKE... "EX-DIRECTOR LLOYD LEFT A MESSAGE WITH THE BIFROST GATEKEEPER FOR JIGGY PEPPER."
OR BETTER YET... "JIGGY IGNORED GARRARD'S ORDERS AND WENT IN SEARCH OF LLOYD." THAT KINDA STUFF.

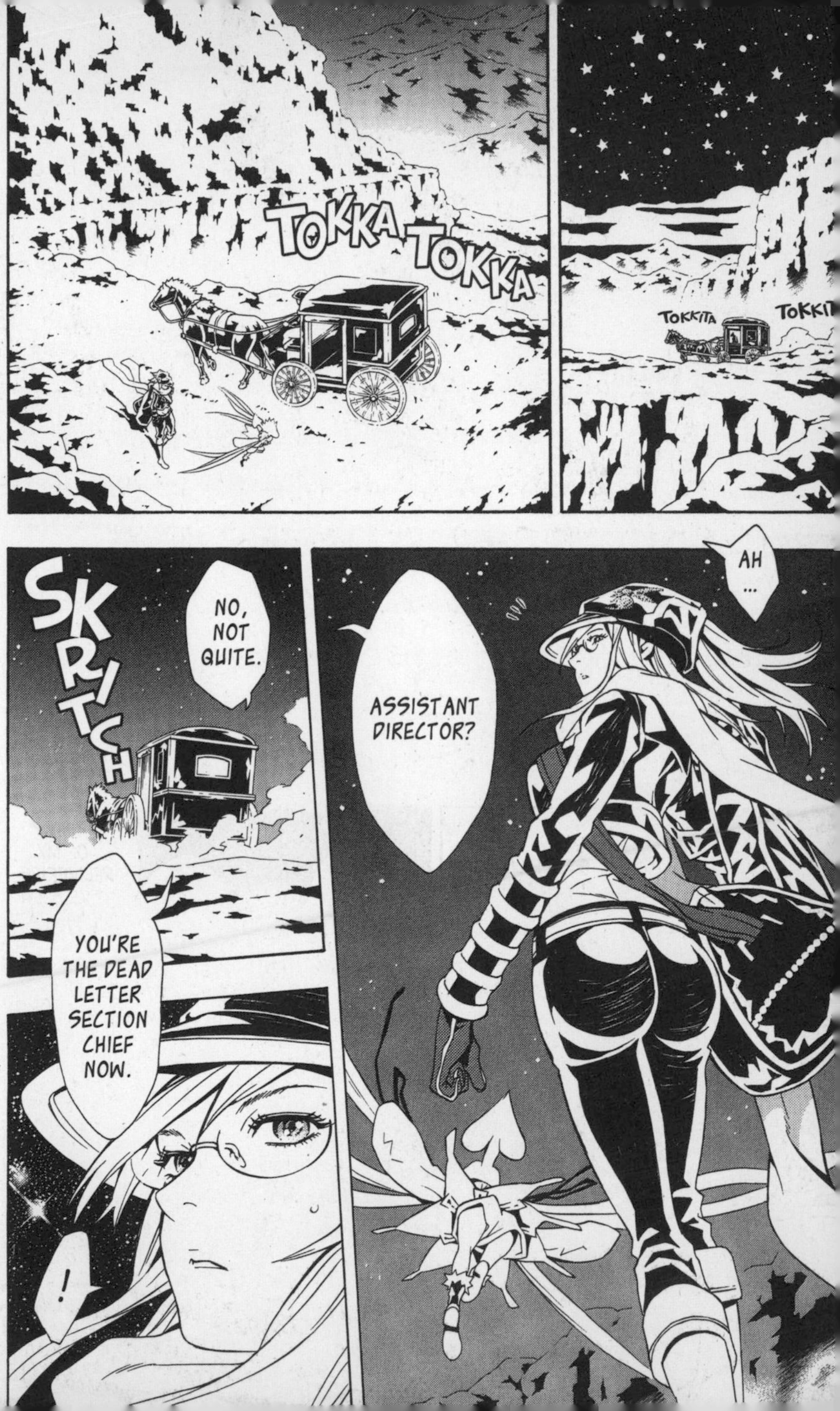

TOKKITA
TOKKITA
TOKKA TOKKA
AH ...
ASSISTANT DIRECTOR?
SKRITCH
NO, NOT QUITE.
YOU'RE THE DEAD LETTER SECTION CHIEF NOW.
!

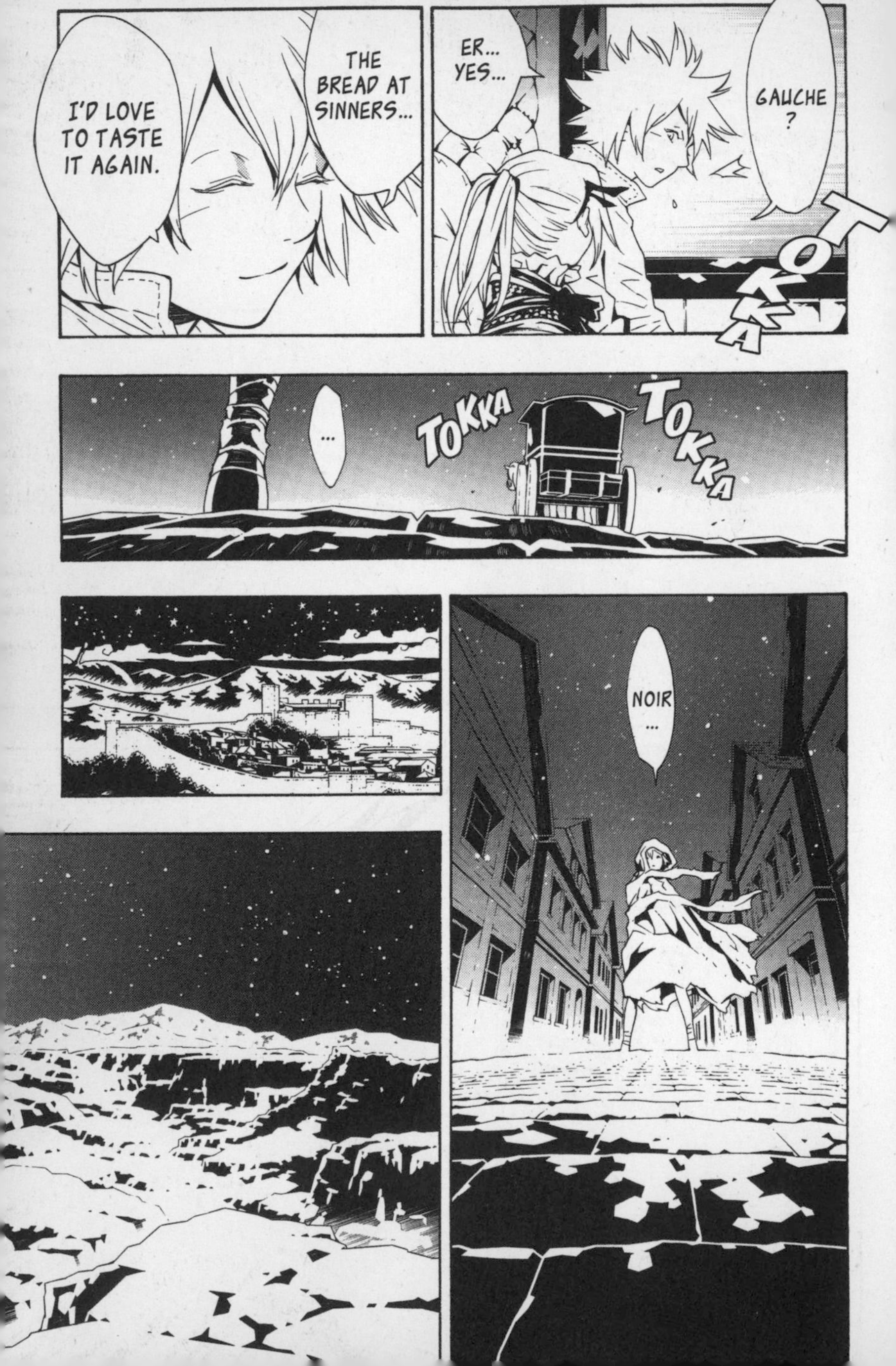
GAUCHE?
TOKKA
ER... YES...
THE BREAD AT SINNERS...
I'D LOVE TO TASTE IT AGAIN.
TOKKA
TOKKA
...
NOIR...

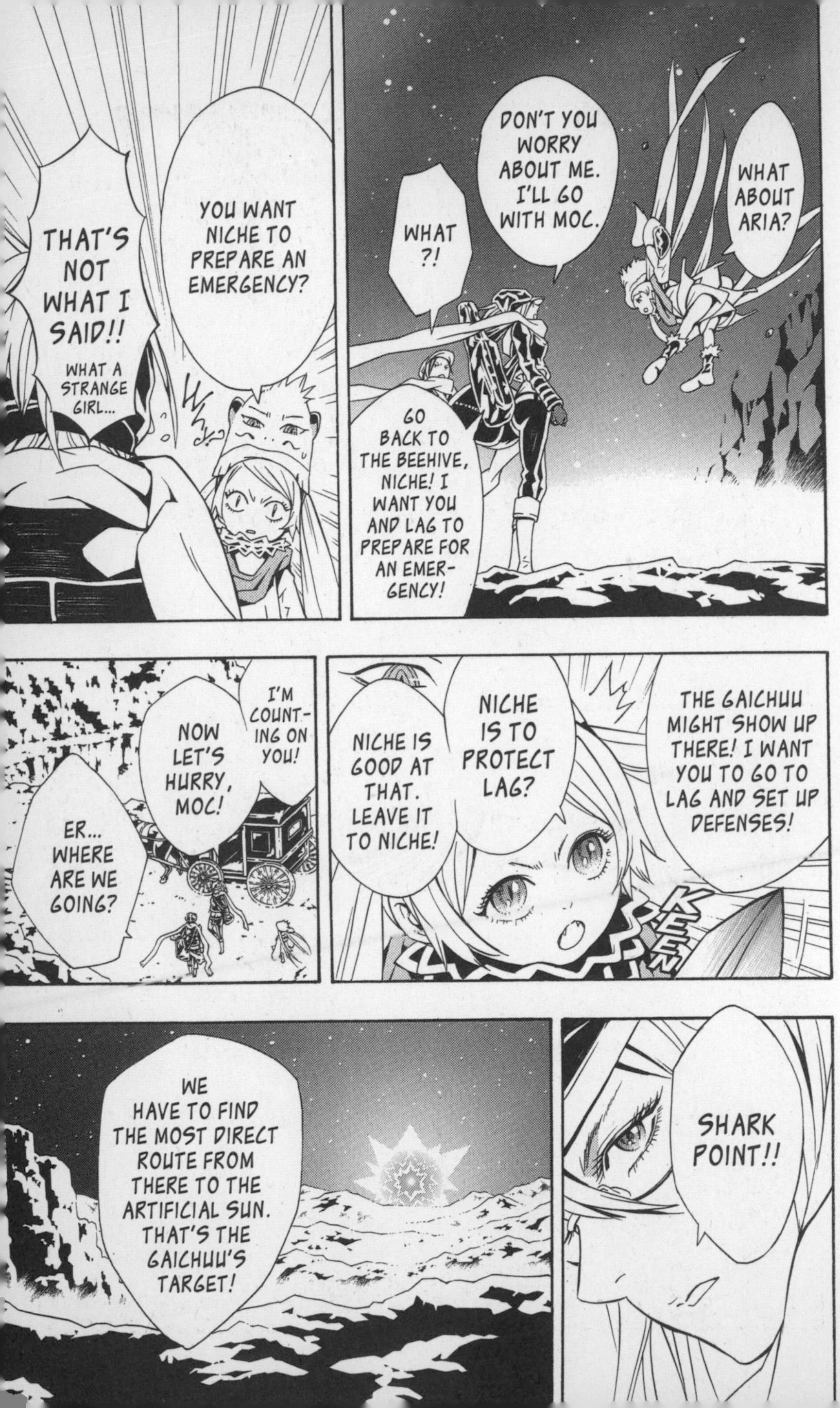
WHAT ABOUT ARIA?
DON'T YOU WORRY ABOUT ME. I'LL GO WITH MOC.
WHAT?!
GO BACK TO THE BEEHIVE, NICHE! I WANT YOU AND LAG TO PREPARE FOR AN EMERGENCY!
YOU WANT NICHE TO PREPARE AN EMERGENCY?
THAT'S NOT WHAT I SAID!!
WHAT A STRANGE GIRL...
THE GAICHUU MIGHT SHOW UP THERE! I WANT YOU TO GO TO LAG AND SET UP DEFENSES!
KEEN
NICHE IS TO PROTECT LAG?
NICHE IS GOOD AT THAT. LEAVE IT TO NICHE!
I'M COUNTING ON YOU!
NOW LET'S HURRY, MOC!
ER... WHERE ARE WE GOING?
SHARK POINT!!
WE HAVE TO FIND THE MOST DIRECT ROUTE FROM THERE TO THE ARTIFICIAL SUN. THAT'S THE GAICHUU'S TARGET!

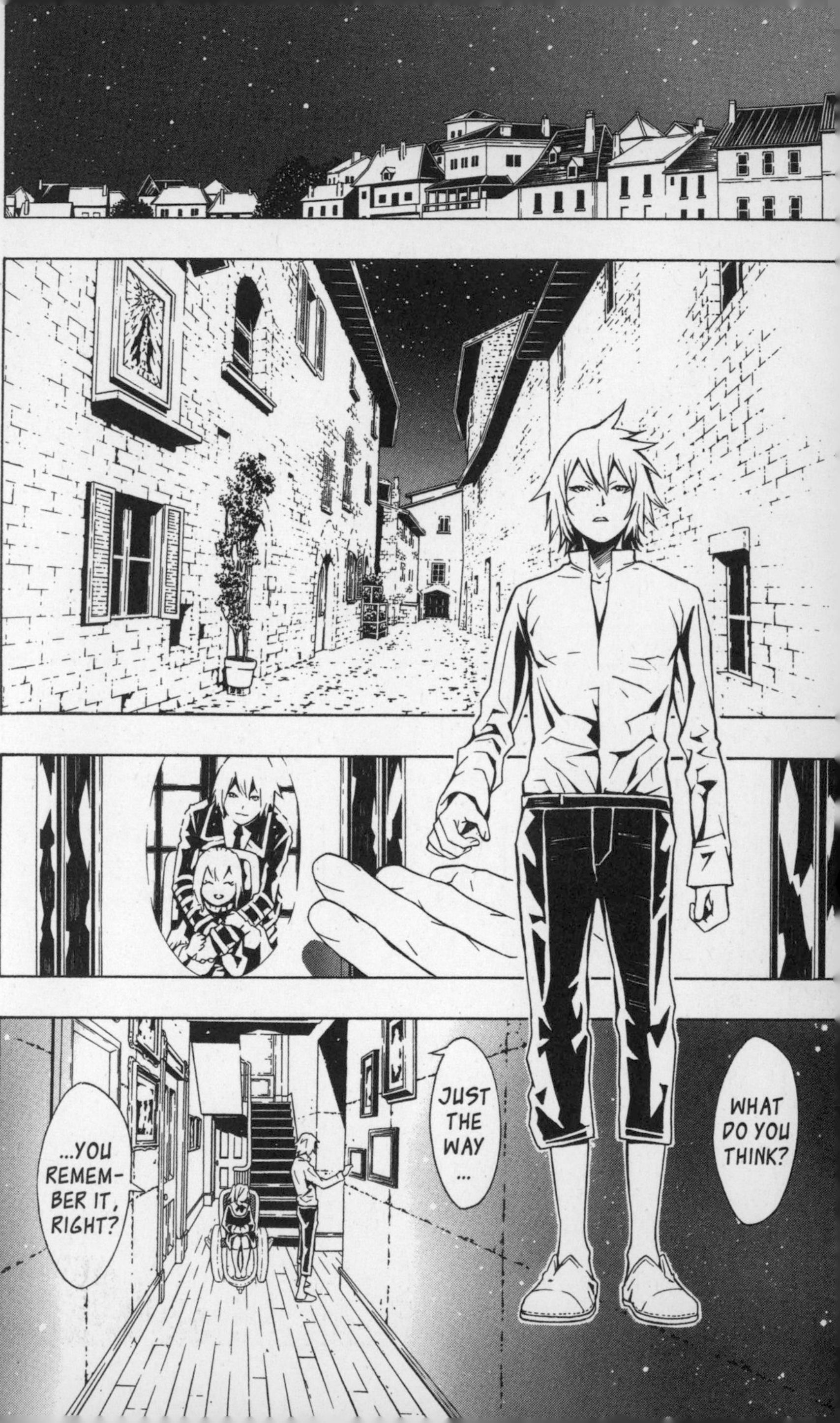
WHAT DO YOU THINK?
JUST THE WAY ...
...YOU REMEMBER IT, RIGHT?

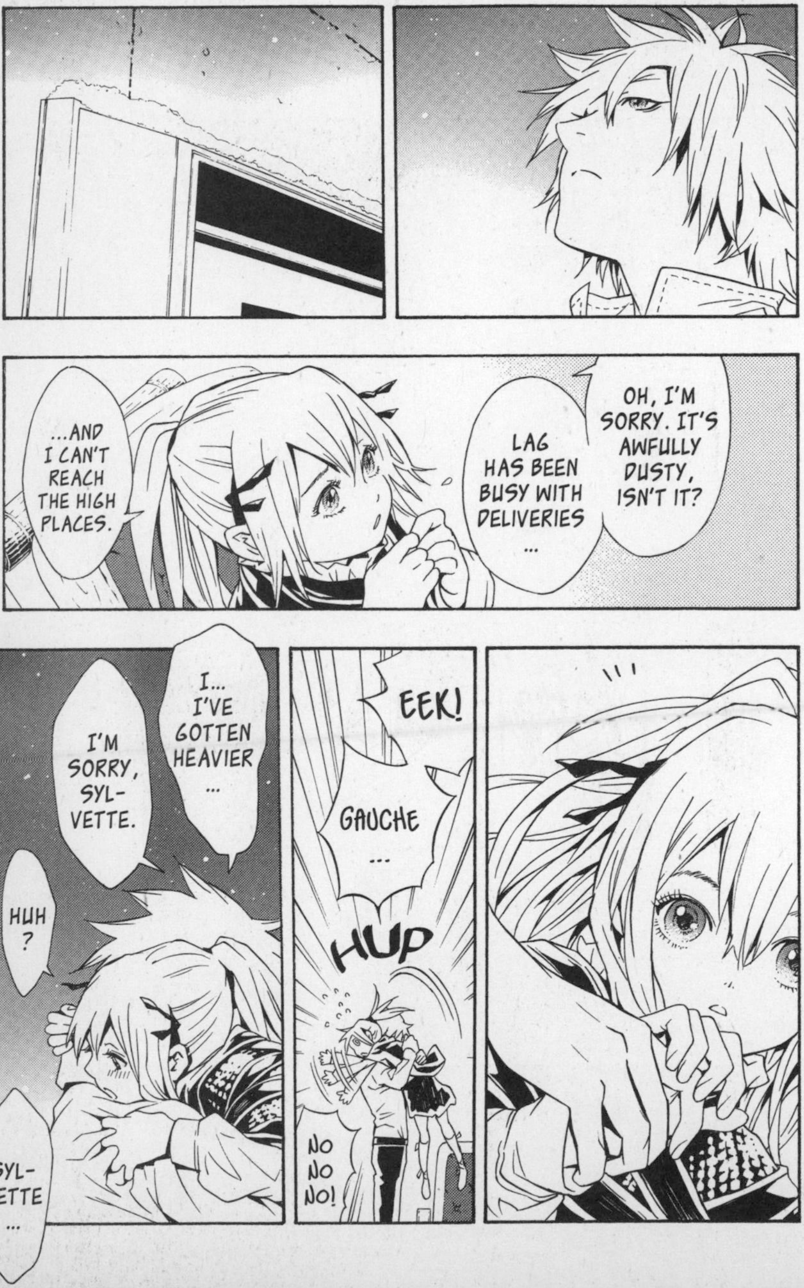

OH, I'M SORRY. IT'S AWFULLY DUSTY, ISN'T IT?
LAG HAS BEEN BUSY WITH DELIVERIES ...
...AND I CAN'T REACH THE HIGH PLACES.
EEK!
GAUCHE ...
HUP
NO NO NO!
I... I'VE GOTTEN HEAVIER ...
I'M SORRY, SYL-VETTE.
HUH ?
SYL-VETTE ...

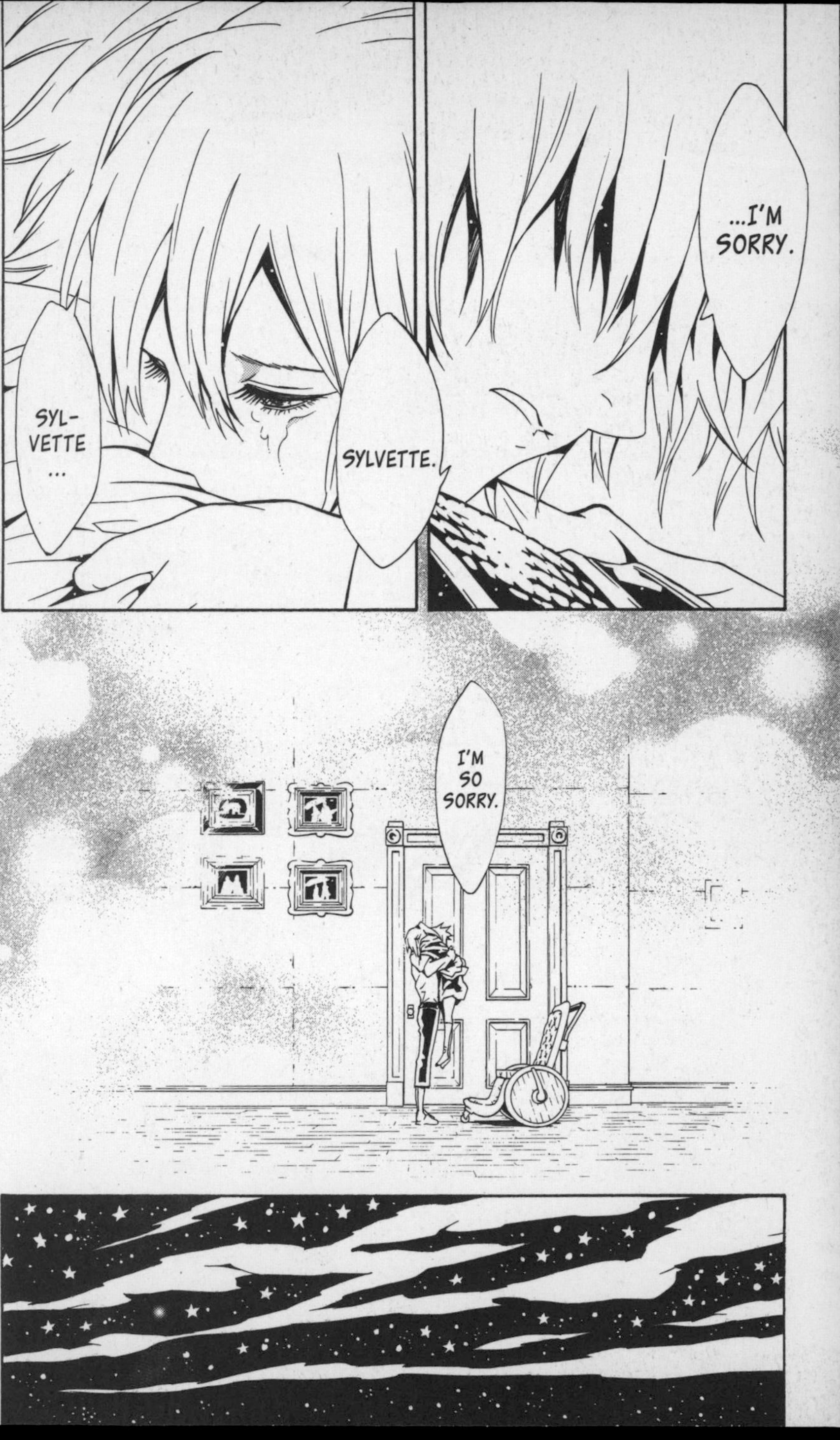
...I'M SORRY.
SYLVETTE.
SYL-VETTE ...
I'M SO SORRY.

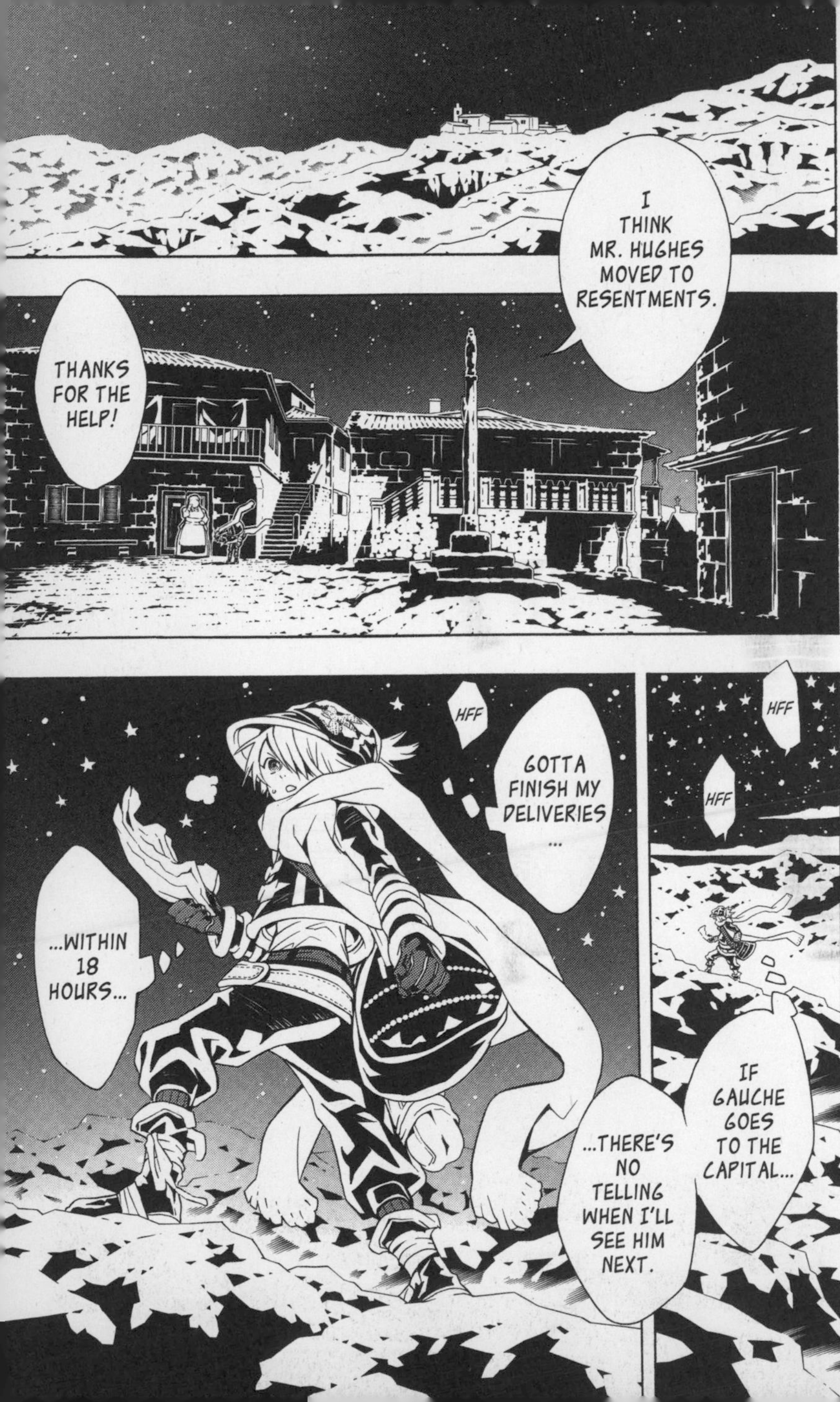
I THINK MR. HUGHES MOVED TO RESENTMENTS.
THANKS FOR THE HELP!
HFF
HFF
HFF
GOTTA FINISH MY DELIVERIES ...
...WITHIN 18 HOURS...
IF GAUCHE GOES TO THE CAPITAL...
...THERE'S NO TELLING WHEN I'LL SEE HIM NEXT.

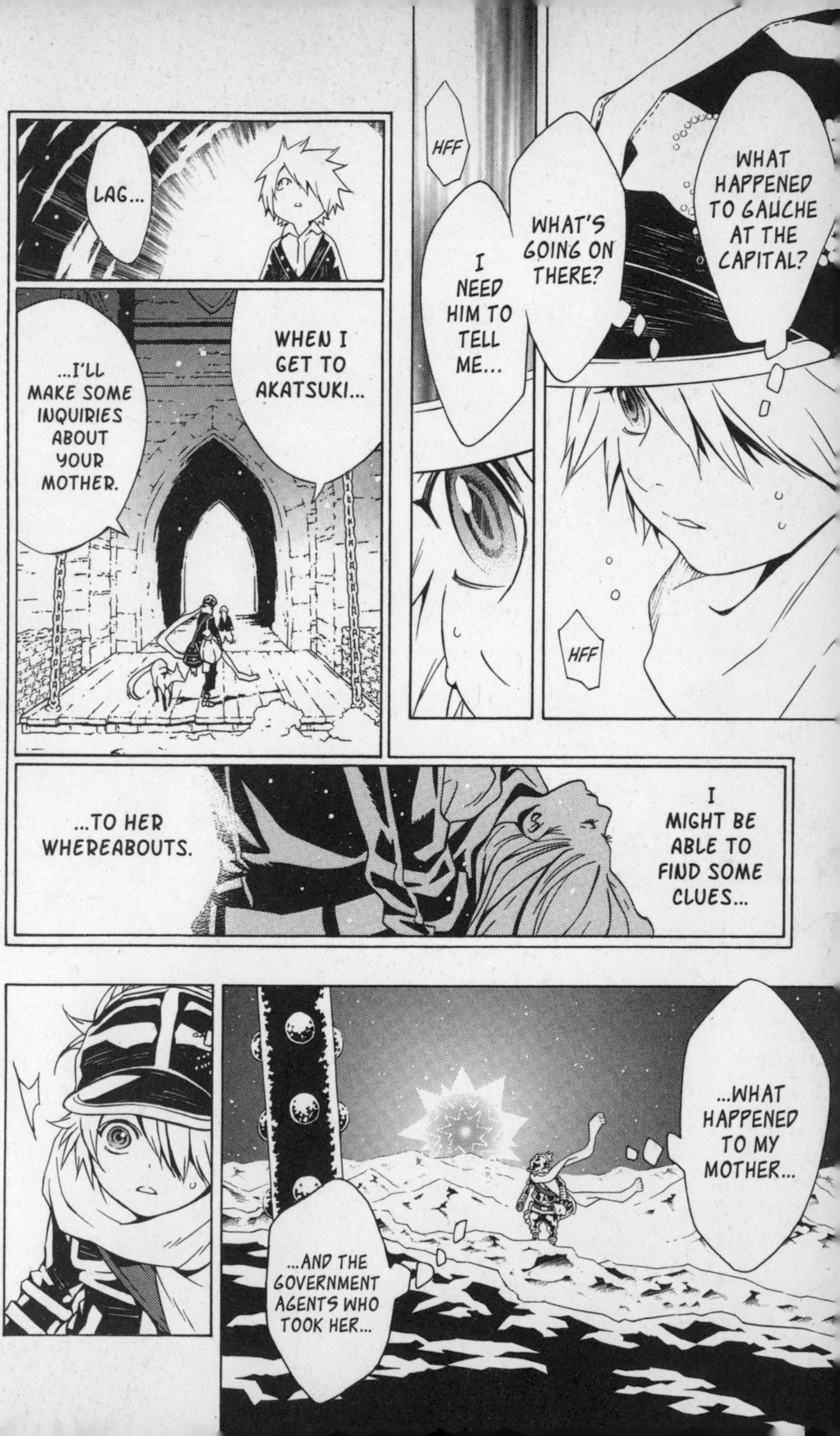
WHAT HAPPENED TO GAUCHE AT THE CAPITAL?
WHAT'S GOING ON THERE?
HFF
I NEED HIM TO TELL ME...
HFF
LAG...
WHEN I GET TO AKATSUKI...
...I'LL MAKE SOME INQUIRIES ABOUT YOUR MOTHER.
I MIGHT BE ABLE TO FIND SOME CLUES...
...TO HER WHEREABOUTS.
...WHAT HAPPENED TO MY MOTHER...
...AND THE GOVERNMENT AGENTS WHO TOOK HER...

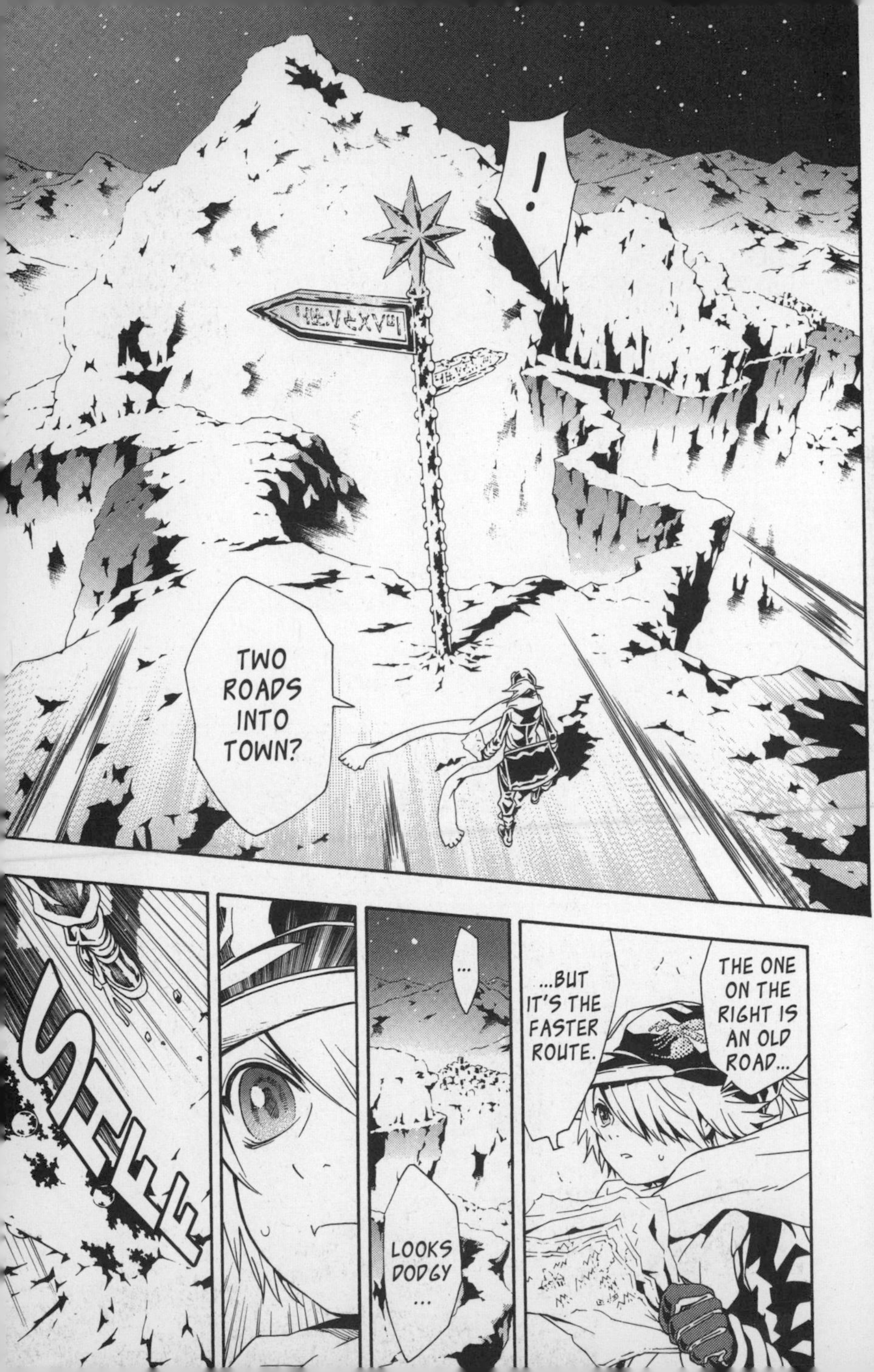
!
TWO ROADS INTO TOWN?
THE ONE ON THE RIGHT IS AN OLD ROAD...
...BUT IT'S THE FASTER ROUTE.
...
LOOKS DODGY ...

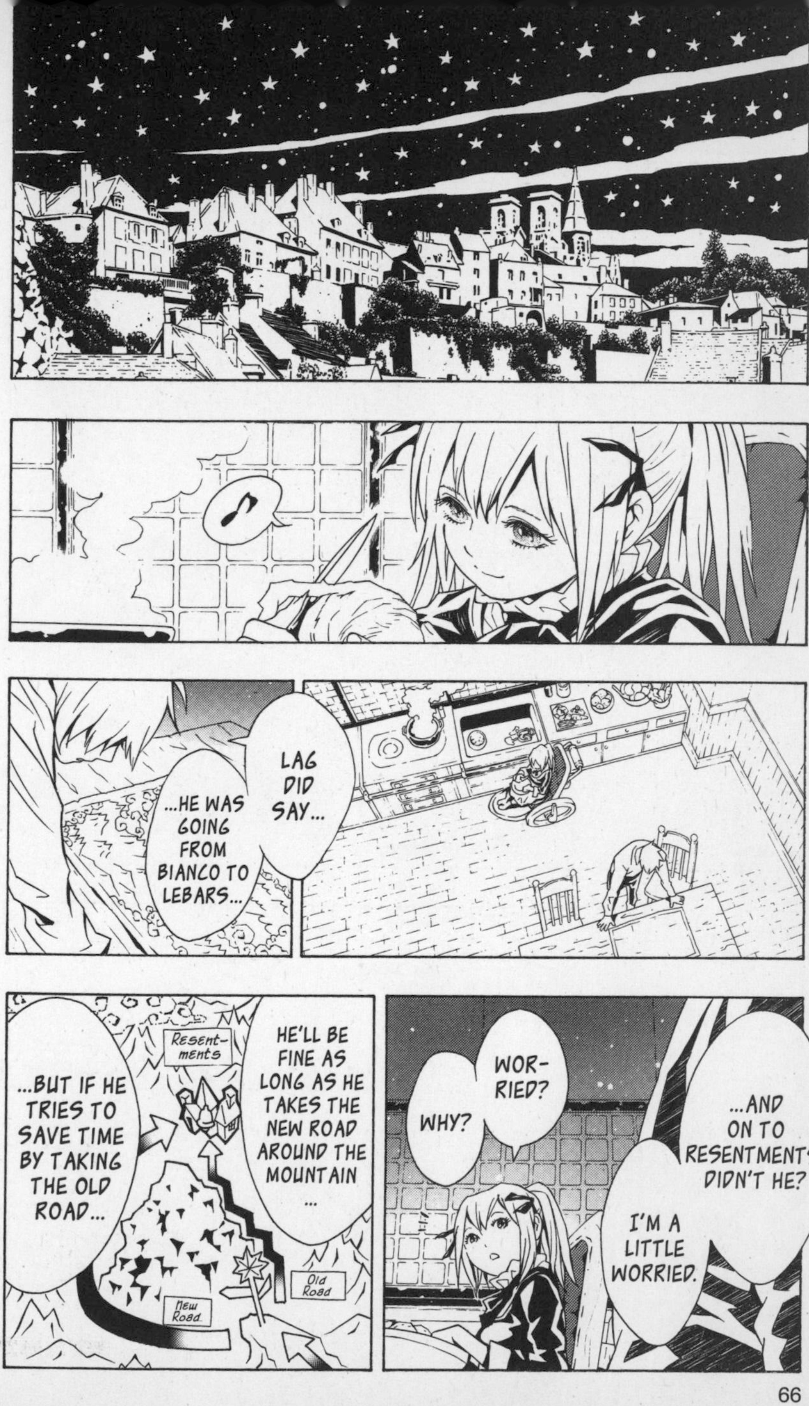
LAG DID SAY...
...HE WAS GOING FROM BIANCO TO LEBARS...
...AND ON TO RESENTMENTS, DIDN'T HE?
I'M A LITTLE WORRIED.
WORRIED?
WHY?
HE'LL BE FINE AS LONG AS HE TAKES THE NEW ROAD AROUND THE MOUNTAIN...
...BUT IF HE TRIES TO SAVE TIME BY TAKING THE OLD ROAD...
Resentments
Old Road
New Road

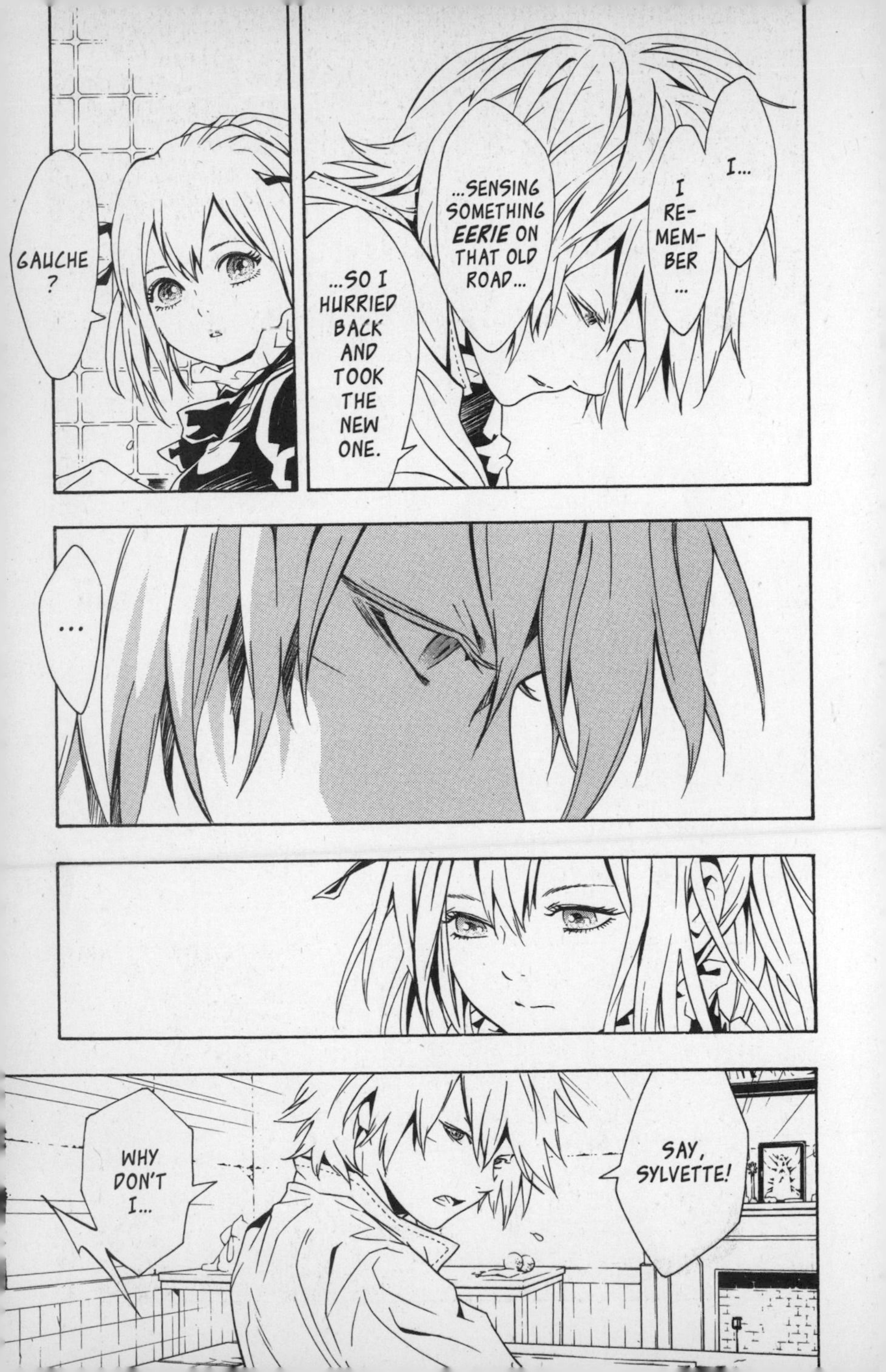
I...
I RE-MEM-BER ...
...SENSING SOMETHING EERIE ON THAT OLD ROAD...
...SO I HURRIED BACK AND TOOK THE NEW ONE.
GAUCHE ?
...
SAY, SYLVETTE!
WHY DON'T I...

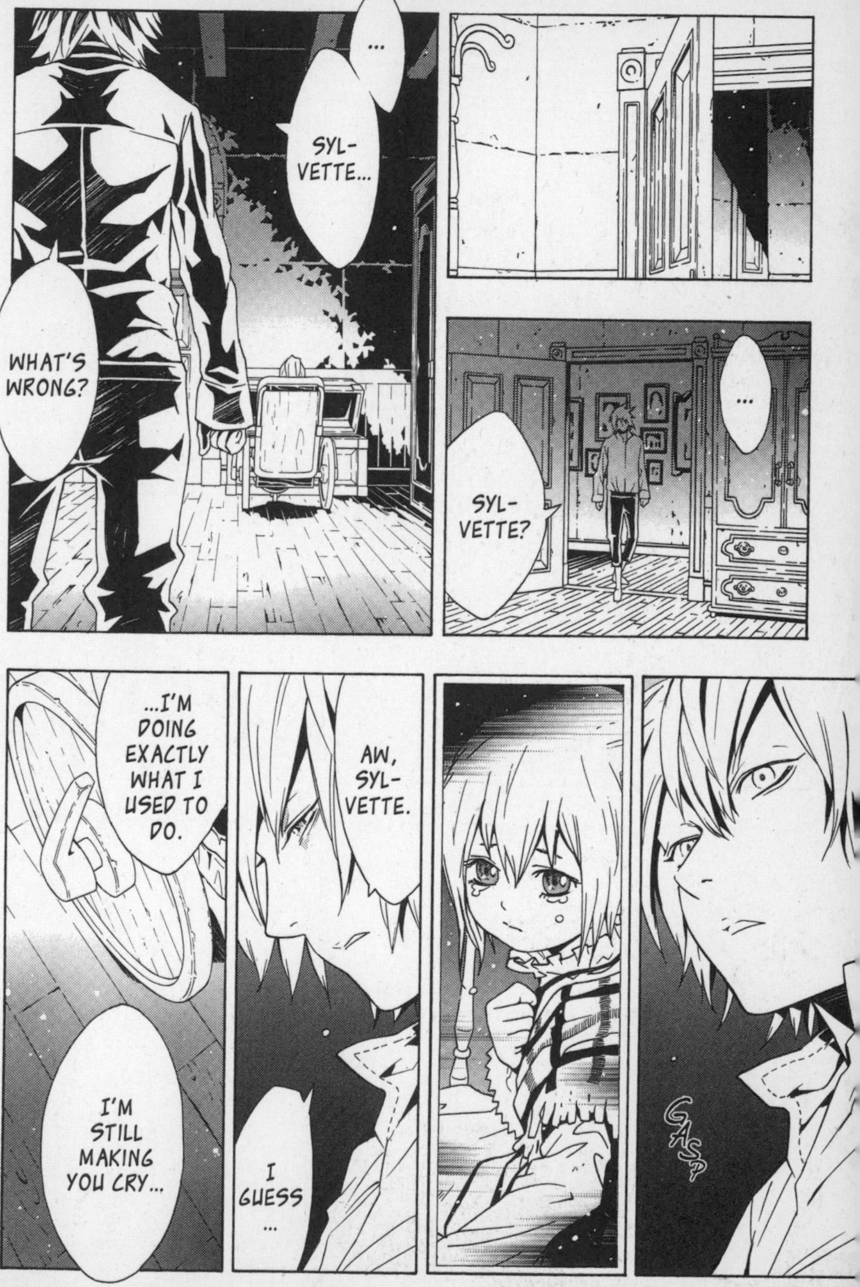
...
SYL-VETTE?
...
SYL-VETTE...
WHAT'S WRONG?
GASP
AW, SYL-VETTE.
I GUESS ...
...I'M DOING EXACTLY WHAT I USED TO DO.
I'M STILL MAKING YOU CRY...

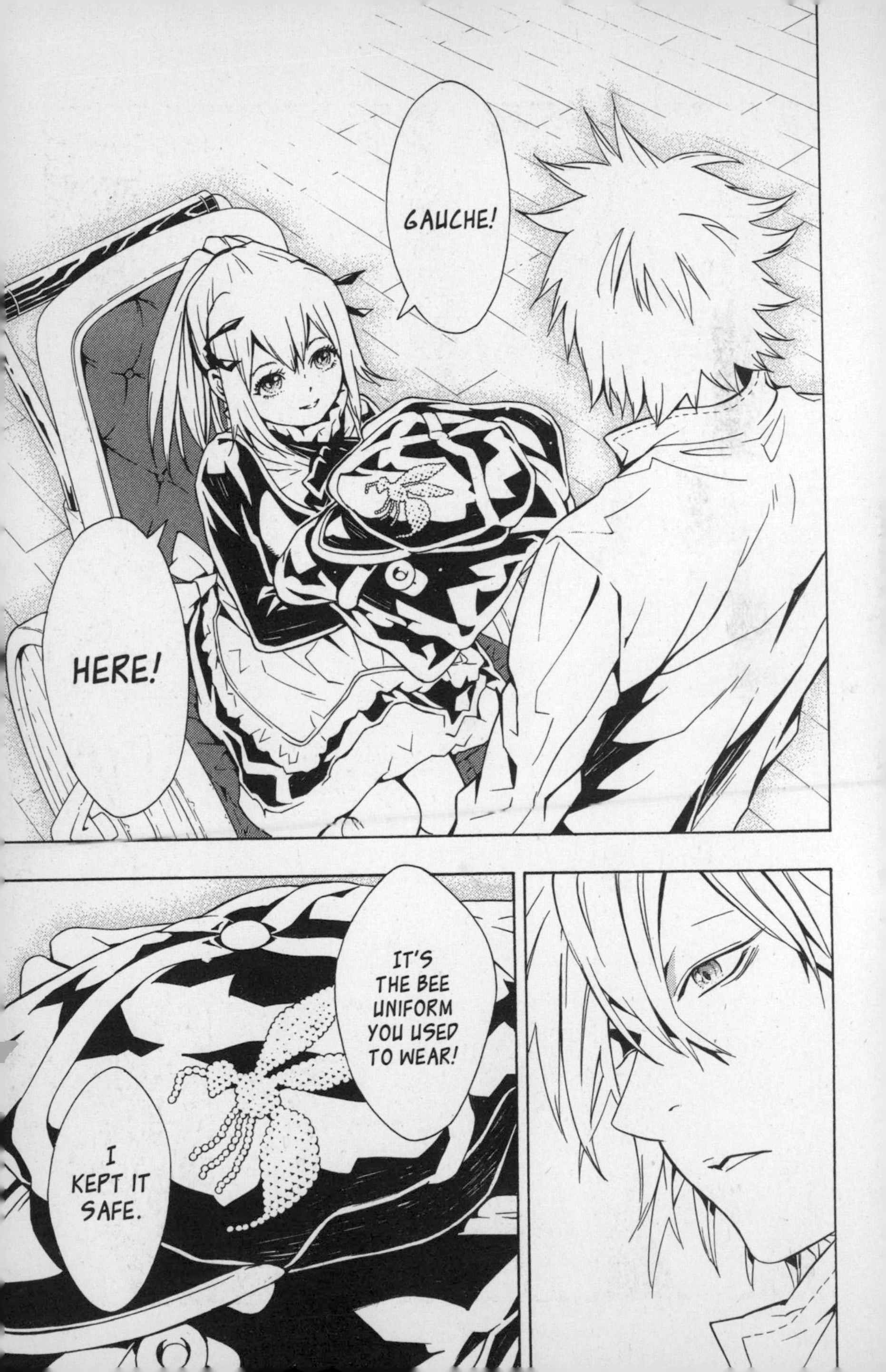
GAUCHE!
HERE!
IT'S THE BEE UNIFORM YOU USED TO WEAR!
I KEPT IT SAFE.

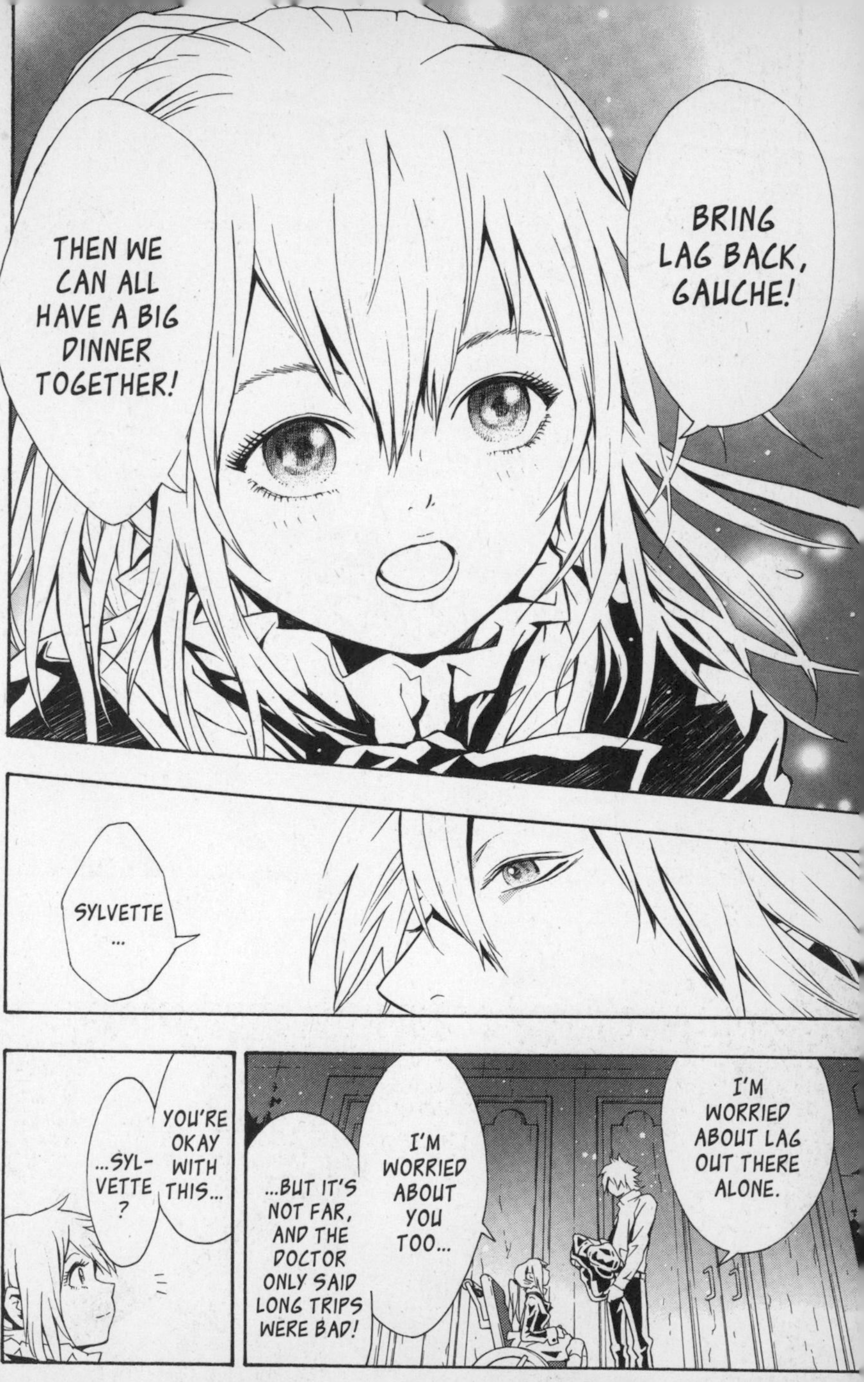
BRING LAG BACK, GAUCHE!
THEN WE CAN ALL HAVE A BIG DINNER TOGETHER!
SYLVETTE ...
I'M WORRIED ABOUT LAG OUT THERE ALONE.
I'M WORRIED ABOUT YOU TOO...
...BUT IT'S NOT FAR, AND THE DOCTOR ONLY SAID LONG TRIPS WERE BAD!
YOU'RE OKAY WITH THIS...
...SYL-VETTE?

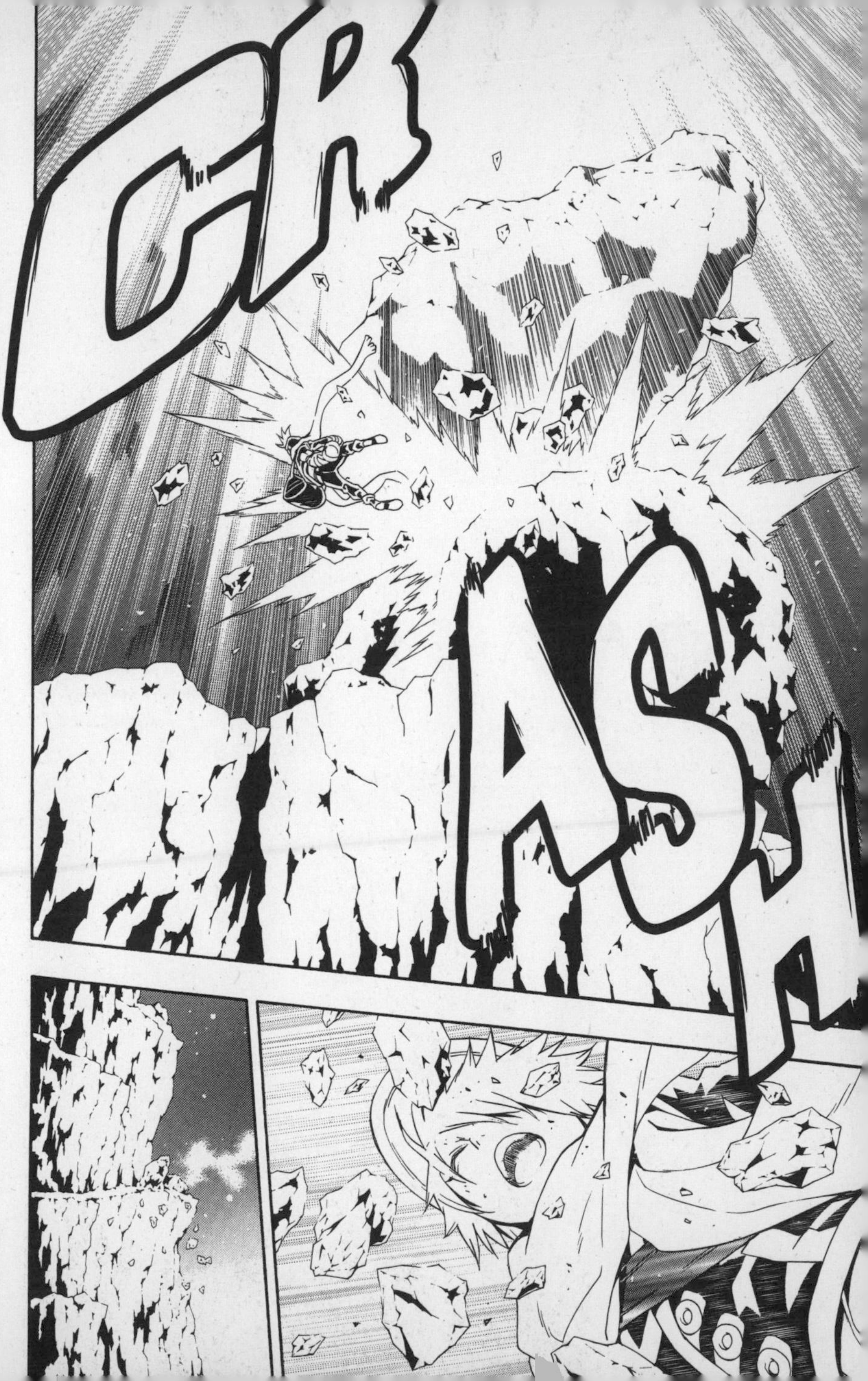
CRASH

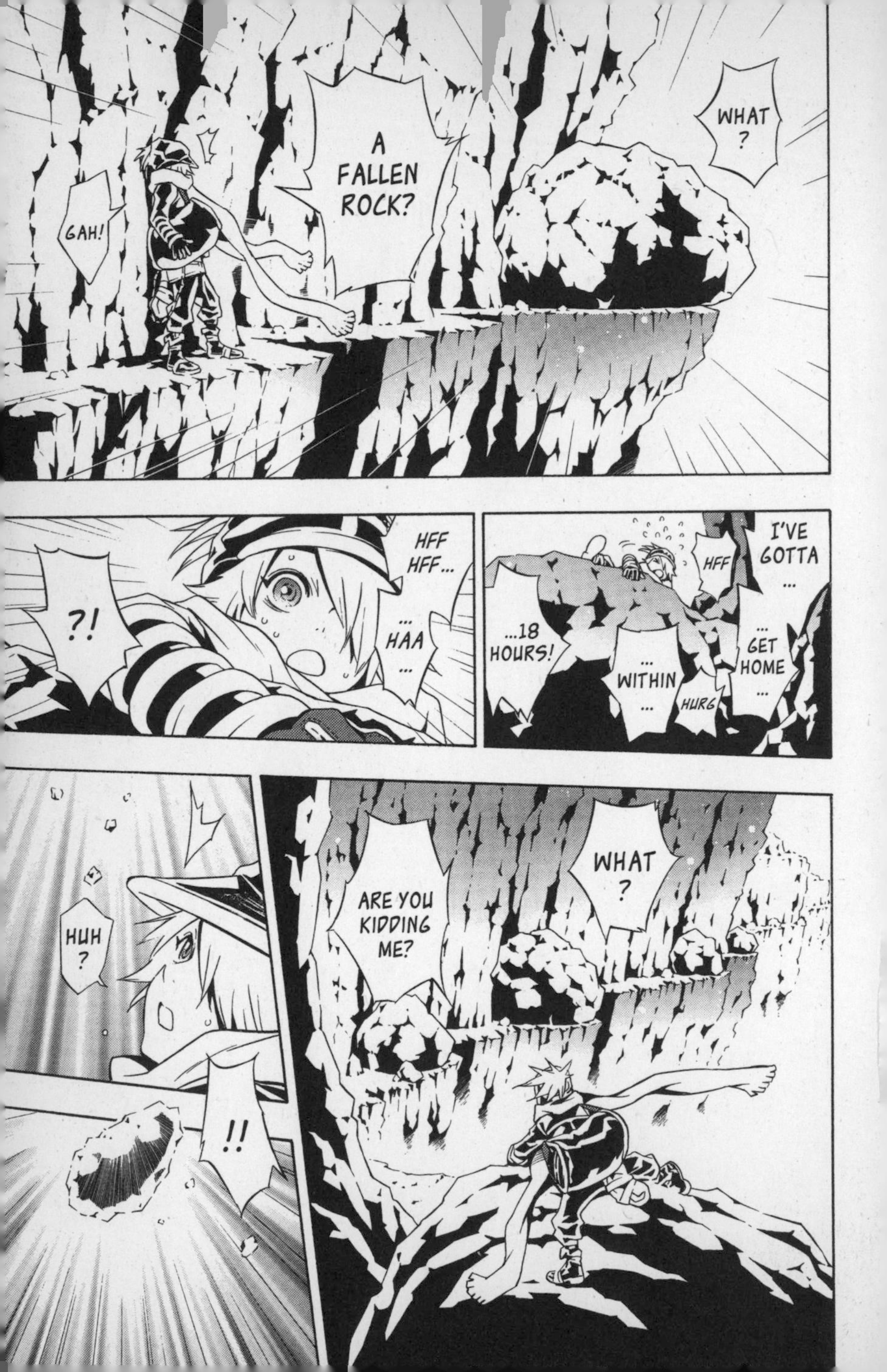
WHAT?
A FALLEN ROCK?
GAH!
I'VE GOTTA...
HFF
...GET HOME...
HURG
...WITHIN...
...18 HOURS!
HFF HFF...
...HAA...
?!
HUH?
!!
WHAT?
ARE YOU KIDDING ME?

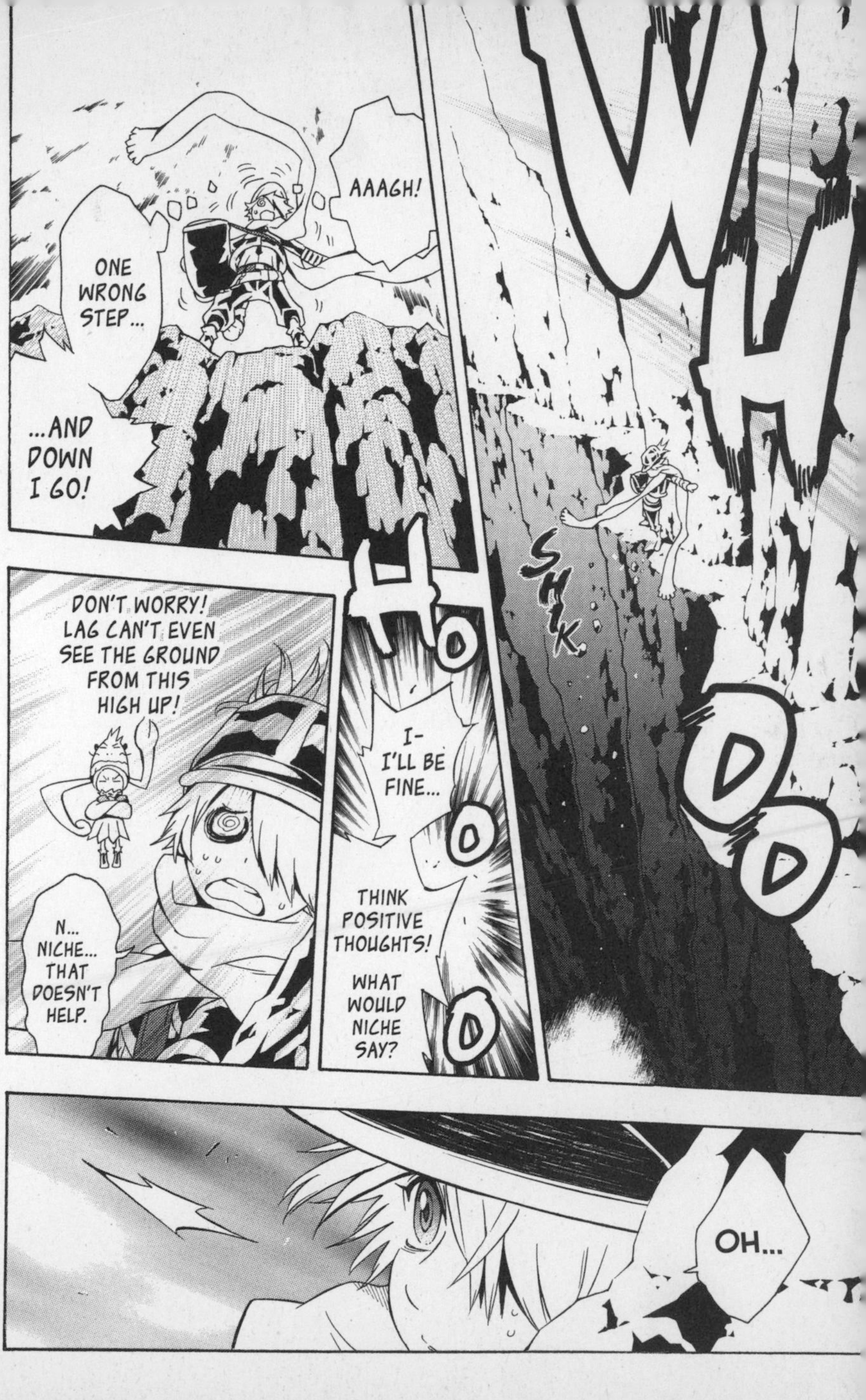
AAAGH!
ONE WRONG STEP...
...AND DOWN I GO!
SHIK
I- I'LL BE FINE...
THINK POSITIVE THOUGHTS!
WHAT WOULD NICHE SAY?
DON'T WORRY! LAG CAN'T EVEN SEE THE GROUND FROM THIS HIGH UP!
N... NICHE... THAT DOESN'T HELP.
OH...

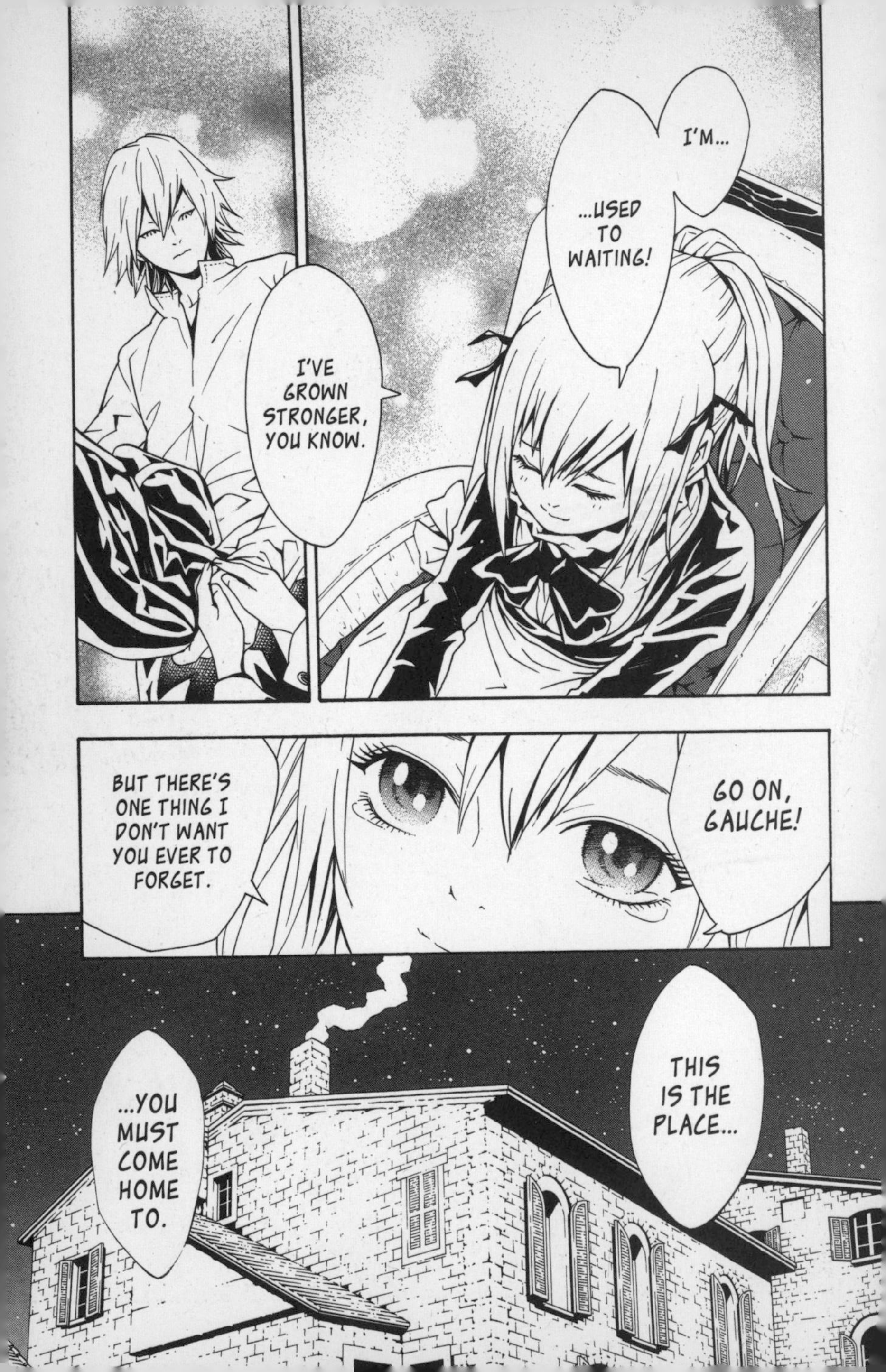
I'M...
...USED TO WAITING!
I'VE GROWN STRONGER, YOU KNOW.
GO ON, GAUCHE!
BUT THERE'S ONE THING I DON'T WANT YOU EVER TO FORGET.
THIS IS THE PLACE...
...YOU MUST COME HOME TO.

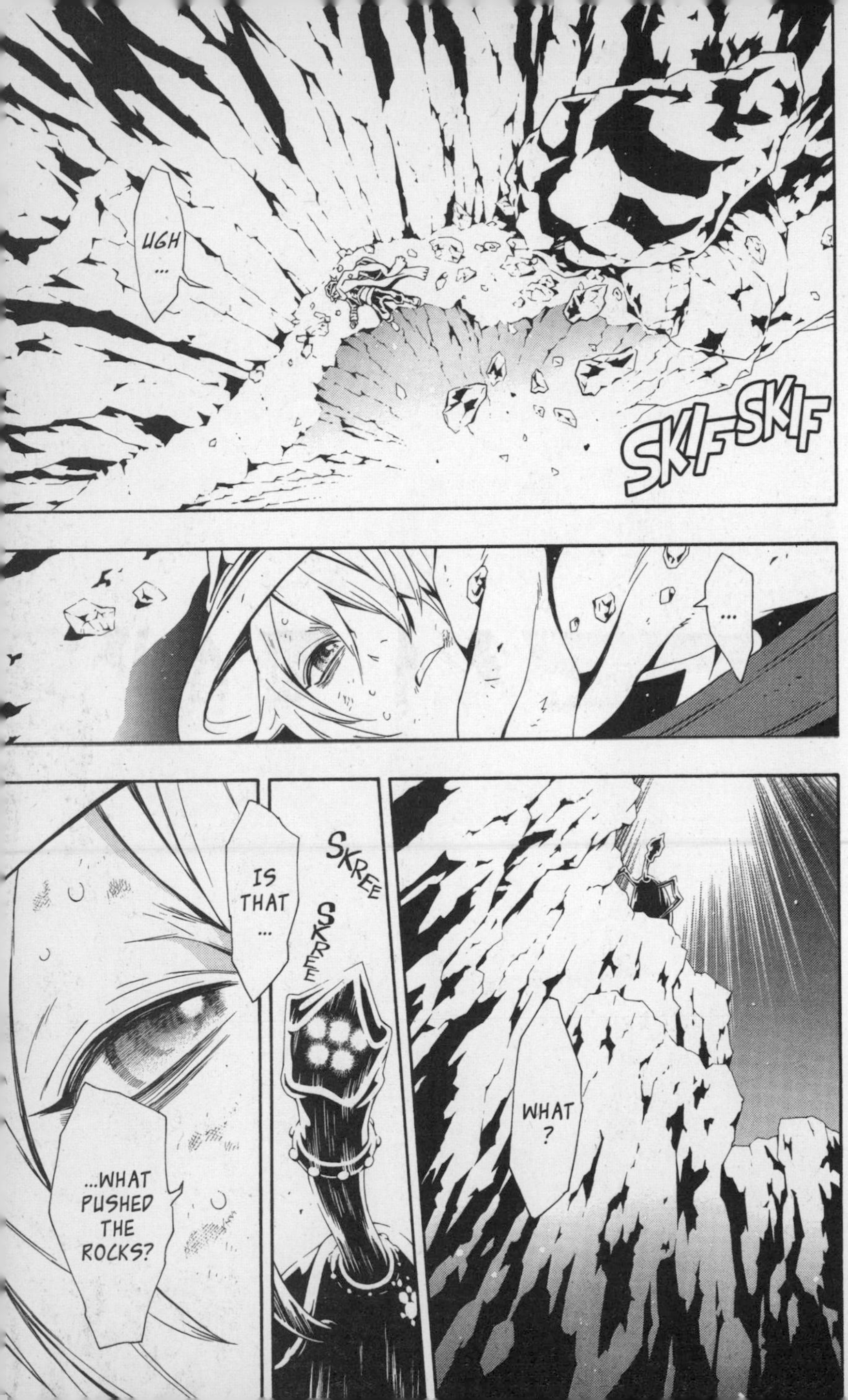
UGH ...
SKIF-SKIF
...
WHAT?
SKREE
SKREE
IS THAT ...
...WHAT PUSHED THE ROCKS?

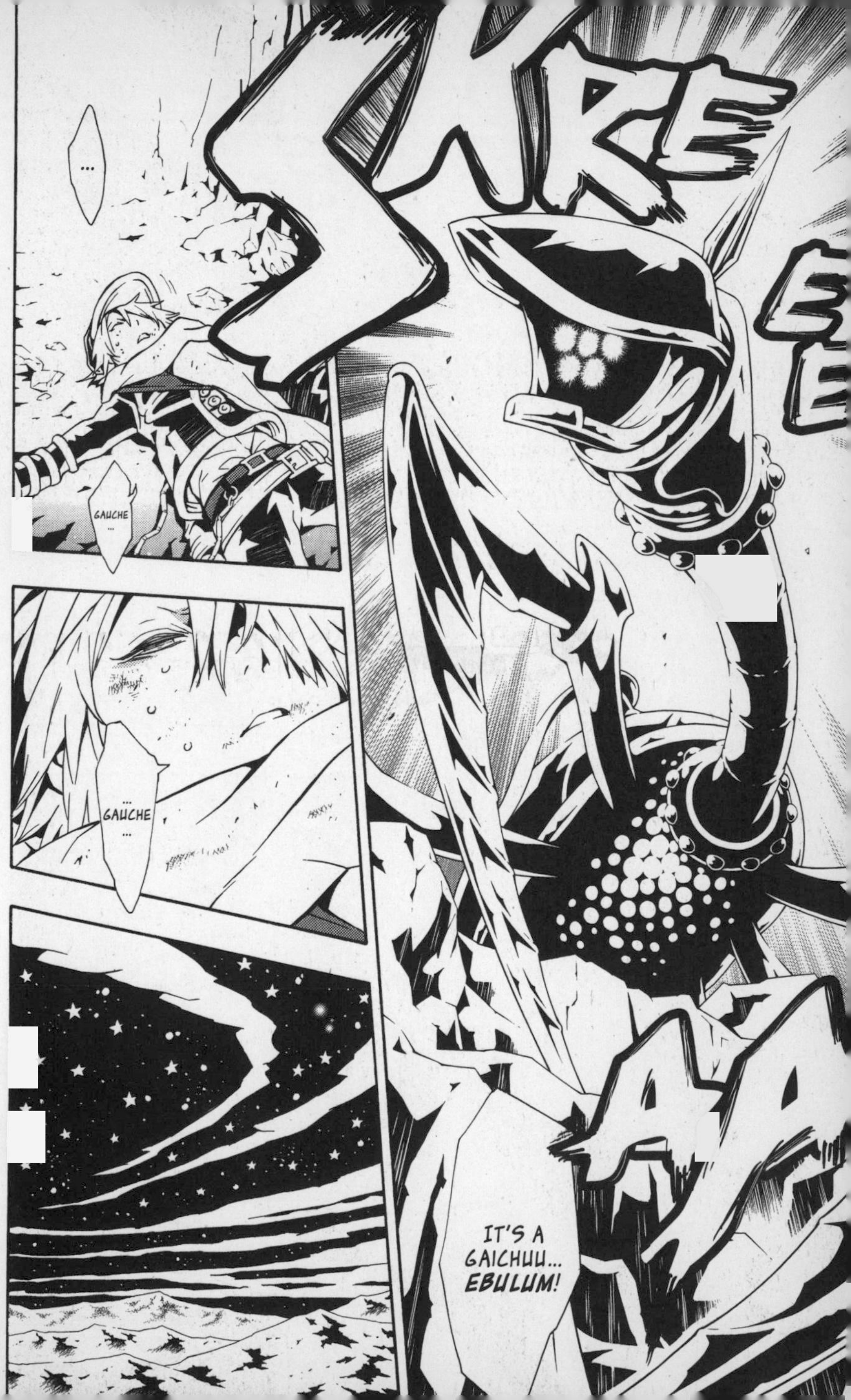
IT'S A GAICHUU... EBULUM!
...
GAUCHE ...
... GAUCHE ...

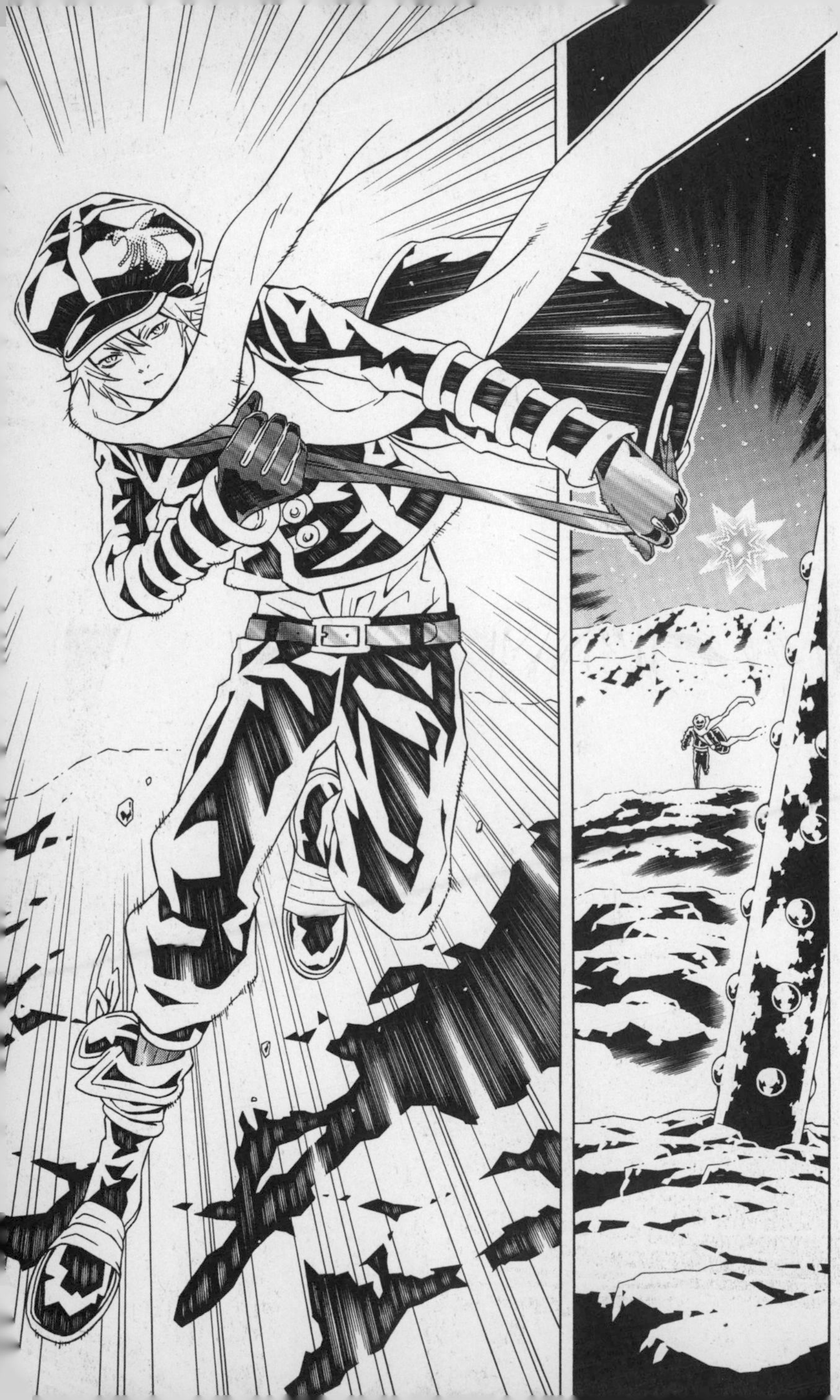

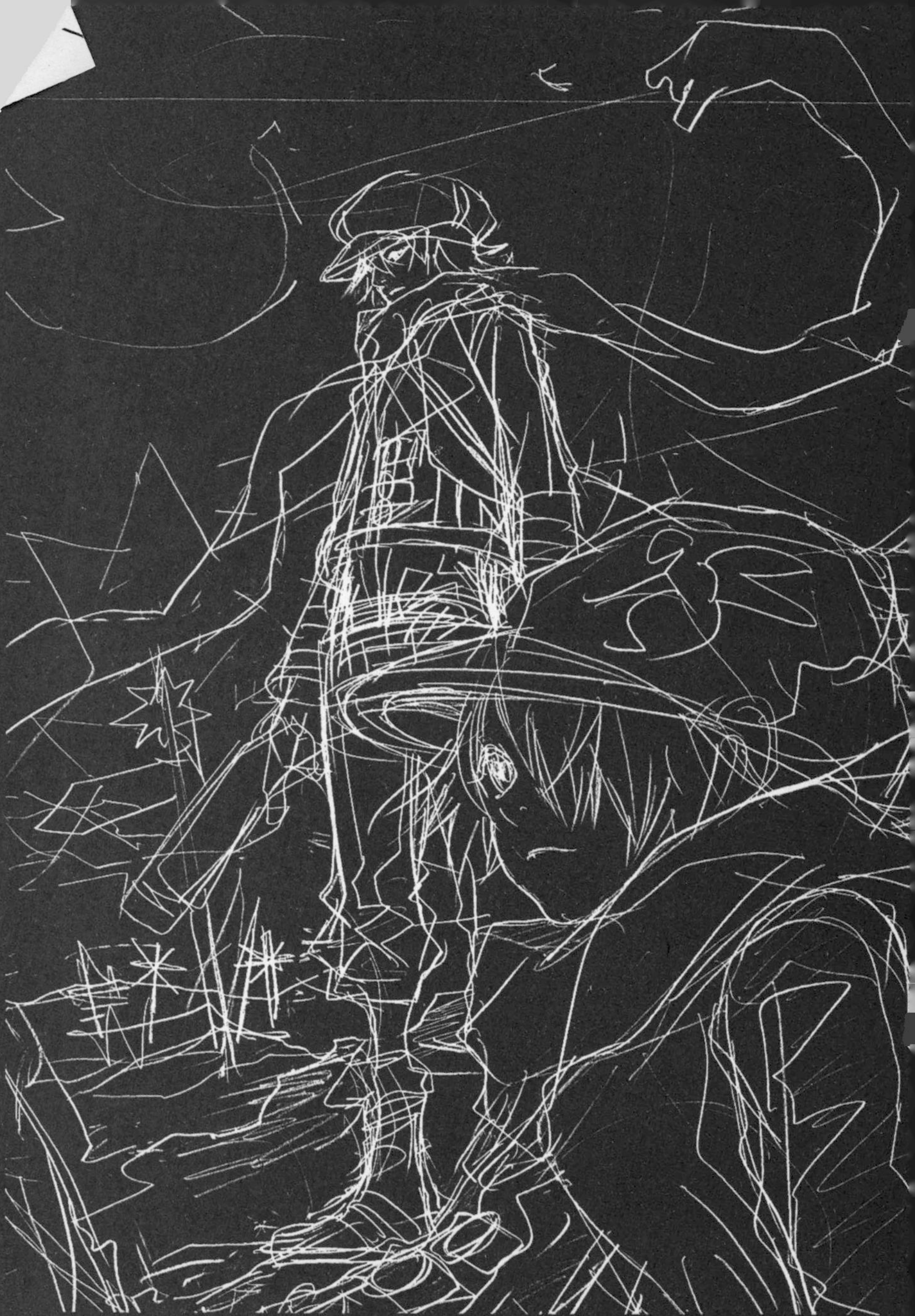

Rough sketch of volume 11 cover.

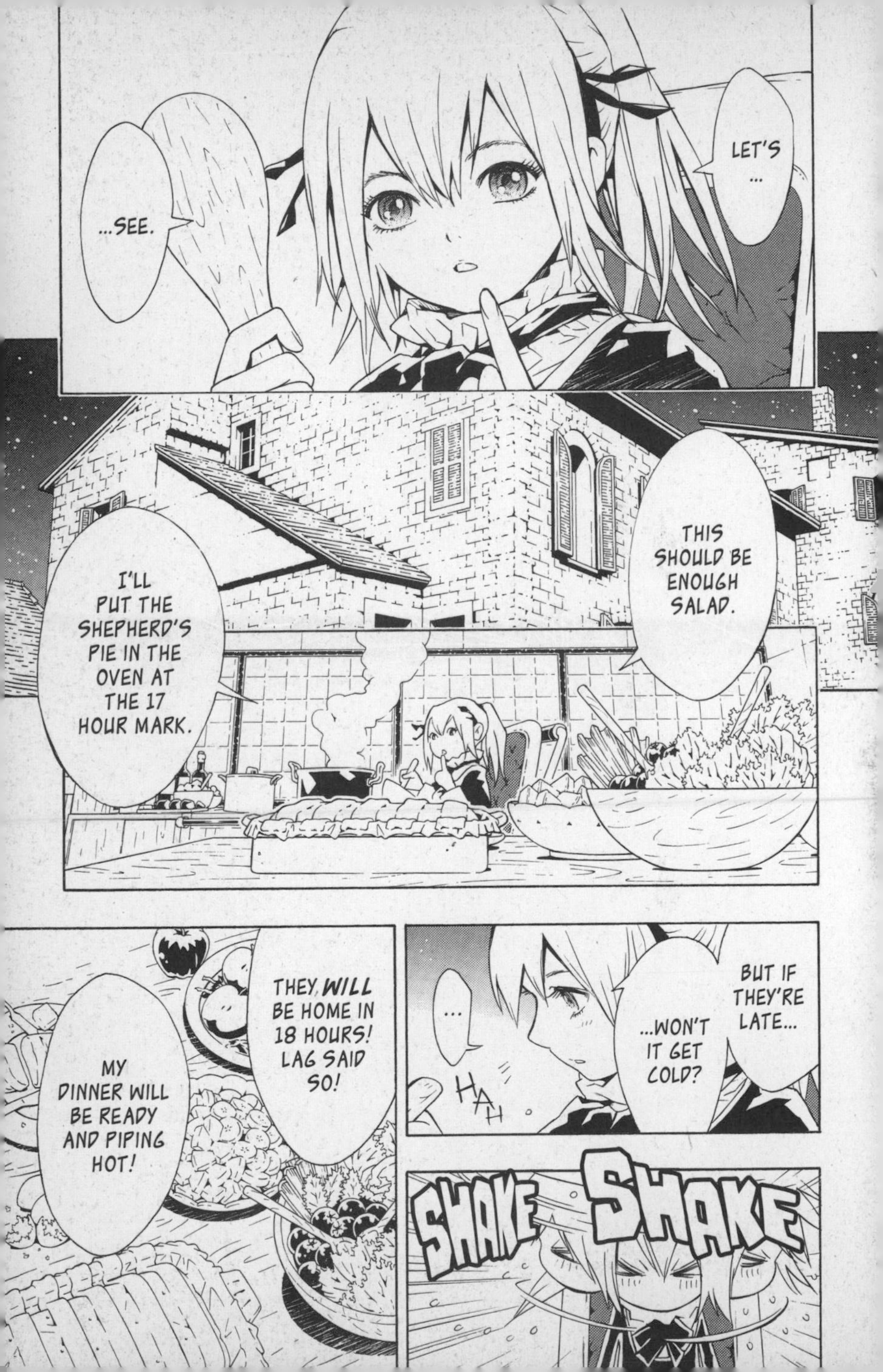
LET'S ...
...SEE.
THIS SHOULD BE ENOUGH SALAD.
I'LL PUT THE SHEPHERD'S PIE IN THE OVEN AT THE 17 HOUR MARK.
BUT IF THEY'RE LATE...
...WON'T IT GET COLD?
...
HAH
SHAKE SHAKE
THEY *WILL* BE HOME IN 18 HOURS! LAG SAID SO!
MY DINNER WILL BE READY AND PIPING HOT!

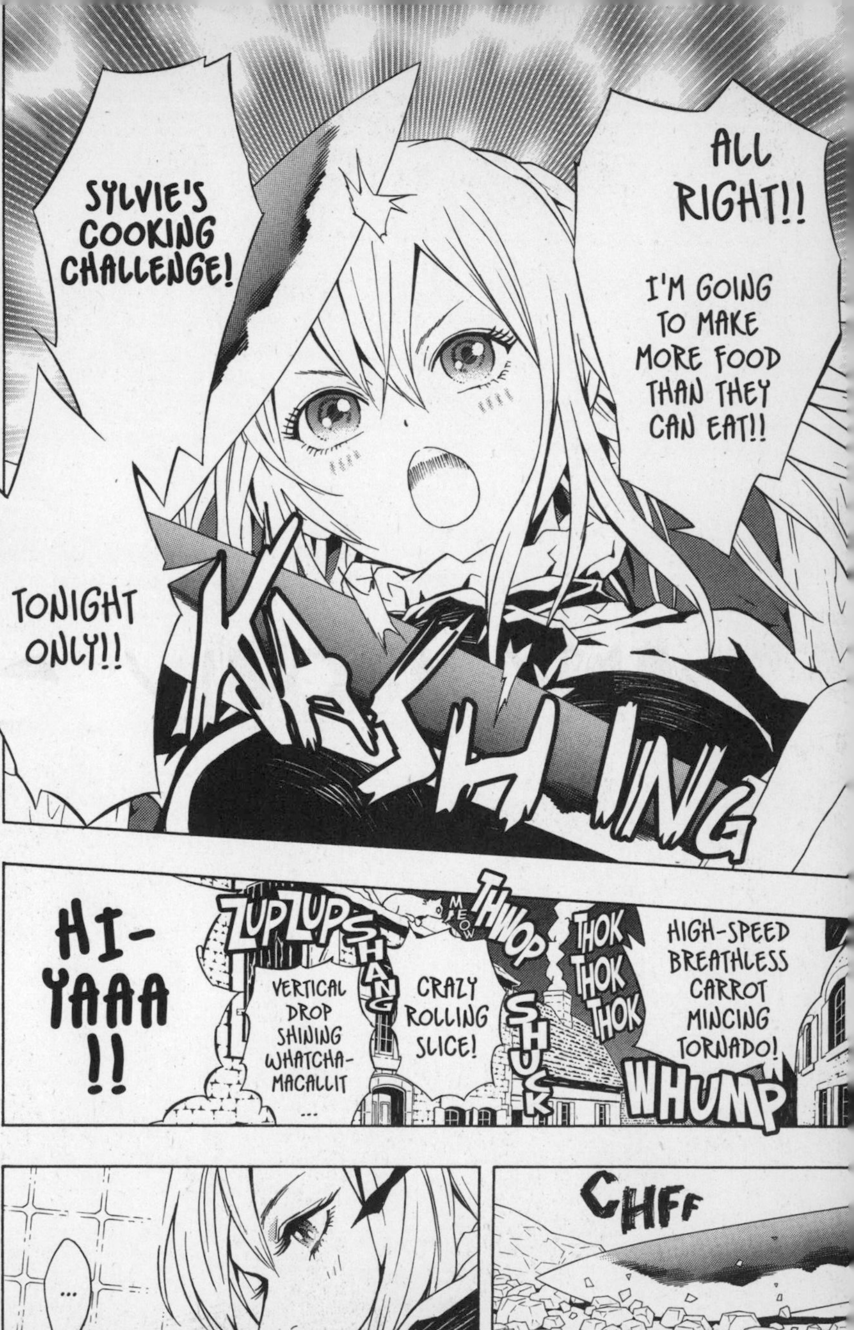
ALL RIGHT!!
I'M GOING TO MAKE MORE FOOD THAN THEY CAN EAT!!
SYLVIE'S COOKING CHALLENGE!
TONIGHT ONLY!!
KASHING
HIGH-SPEED BREATHLESS CARROT MINCING TORNADO!
WHUMP
THOK THOK THOK
SHUCK
THWOP
MEOW
CRAZY ROLLING SLICE!
SHANG
VERTICAL DROP SHINING WHATCHA-MACALLIT ...
ZUP ZUP
HI-YAAA!!
CHFF
...

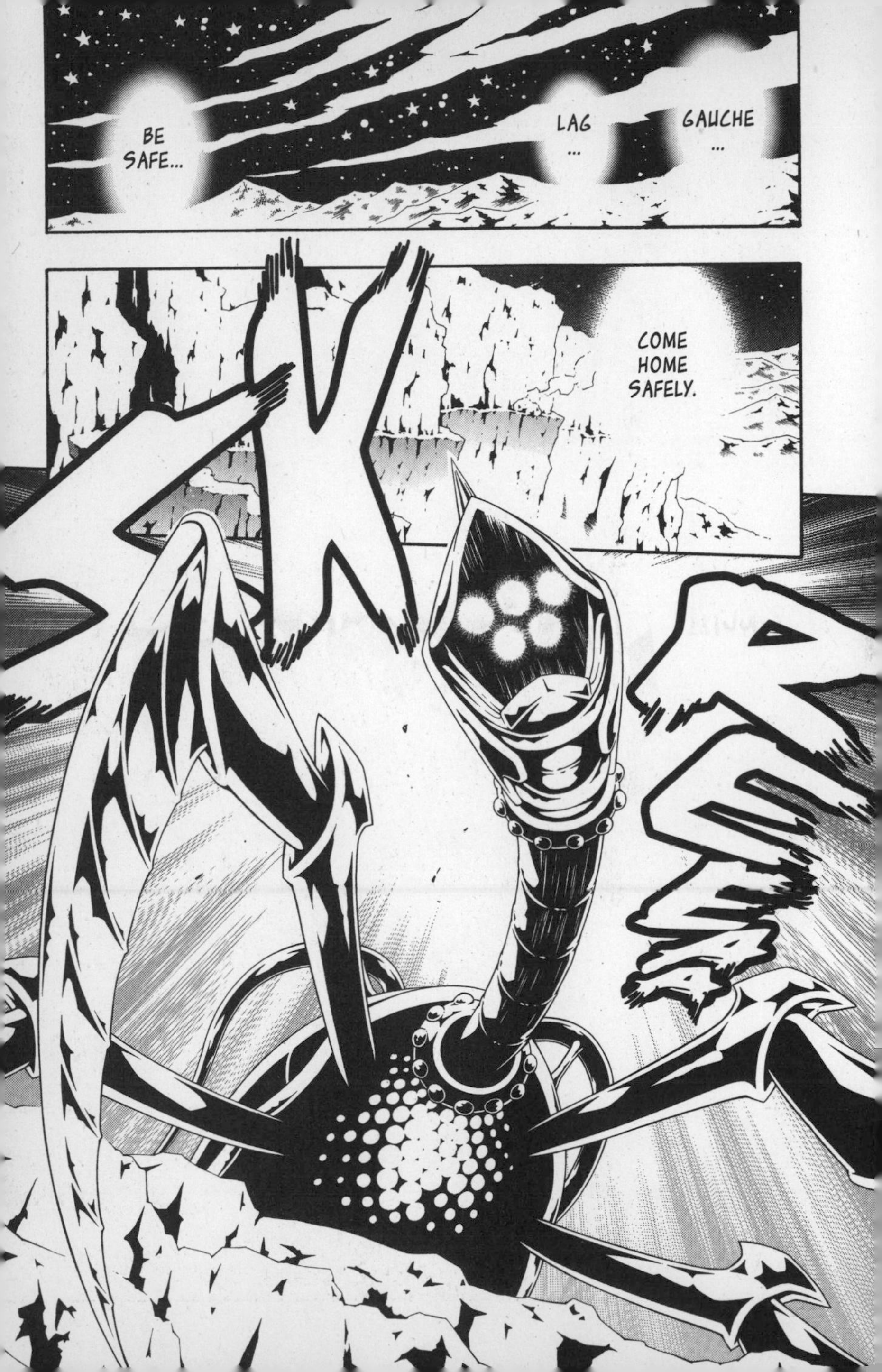
GAUCHE ...
LAG ...
BE SAFE...
COME HOME SAFELY.

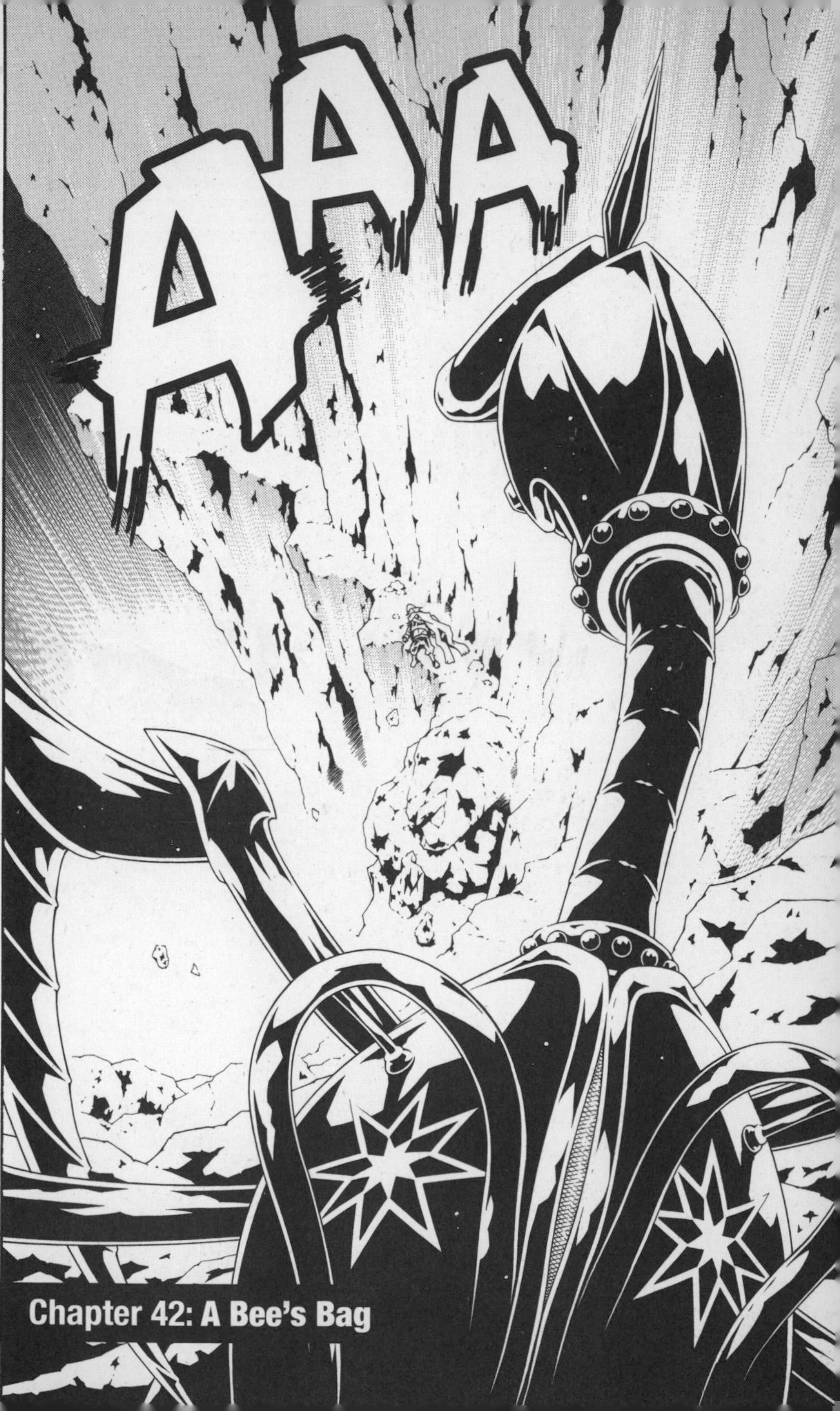
AAAA

Chapter 42: A Bee's Bag

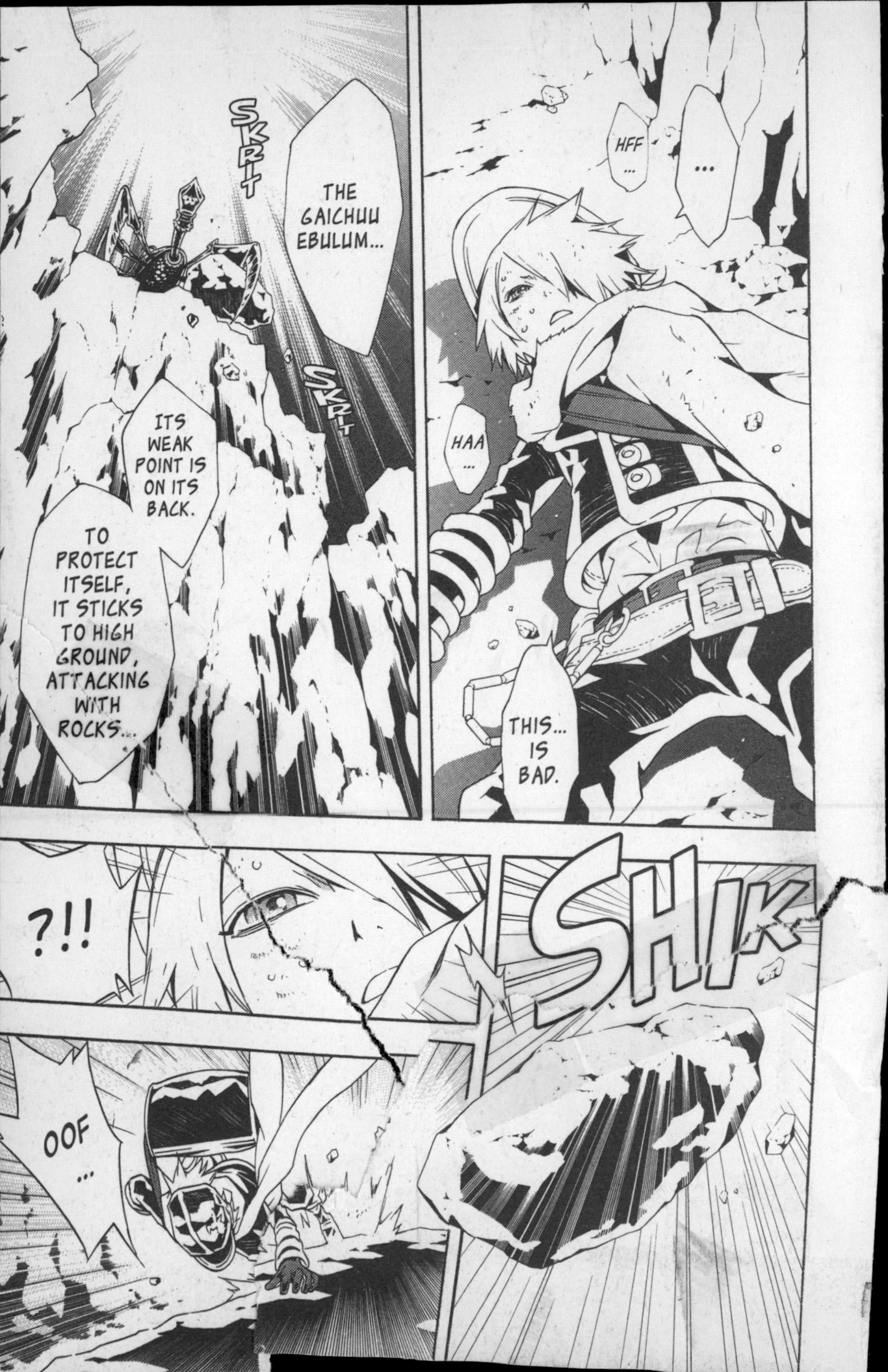

HFF...
...
HAA...
THIS... IS BAD.
SKRIT
THE GAICHUU EBULUM...
SKRIT
ITS WEAK POINT IS ON ITS BACK.
TO PROTECT ITSELF, IT STICKS TO HIGH GROUND, ATTACKING WITH ROCKS...
?!!
SHIK
OOF...

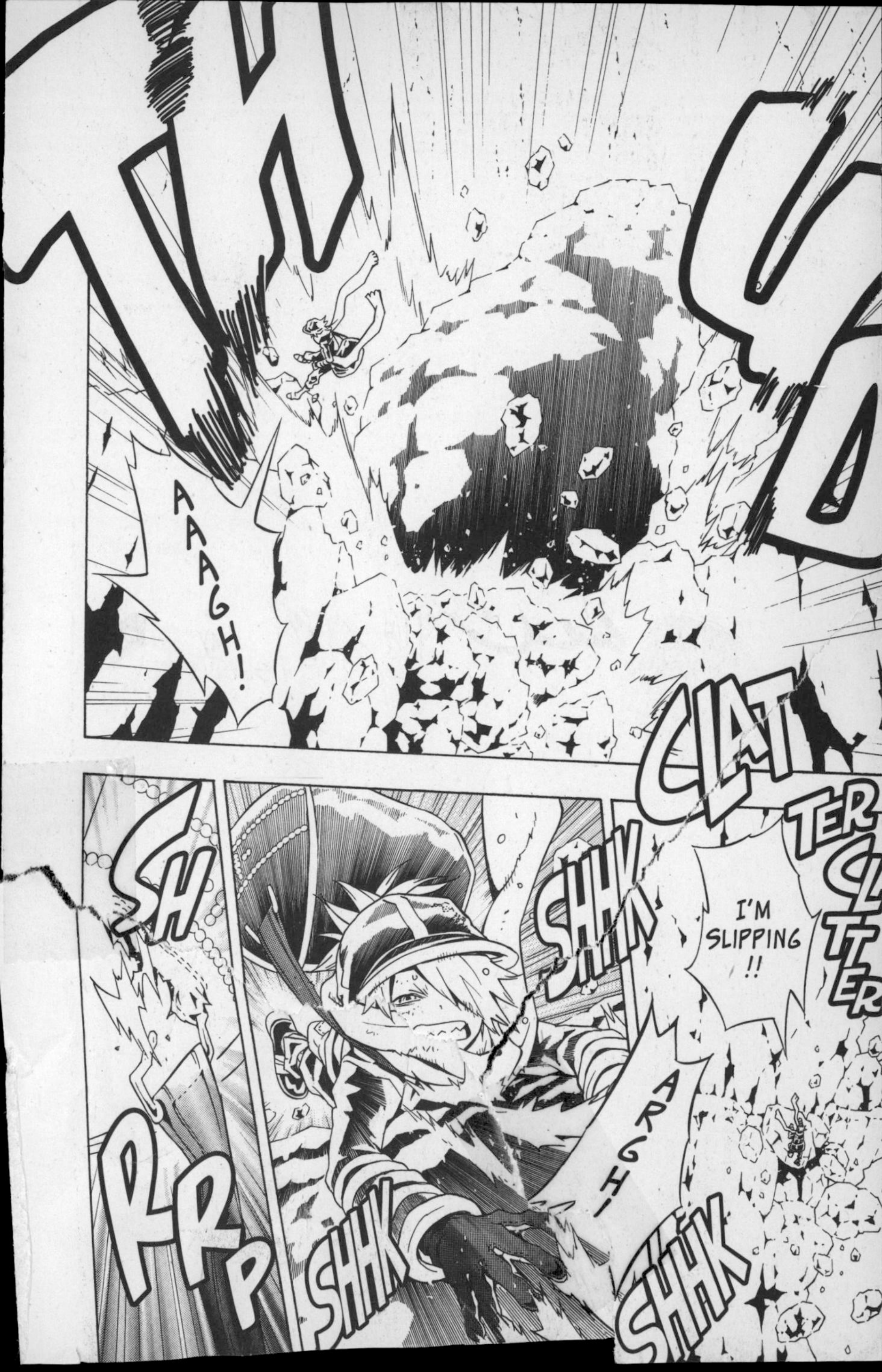
AAAGH!
CLATTER
CLATTER
I'M SLIPPING !!
SHHK
ARGH!
SHHK
SHHK
SH
RRP

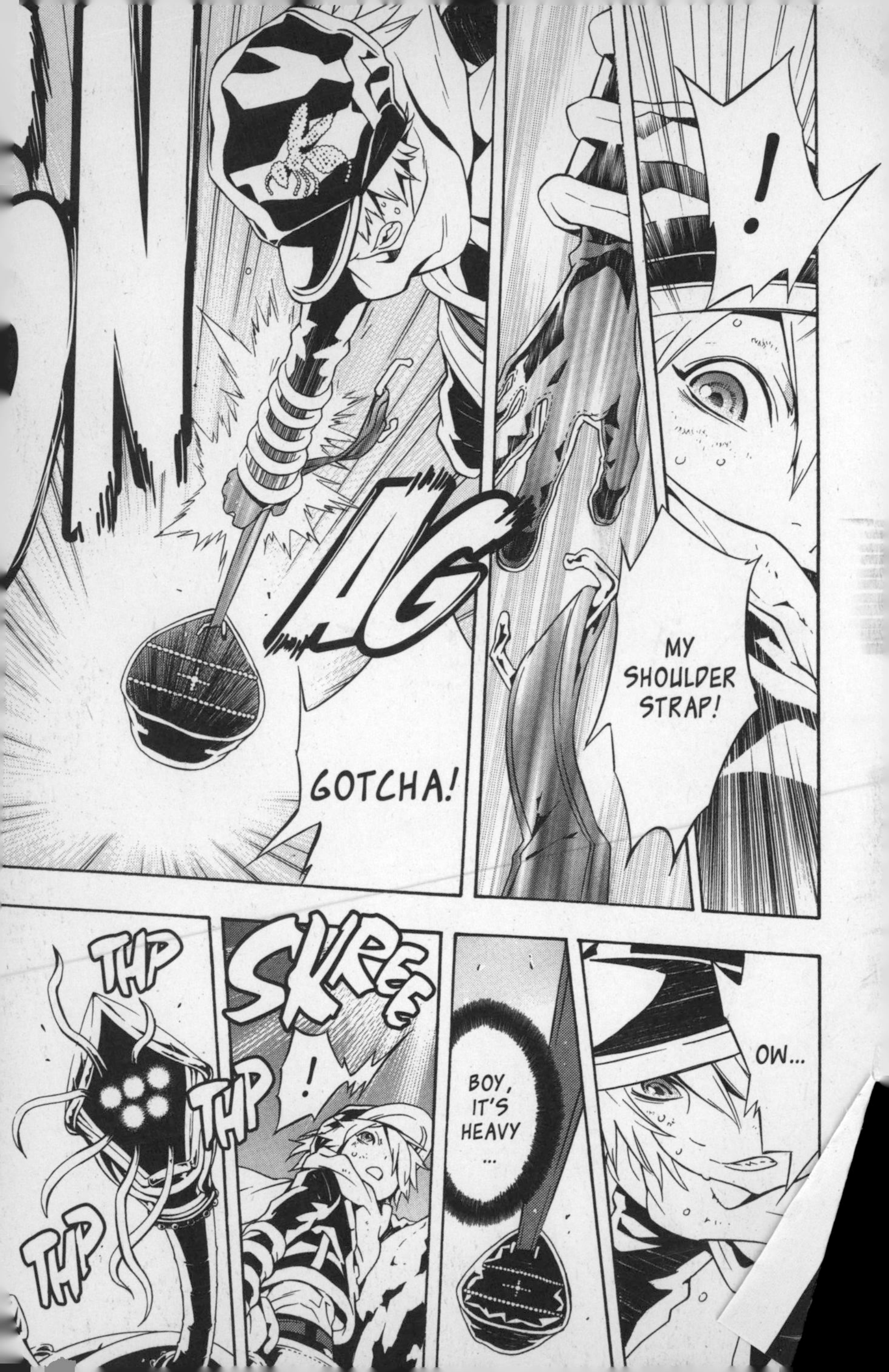
!
MY SHOULDER STRAP!
AG
GOTCHA!
OW...
BOY, IT'S HEAVY ...
SKREE
!
THP
THP
THP

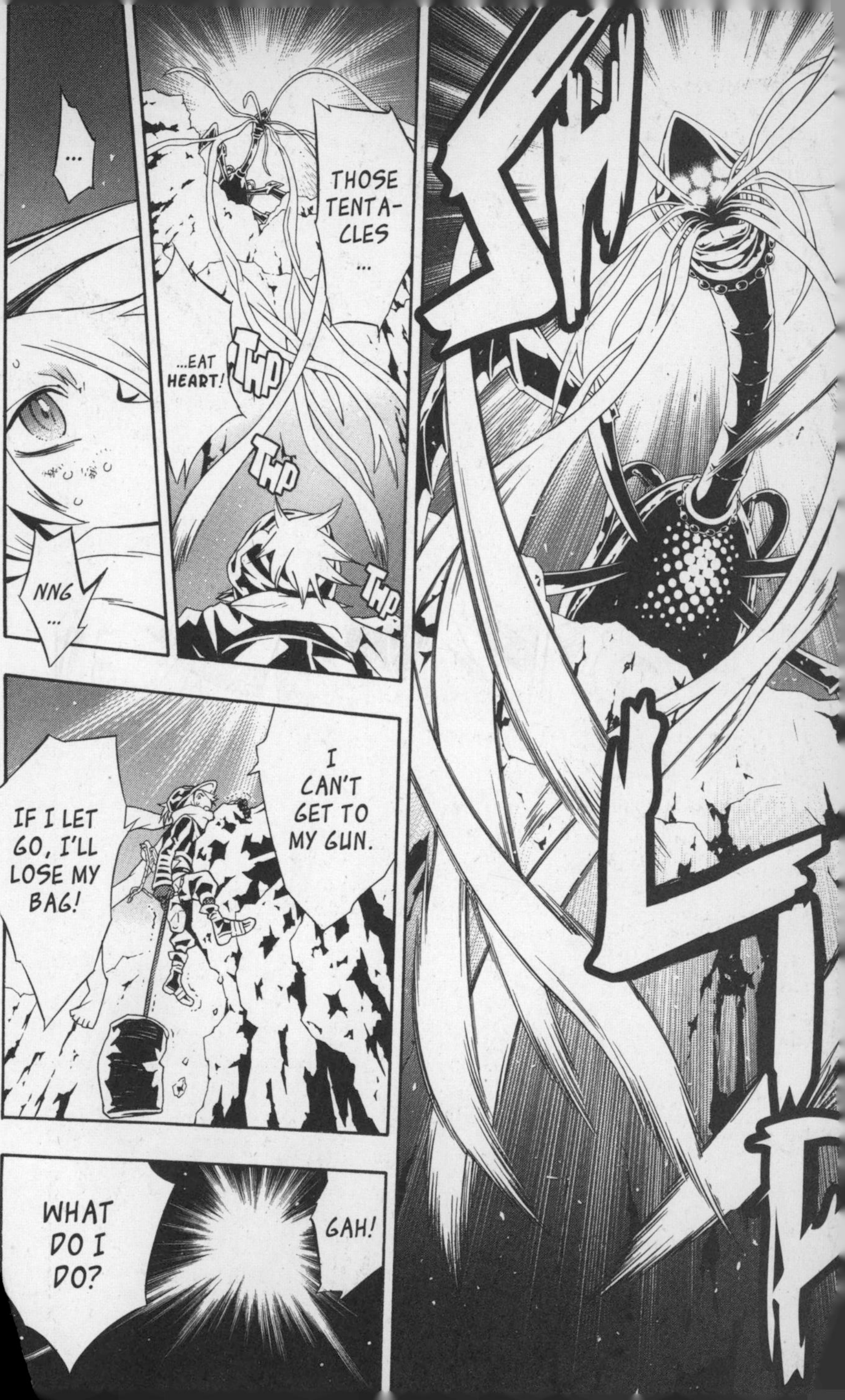
THOSE TENTA-CLES ...
...EAT HEART!
THP
THP
THP
...
NNG ...
I CAN'T GET TO MY GUN.
IF I LET GO, I'LL LOSE MY BAG!
GAH!
WHAT DO I DO?

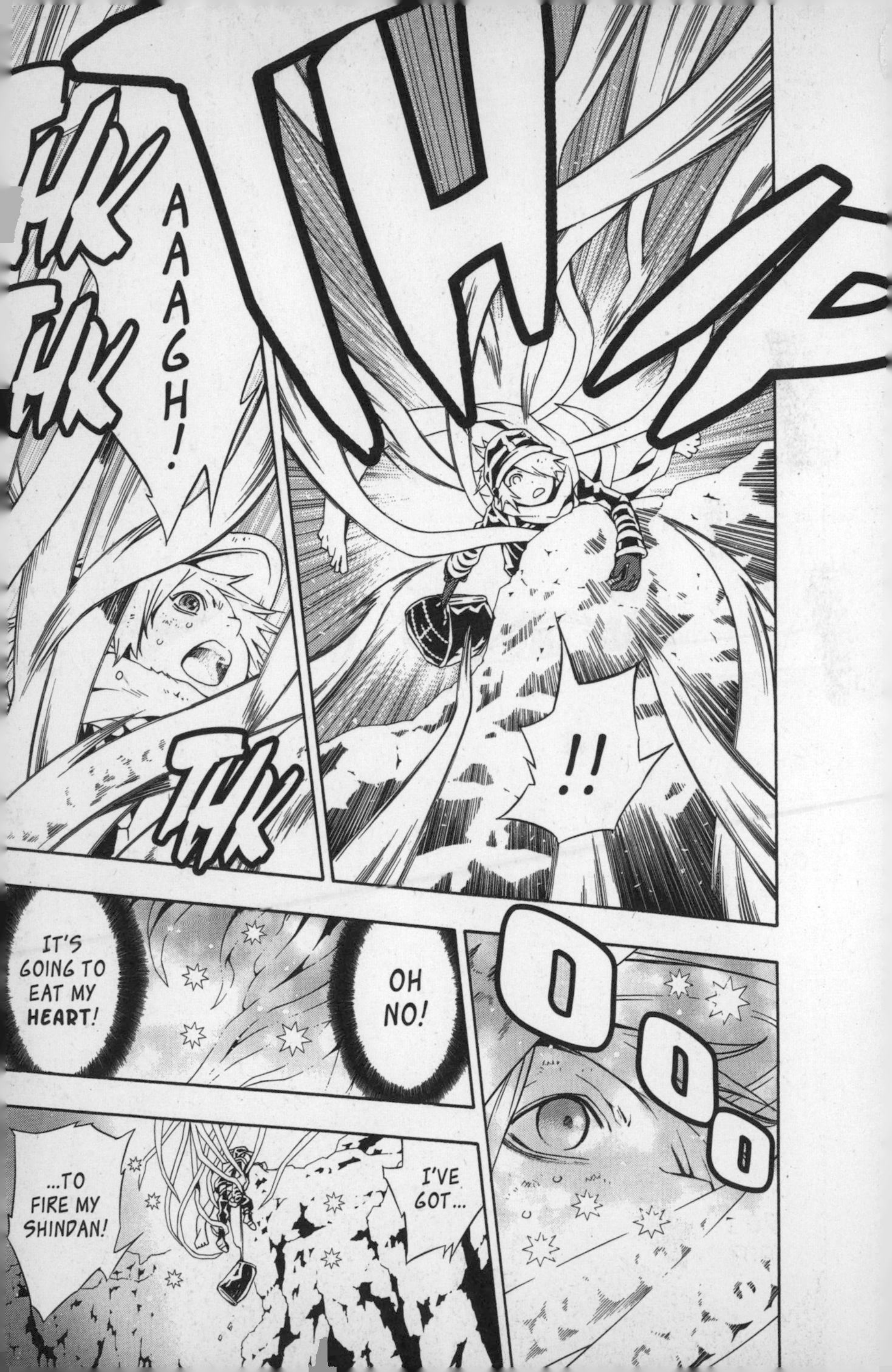
!!
THK
AAAAGH!
THK THK
OH NO!
IT'S GOING TO EAT MY HEART!
I'VE GOT...
...TO FIRE MY SHINDAN!

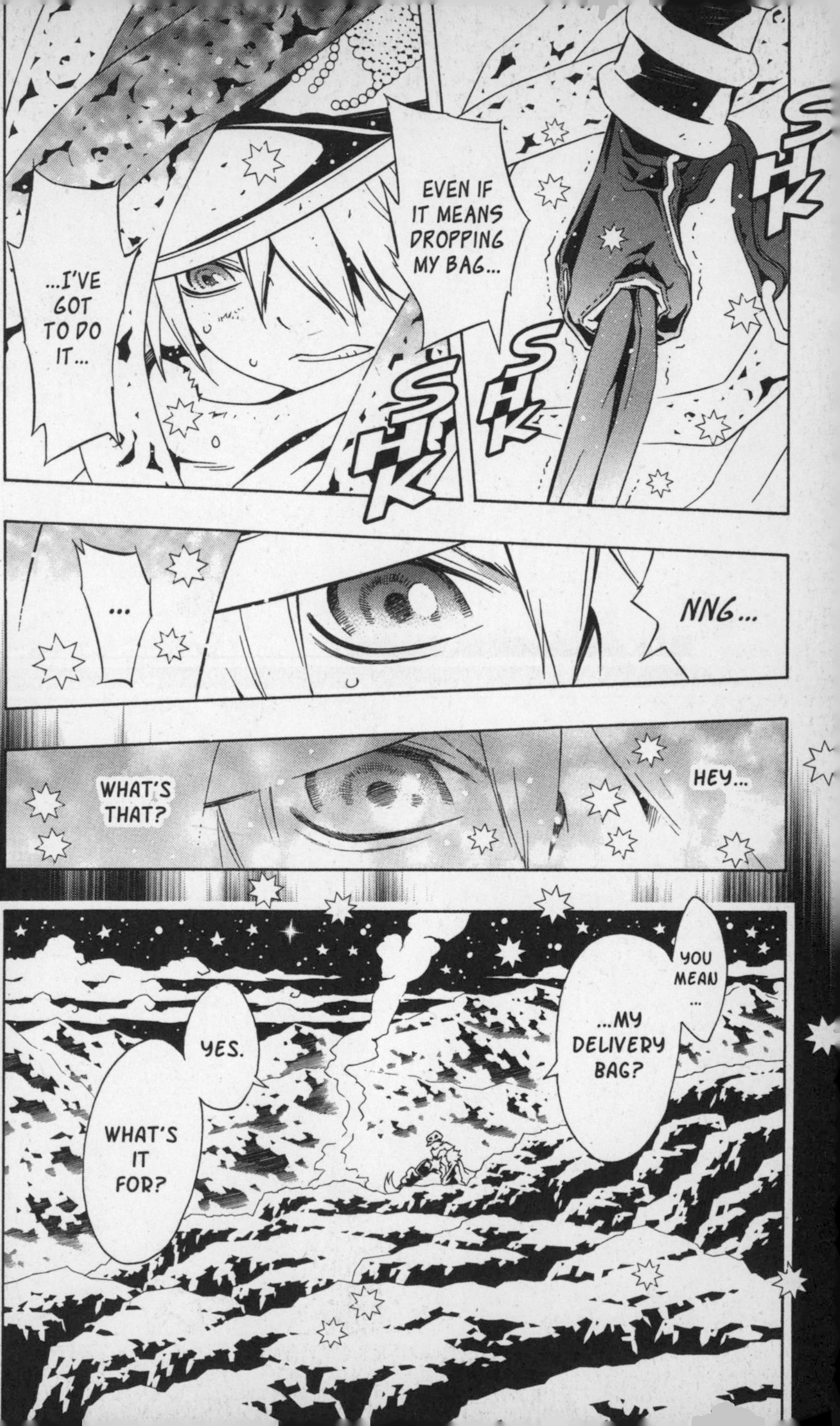
SHK
EVEN IF IT MEANS DROPPING MY BAG...
SHK
SHK
...I'VE GOT TO DO IT...
NNG...
...
HEY...
WHAT'S THAT?
YOU MEAN...
...MY DELIVERY BAG?
YES.
WHAT'S IT FOR?

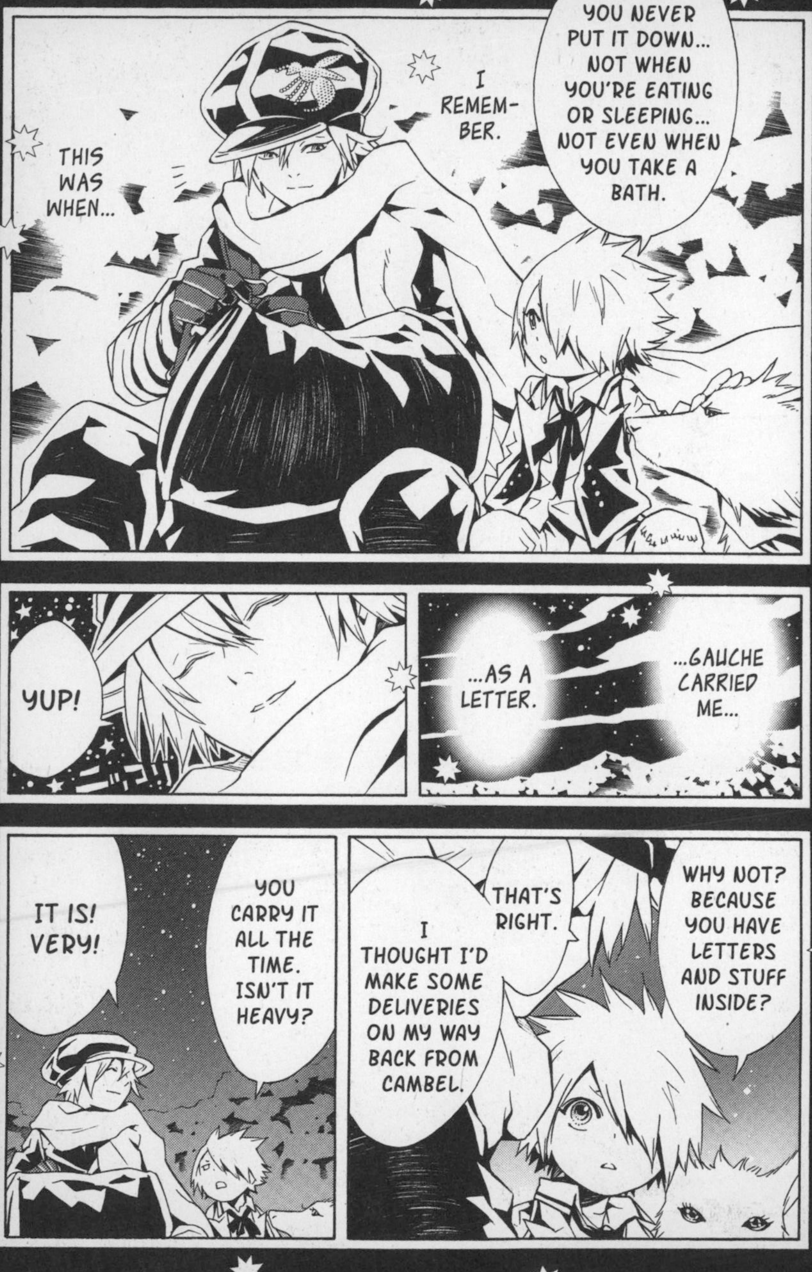
YOU NEVER PUT IT DOWN... NOT WHEN YOU'RE EATING OR SLEEPING... NOT EVEN WHEN YOU TAKE A BATH.
I REMEM-BER.
THIS WAS WHEN...
...GAUCHE CARRIED ME...
...AS A LETTER.
YUP!
WHY NOT? BECAUSE YOU HAVE LETTERS AND STUFF INSIDE?
THAT'S RIGHT.
I THOUGHT I'D MAKE SOME DELIVERIES ON MY WAY BACK FROM CAMBEL.
YOU CARRY IT ALL THE TIME. ISN'T IT HEAVY?
IT IS! VERY!

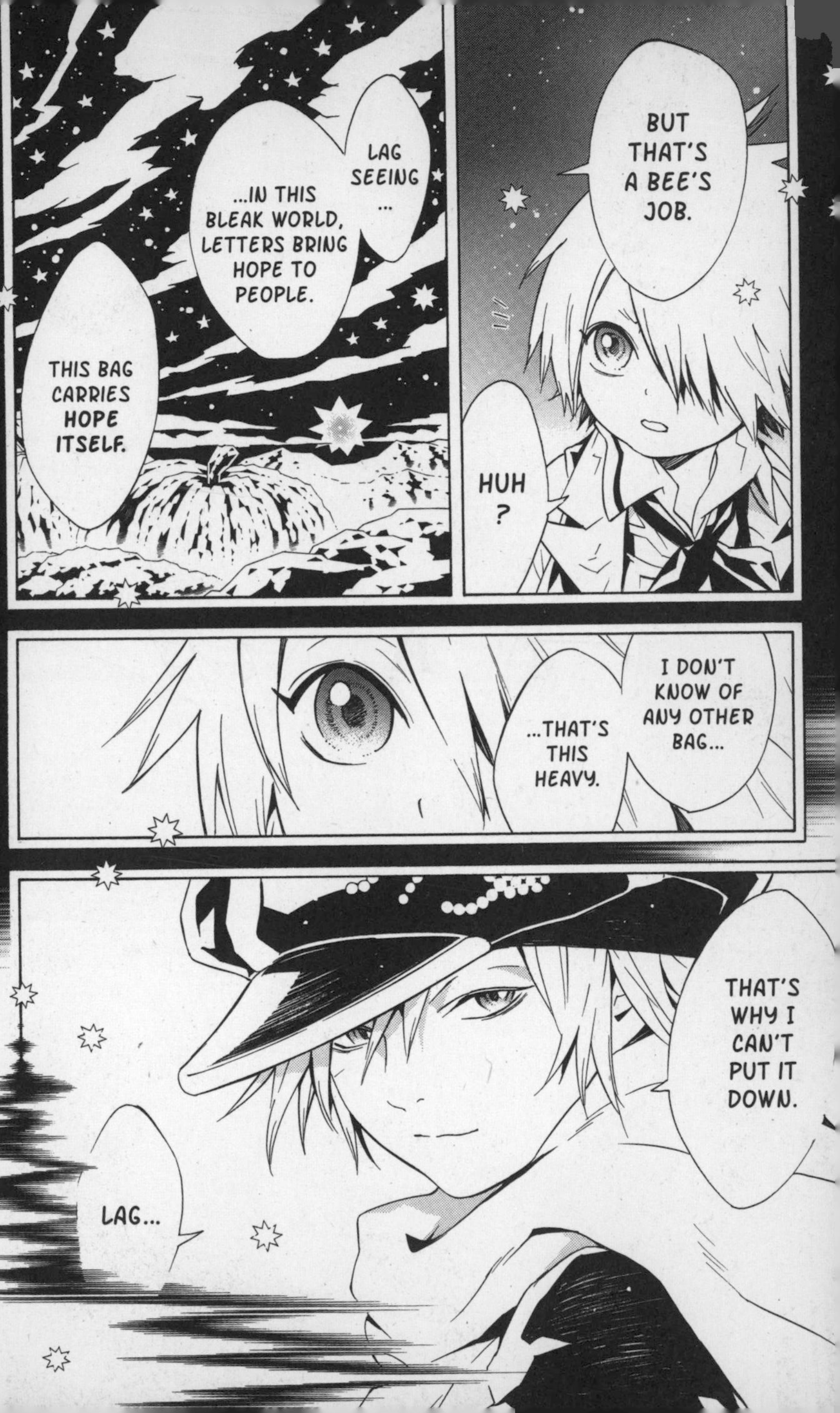
BUT THAT'S A BEE'S JOB.
HUH?
LAG SEEING...
...IN THIS BLEAK WORLD, LETTERS BRING HOPE TO PEOPLE.
THIS BAG CARRIES HOPE ITSELF.
I DON'T KNOW OF ANY OTHER BAG...
...THAT'S THIS HEAVY.
THAT'S WHY I CAN'T PUT IT DOWN.
LAG...

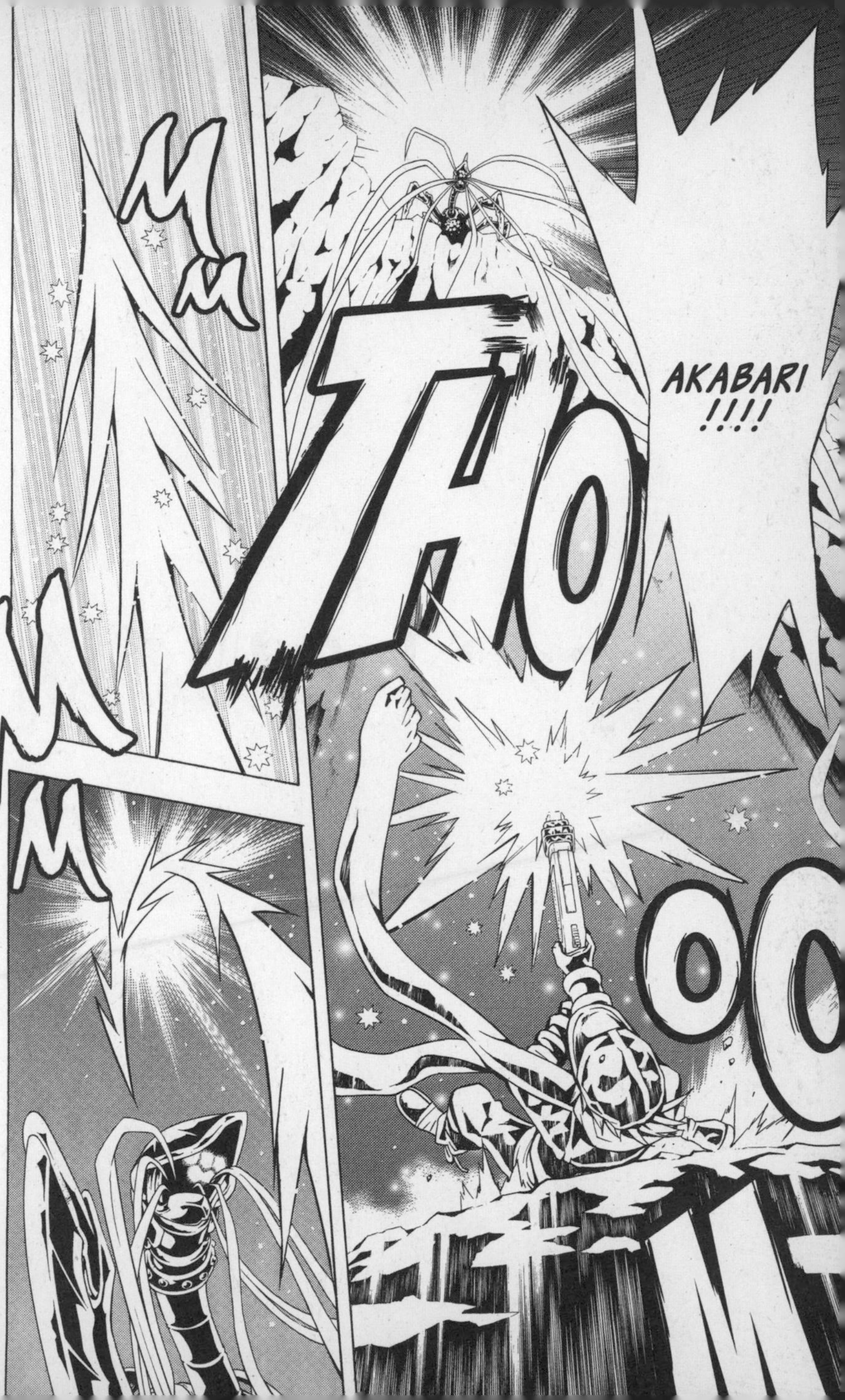
AKABARI
!!!!
THOO
MMMM

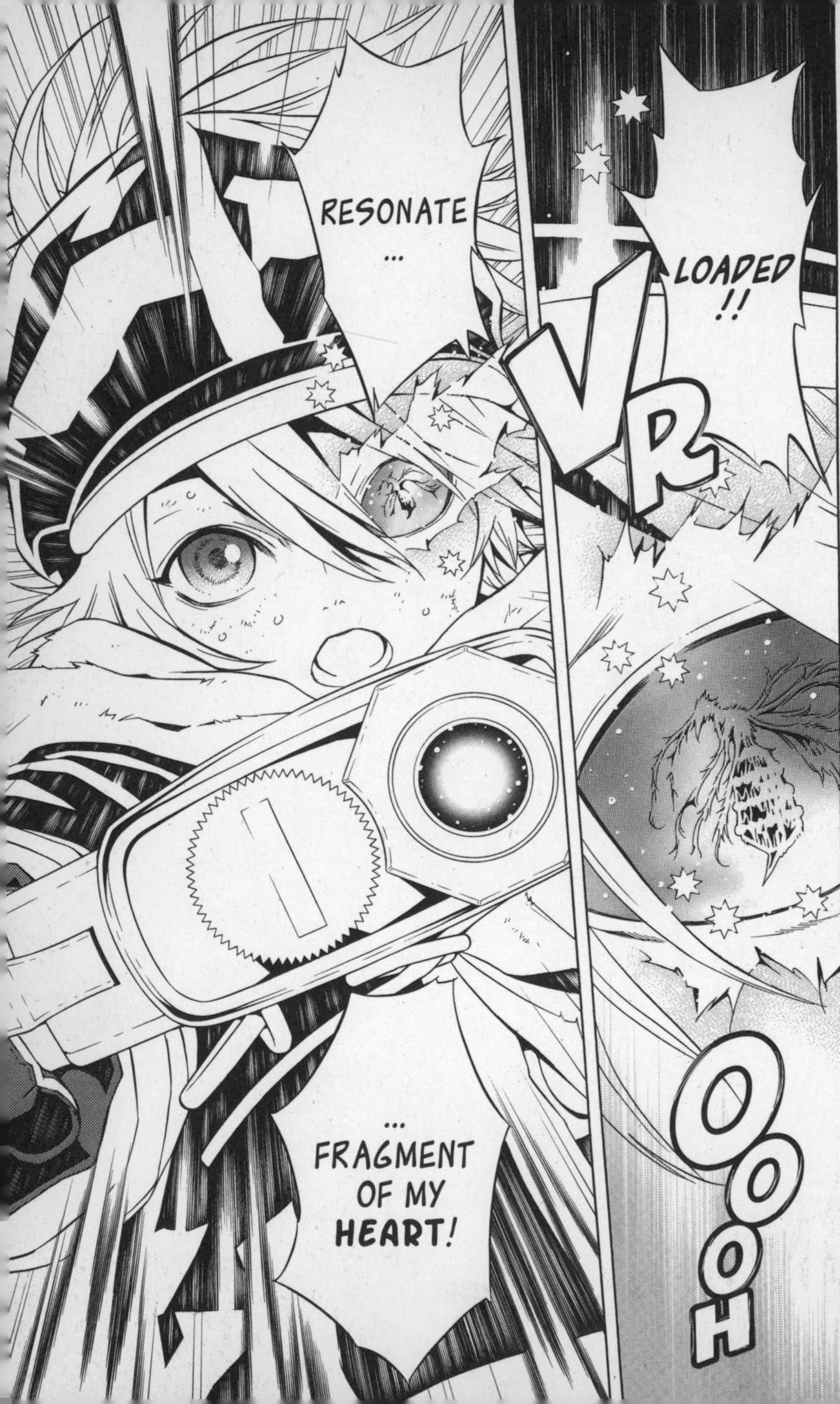
LOADED !!
RESONATE ...
VR
... FRAGMENT OF MY HEART!
OOOOH

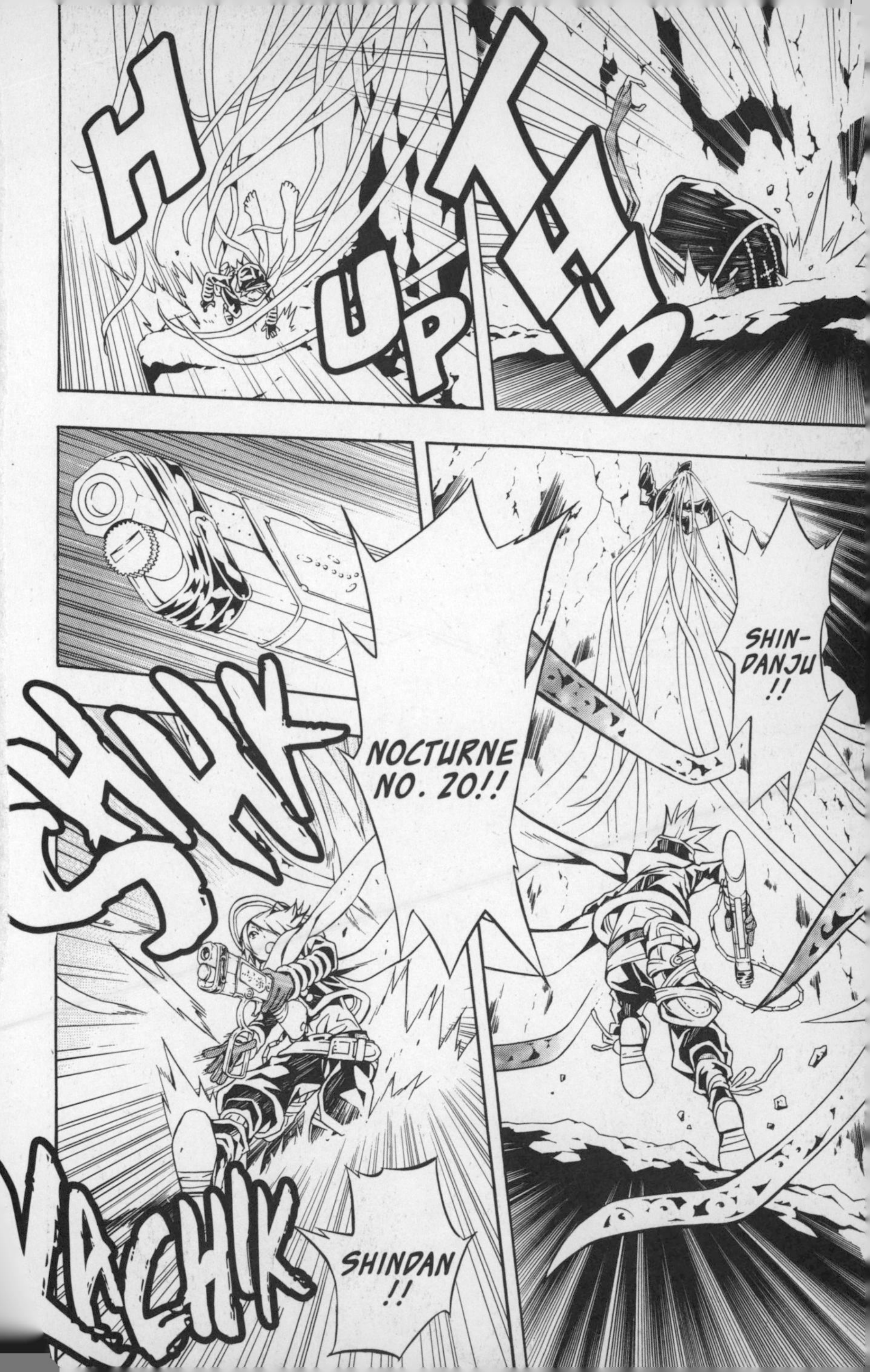
SHIN-DANJU !!
NOCTURNE NO. 20!!
SHINDAN !!

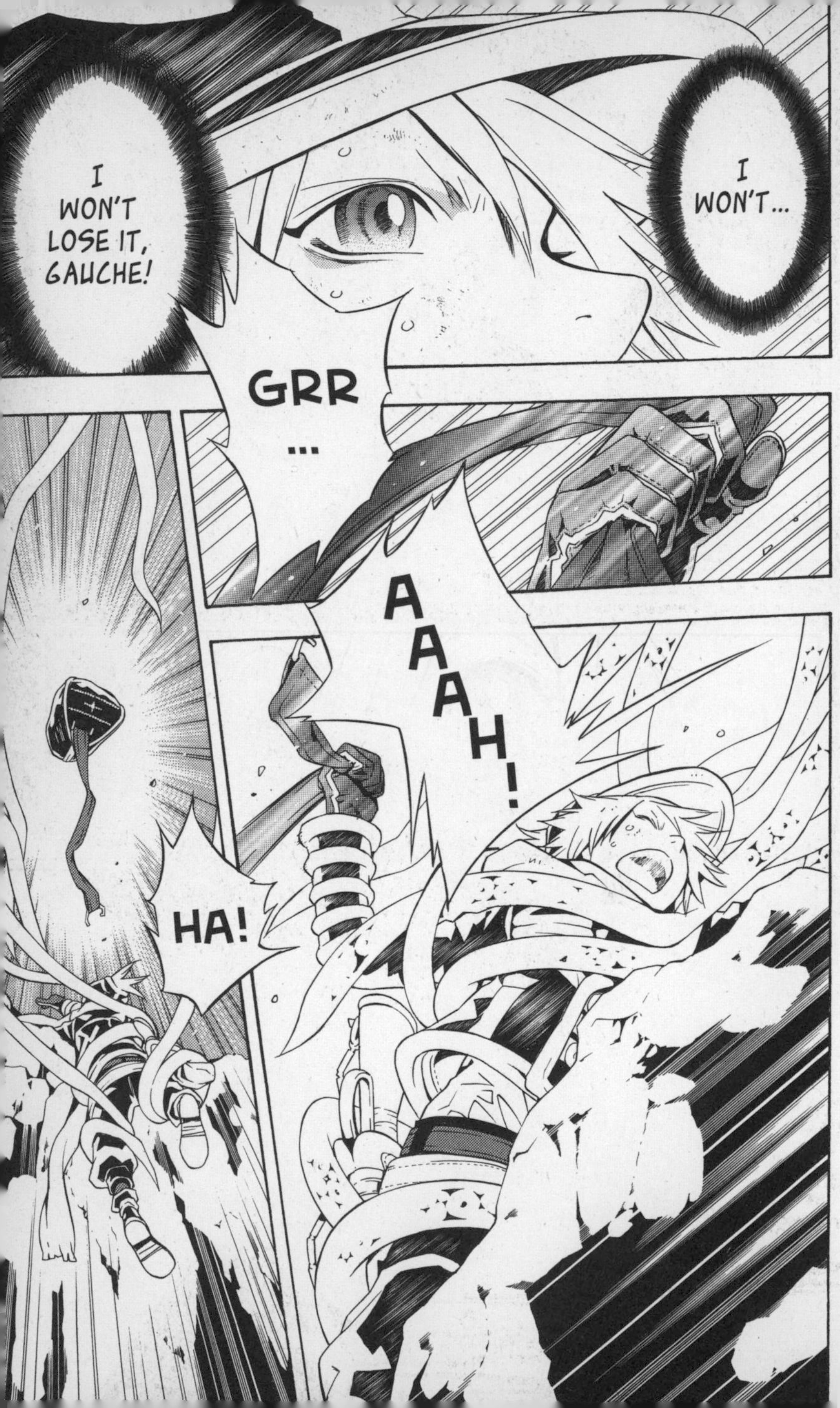
I WON'T...
I WON'T LOSE IT, GAUCHE!
GRR ...
AAAH!
HA!

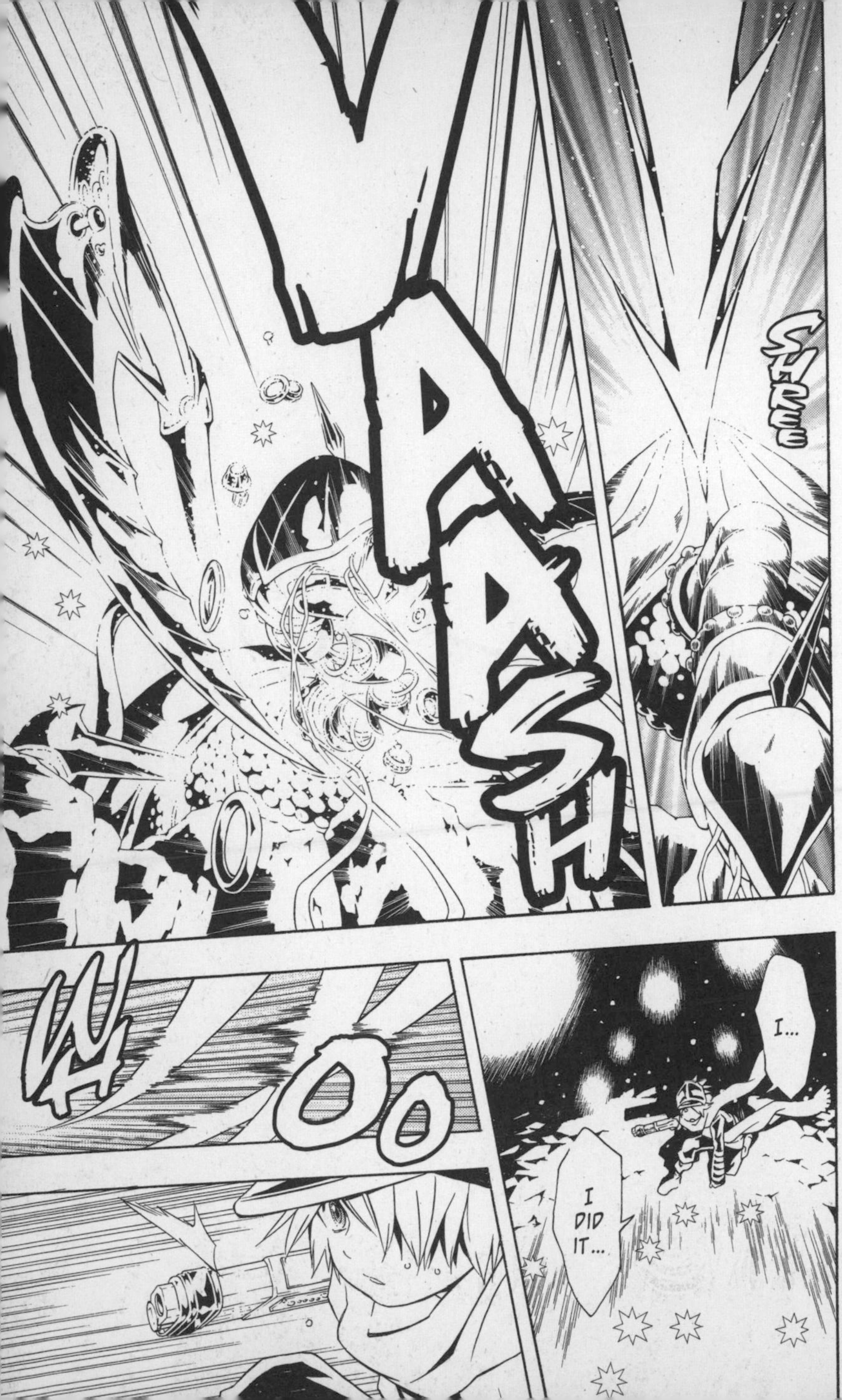
SHREE
VASH
I...
I DID IT...
WOO

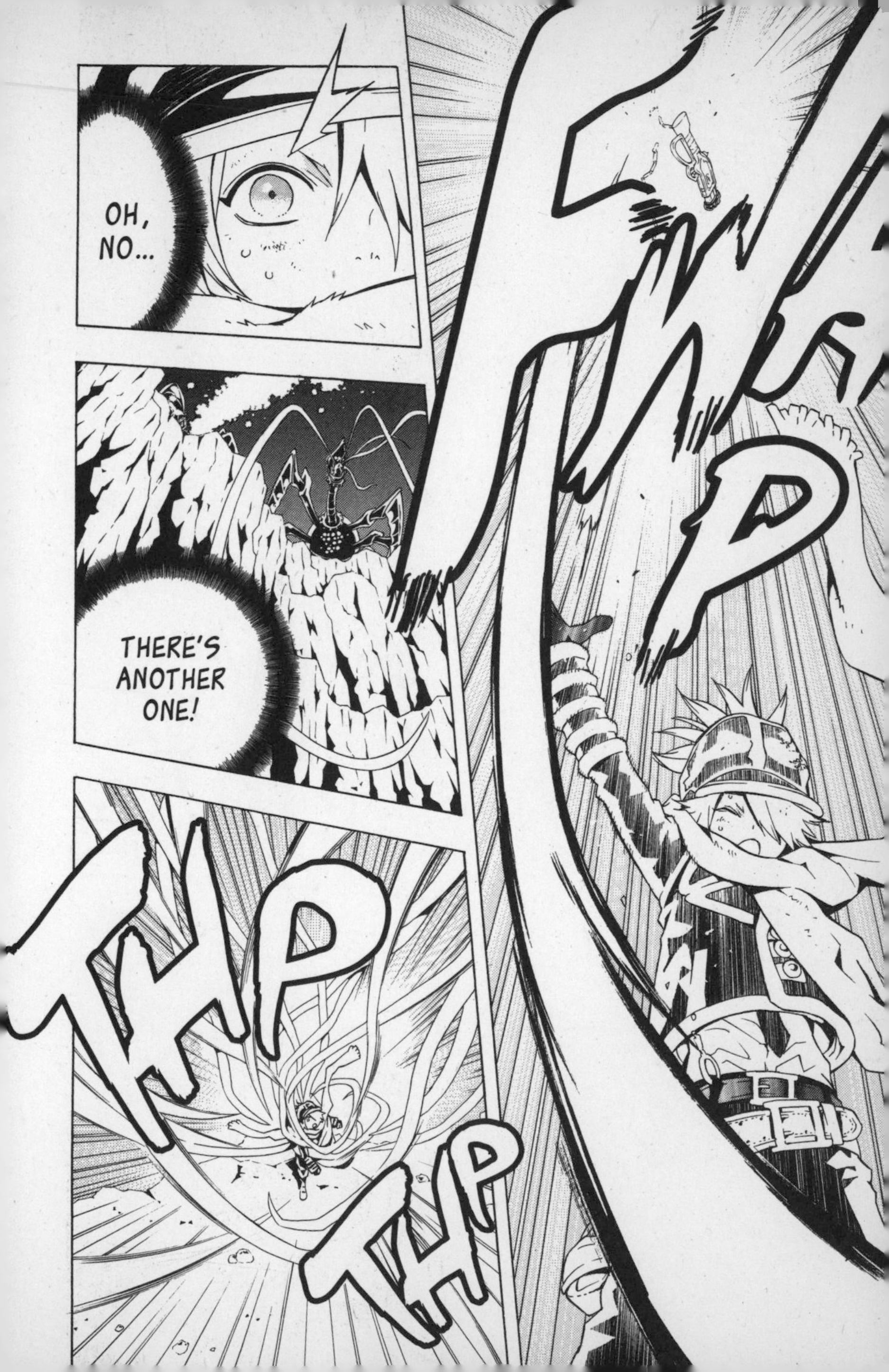
OH, NO...
THERE'S ANOTHER ONE!
THP
THP

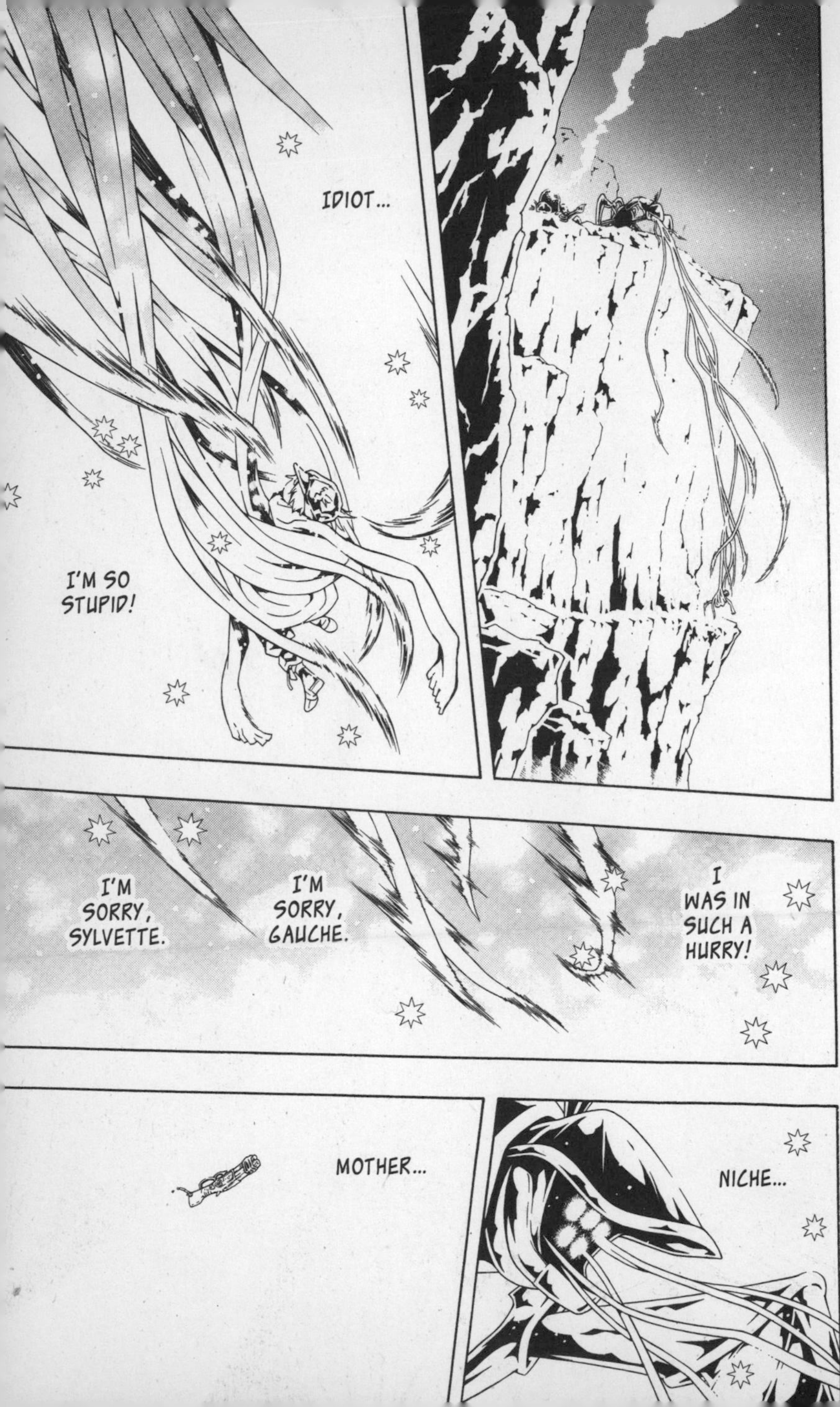
IDIOT...
I'M SO STUPID!
I WAS IN SUCH A HURRY!
I'M SORRY, GAUCHE.
I'M SORRY, SYLVETTE.
NICHE...
MOTHER...

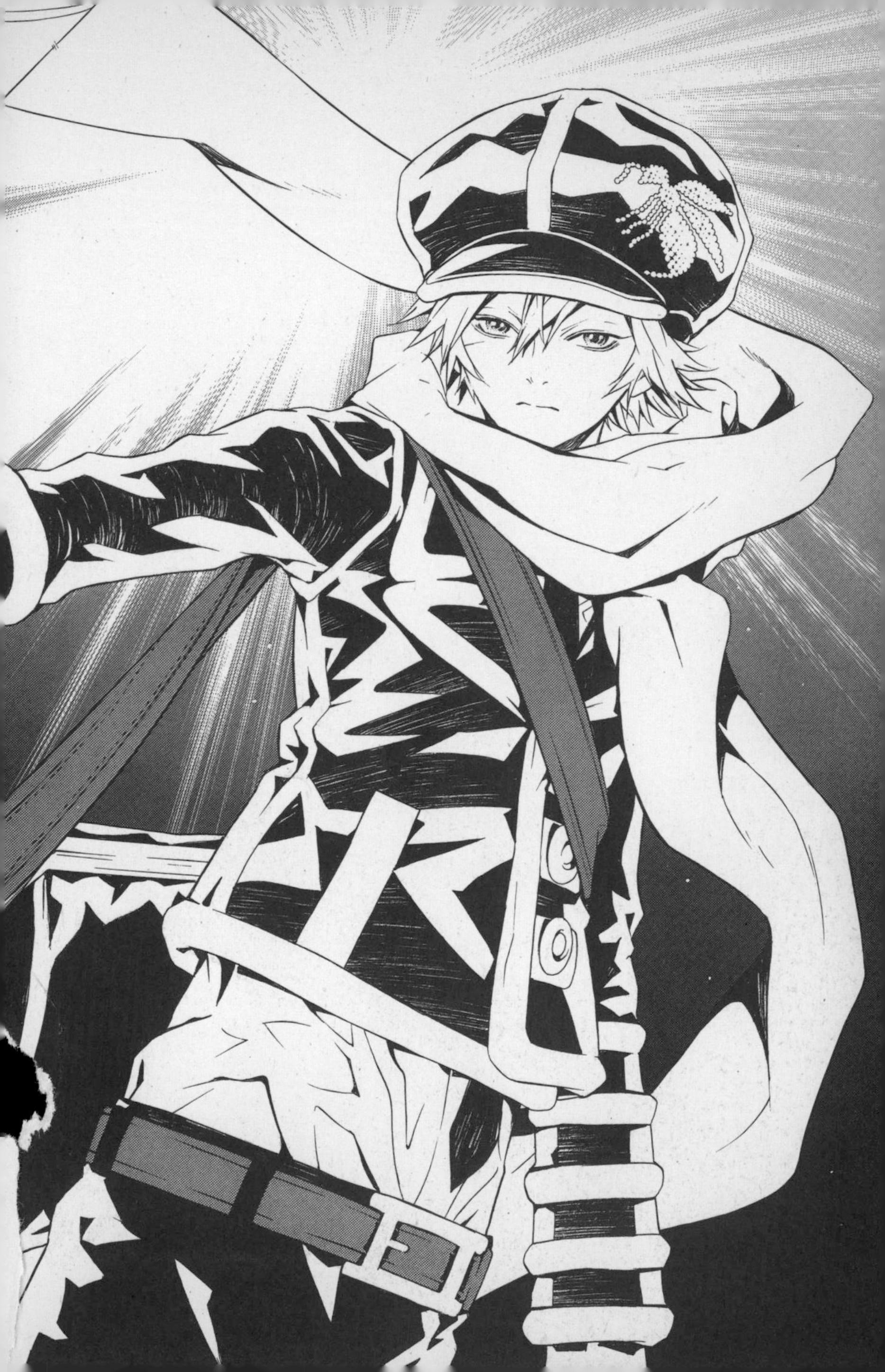

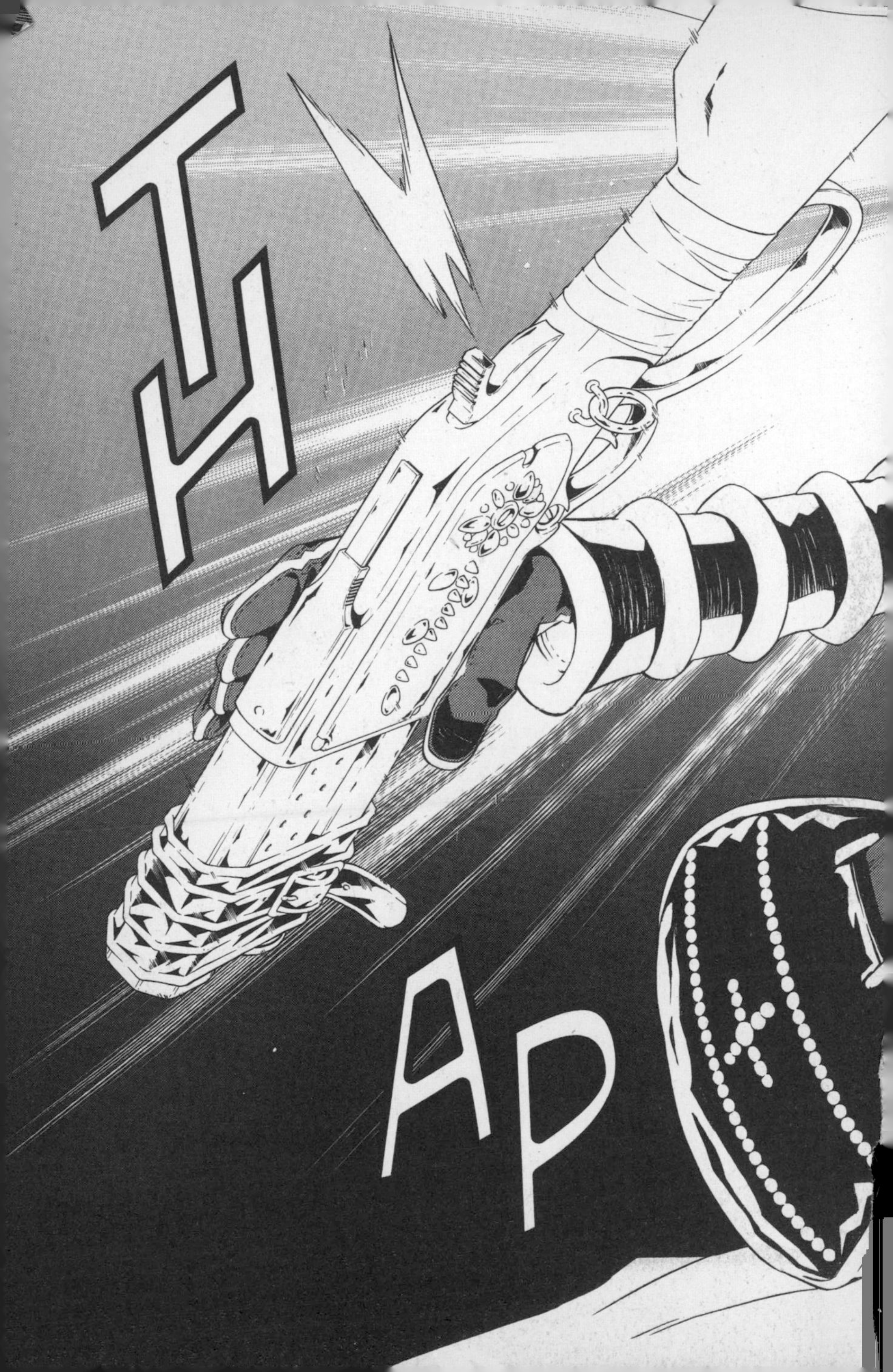
TH
AP

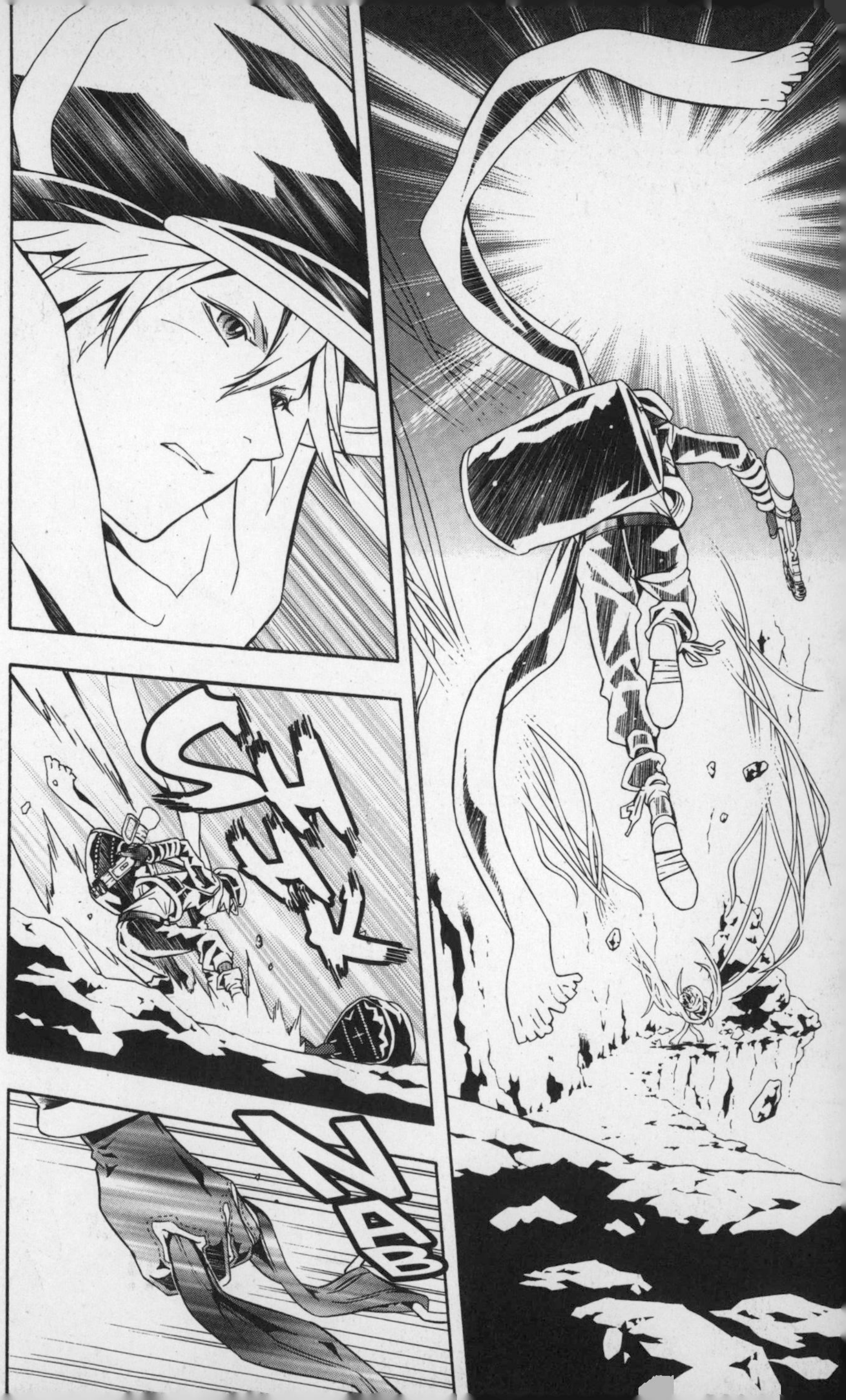
SHK
ZAB

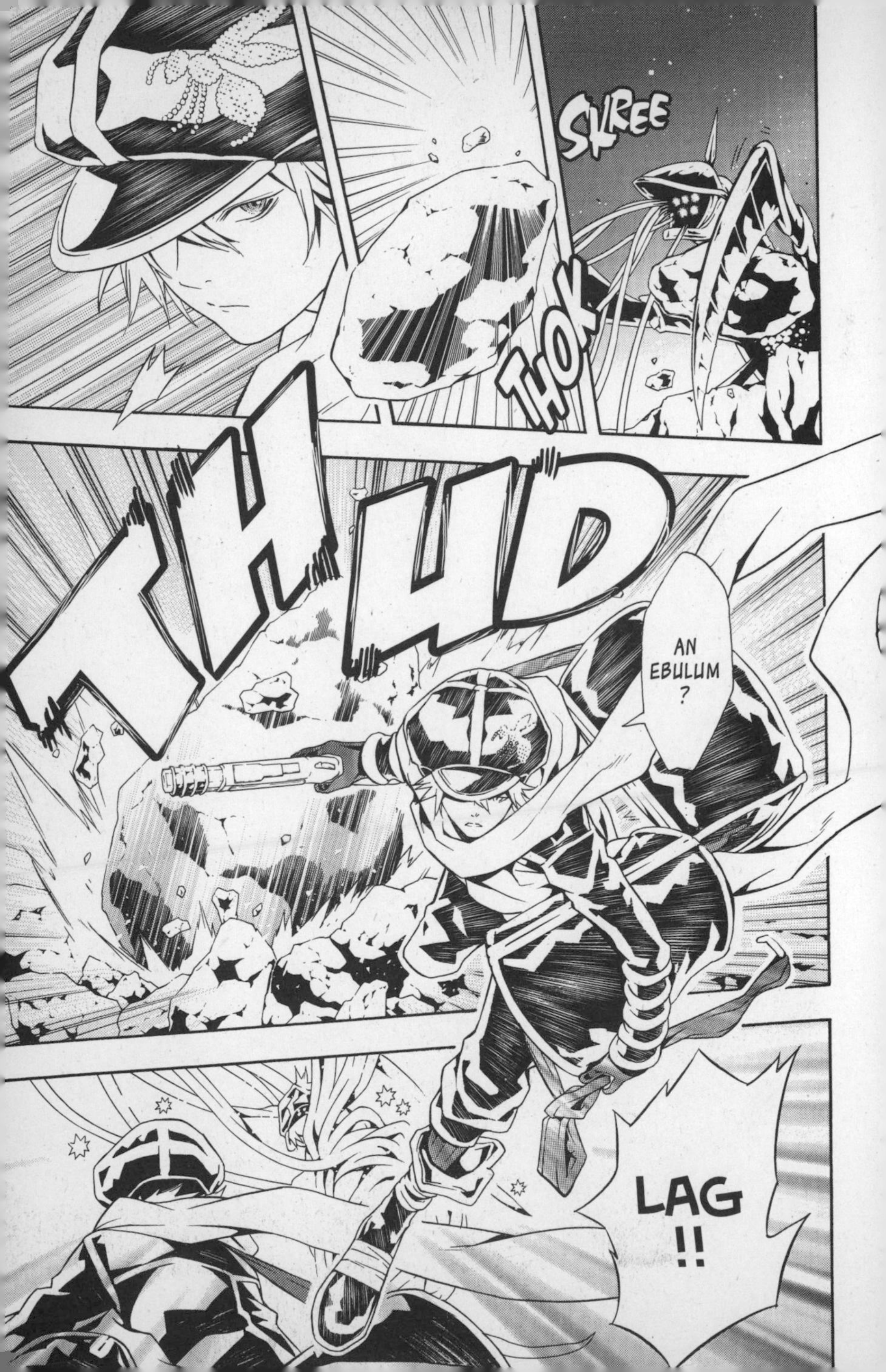
SKREE
THOK
THUD
AN EBULUM?
LAG!!

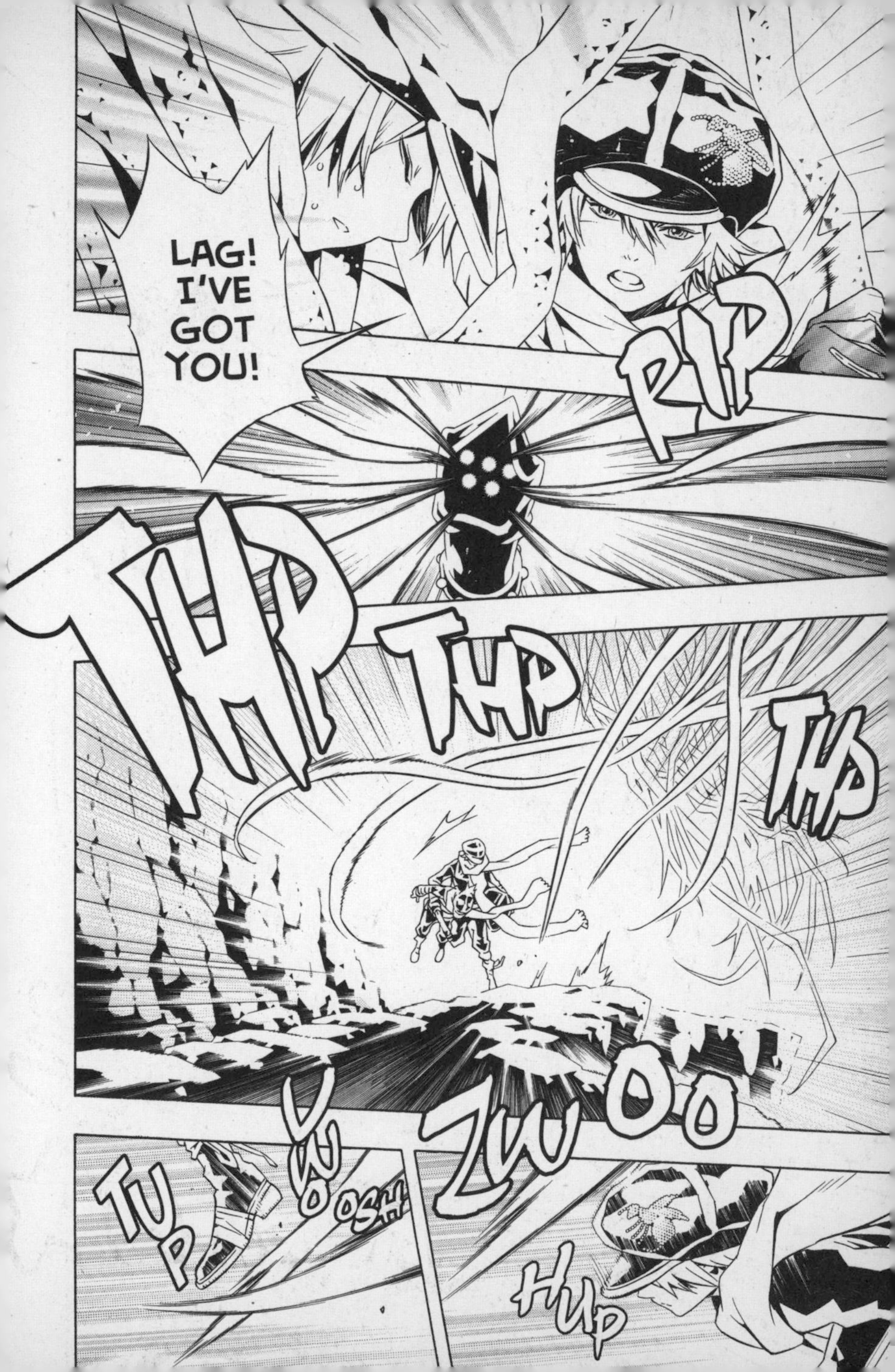
LAG! I'VE GOT YOU!
RIP
THP
THP
THP
ZUOO
YOOSH
TUP
HUP

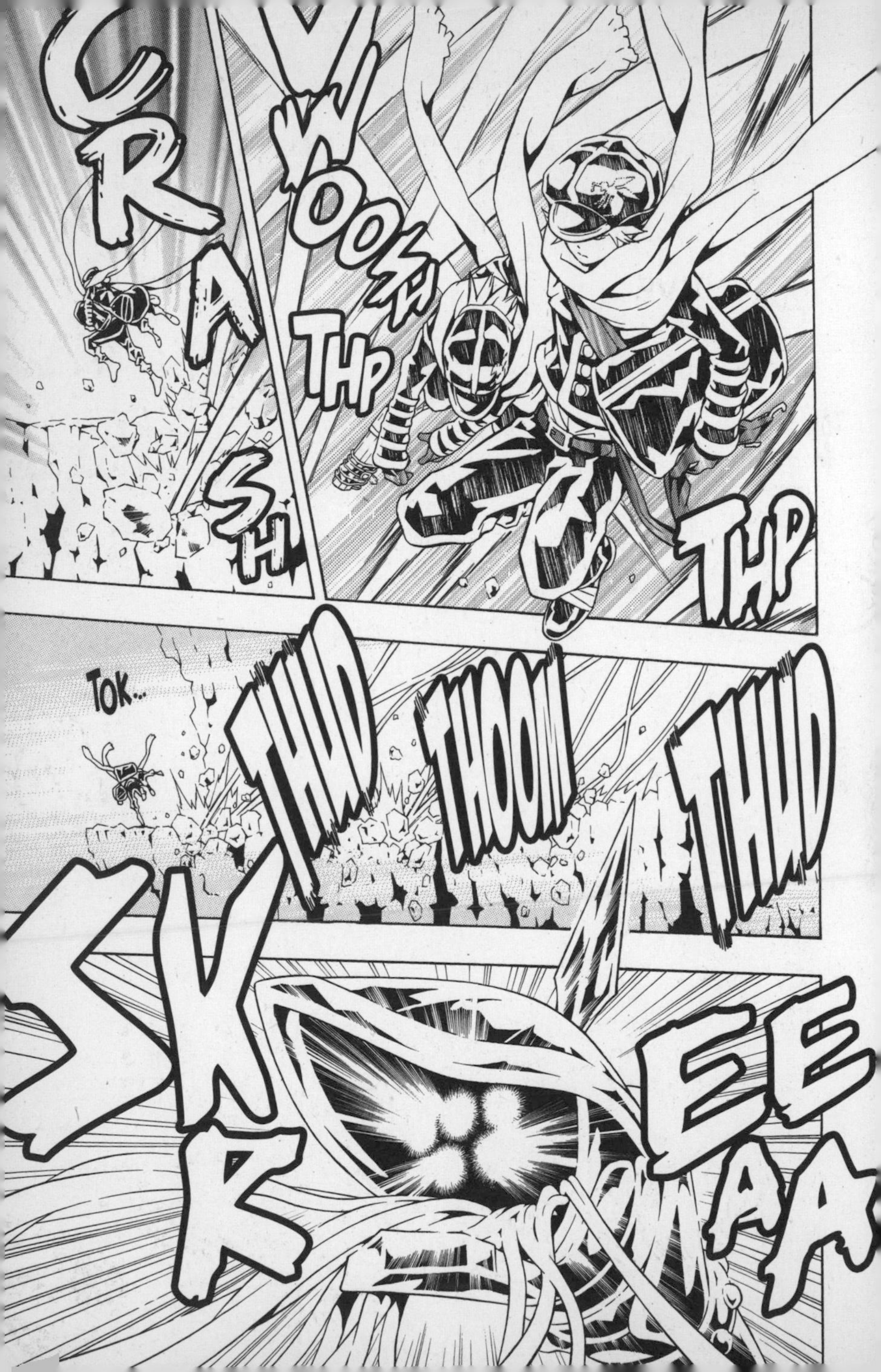
WOOOSH
THP
THP
CRA
SH
TOK...
THUD
THOOM
THUD
KR
EE

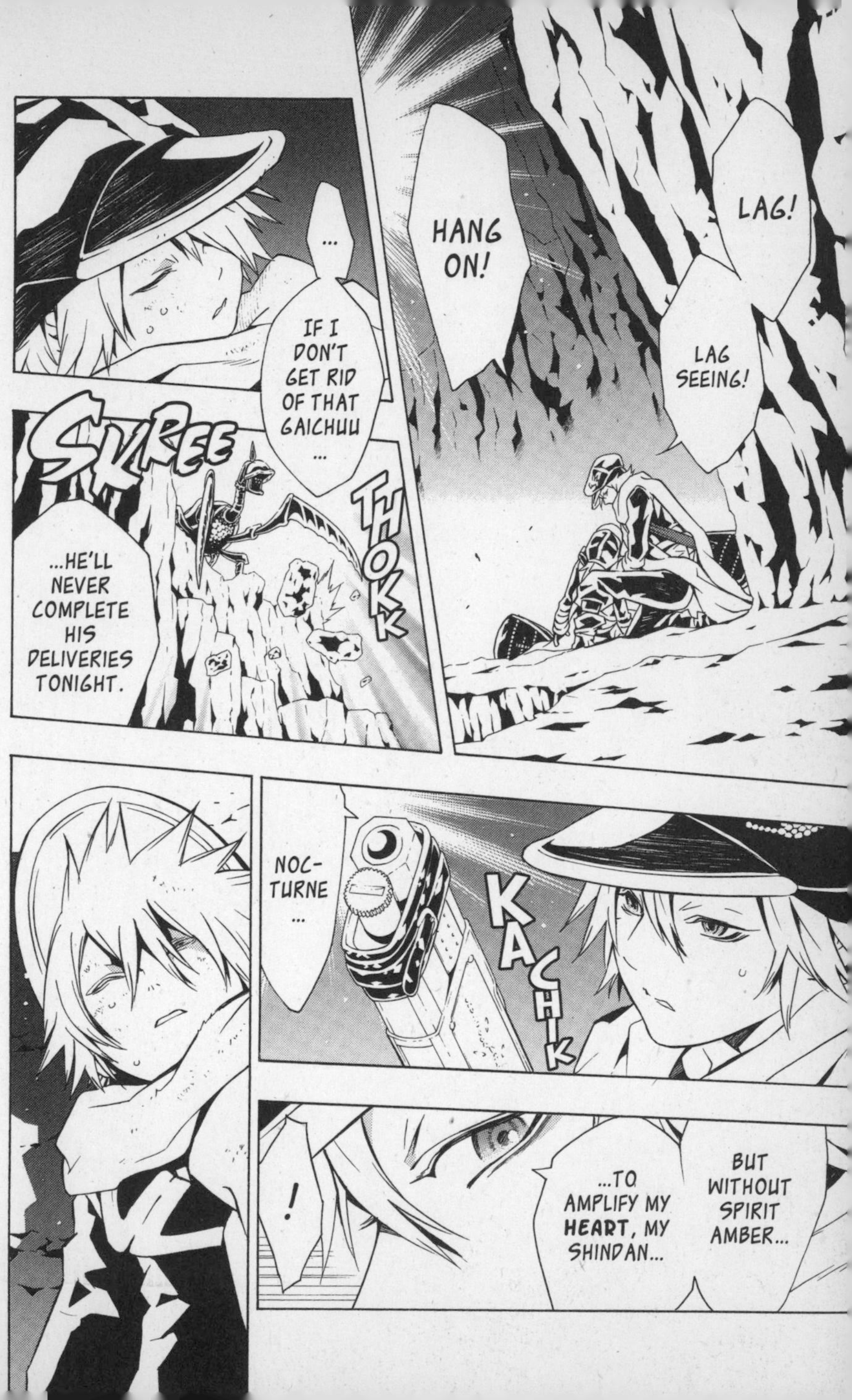
LAG!
LAG SEEING!
HANG ON!
...
IF I DON'T GET RID OF THAT GAICHUU ...
SKREE
THOKK
...HE'LL NEVER COMPLETE HIS DELIVERIES TONIGHT.
KACHIK
NOC-TURNE ...
BUT WITHOUT SPIRIT AMBER...
...TO AMPLIFY MY **HEART**, MY SHINDAN...
!

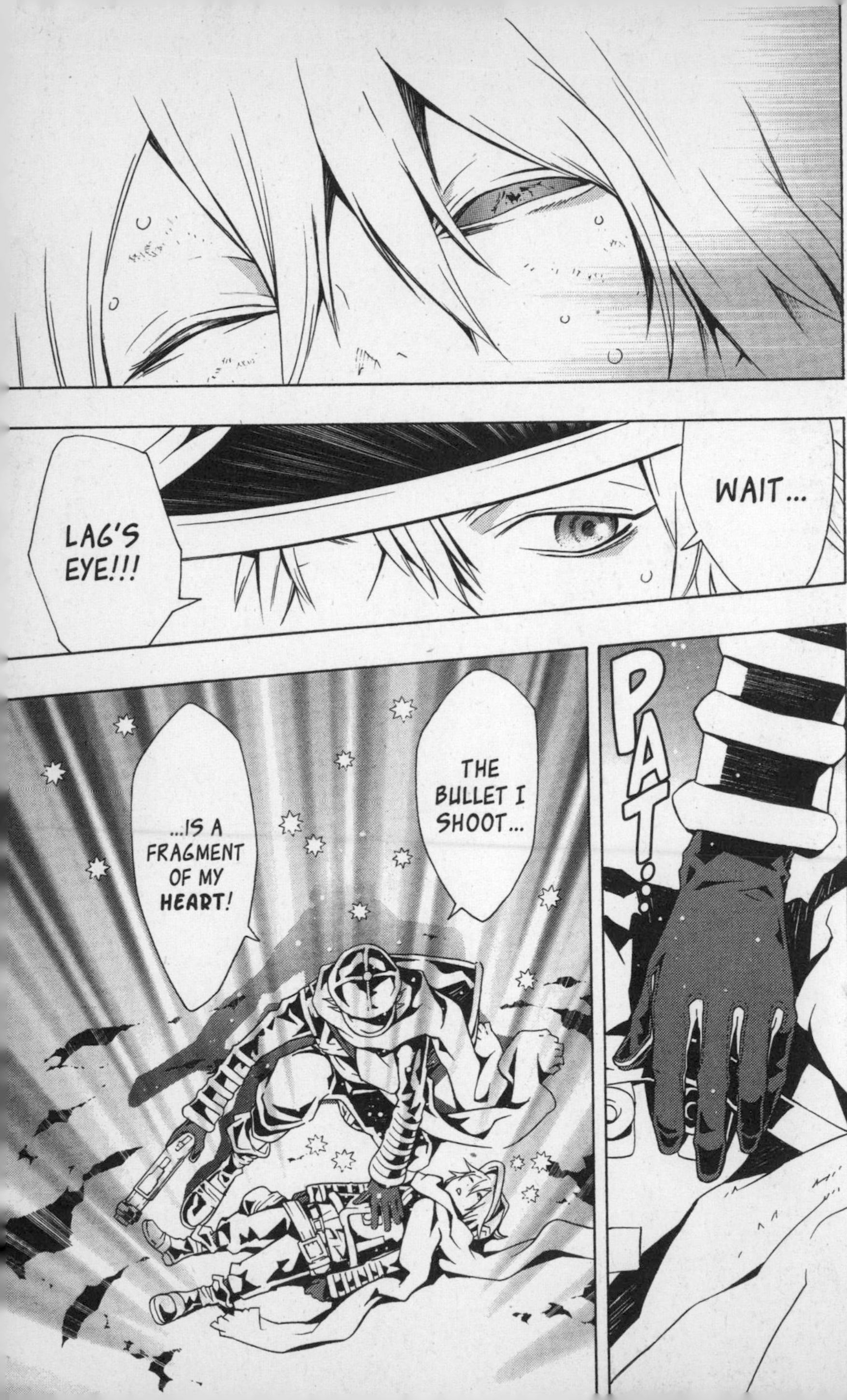

WAIT...
LAG'S EYE!!!
PAT
THE BULLET I SHOOT...
...IS A FRAGMENT OF MY HEART!

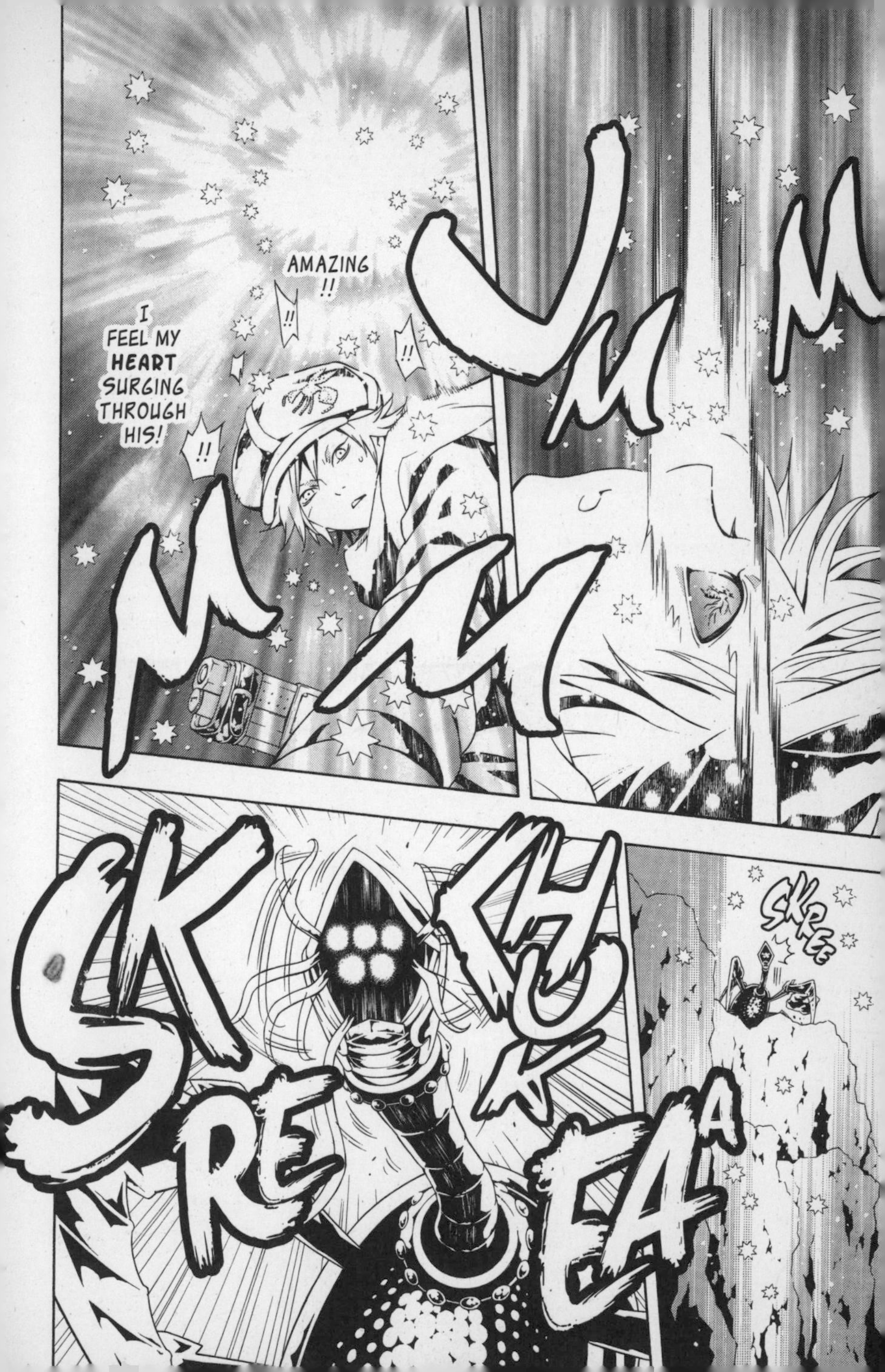
AMAZING !!
I FEEL MY HEART SURGING THROUGH HIS!
!!
!!
!!
SKREE

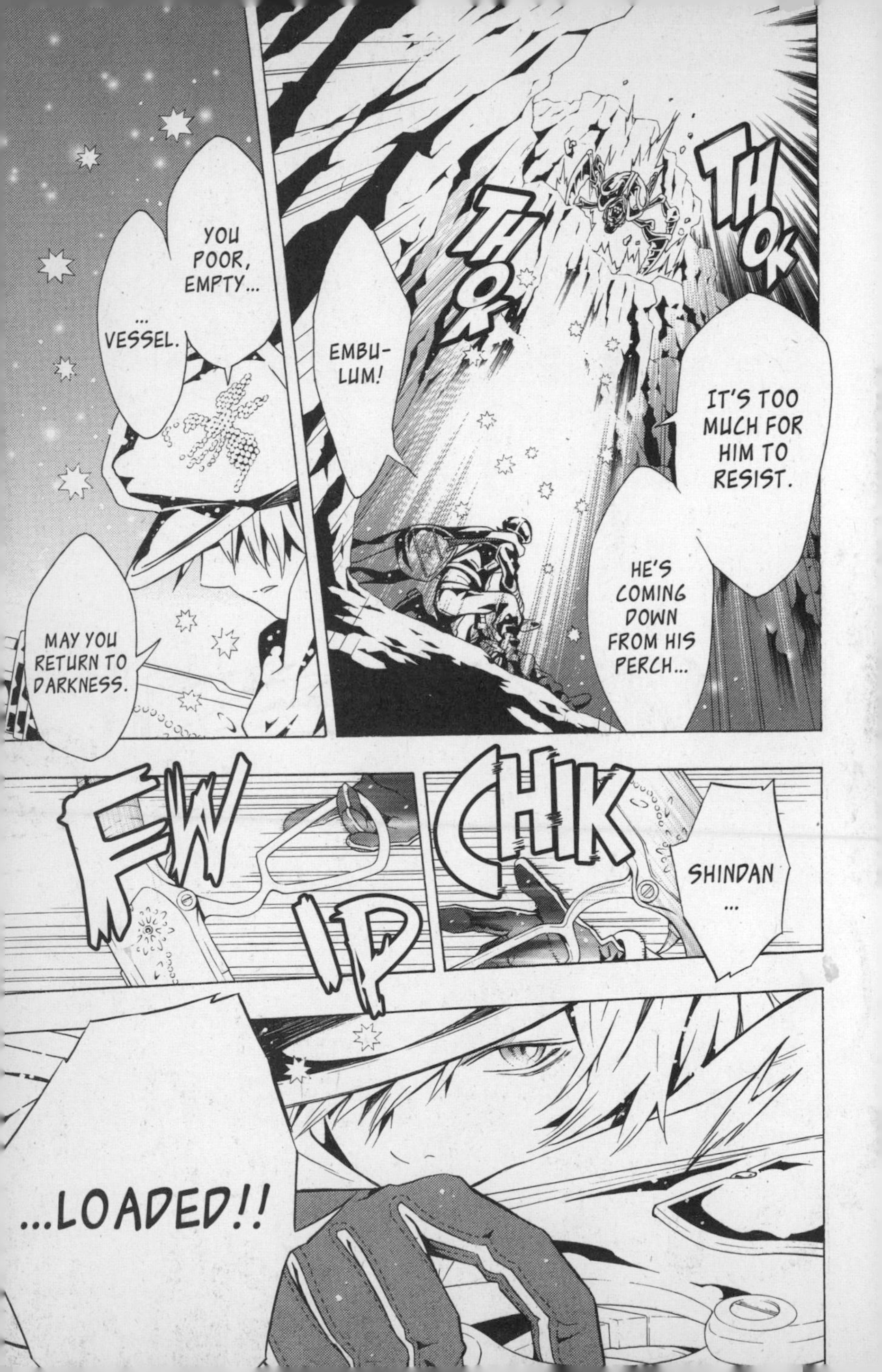
THOK
IT'S TOO MUCH FOR HIM TO RESIST.
HE'S COMING DOWN FROM HIS PERCH...
THOK
EMBU-LUM!
YOU POOR, EMPTY...
...VESSEL.
MAY YOU RETURN TO DARKNESS.
SHINDAN...
CHIK
FWIP
...LOADED!!

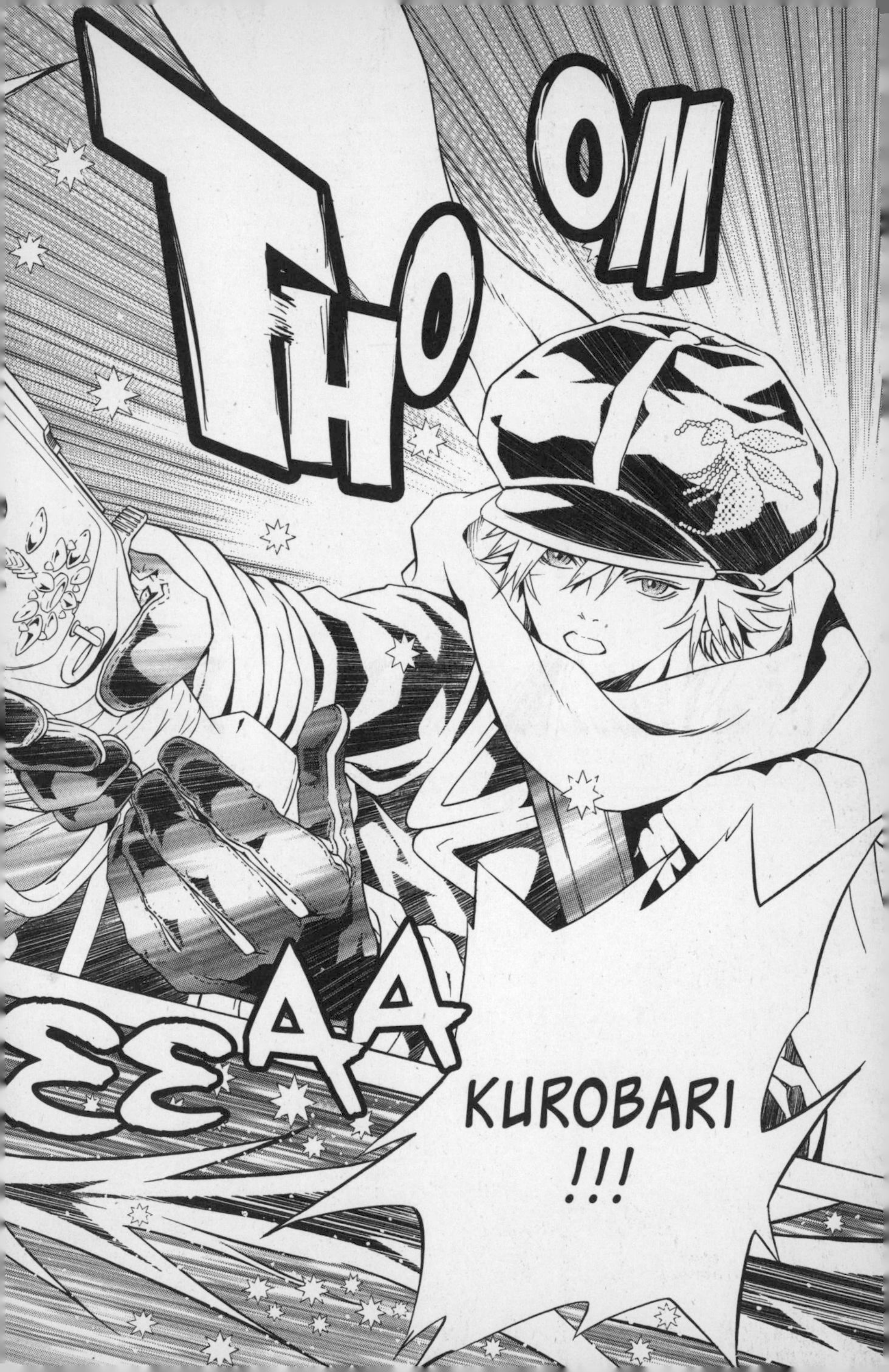
THOOM
KUROBARI
!!!

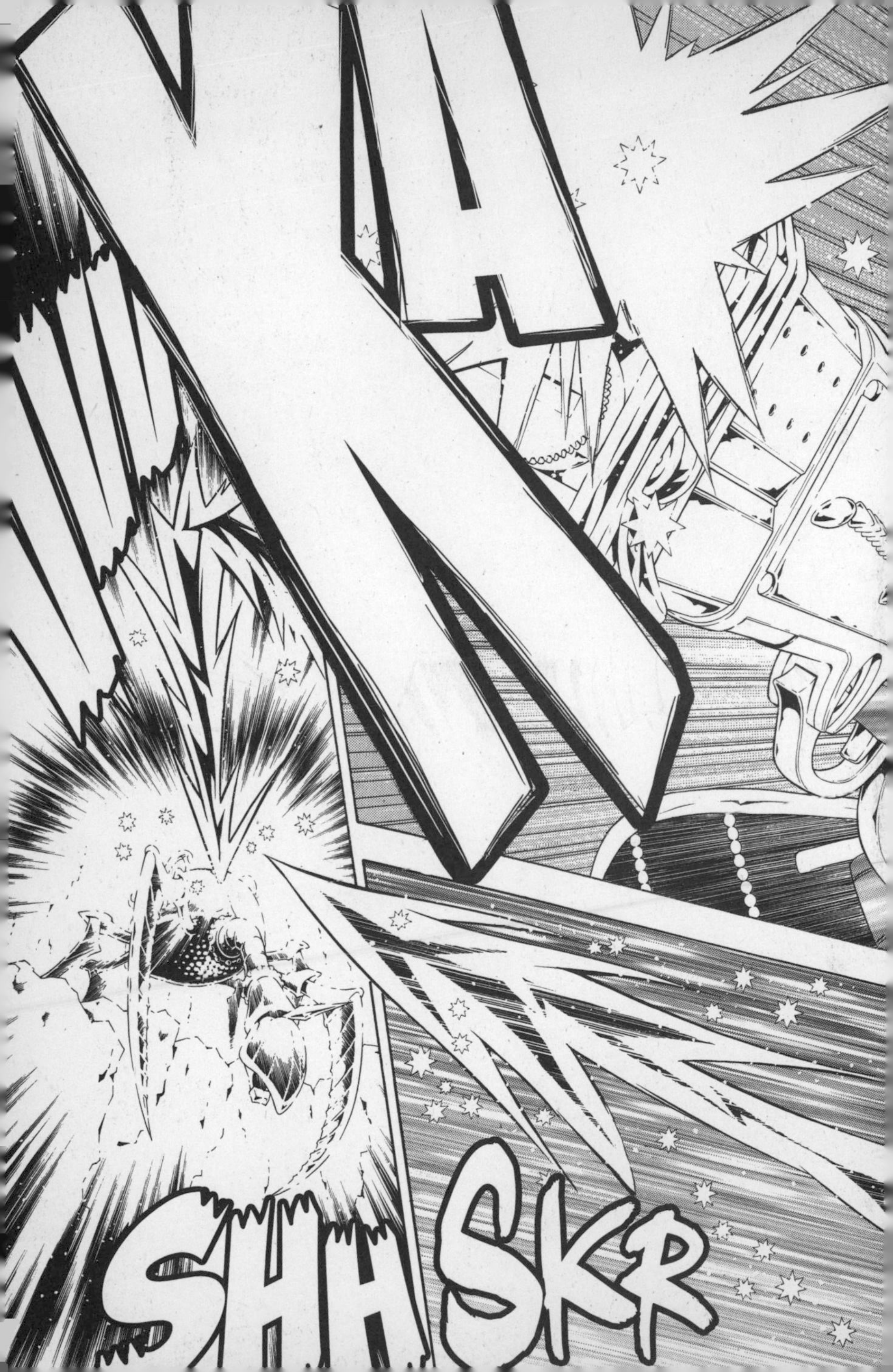
SKR

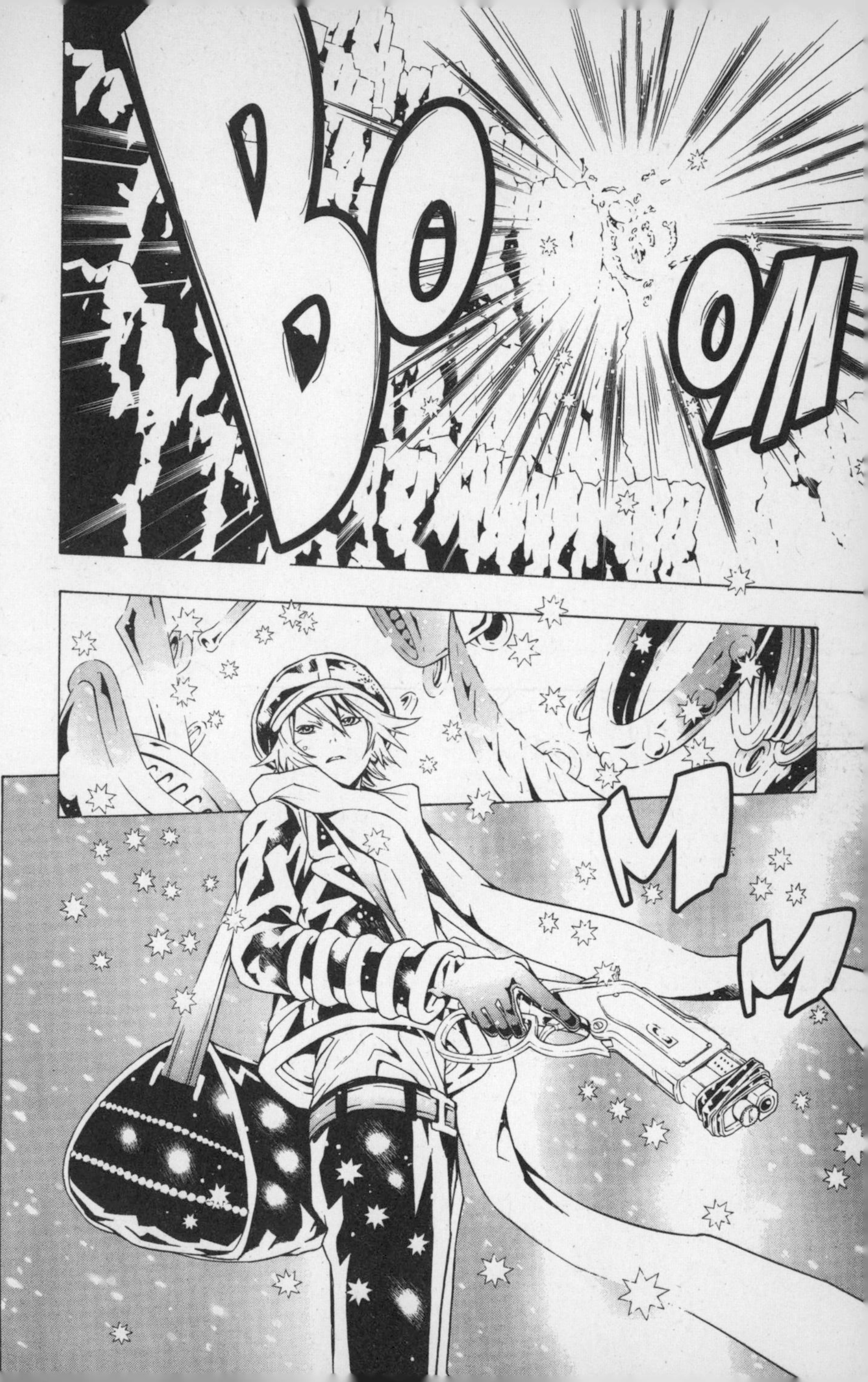
BOOM
MM

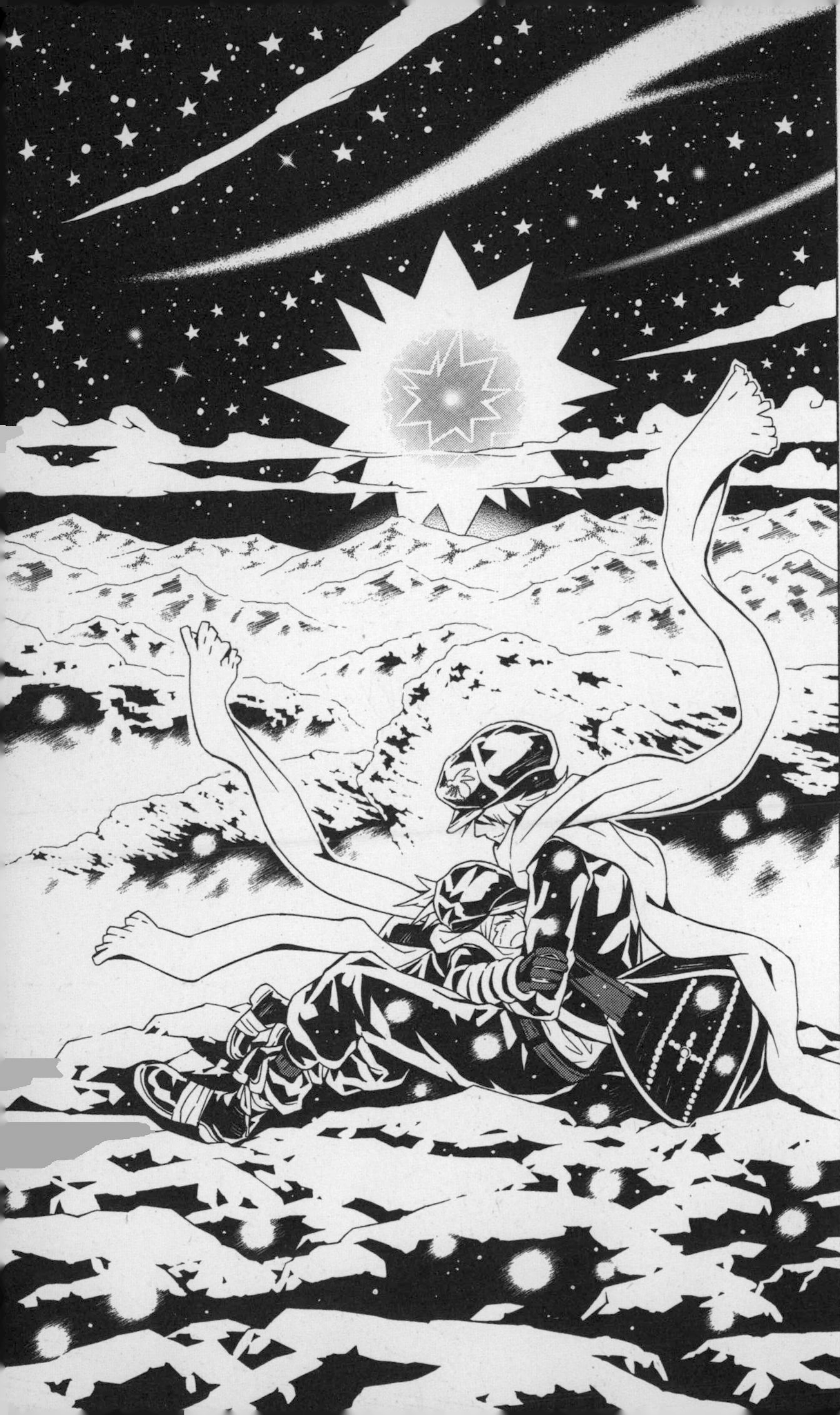

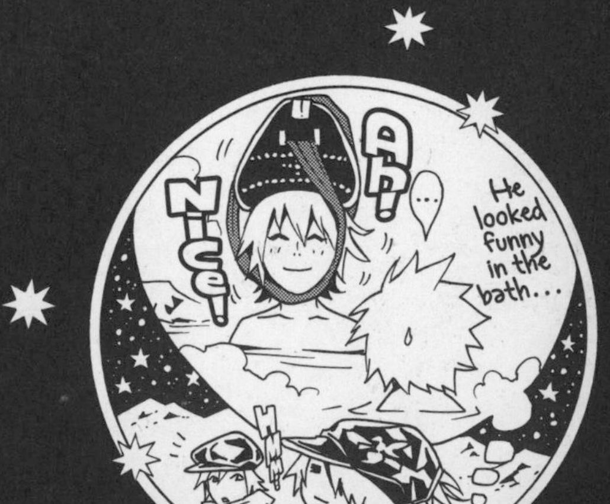
He looked funny in the bath...
Ah!
...
Nice!
HMM

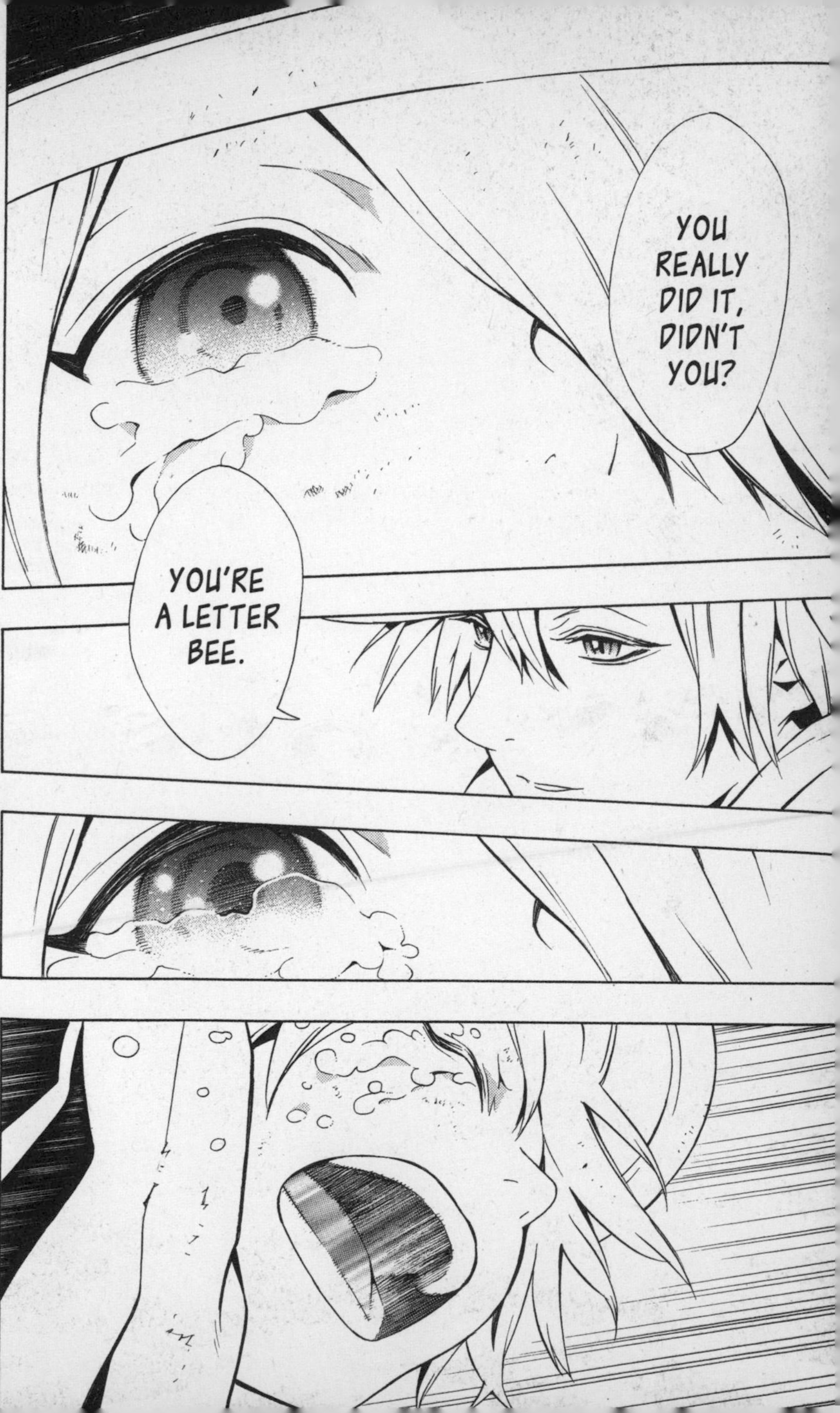
YOU REALLY DID IT, DIDN'T YOU?
YOU'RE A LETTER BEE.

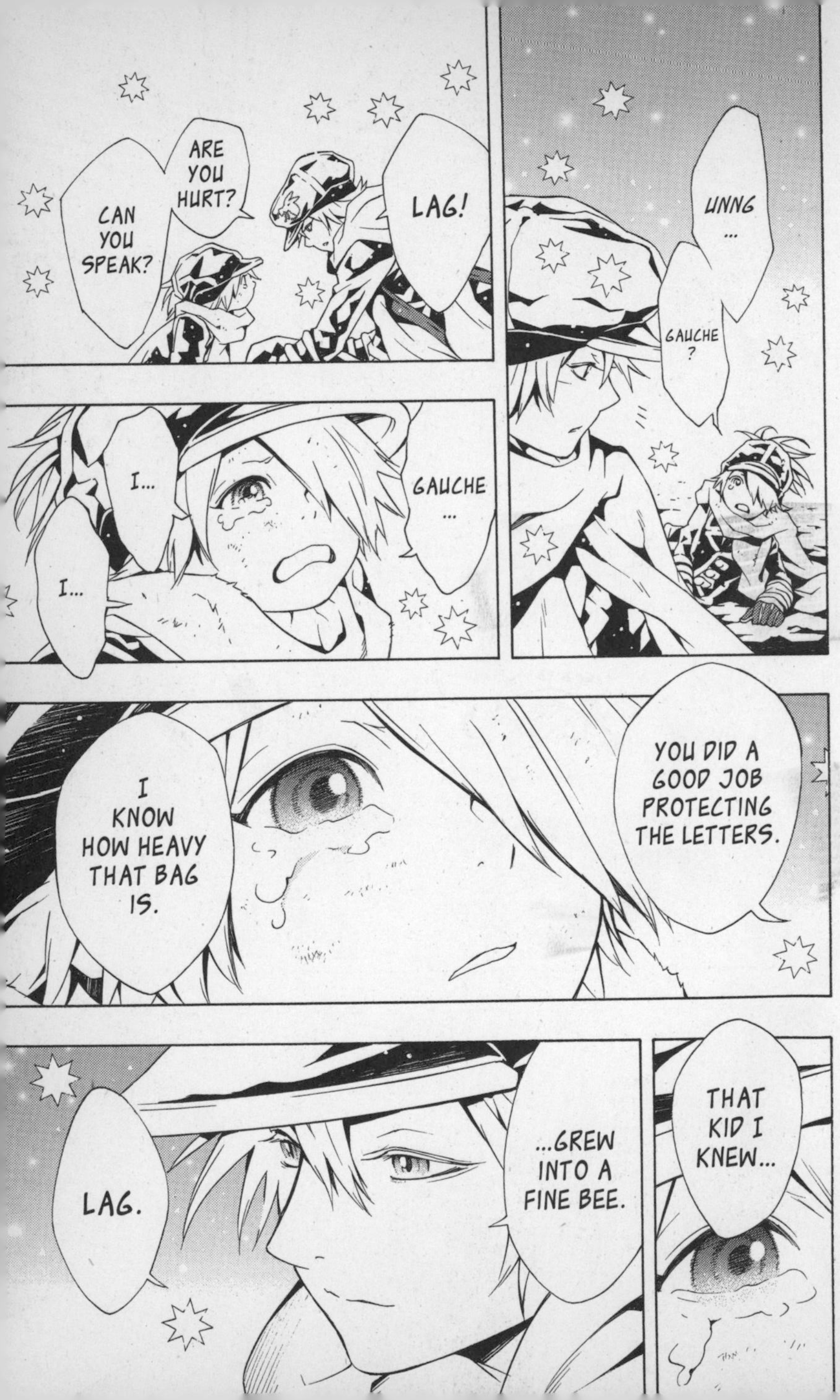
UNNG ...
GAUCHE ?
LAG!
ARE YOU HURT?
CAN YOU SPEAK?
GAUCHE ...
I...
I...
YOU DID A GOOD JOB PROTECTING THE LETTERS.
I KNOW HOW HEAVY THAT BAG IS.
THAT KID I KNEW...
...GREW INTO A FINE BEE.
LAG.

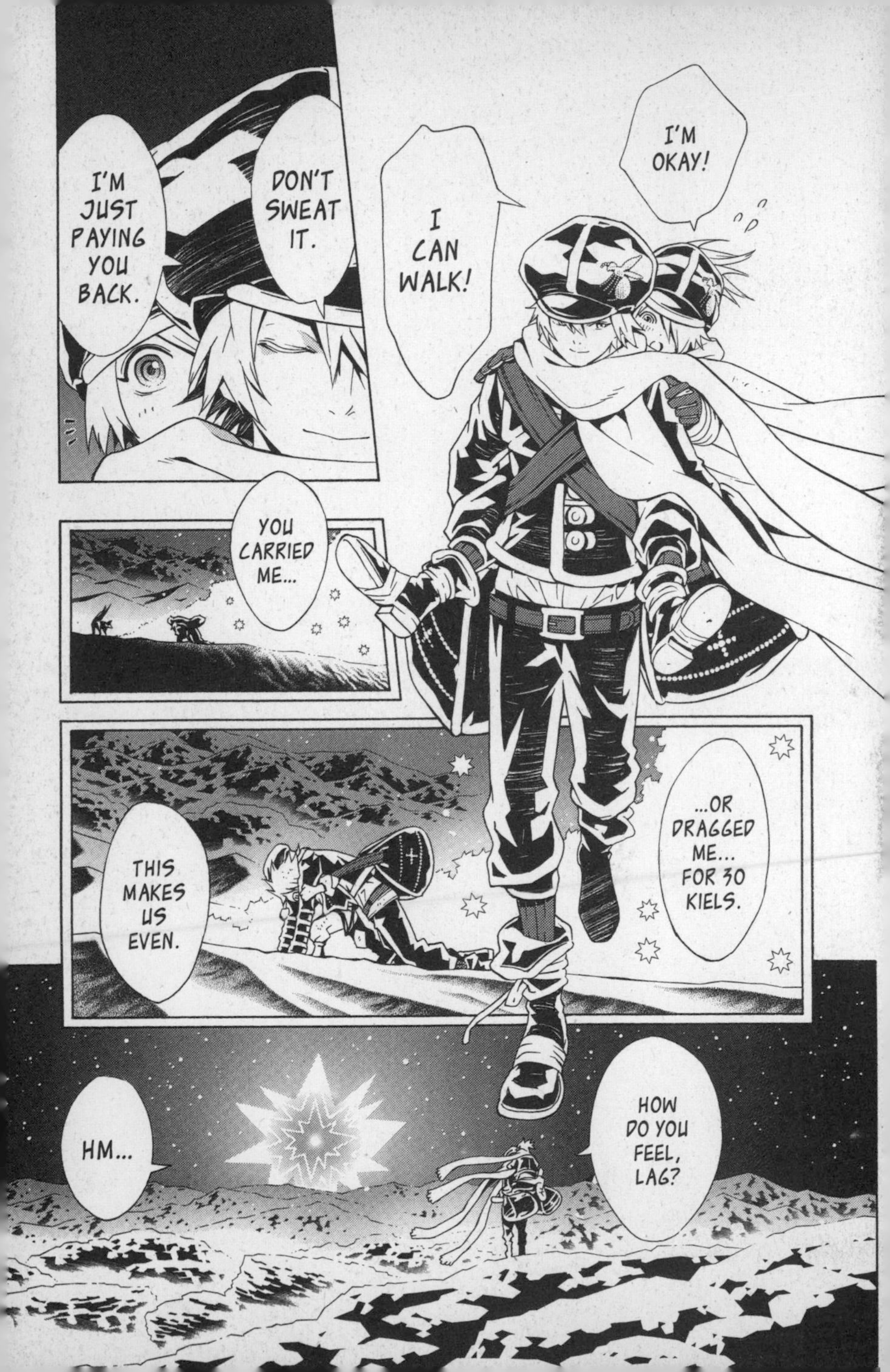
I'M OKAY!
I CAN WALK!
DON'T SWEAT IT.
I'M JUST PAYING YOU BACK.
YOU CARRIED ME...
...OR DRAGGED ME... FOR 30 KIELS.
THIS MAKES US EVEN.
HOW DO YOU FEEL, LAG?
HM...

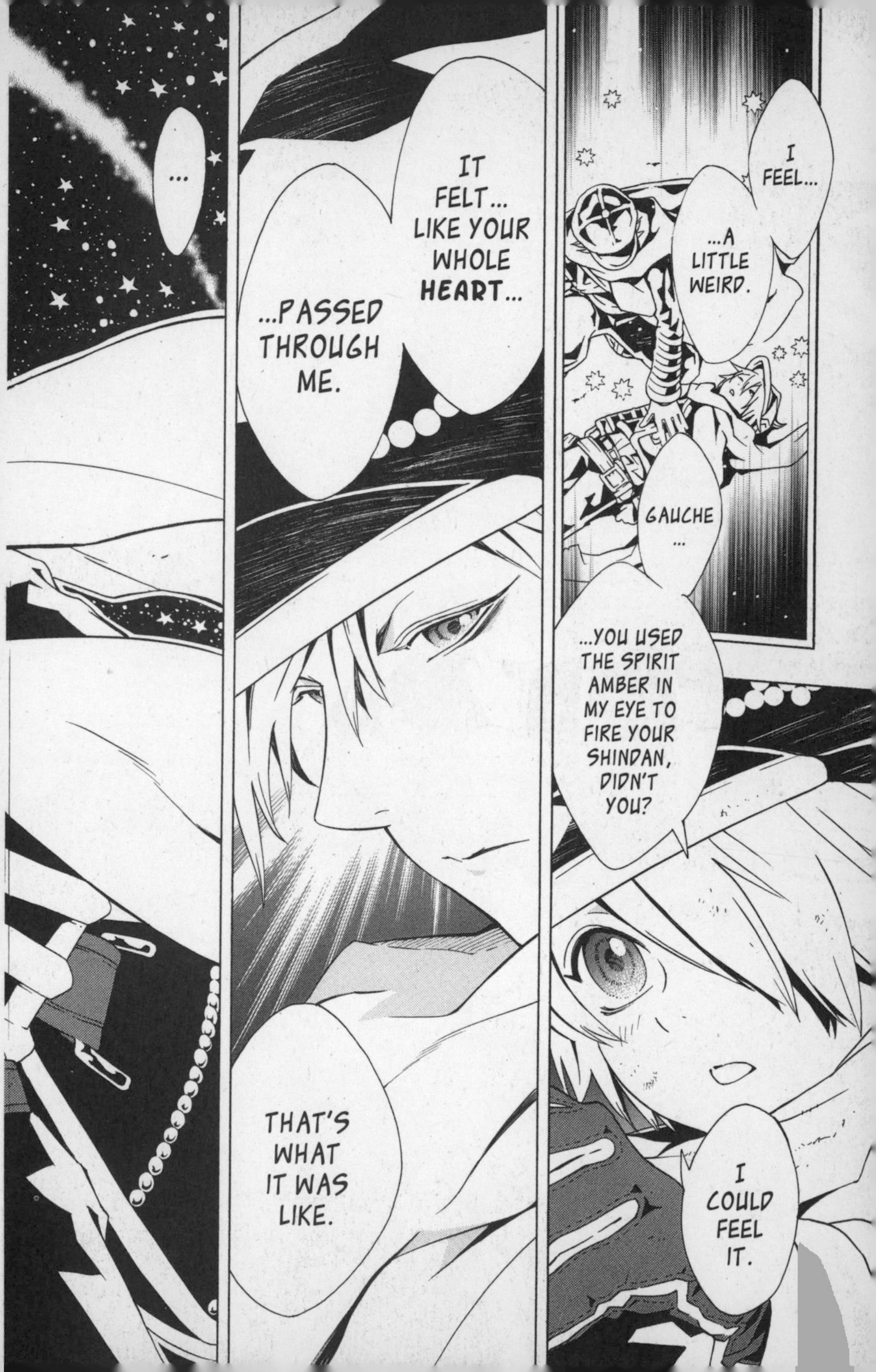
I FEEL...
...A LITTLE WEIRD.
GAUCHE...
...YOU USED THE SPIRIT AMBER IN MY EYE TO FIRE YOUR SHINDAN, DIDN'T YOU?
I COULD FEEL IT.
IT FELT... LIKE YOUR WHOLE HEART...
...PASSED THROUGH ME.
THAT'S WHAT IT WAS LIKE.
...

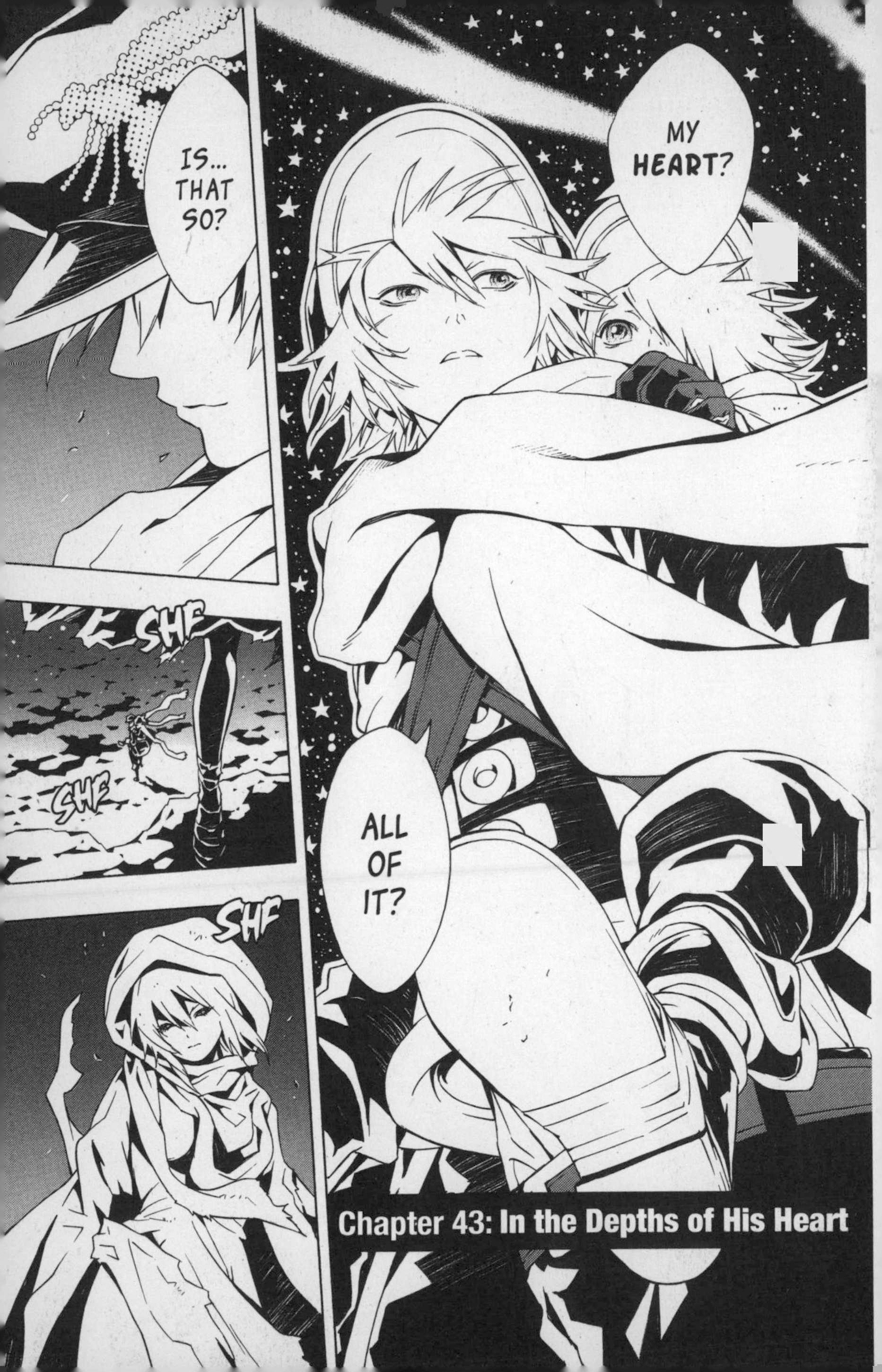
MY HEART?
...
IS... THAT SO?
ALL OF IT?
SHF
SHF
SHF
Chapter 43: In the Depths of His Heart

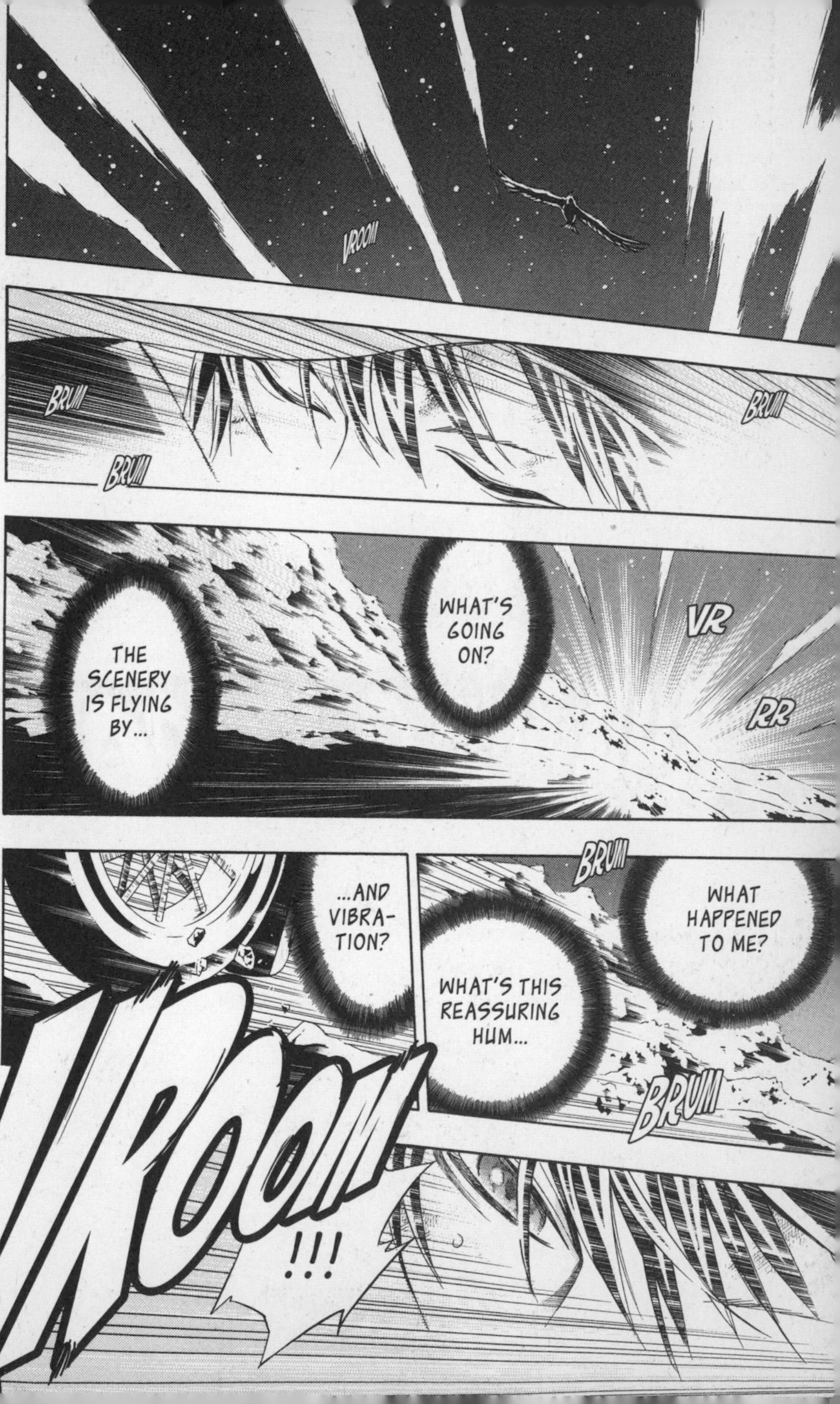
VROOM
BRUM
BRUM
BRUM
VR
RR
WHAT'S GOING ON?
THE SCENERY IS FLYING BY...
BRUM
WHAT HAPPENED TO ME?
WHAT'S THIS REASSURING HUM...
...AND VIBRATION?
BRUM
VROOM
!!!

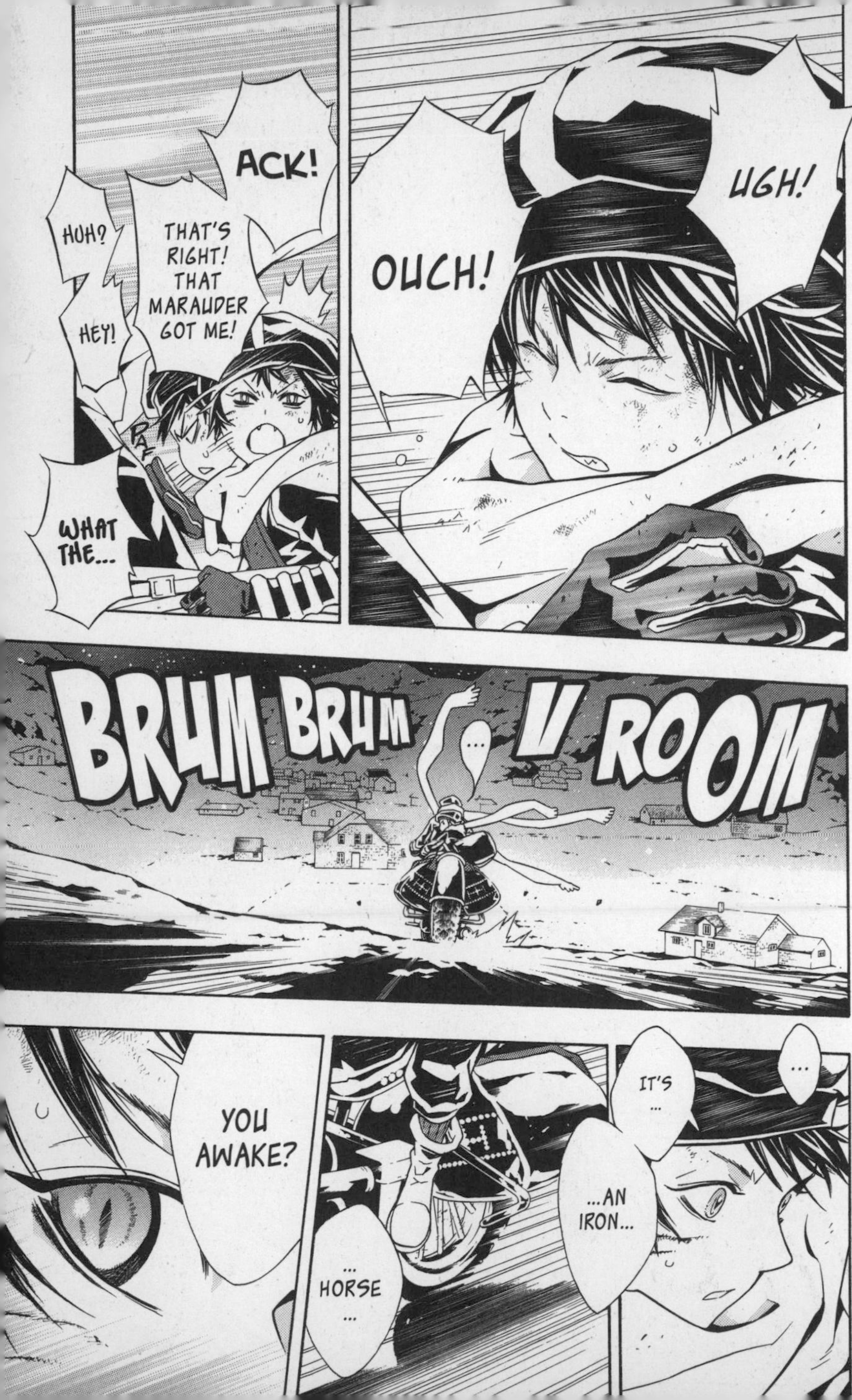
UGH!
OUCH!
ACK!
THAT'S RIGHT! THAT MARAUDER GOT ME!
HUH?
HEY!
PAF
WHAT THE...
BRUM BRUM
V ROOM
...
...
IT'S ...
...AN IRON...
... HORSE ...
YOU AWAKE?

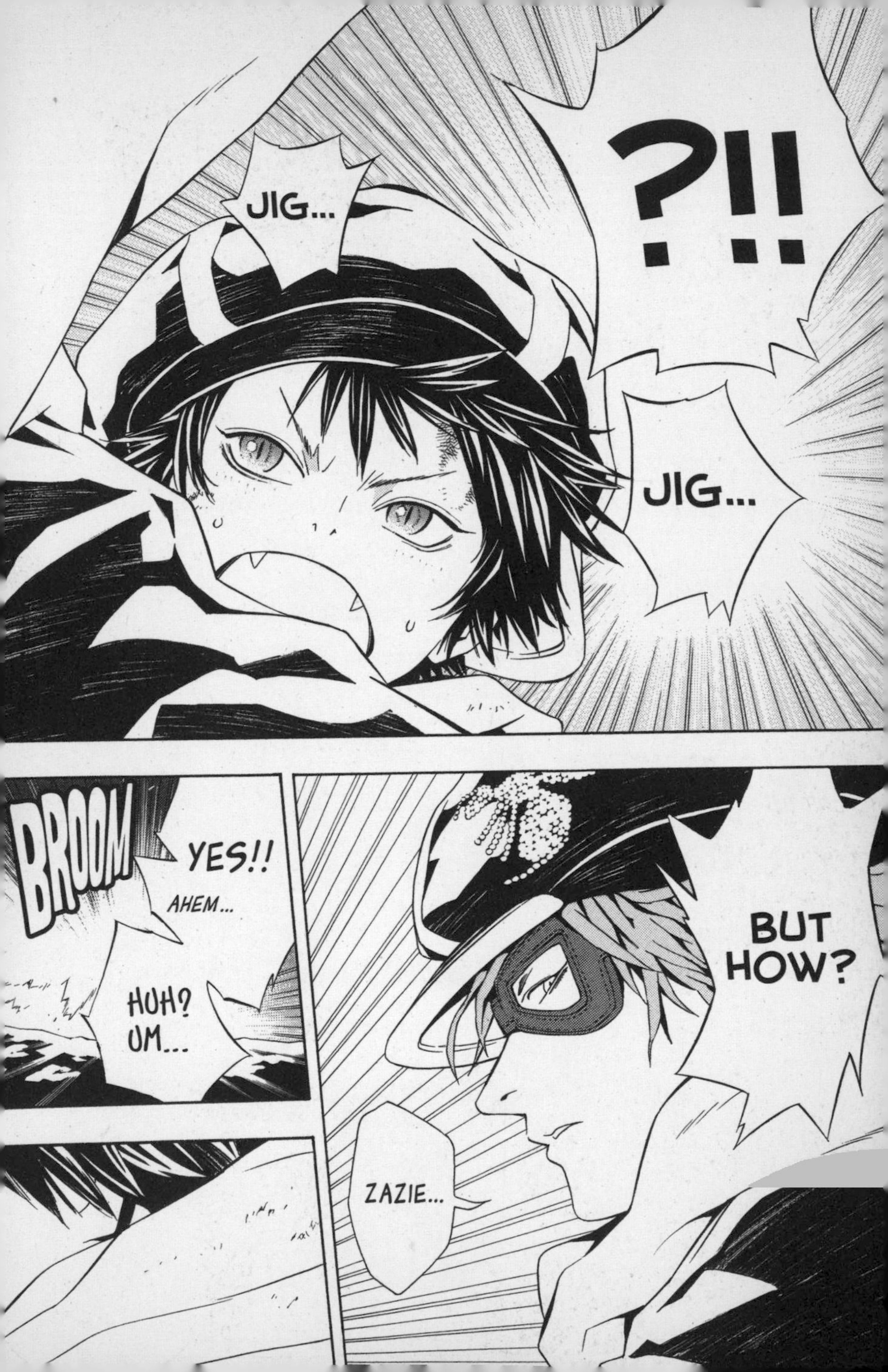
?!!
JIG...
JIG...
BUT HOW?
ZAZIE...
BROOM
YES!!
AHEM...
HUH? UM...

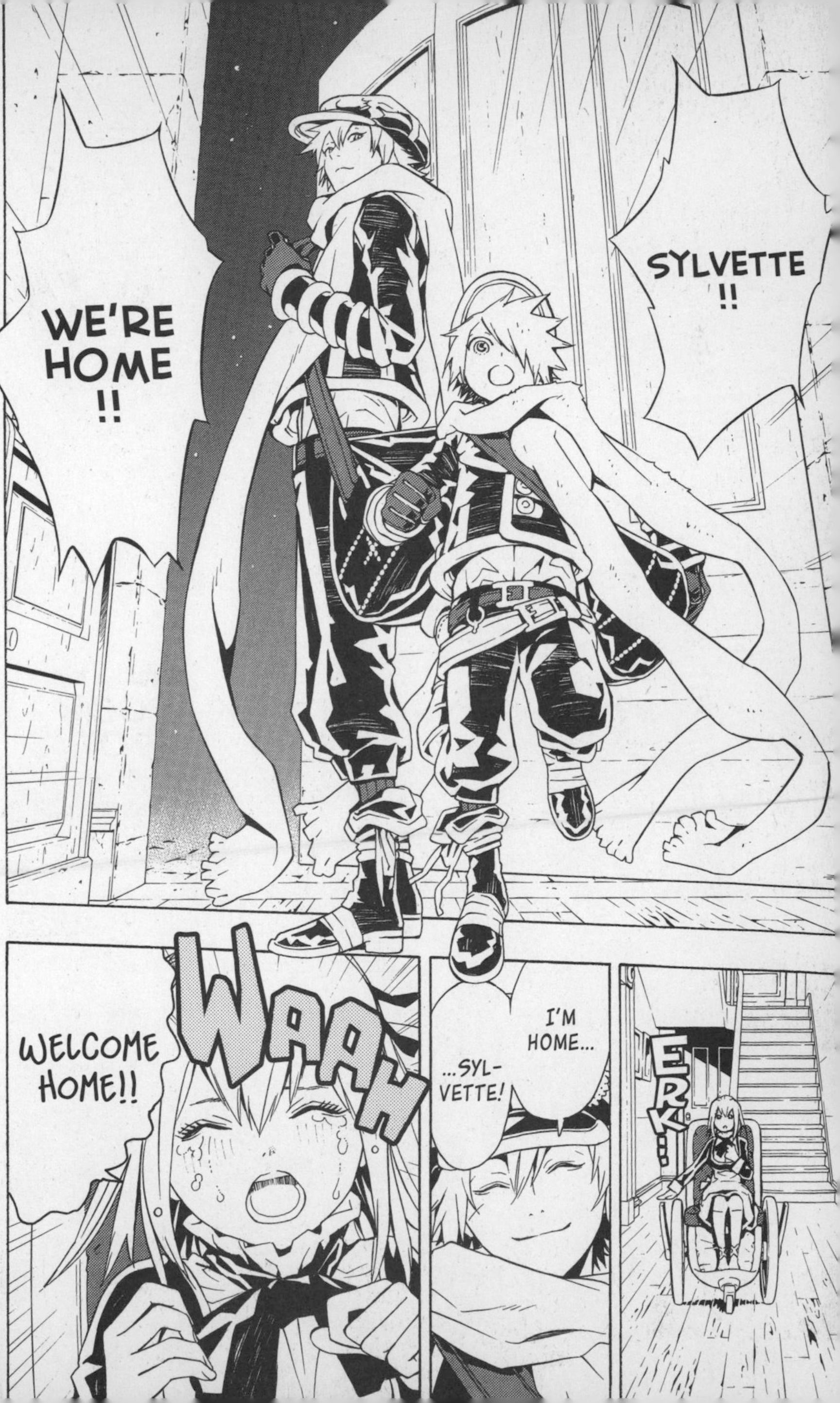
SYLVETTE !!
WE'RE HOME !!
ERK...
I'M HOME...
...SYL-VETTE!
WAAAH
WELCOME HOME!!

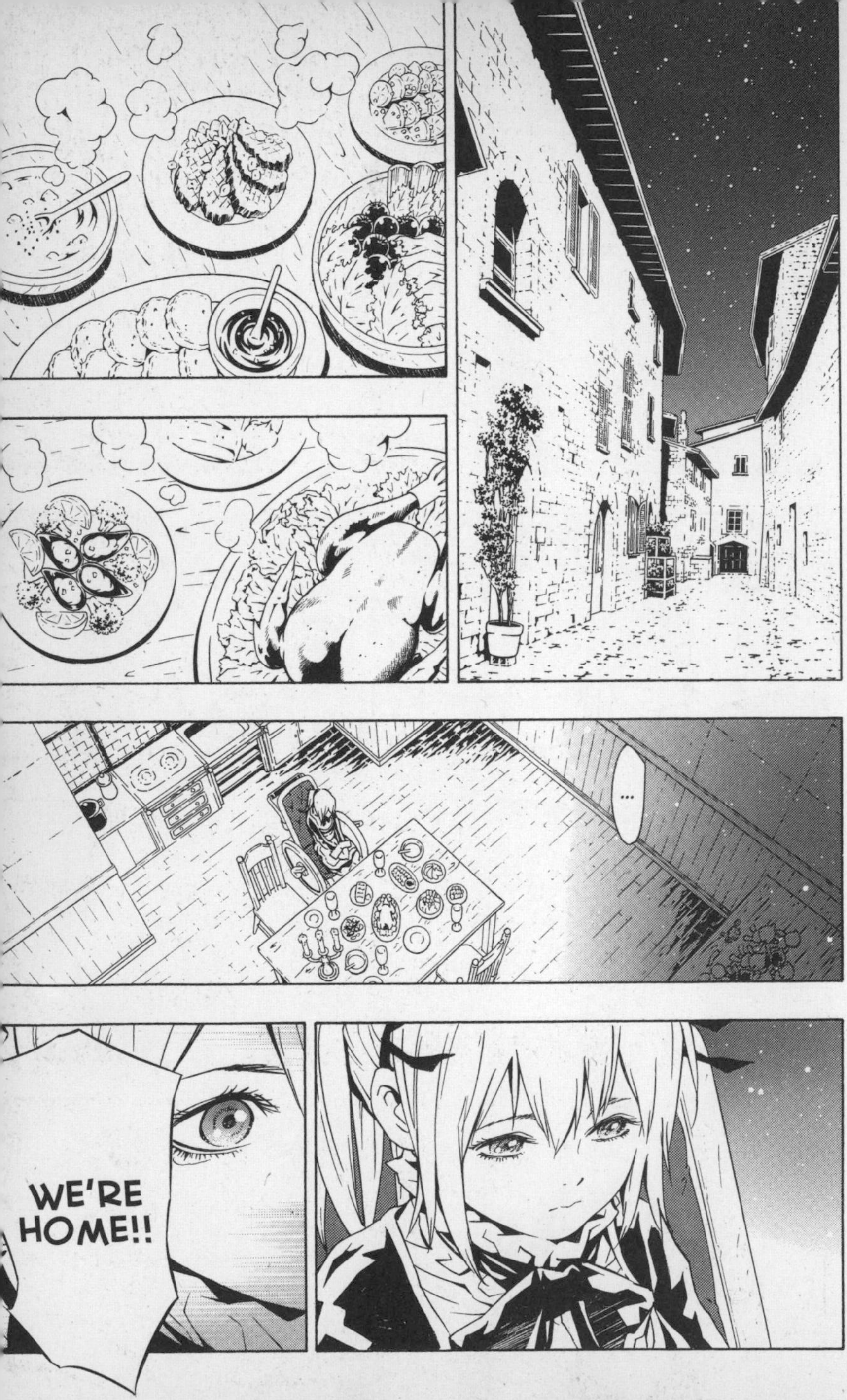
...
WE'RE HOME!!

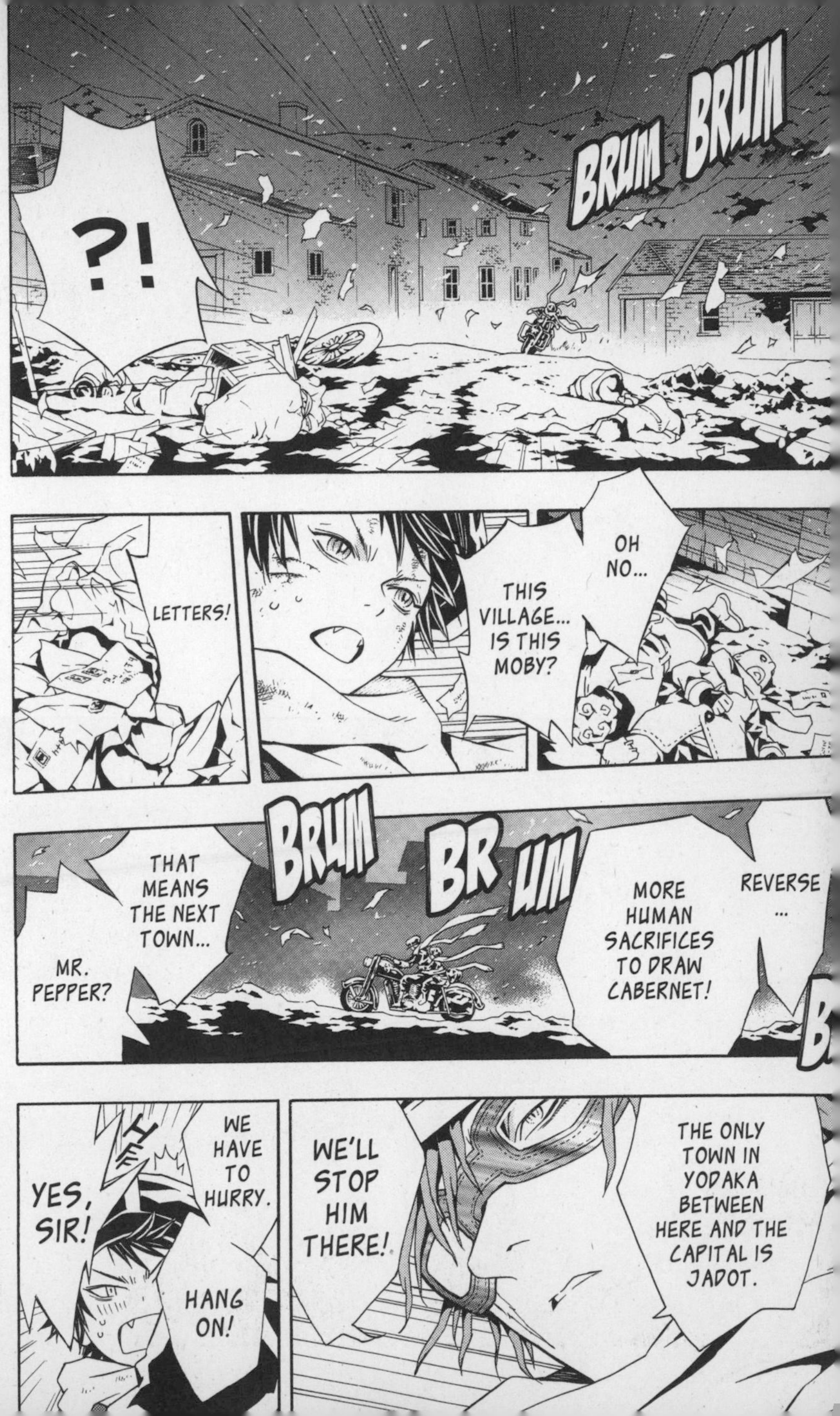
BRUM BRUM
?!
OH NO...
THIS VILLAGE... IS THIS MOBY?
LETTERS!
REVERSE ...
MORE HUMAN SACRIFICES TO DRAW CABERNET!
BRUM
BR UM
THAT MEANS THE NEXT TOWN...
MR. PEPPER?
THE ONLY TOWN IN YODAKA BETWEEN HERE AND THE CAPITAL IS JADOT.
WE'LL STOP HIM THERE!
WE HAVE TO HURRY.
HE
YES, SIR!
HANG ON!

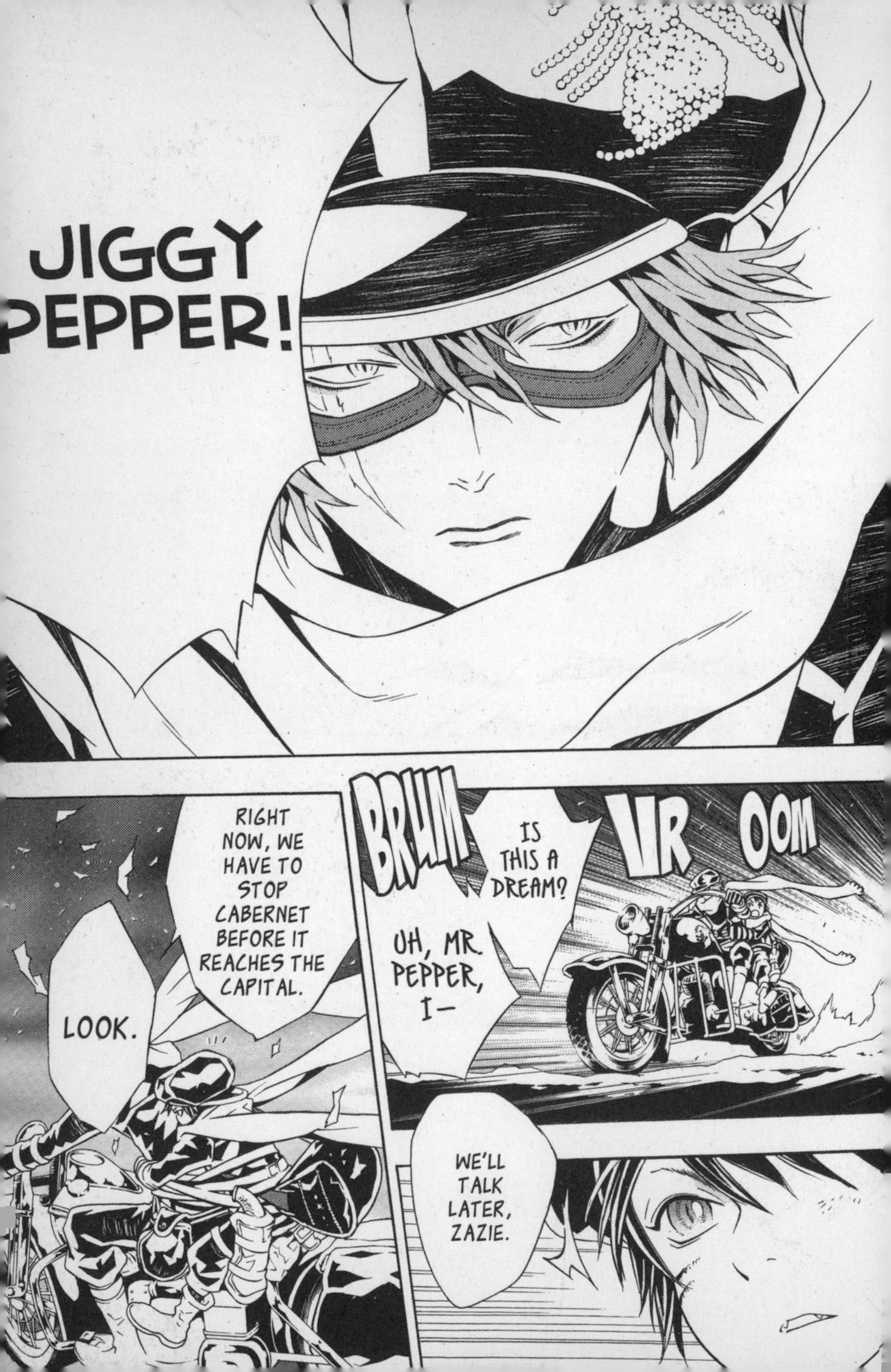

JIGGY PEPPER!
VR OOM
IS THIS A DREAM?
BRUM
UH, MR. PEPPER, I—
WE'LL TALK LATER, ZAZIE.
RIGHT NOW, WE HAVE TO STOP CABERNET BEFORE IT REACHES THE CAPITAL.
LOOK.

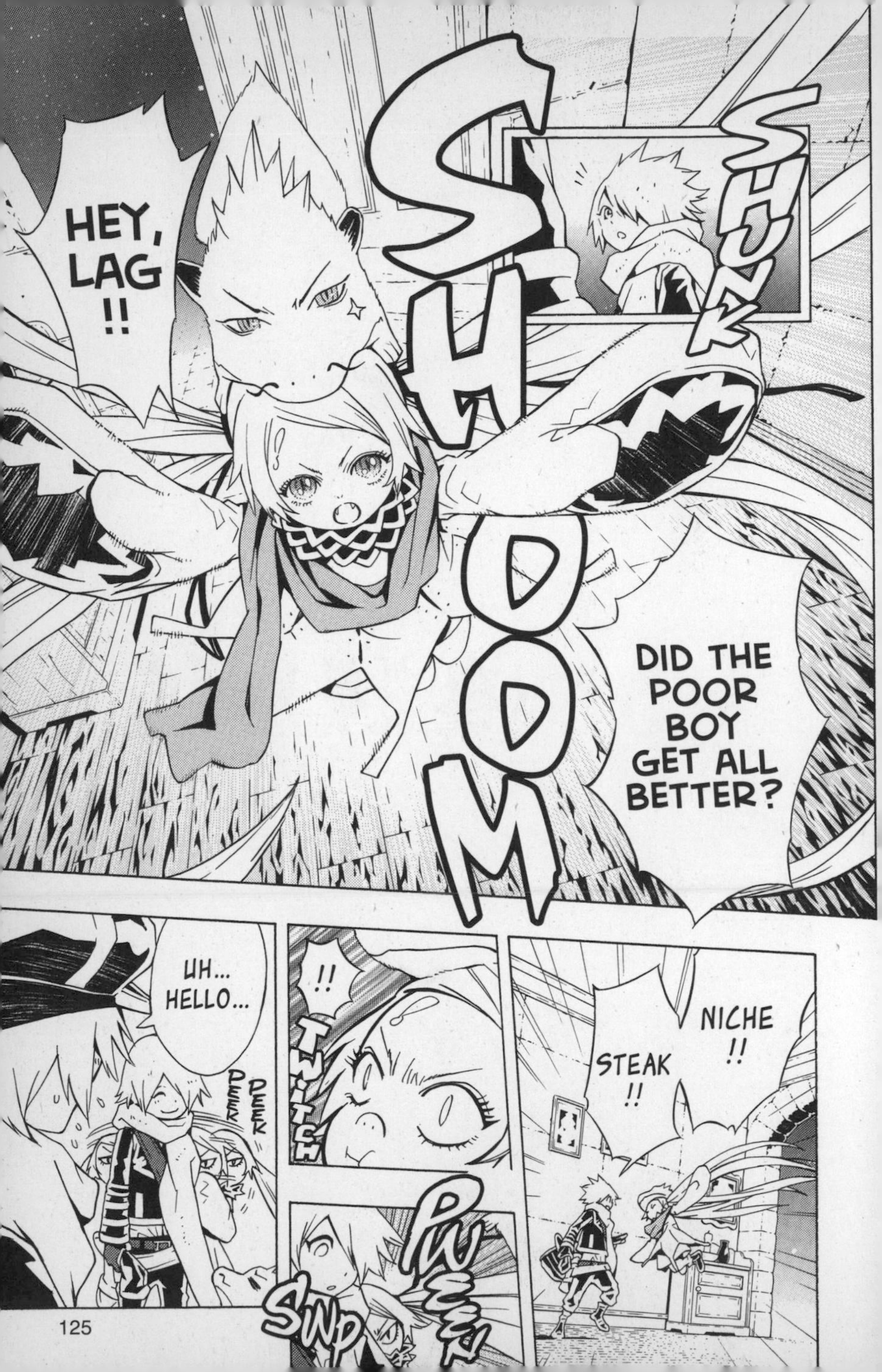

SHUNK
SHOOM
DID THE POOR BOY GET ALL BETTER?
HEY, LAG!!
NICHE!!
STEAK!!
!!
TWITCH
PWEEE
SNP
UH... HELLO...
PEEK PEEK

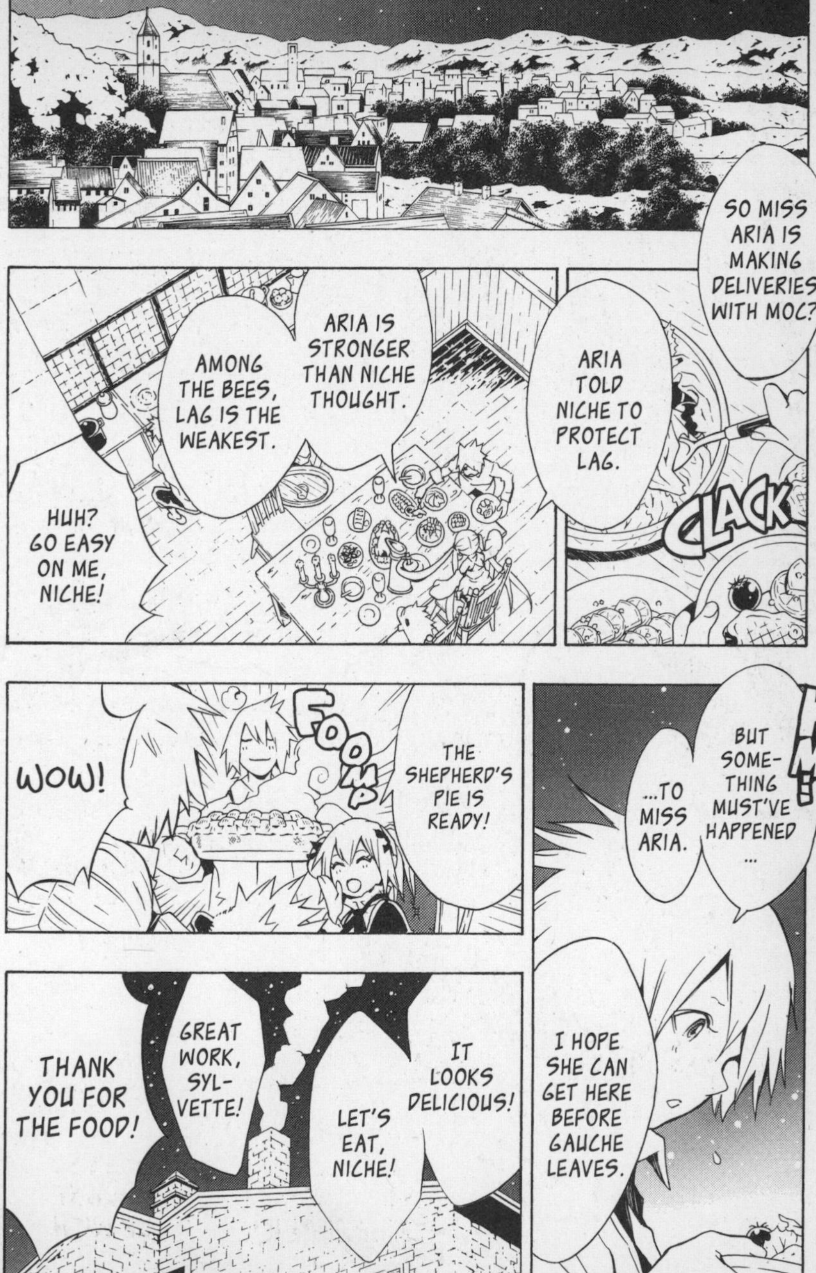
SO MISS ARIA IS MAKING DELIVERIES WITH MOC?
CLACK
ARIA TOLD NICHE TO PROTECT LAG.
ARIA IS STRONGER THAN NICHE THOUGHT.
AMONG THE BEES, LAG IS THE WEAKEST.
HUH? GO EASY ON ME, NICHE!
HM!
BUT SOME-THING MUST'VE HAPPENED ...
...TO MISS ARIA.
I HOPE SHE CAN GET HERE BEFORE GAUCHE LEAVES.
THE SHEPHERD'S PIE IS READY!
FOOMP
WOW!
IT LOOKS DELICIOUS!
LET'S EAT, NICHE!
GREAT WORK, SYL-VETTE!
THANK YOU FOR THE FOOD!

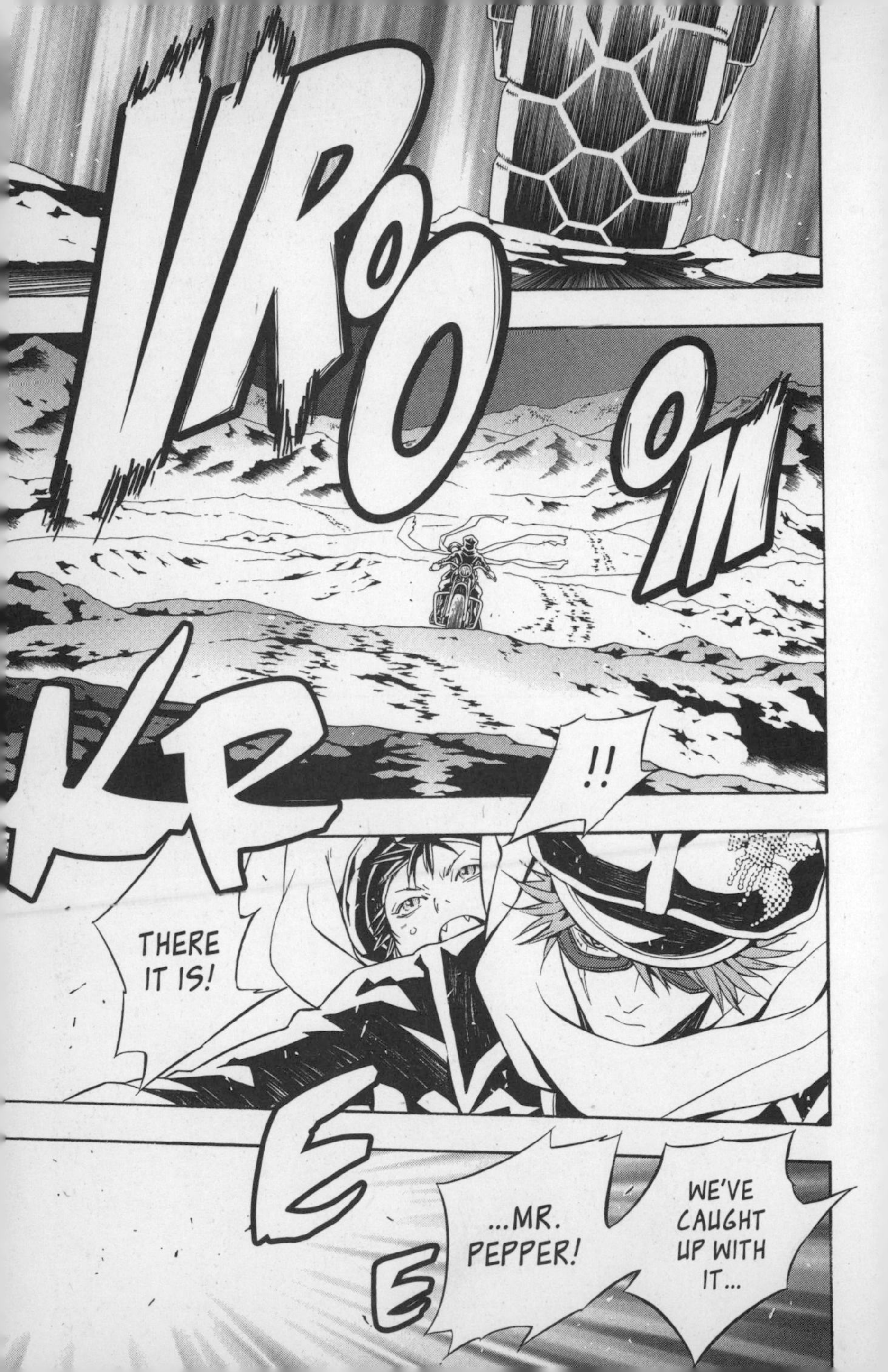
VROOM
VROOM
!!
THERE IT IS!
WE'VE CAUGHT UP WITH IT...
...MR. PEPPER!

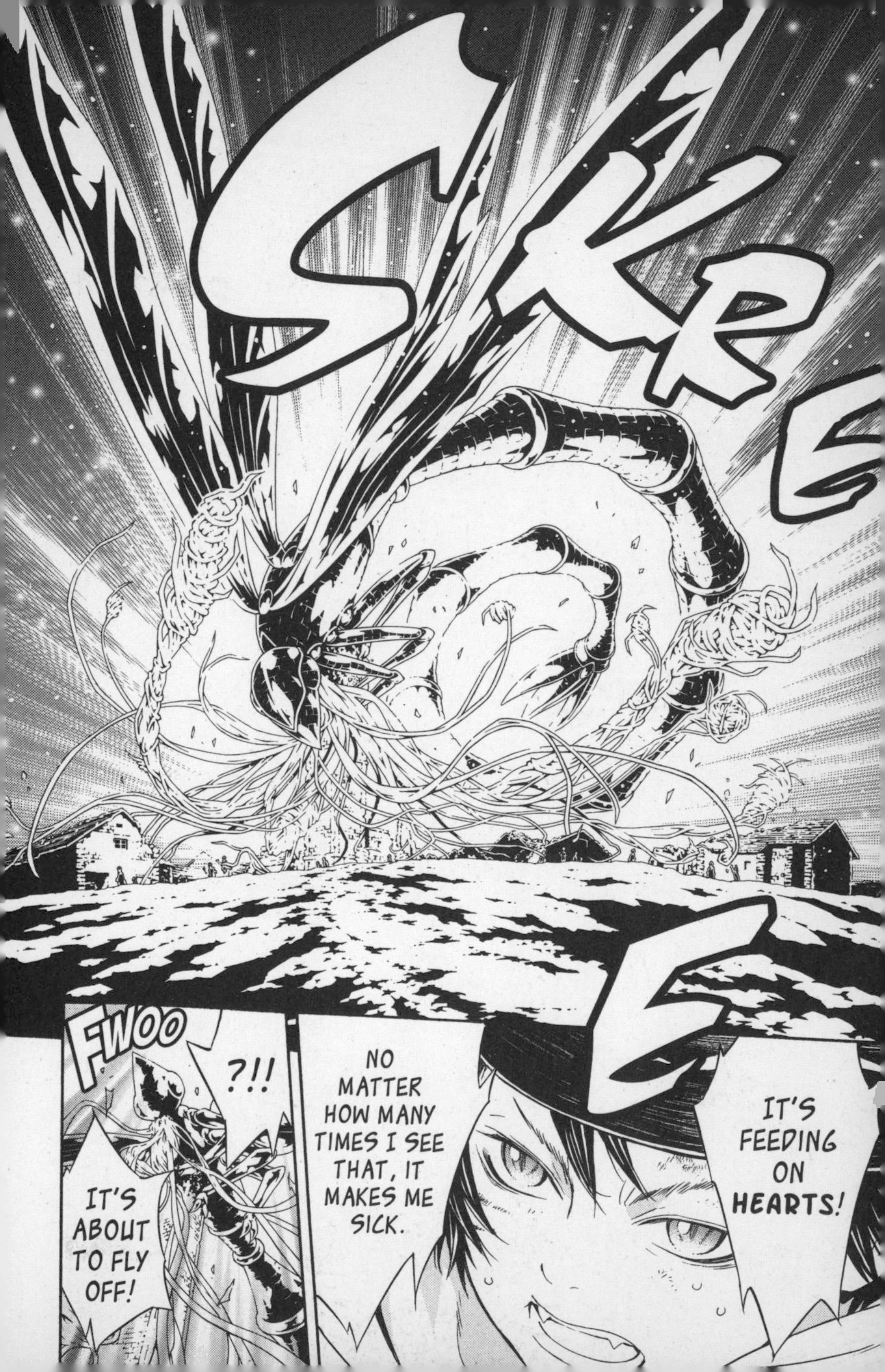
SKREE
FWOO
?!!
NO MATTER HOW MANY TIMES I SEE THAT, IT MAKES ME SICK.
IT'S FEEDING ON HEARTS!
IT'S ABOUT TO FLY OFF!

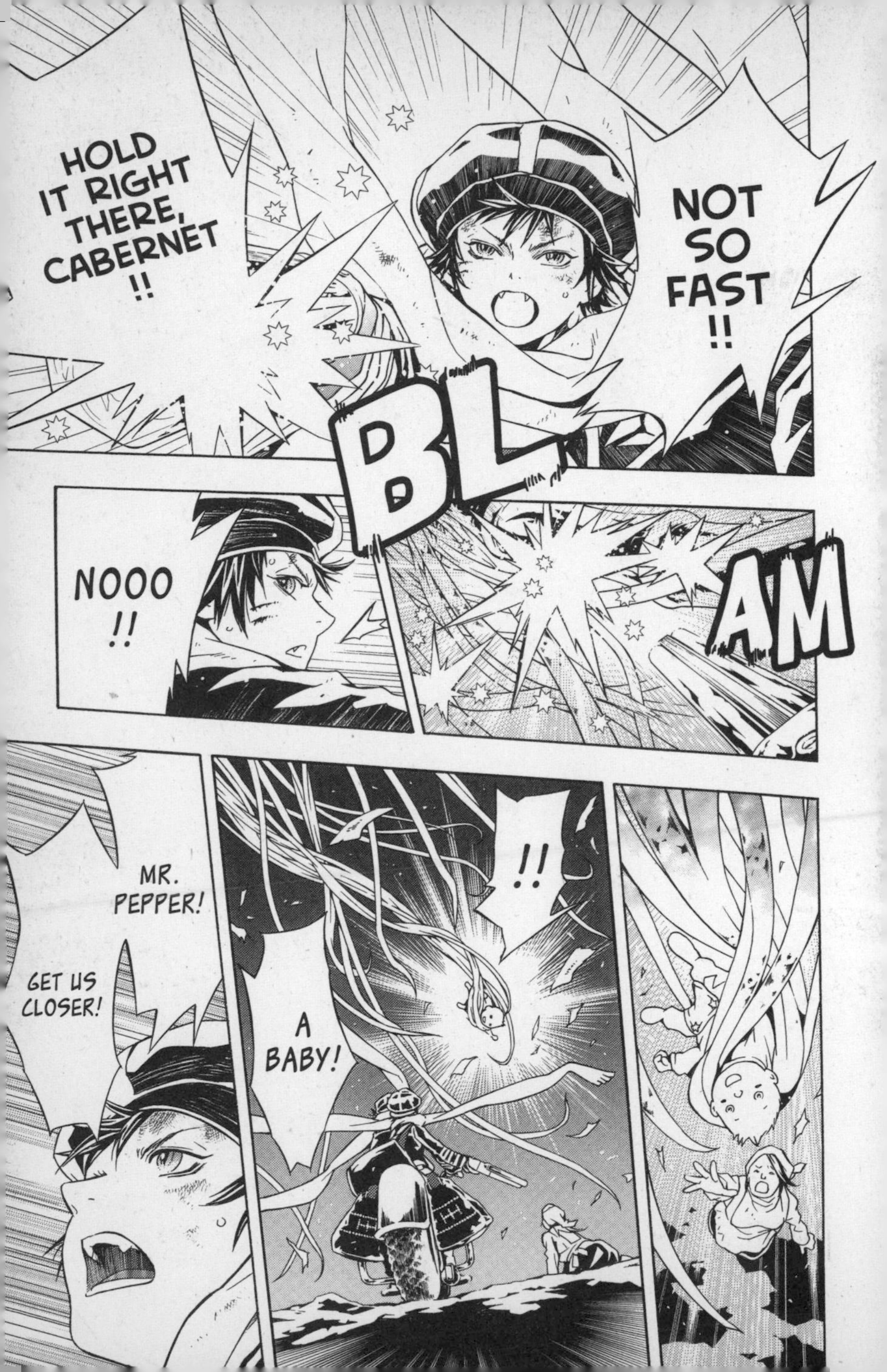
NOT SO FAST !!
HOLD IT RIGHT THERE, CABERNET !!
BLAM
NOOO !!
!!
A BABY!
MR. PEPPER!
GET US CLOSER!

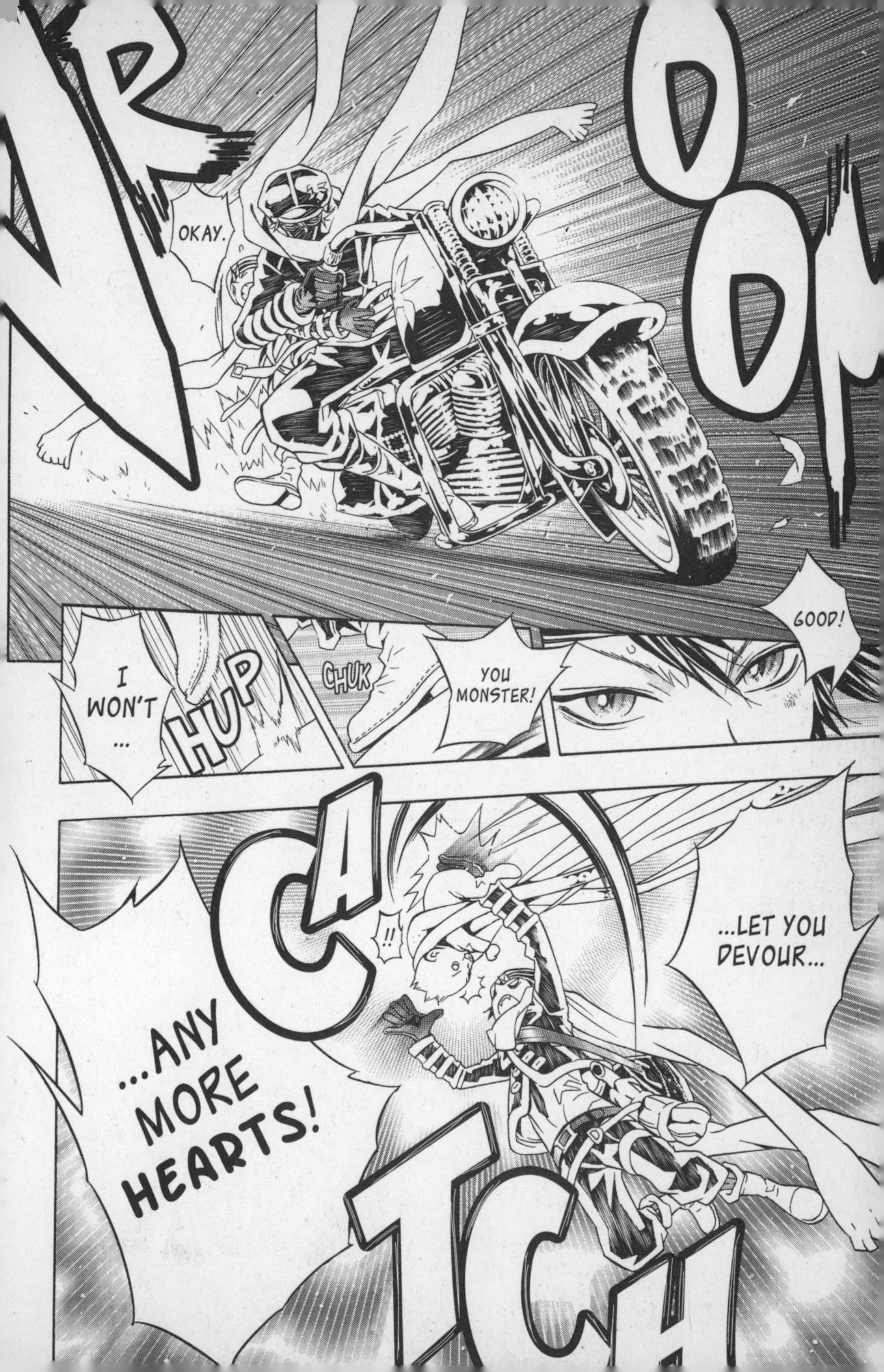
OKAY.
GOOD!
YOU MONSTER!
CHUK
I WON'T ...
HUP
...LET YOU DEVOUR...
!!
CATCH
...ANY MORE HEARTS!

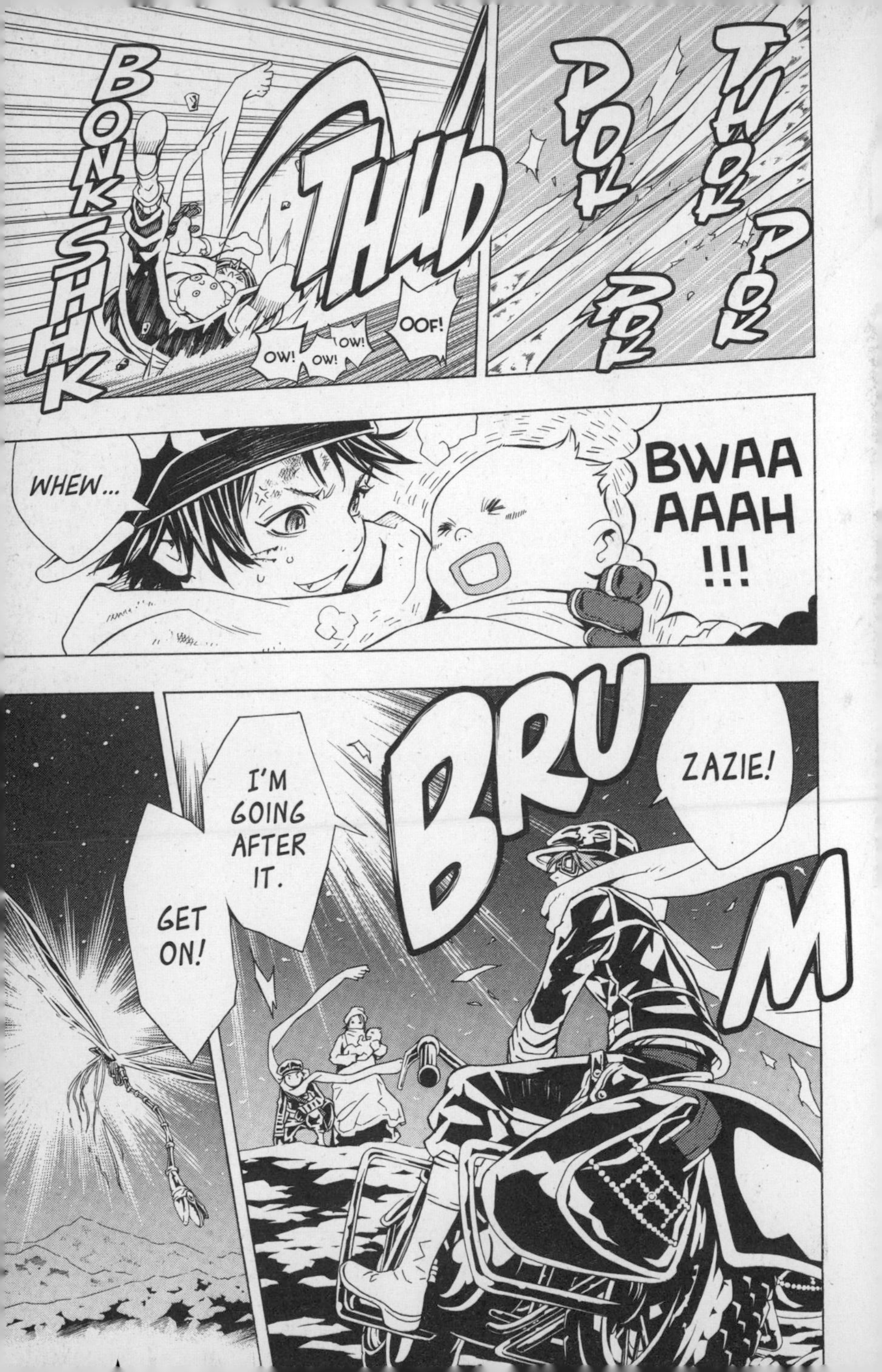
THOK
POK
POK
POK
THUD
BONK
SHHK
OOF!
OW!
OW!
OW!
BWAA AAAH!!!
WHEW...
ZAZIE!
BRUM
I'M GOING AFTER IT.
GET ON!

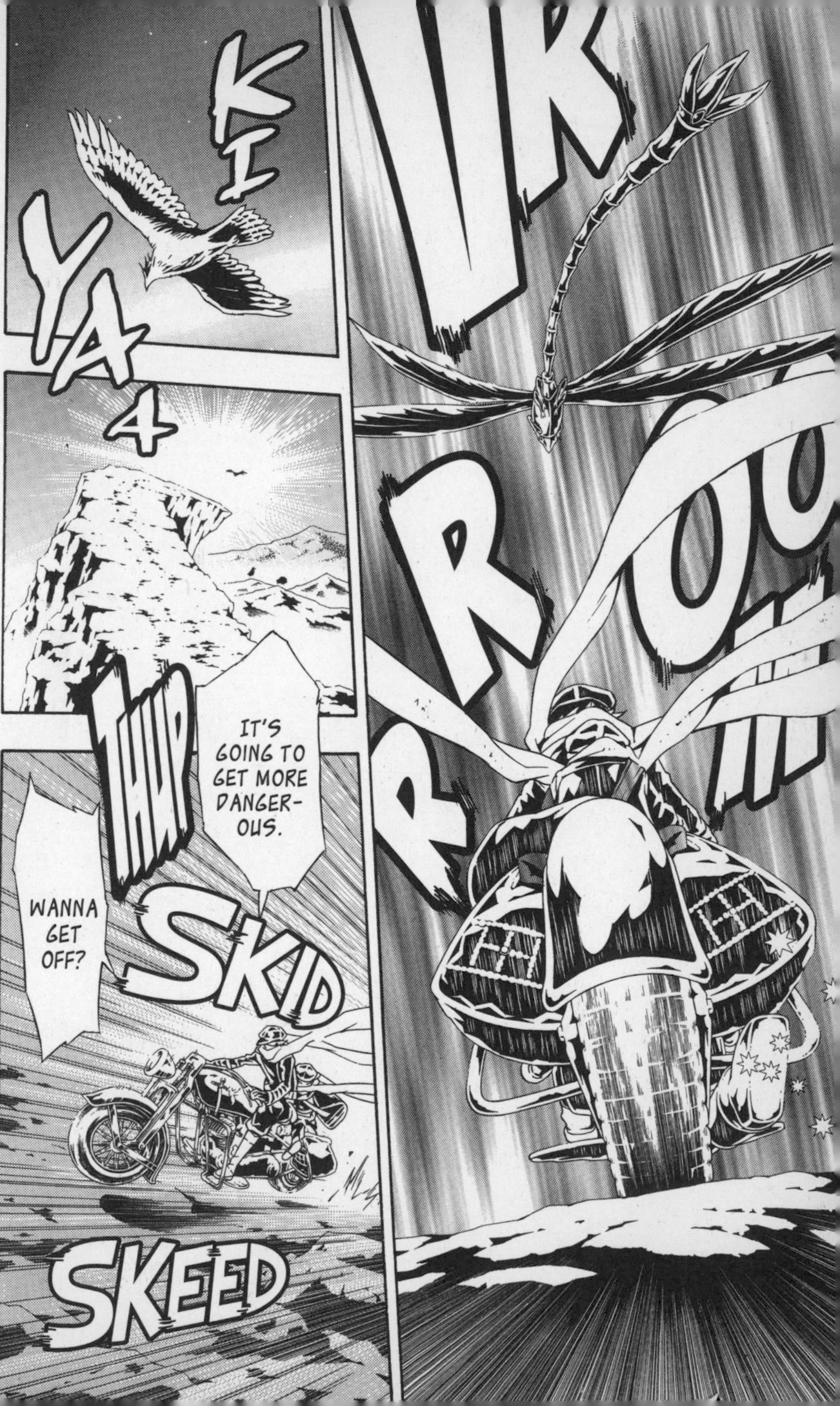
VRRROOOM
KIYA 4
KI YA 4
THUD
IT'S GOING TO GET MORE DANGER-OUS.
WANNA GET OFF?
SKID
SKEED

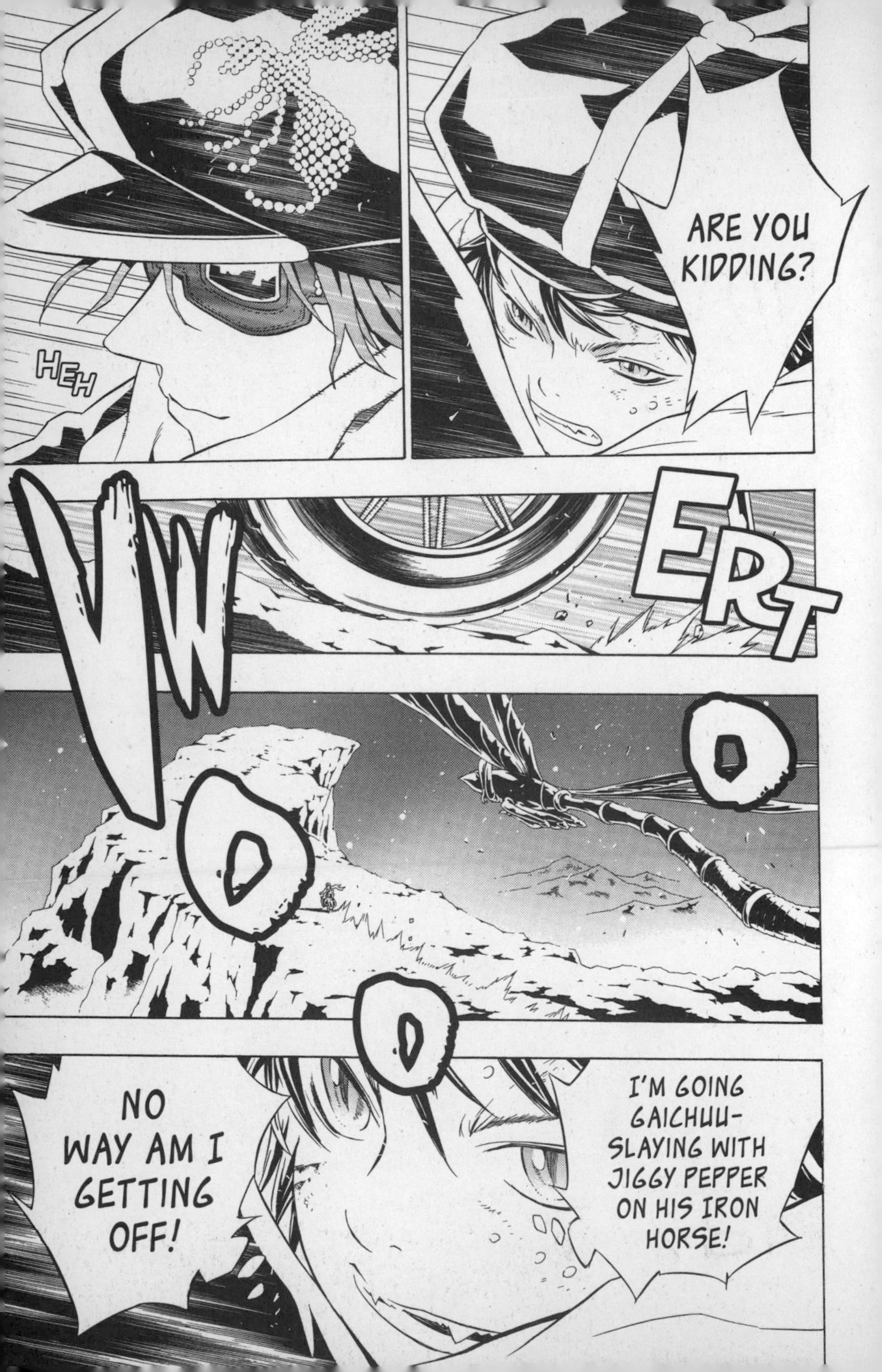
ARE YOU KIDDING?
HEH
VVVV
ERT
OOOO
I'M GOING GAICHUU-SLAYING WITH JIGGY PEPPER ON HIS IRON HORSE!
NO WAY AM I GETTING OFF!

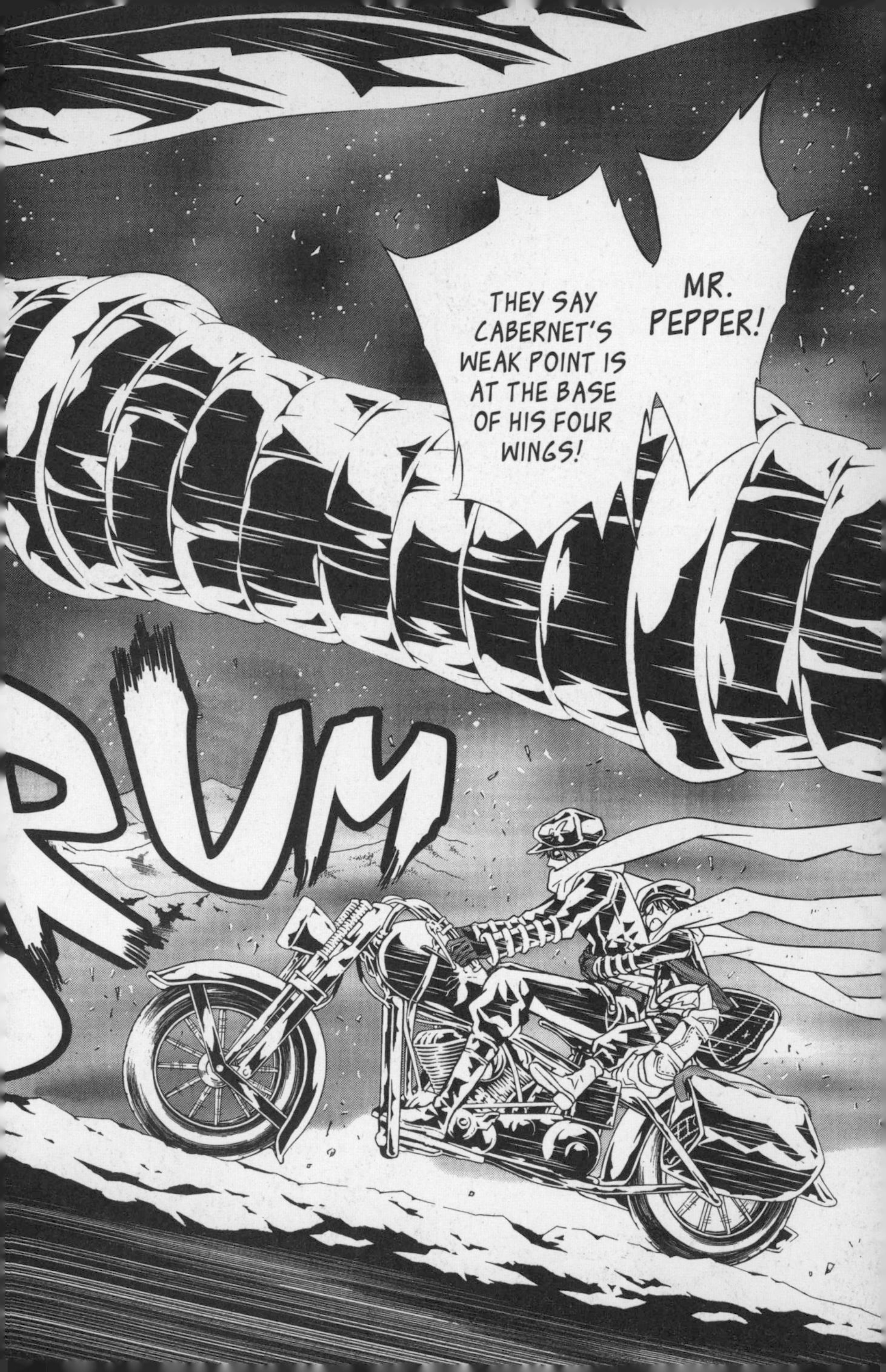
MR. PEPPER!
THEY SAY CABERNET'S WEAK POINT IS AT THE BASE OF HIS FOUR WINGS!
RUM

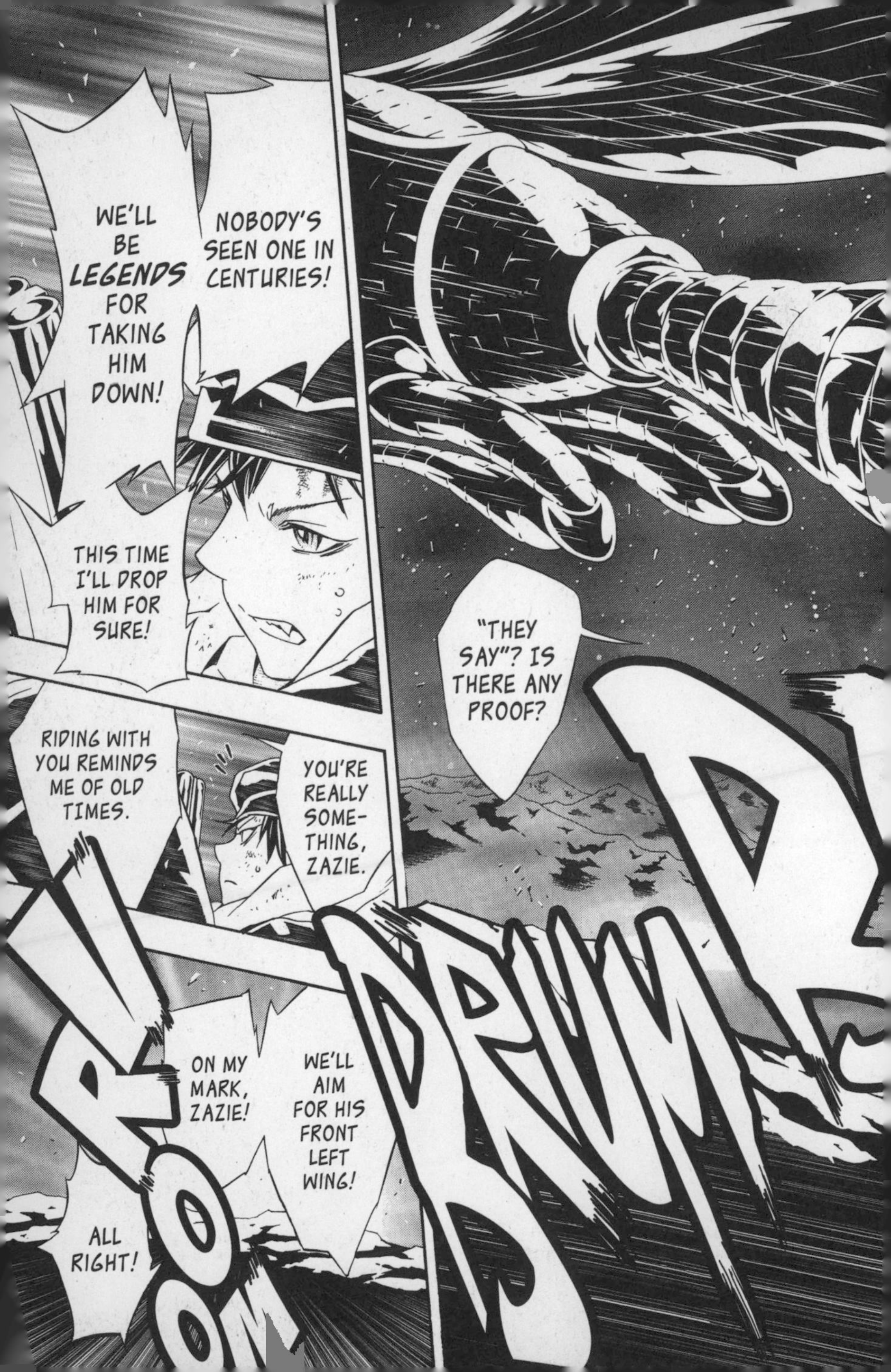
"THEY SAY"? IS THERE ANY PROOF?
NOBODY'S SEEN ONE IN CENTURIES!
WE'LL BE *LEGENDS* FOR TAKING HIM DOWN!
THIS TIME I'LL DROP HIM FOR SURE!
YOU'RE REALLY SOME-THING, ZAZIE.
RIDING WITH YOU REMINDS ME OF OLD TIMES.
WE'LL AIM FOR HIS FRONT LEFT WING!
ON MY MARK, ZAZIE!
ALL RIGHT!

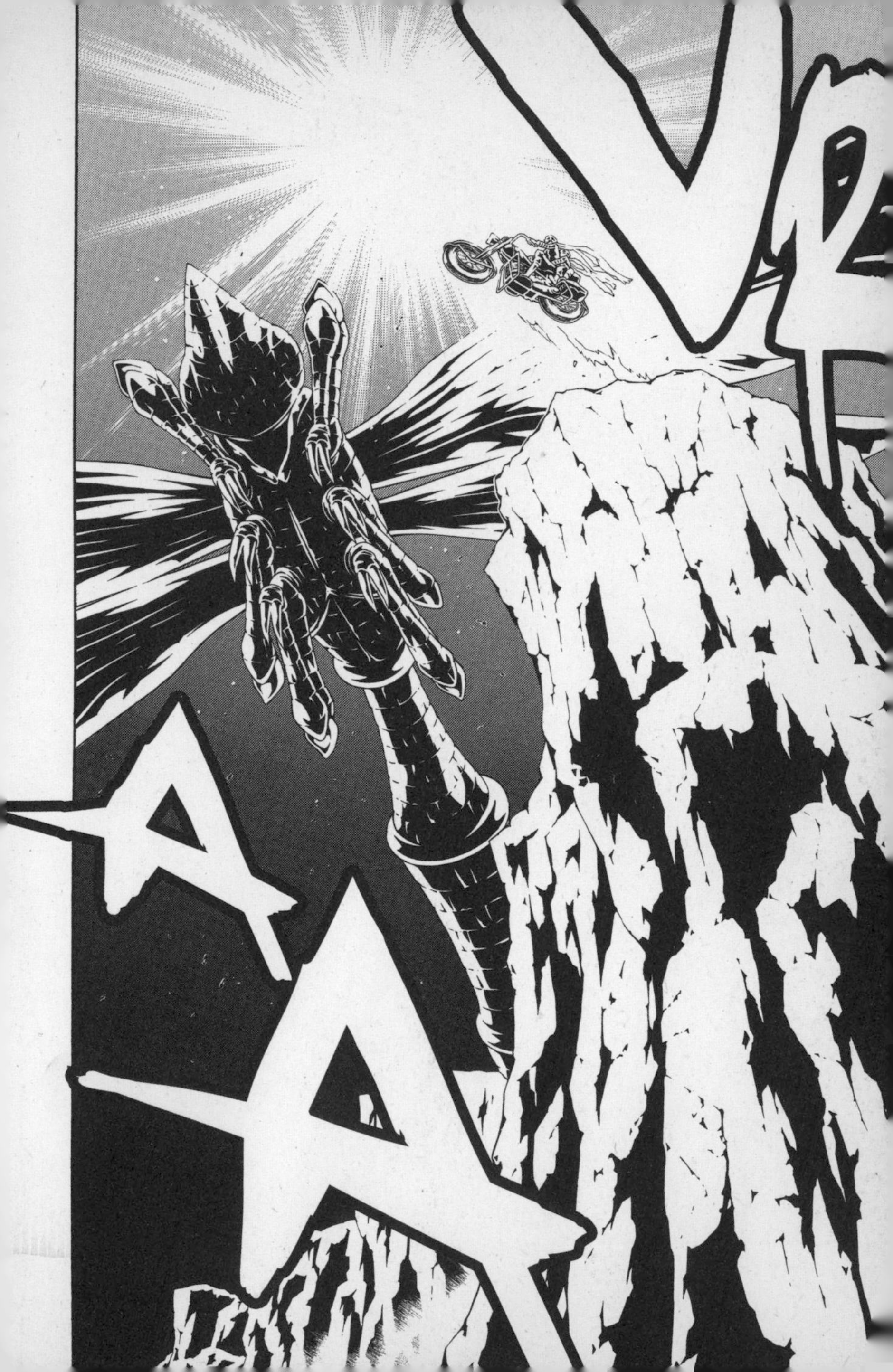

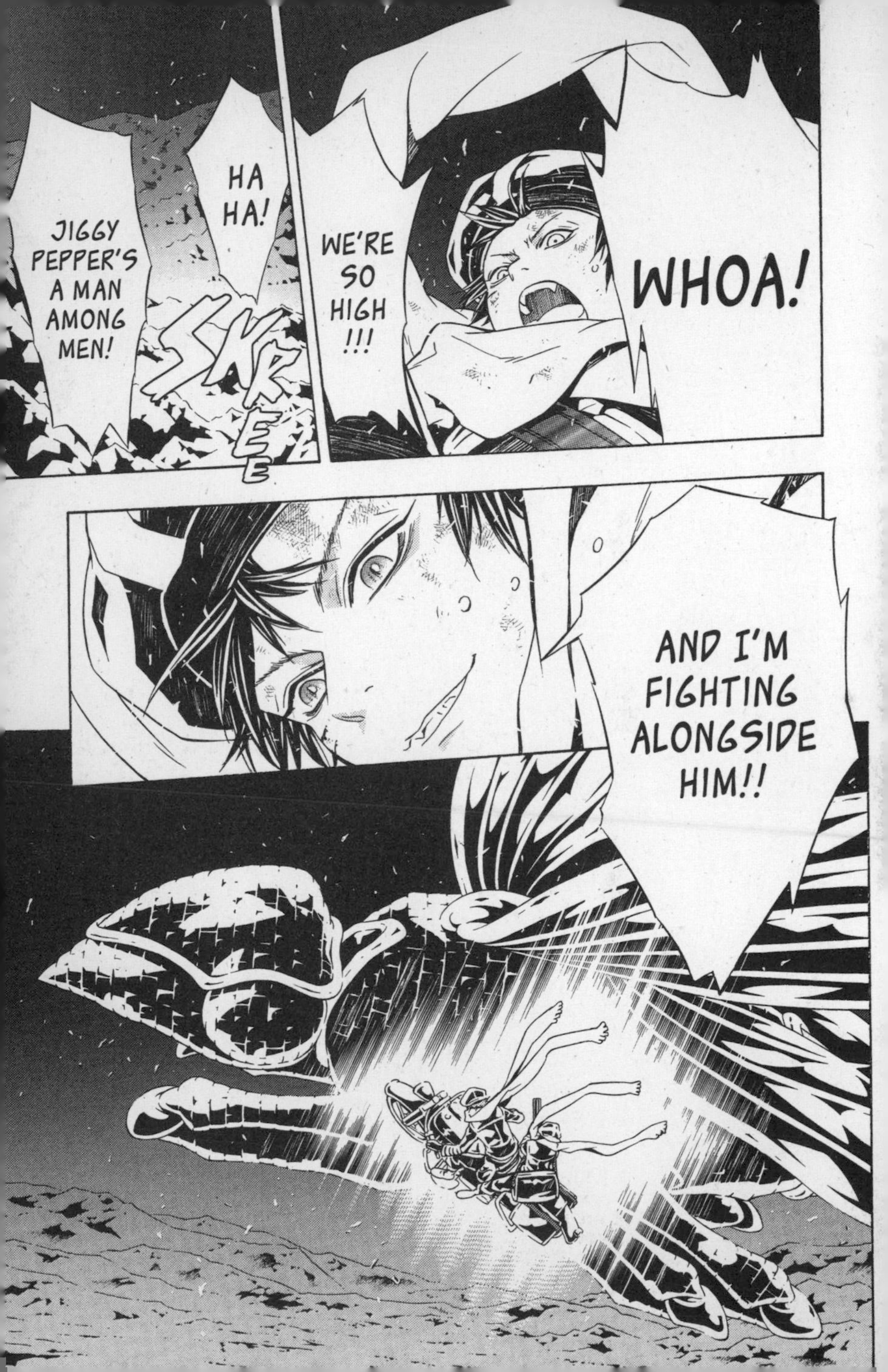
WHOA!
WE'RE SO HIGH!!!
HA HA!
JIGGY PEPPER'S A MAN AMONG MEN!
SKREEE
AND I'M FIGHTING ALONGSIDE HIM!!

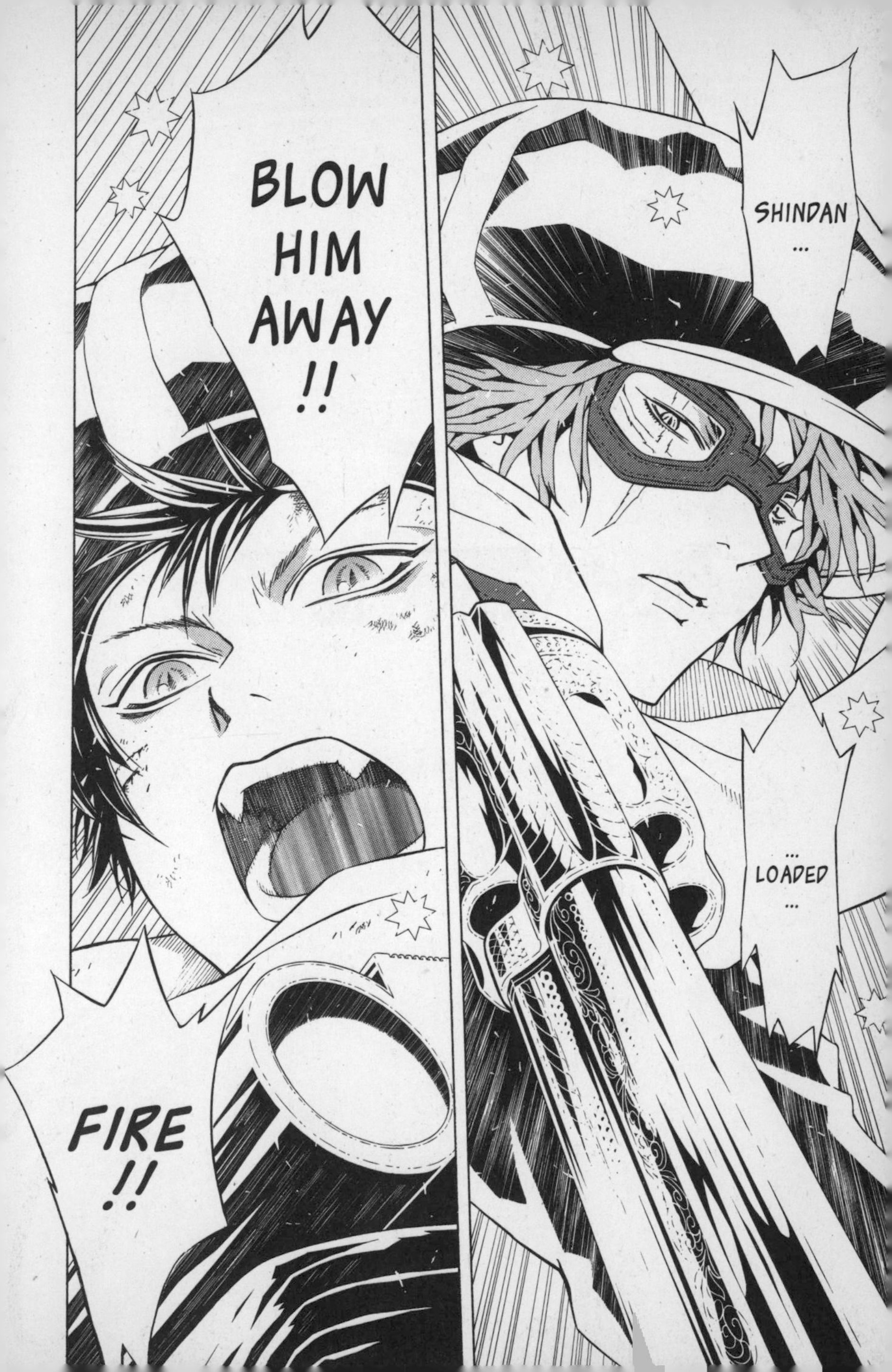
SHINDAN ...
BLOW HIM AWAY !!
... LOADED ...
FIRE !!

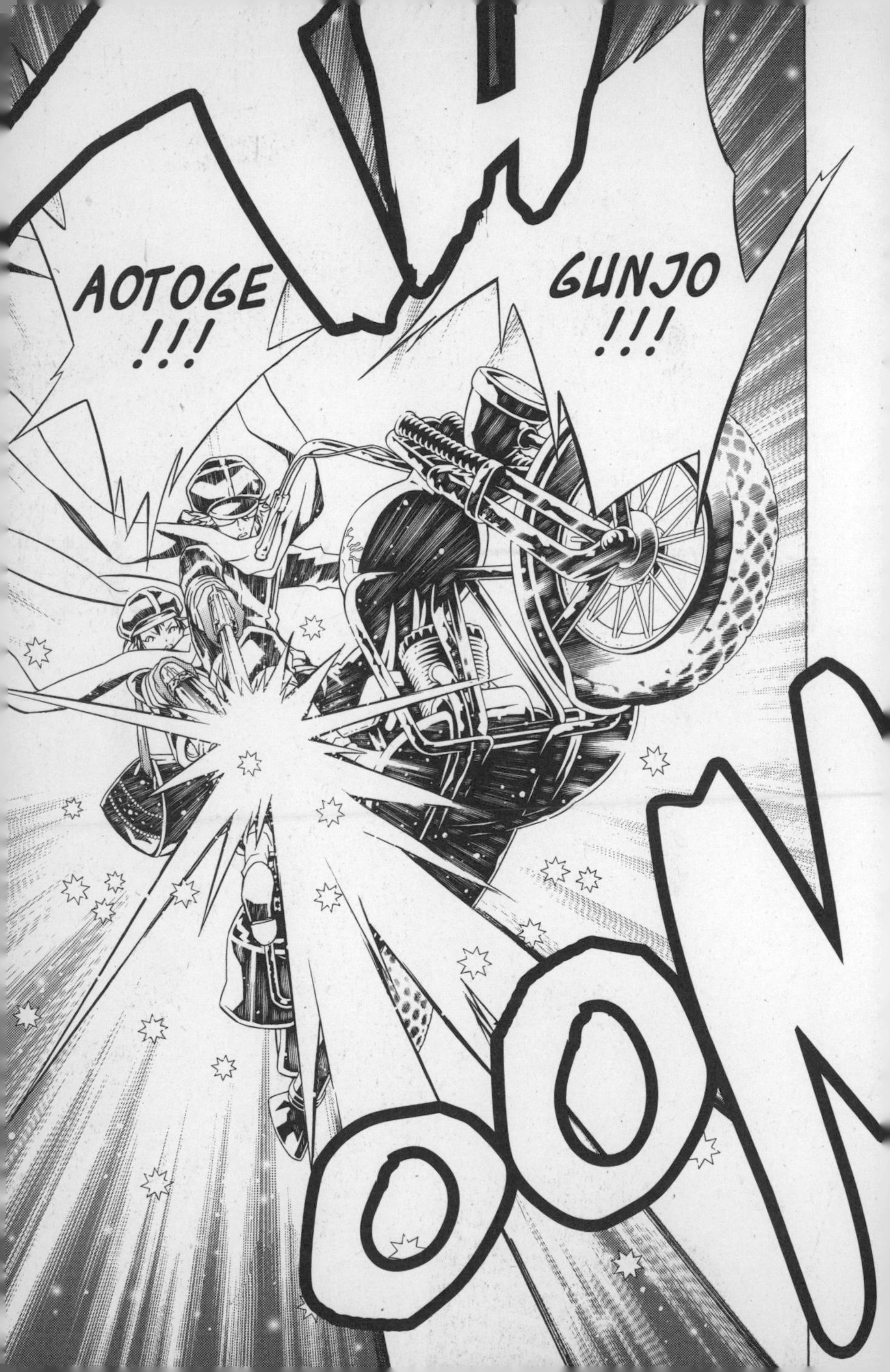
GUNJO !!!
AOTOGE !!!

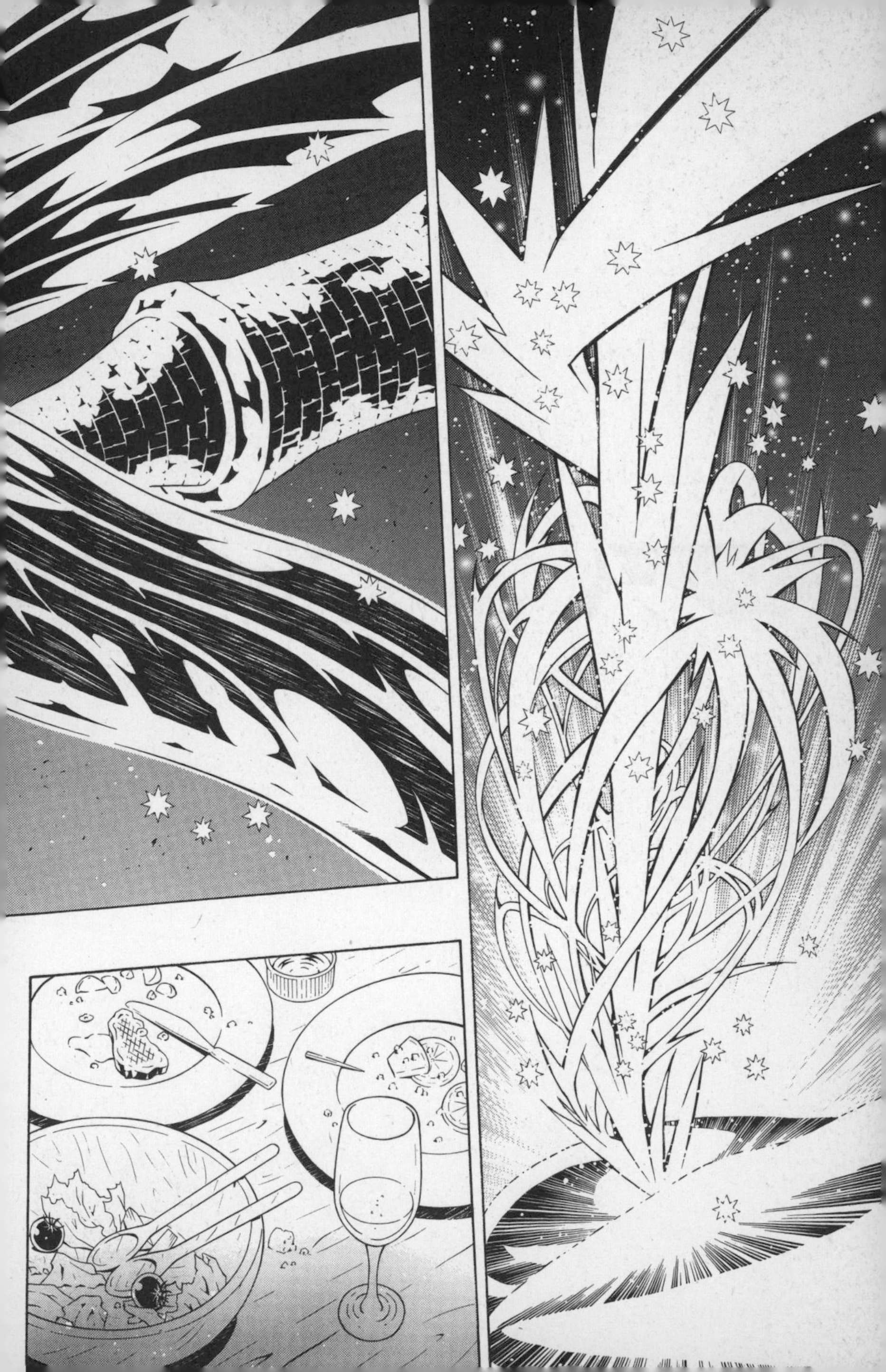

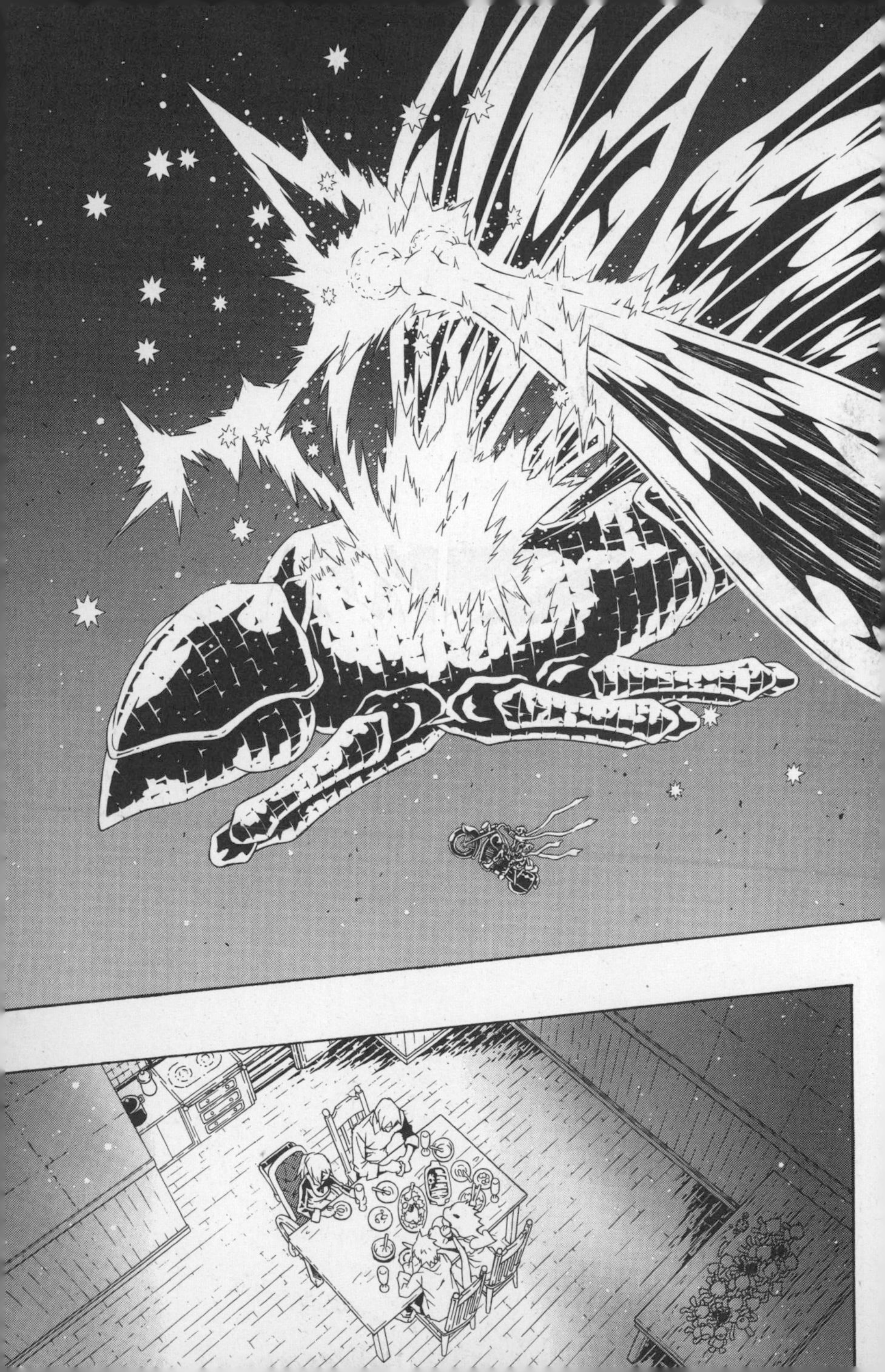

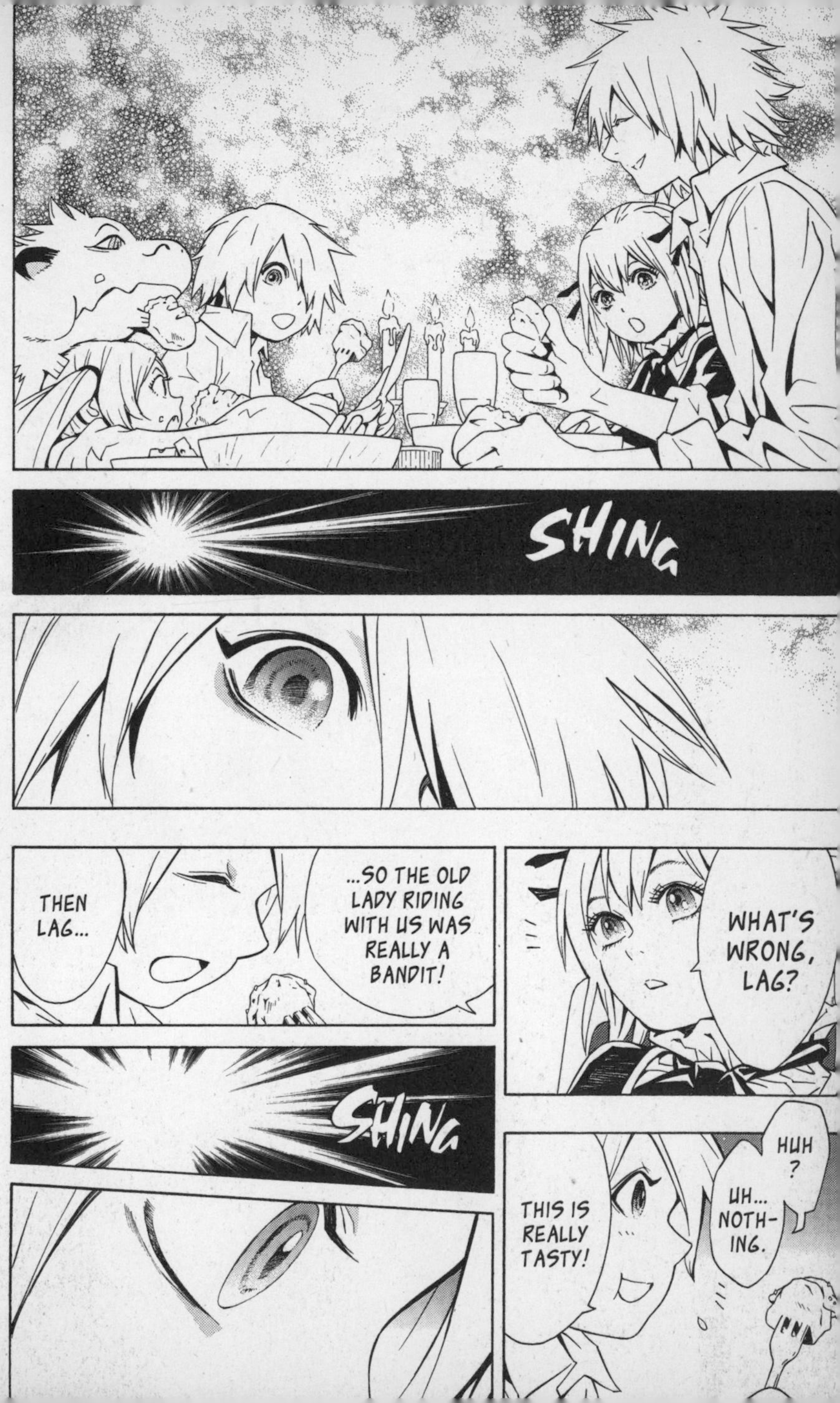
SHING
WHAT'S WRONG, LAG?
...SO THE OLD LADY RIDING WITH US WAS REALLY A BANDIT!
THEN LAG...
SHING
HUH?
UH... NOTHING.
THIS IS REALLY TASTY!

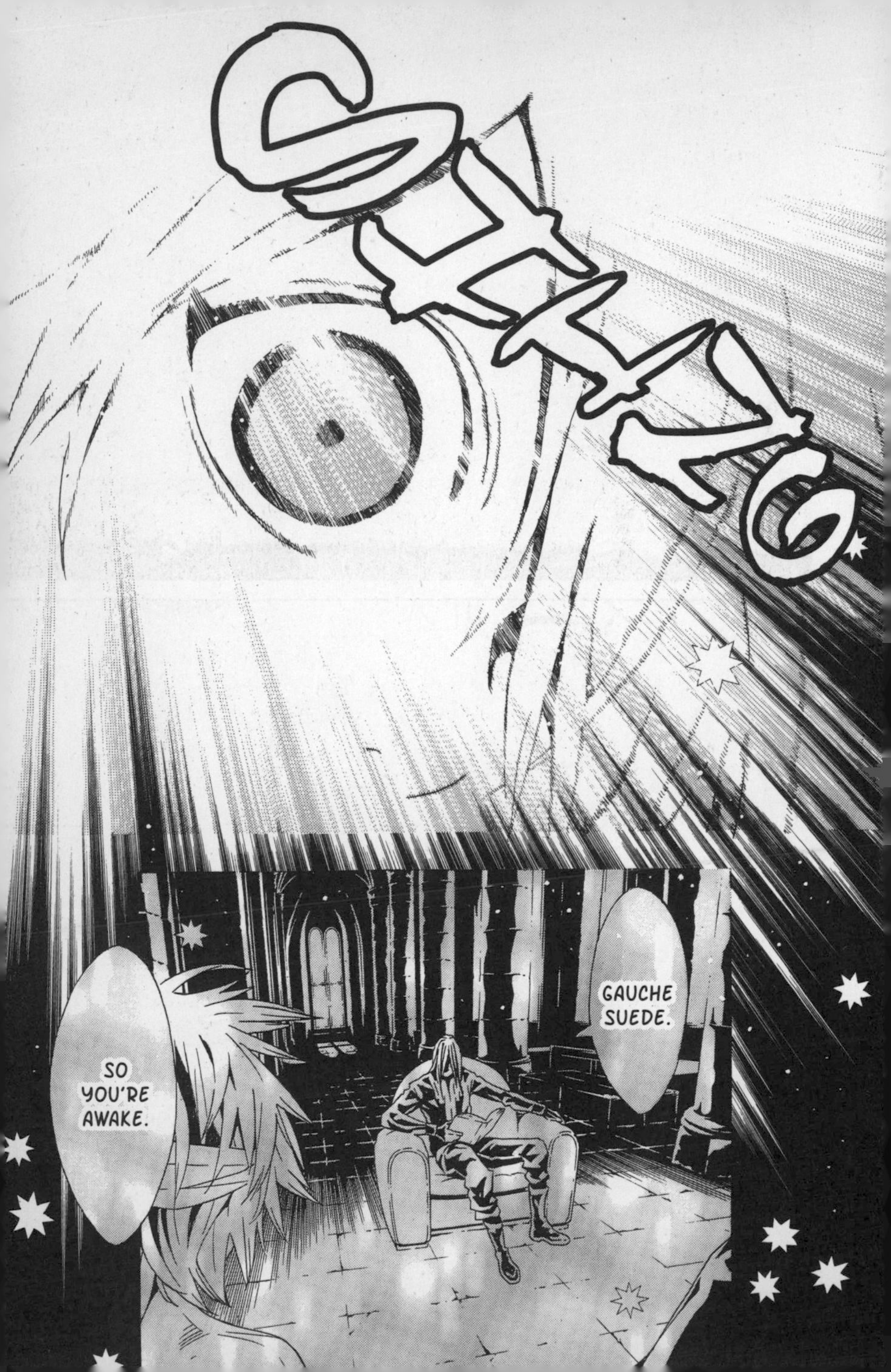
GAUCHE SUEDE.
SO YOU'RE AWAKE.

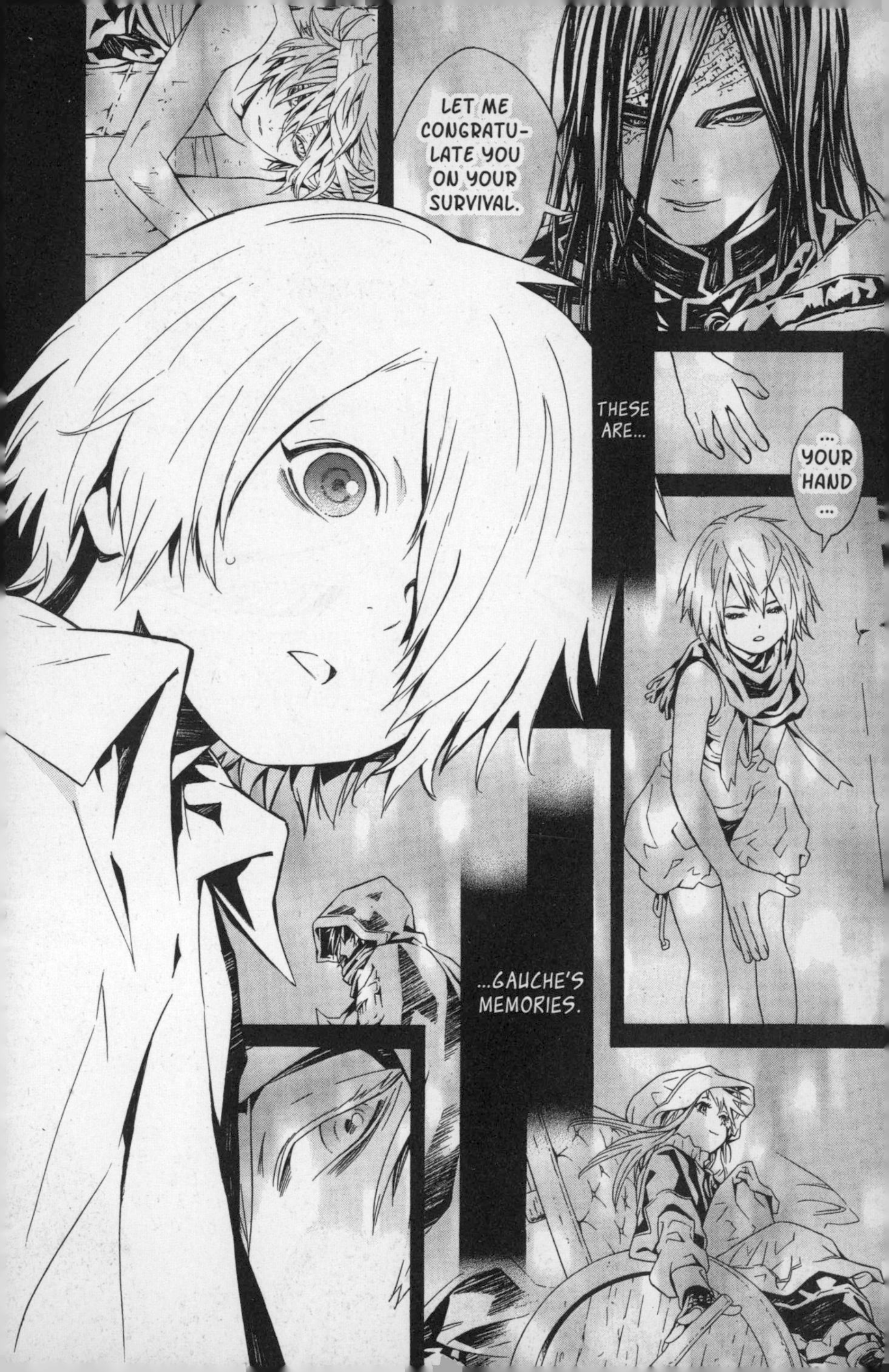
LET ME CONGRATU-LATE YOU ON YOUR SURVIVAL.
THESE ARE...
... YOUR HAND ...
...GAUCHE'S MEMORIES.

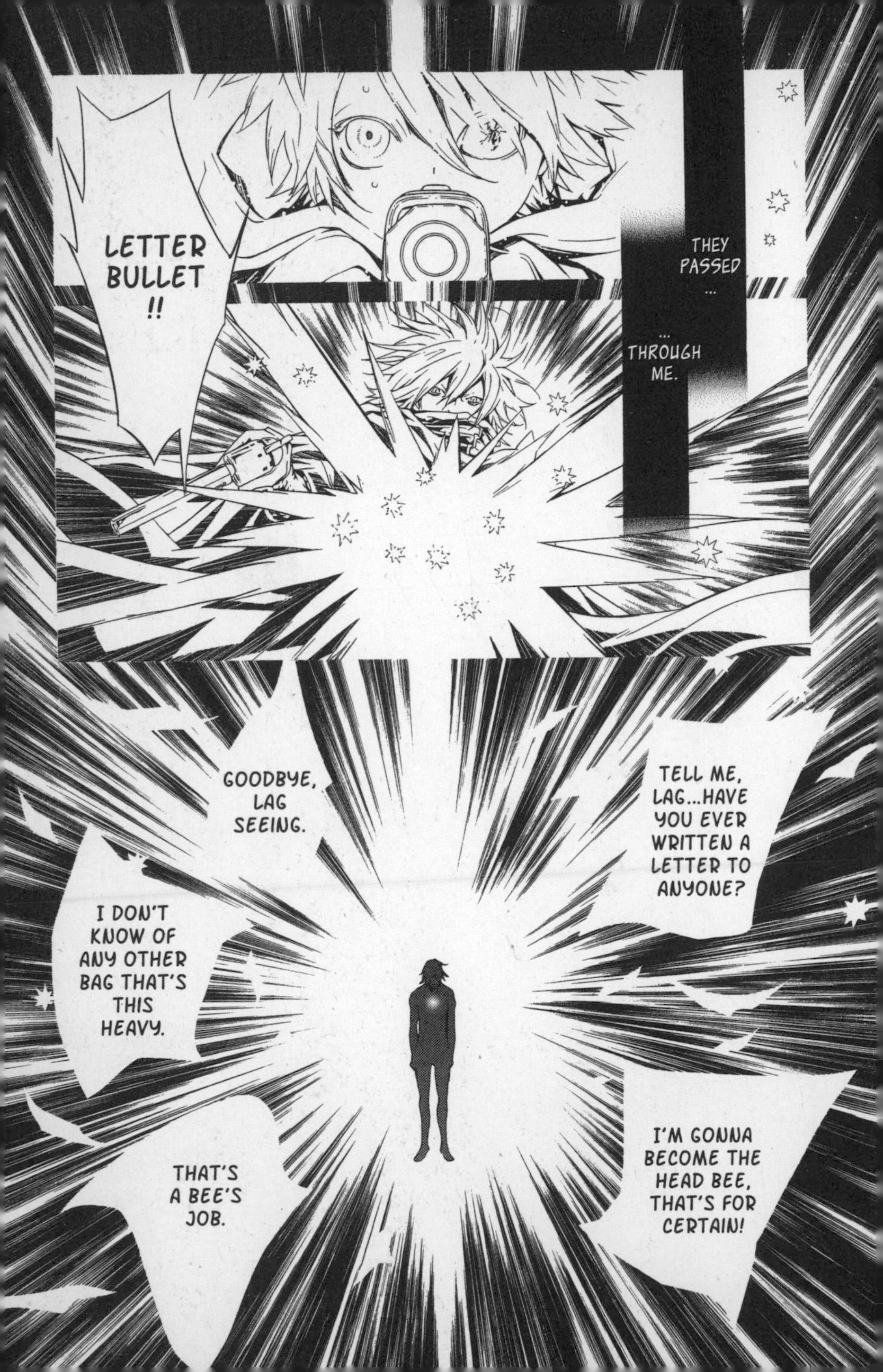
THEY PASSED ...
... THROUGH ME.
LETTER BULLET !!
TELL ME, LAG...HAVE YOU EVER WRITTEN A LETTER TO ANYONE?
GOODBYE, LAG SEEING.
I DON'T KNOW OF ANY OTHER BAG THAT'S THIS HEAVY.
I'M GONNA BECOME THE HEAD BEE, THAT'S FOR CERTAIN!
THAT'S A BEE'S JOB.

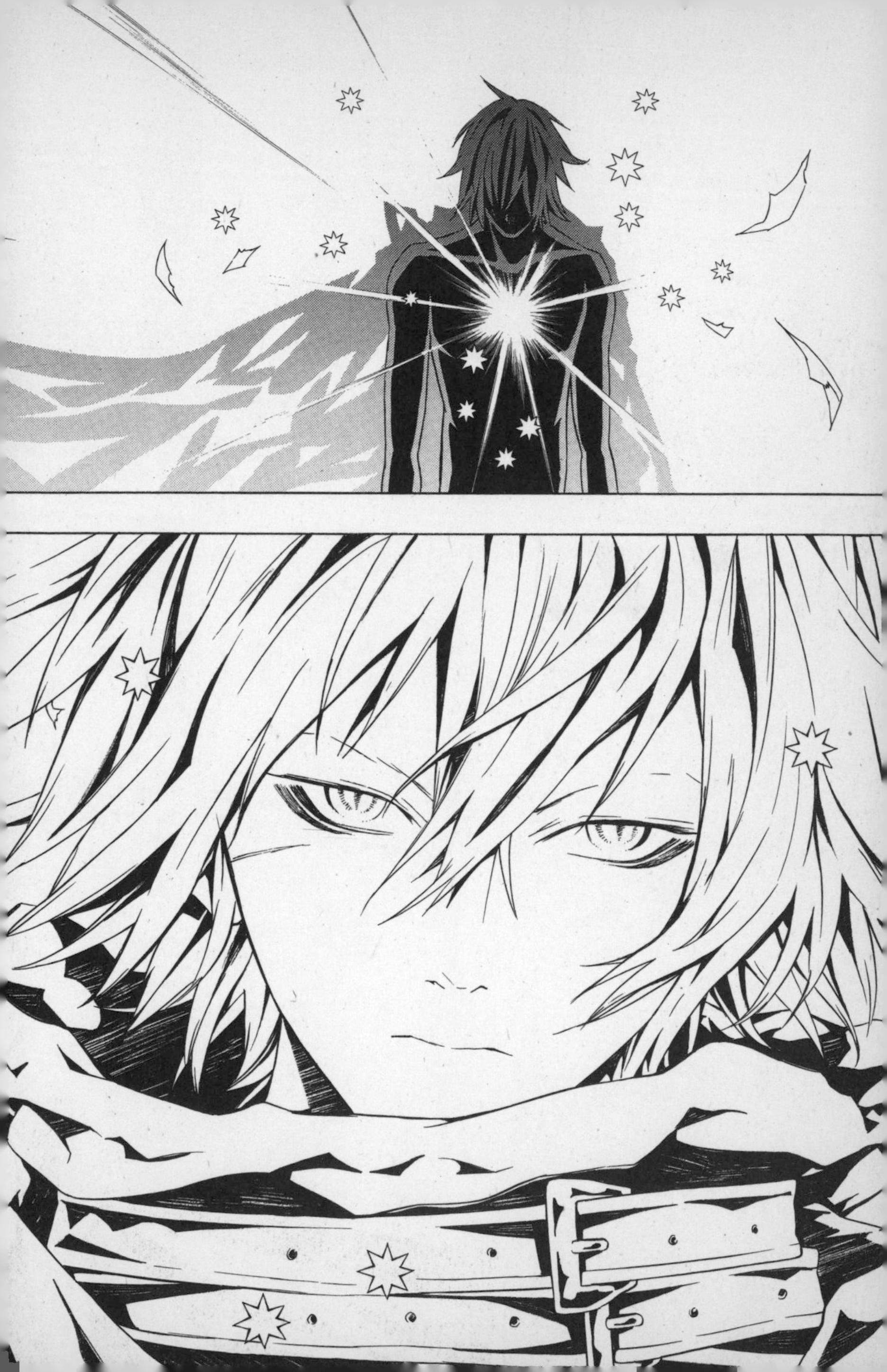

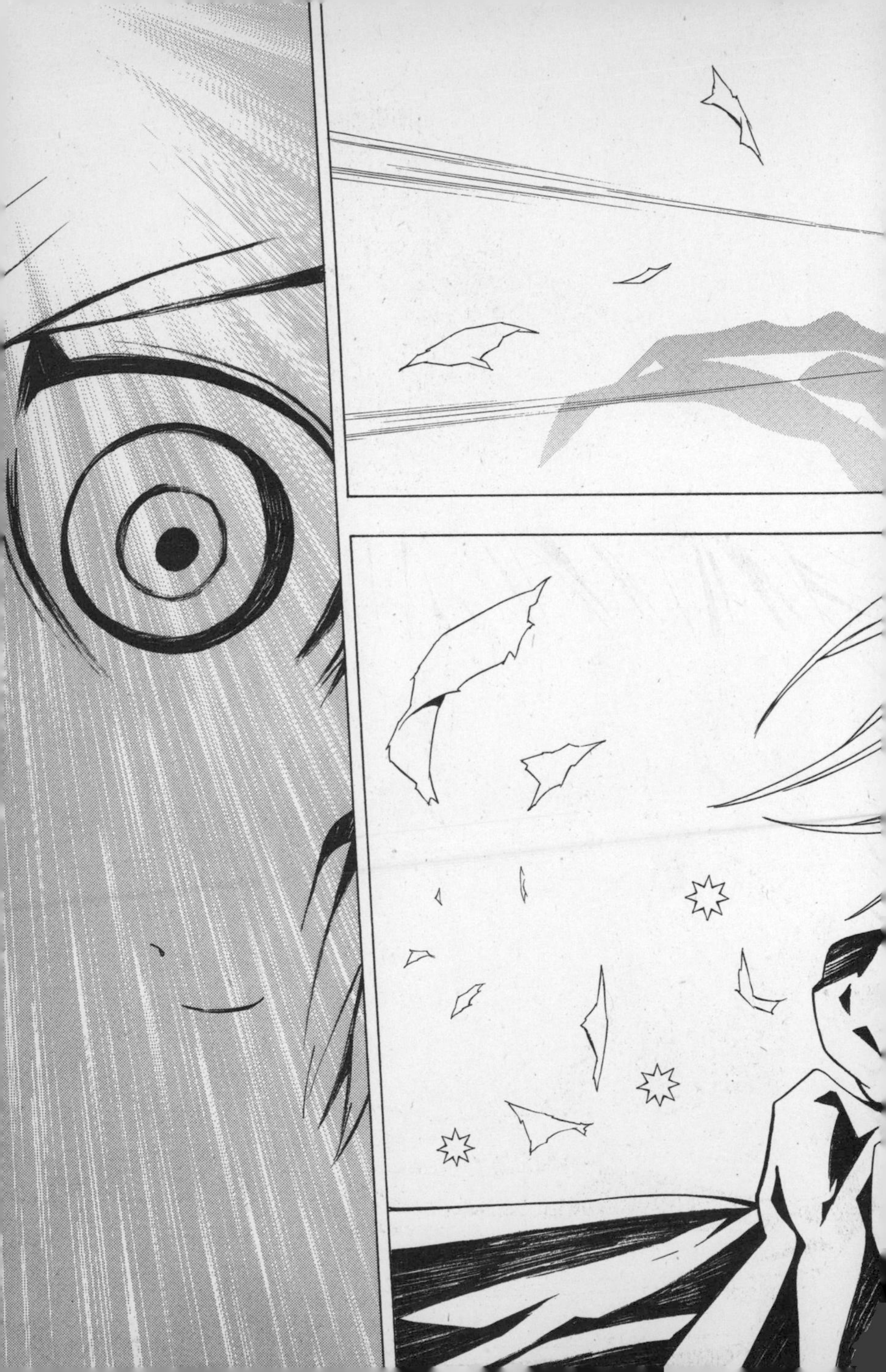

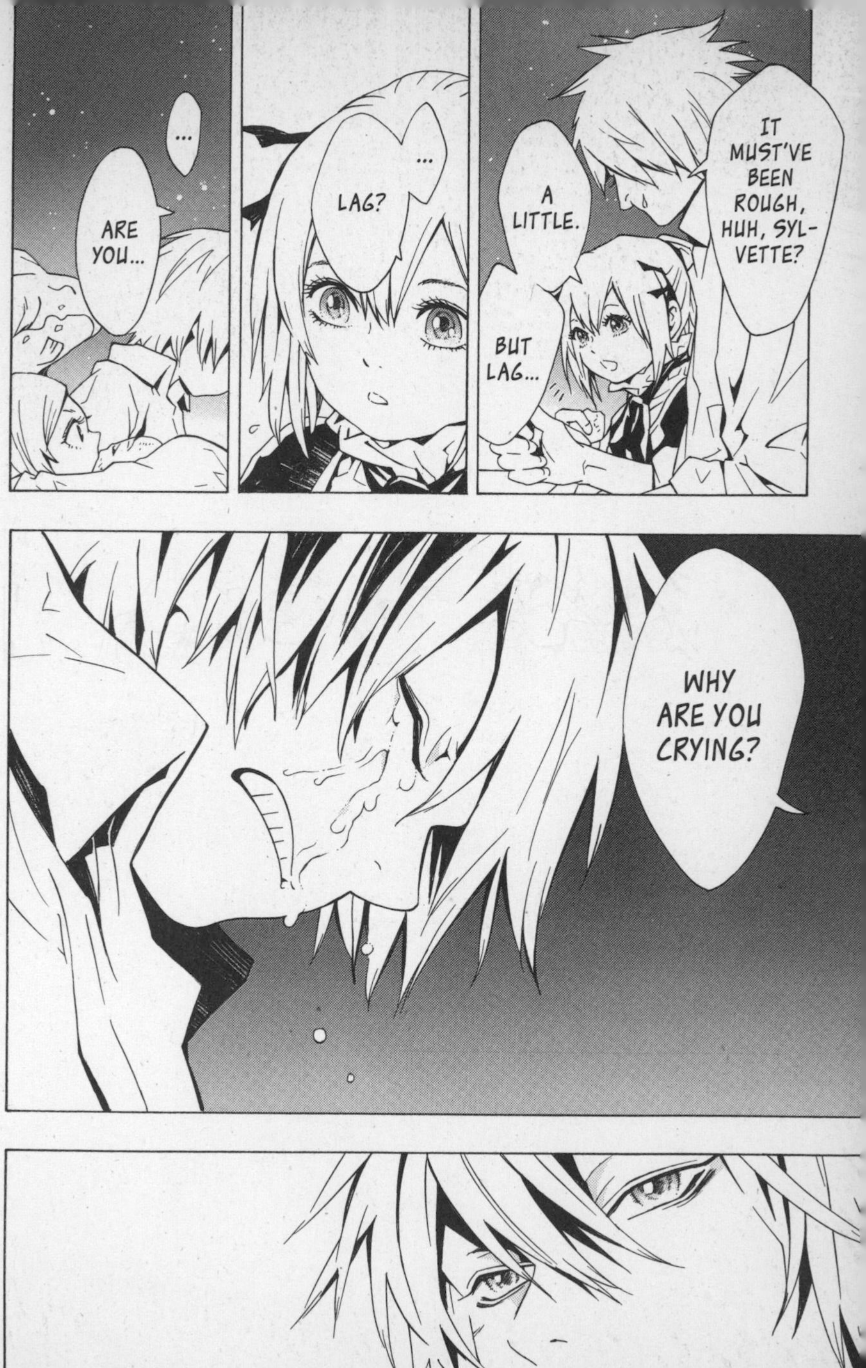
IT MUST'VE BEEN ROUGH, HUH, SYL-VETTE?
A LITTLE.
BUT LAG...
...
LAG?
...
ARE YOU...
WHY ARE YOU CRYING?

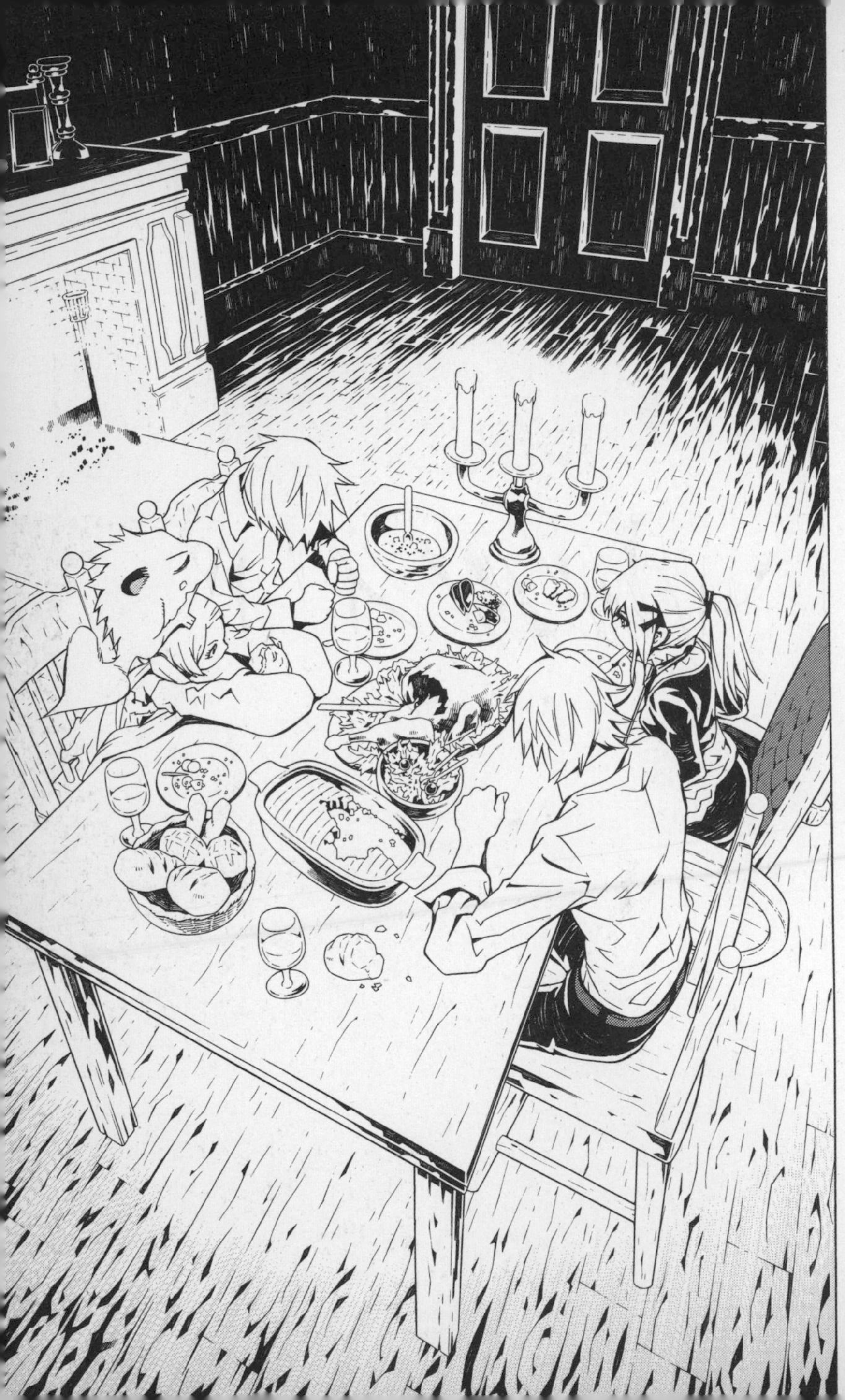

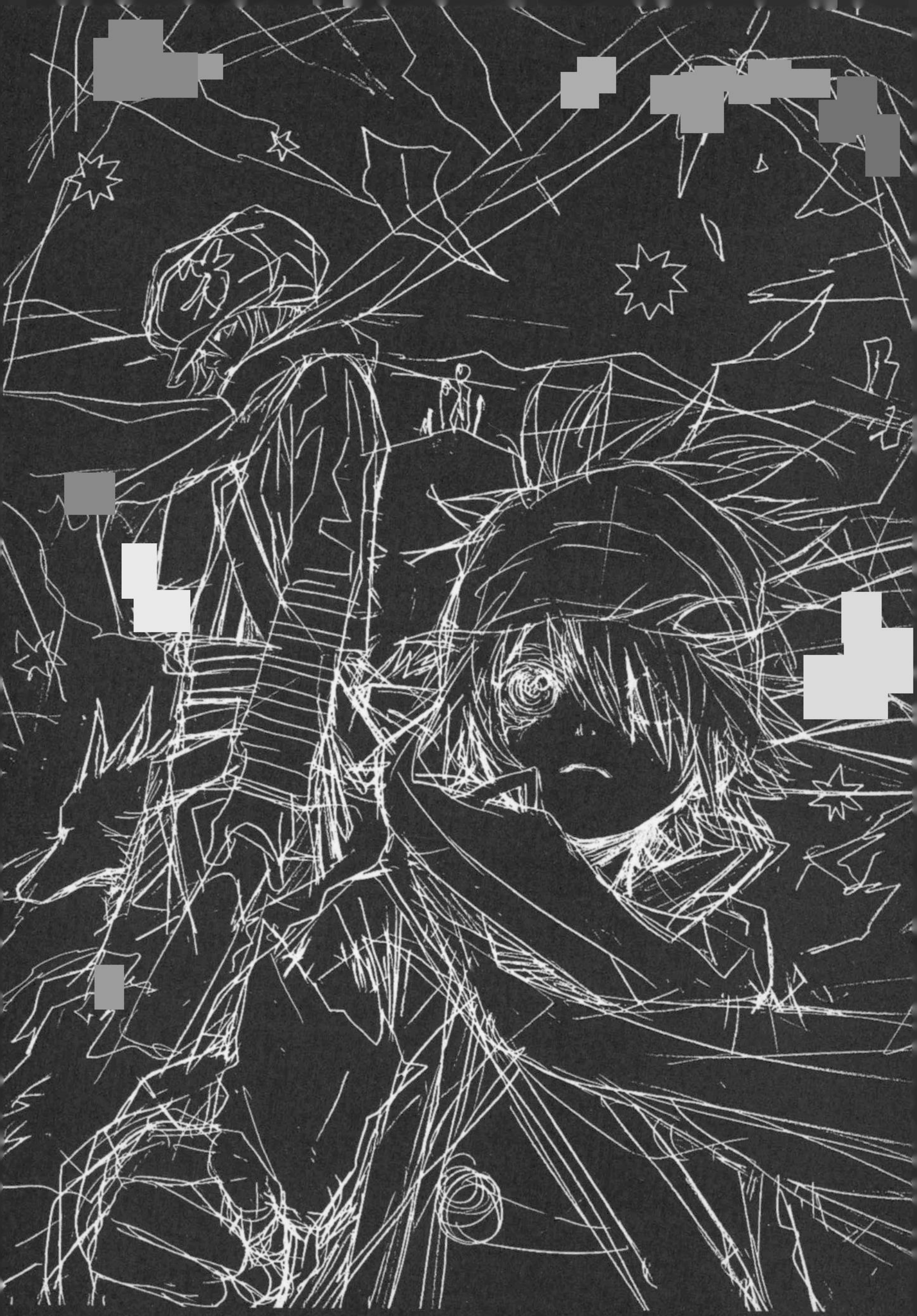

Rough sketch of volume 1 cover.

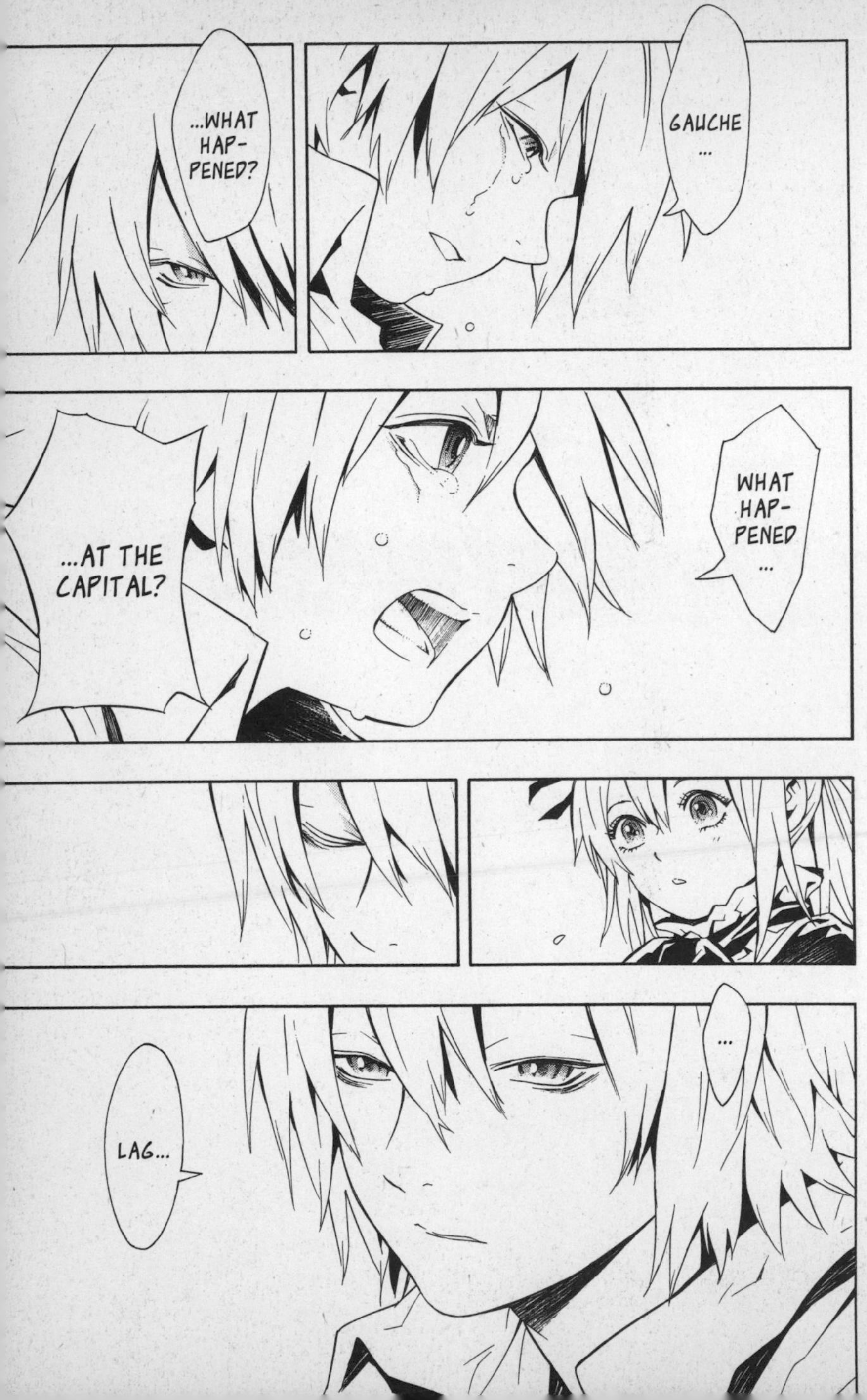
GAUCHE ...
...WHAT HAP-PENED?
WHAT HAP-PENED ...
...AT THE CAPITAL?
...
LAG...

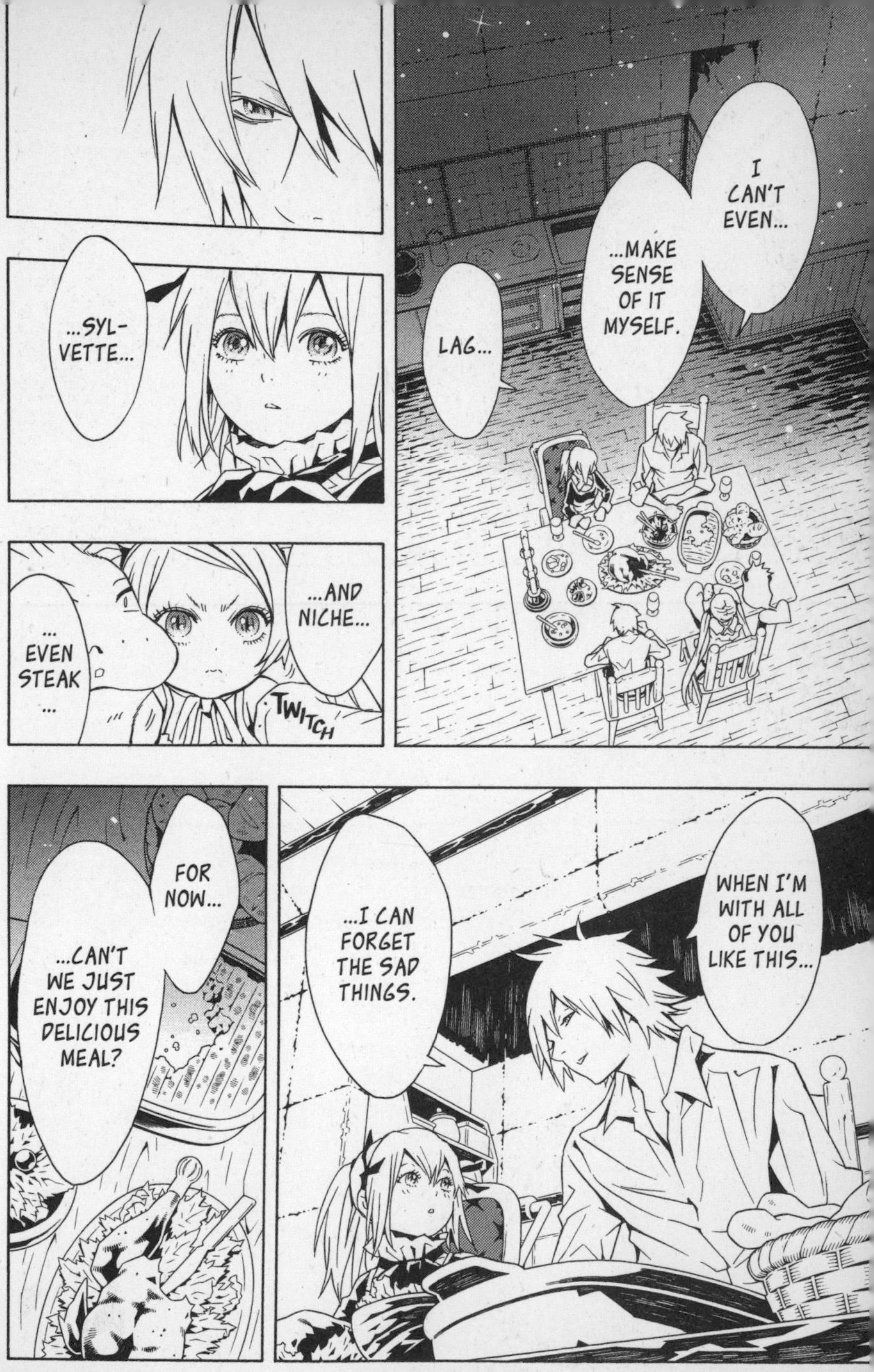
I CAN'T EVEN...
...MAKE SENSE OF IT MYSELF.
LAG...
...SYL-VETTE...
...AND NICHE...
... EVEN STEAK ...
TWITCH
WHEN I'M WITH ALL OF YOU LIKE THIS...
...I CAN FORGET THE SAD THINGS.
FOR NOW...
...CAN'T WE JUST ENJOY THIS DELICIOUS MEAL?

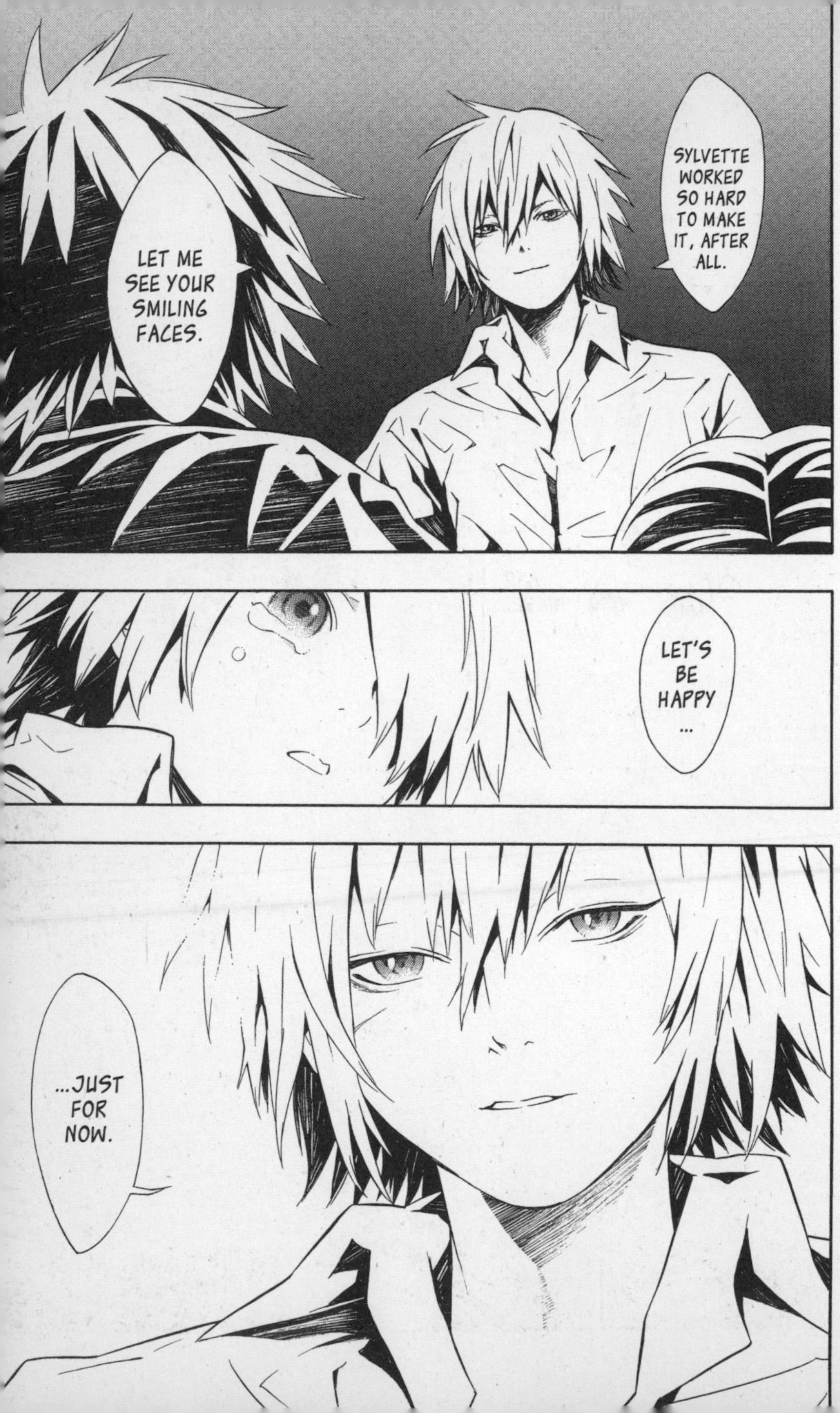
SYLVETTE WORKED SO HARD TO MAKE IT, AFTER ALL.
LET ME SEE YOUR SMILING FACES.
LET'S BE HAPPY ...
...JUST FOR NOW.

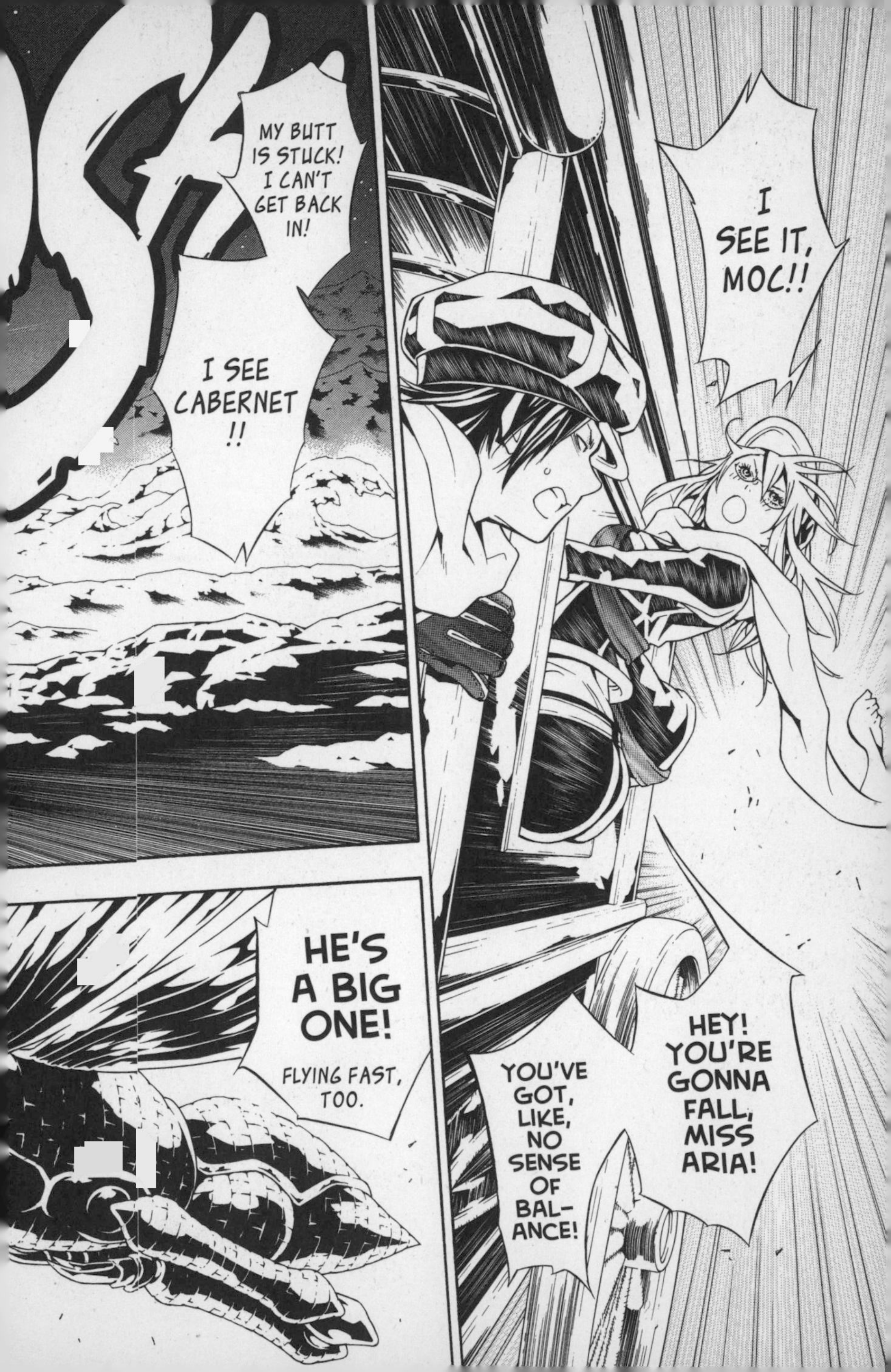
I SEE IT, MOC!!
MY BUTT IS STUCK! I CAN'T GET BACK IN!
I SEE CABERNET !!
HEY! YOU'RE GONNA FALL, MISS ARIA!
YOU'VE GOT, LIKE, NO SENSE OF BAL-ANCE!
HE'S A BIG ONE!
FLYING FAST, TOO.

Chapter 44: Silence and Pursuit

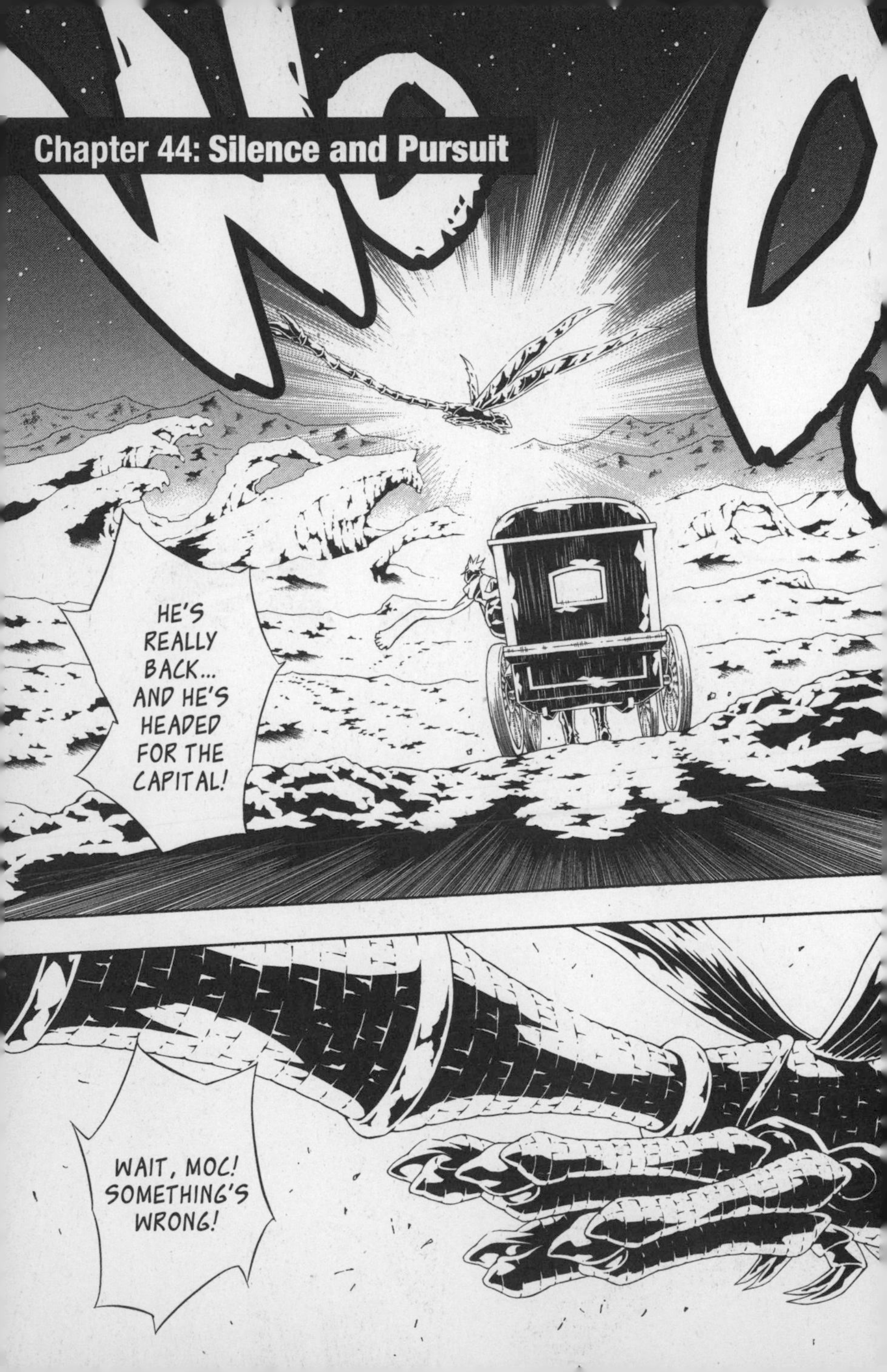
HE'S REALLY BACK... AND HE'S HEADED FOR THE CAPITAL!
WAIT, MOC! SOMETHING'S WRONG!

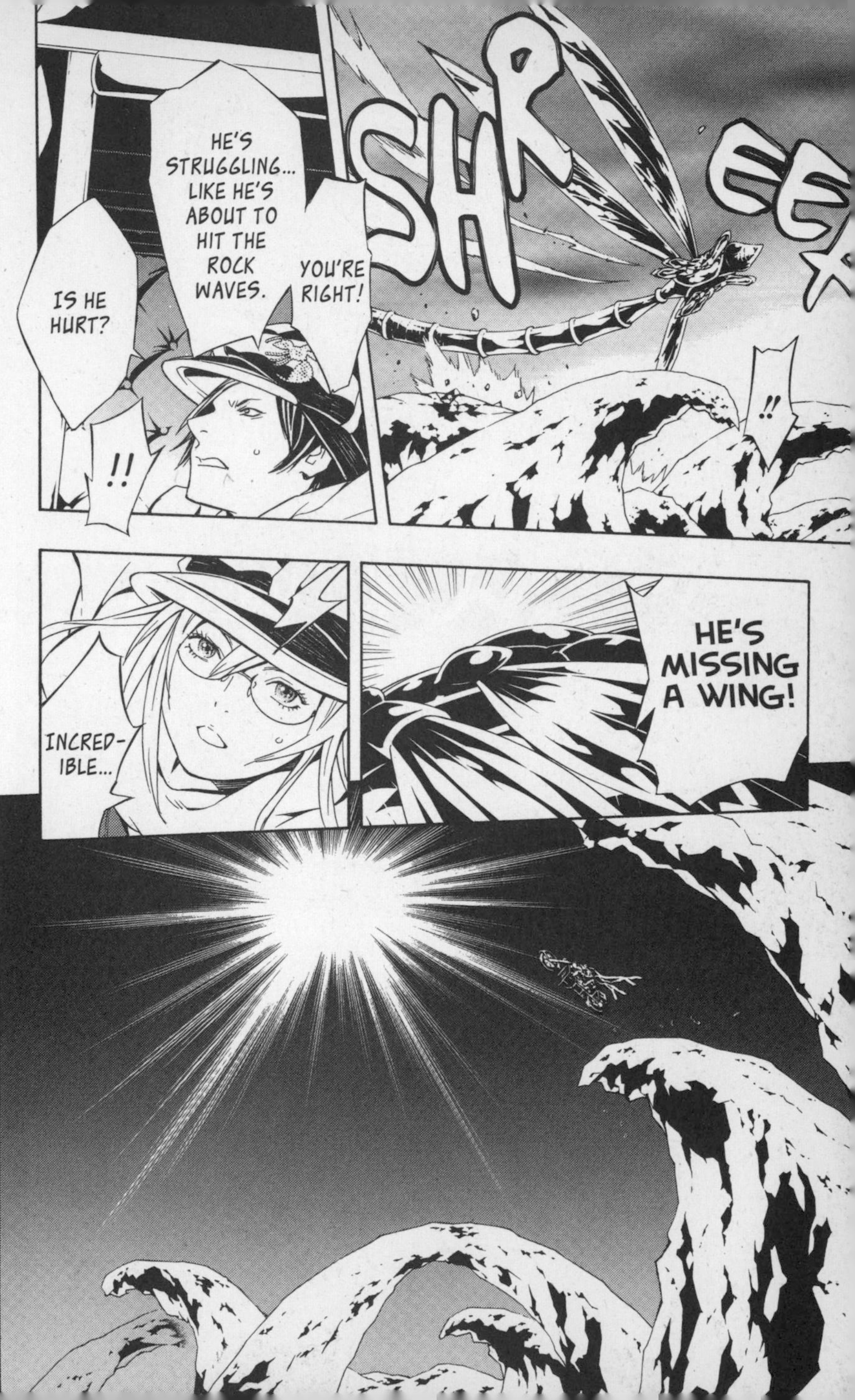
SHREEX
!!
HE'S STRUGGLING... LIKE HE'S ABOUT TO HIT THE ROCK WAVES.
YOU'RE RIGHT!
IS HE HURT?
!!
HE'S MISSING A WING!
INCRED-IBLE...

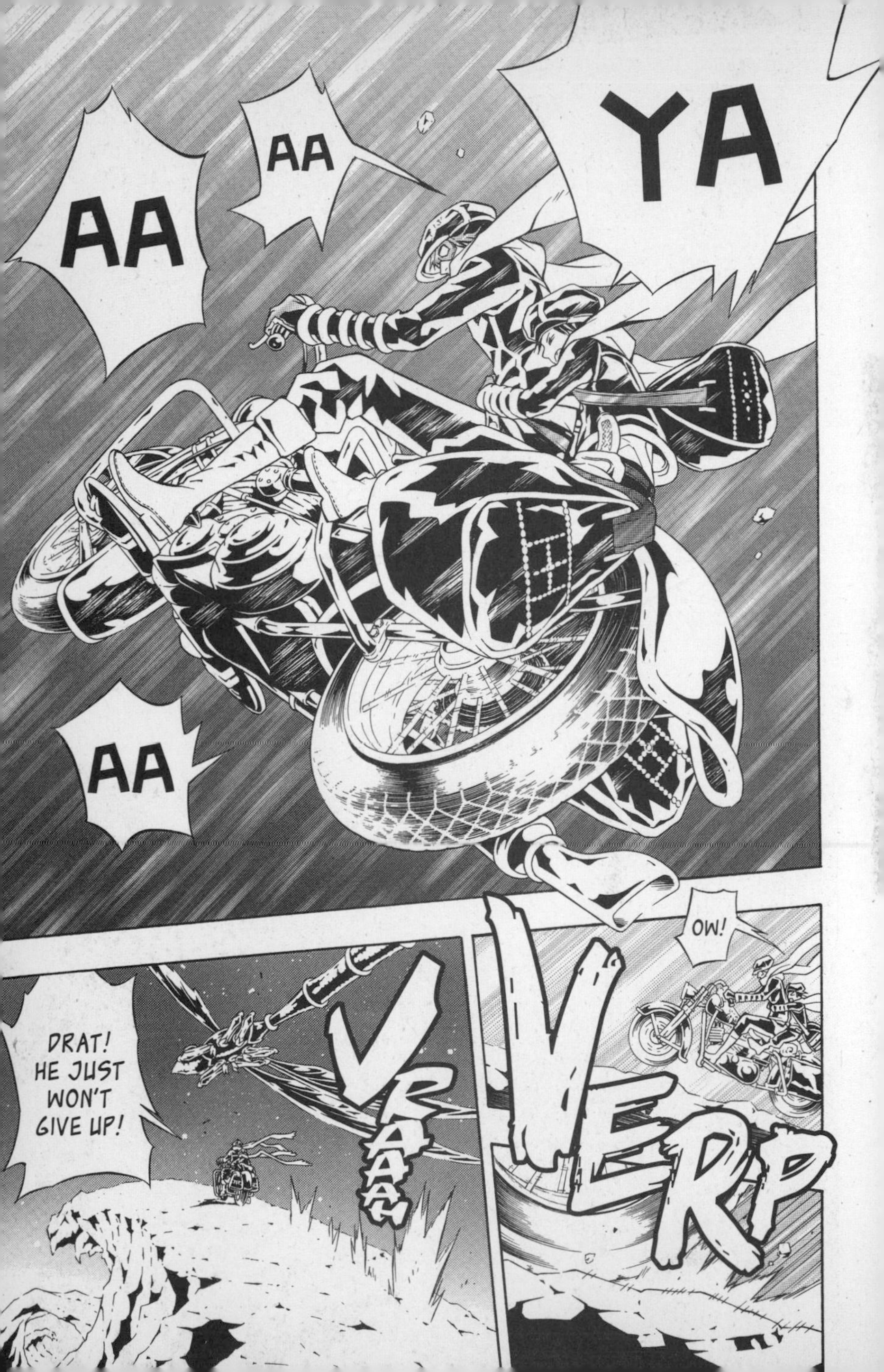
YA
AA
AA
AA
OW!
VERP
VRAAAH
DRAT! HE JUST WON'T GIVE UP!

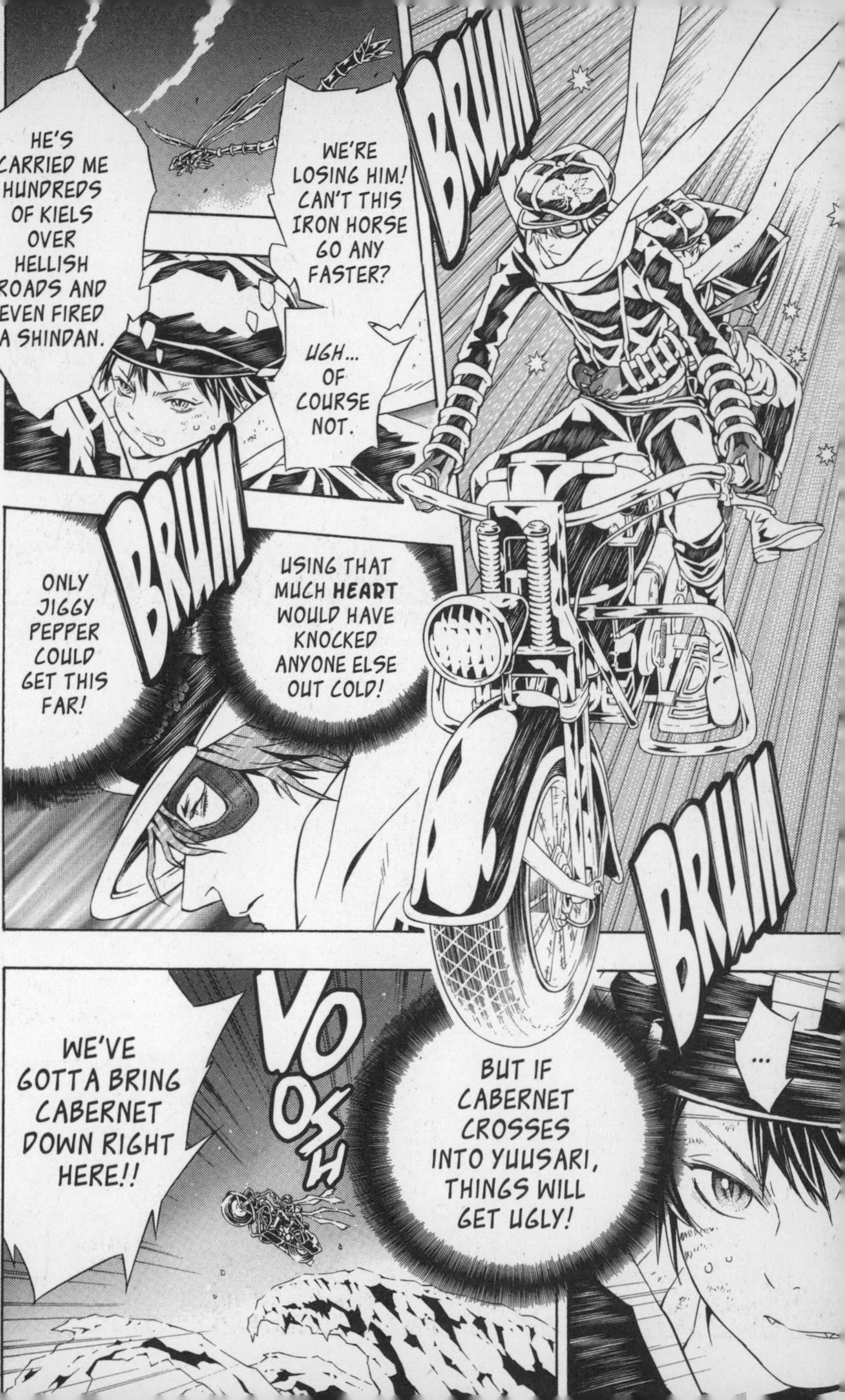
BRUM
WE'RE LOSING HIM! CAN'T THIS IRON HORSE GO ANY FASTER?
UGH... OF COURSE NOT.
HE'S CARRIED ME HUNDREDS OF KIELS OVER HELLISH ROADS AND EVEN FIRED A SHINDAN.
BRUM
BRUM
USING THAT MUCH **HEART** WOULD HAVE KNOCKED ANYONE ELSE OUT COLD!
ONLY JIGGY PEPPER COULD GET THIS FAR!
...
BUT IF CABERNET CROSSES INTO YUUSARI, THINGS WILL GET UGLY!
VOOSH
WE'VE GOTTA BRING CABERNET DOWN RIGHT HERE!!

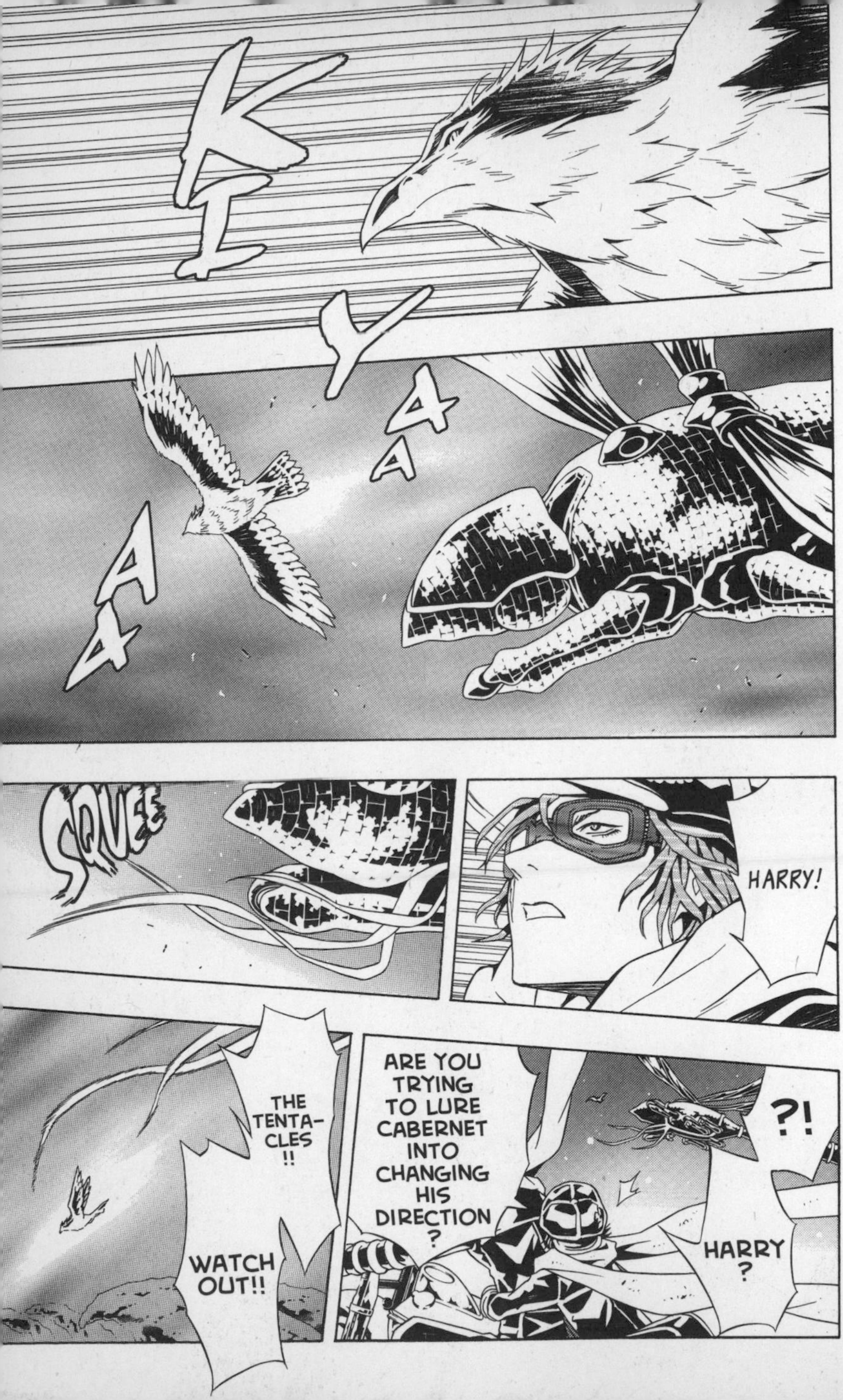
KIYAAAA
SQUEE
HARRY!
ARE YOU TRYING TO LURE CABERNET INTO CHANGING HIS DIRECTION?
HARRY?
?!
THE TENTA-CLES!!
WATCH OUT!!

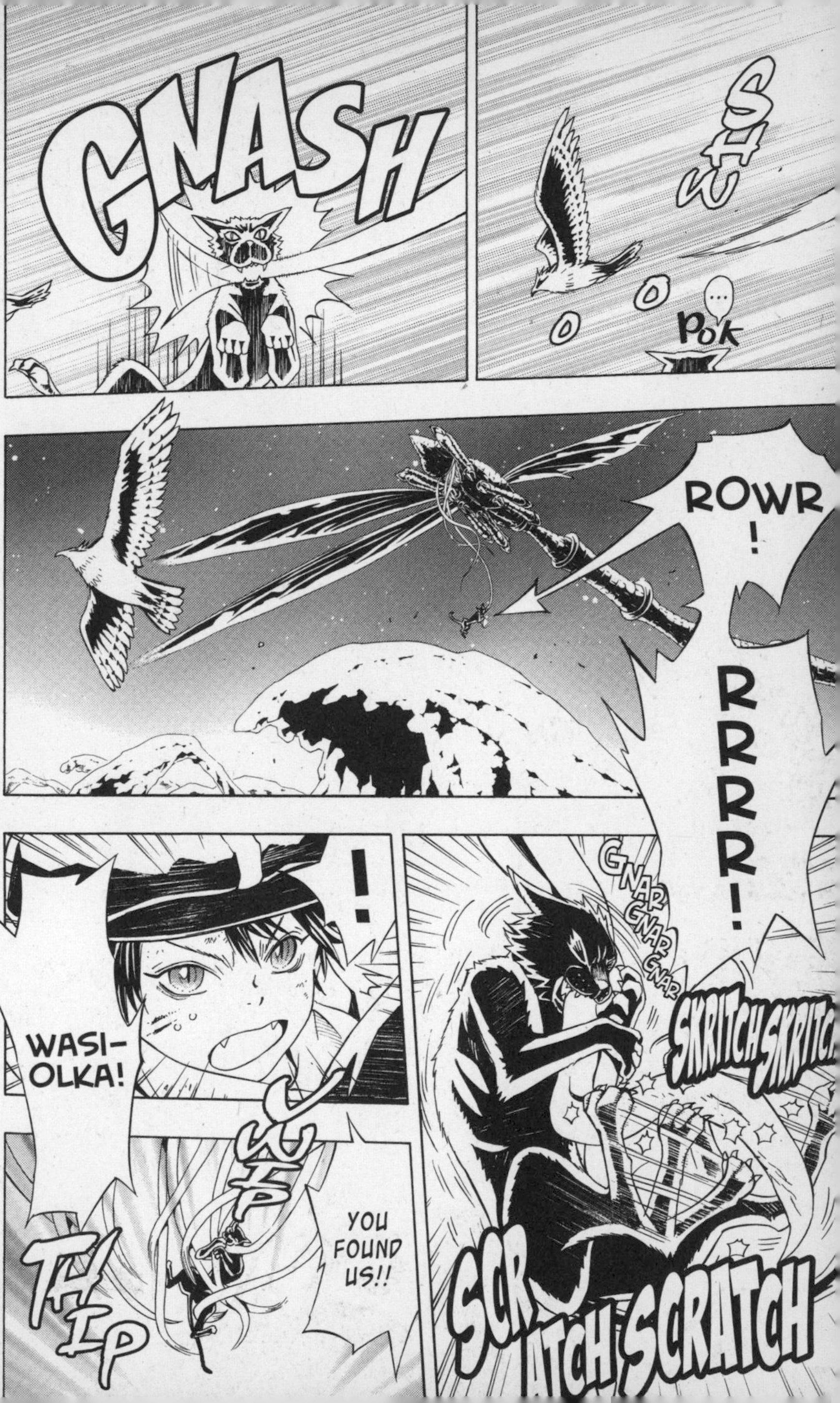
GNASH
SHU
O O
...
POK
ROWR!
RRRRR!
!
WASI-OLKA!
GNAR GNAR GNAR GNAR
SKRITCH SKRITCH
WIP
YOU FOUND US!!
THIP
SCRATCH SCRATCH

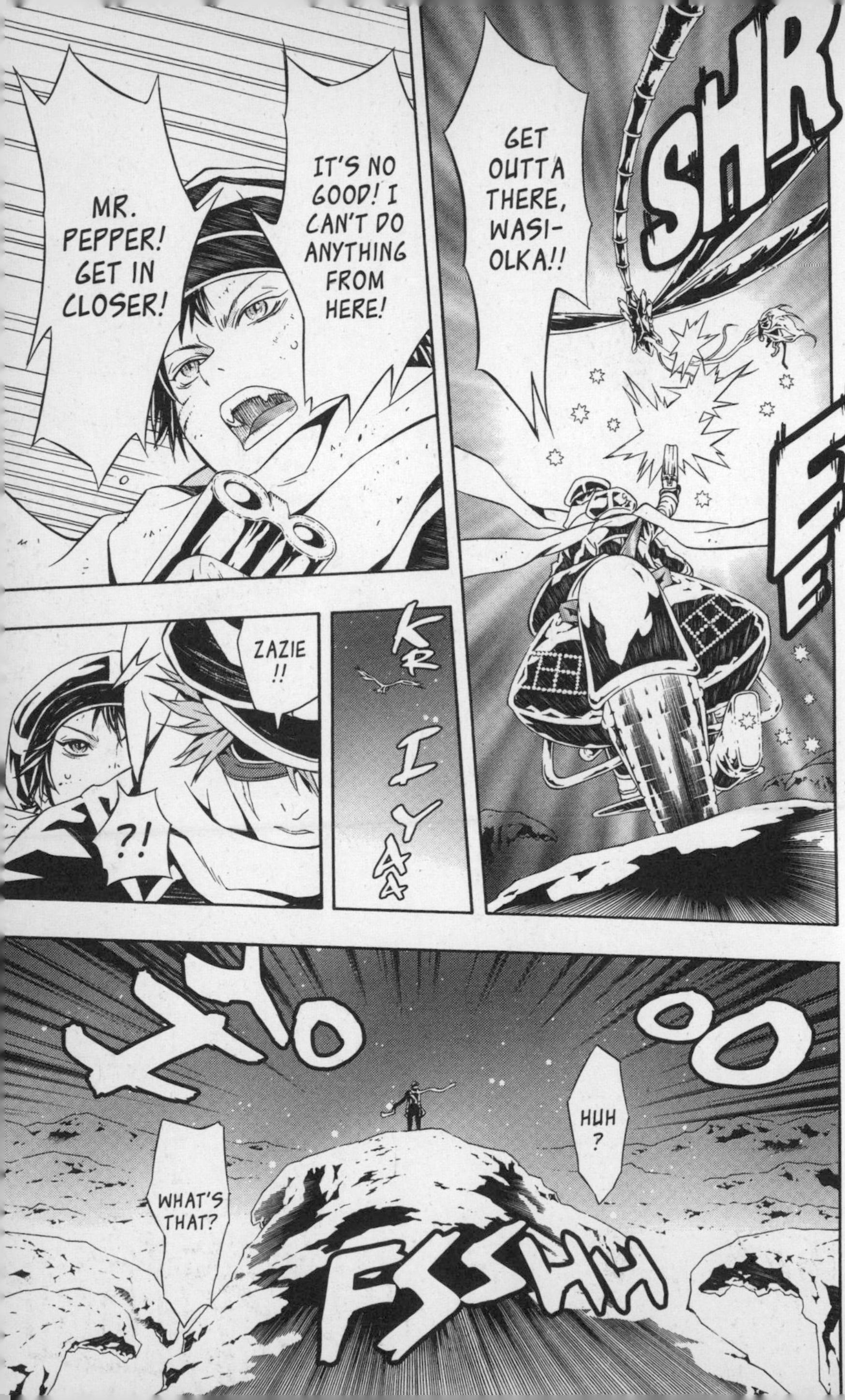
GET OUTTA THERE, WASI-OLKA!!
SHR
EE
IT'S NO GOOD! I CAN'T DO ANYTHING FROM HERE!
MR. PEPPER! GET IN CLOSER!
KRIYAA
ZAZIE !!
?!
YO
OO
HUH ?
WHAT'S THAT?
FSSHH

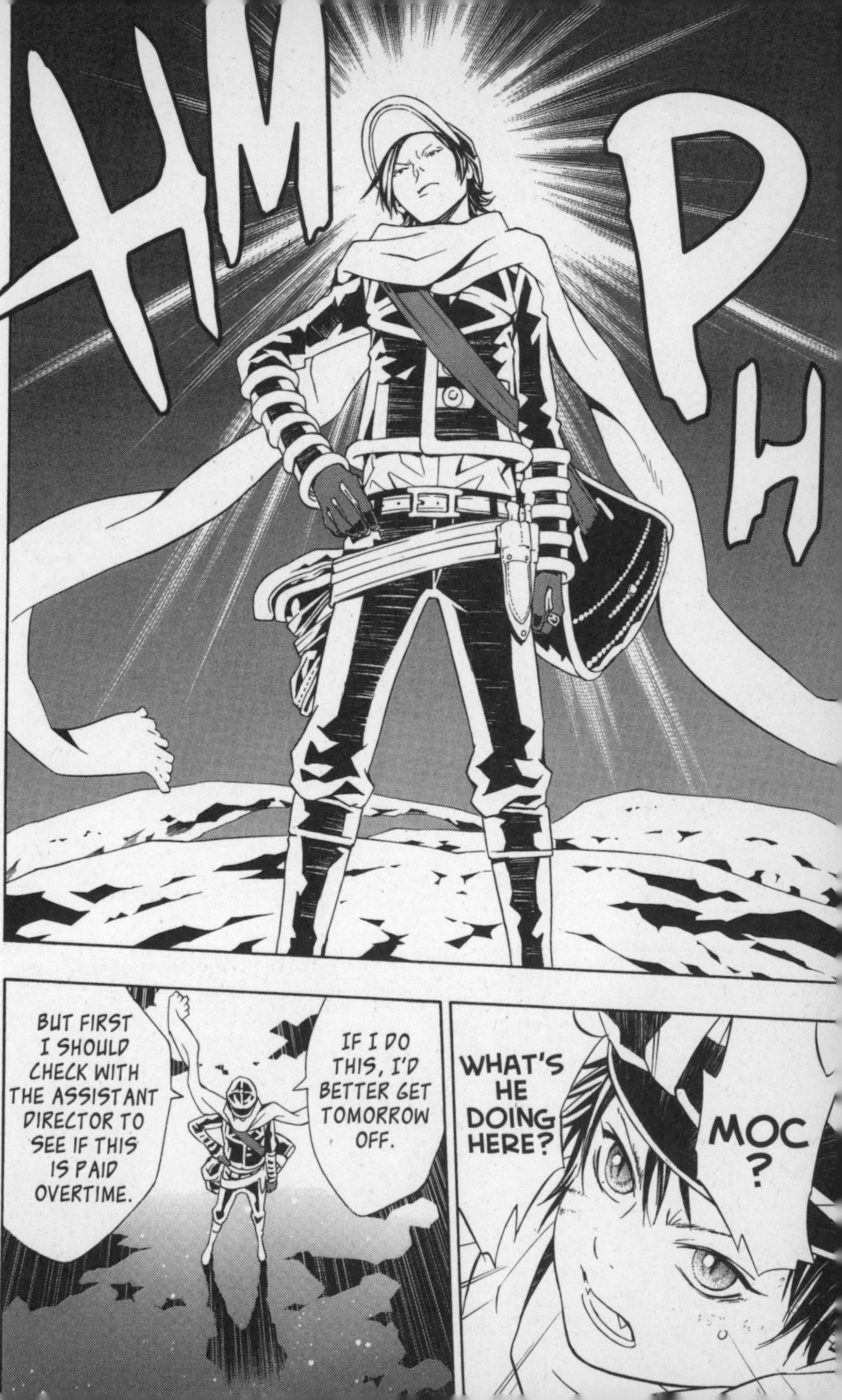
HMPH
MOC?
WHAT'S HE DOING HERE?
IF I DO THIS, I'D BETTER GET TOMORROW OFF.
BUT FIRST I SHOULD CHECK WITH THE ASSISTANT DIRECTOR TO SEE IF THIS IS PAID OVERTIME.

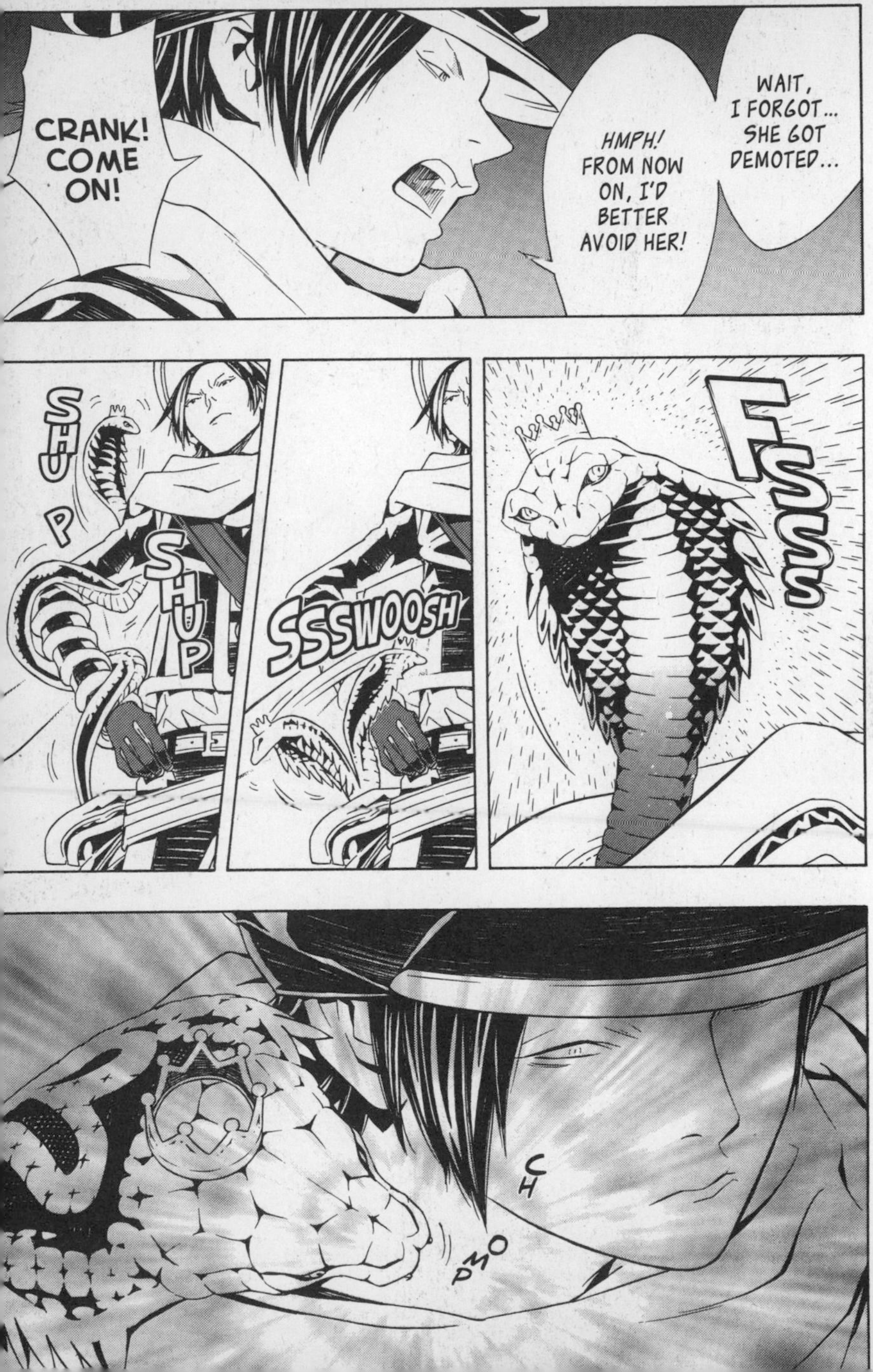
WAIT, I FORGOT... SHE GOT DEMOTED...
HMPH! FROM NOW ON, I'D BETTER AVOID HER!
CRANK! COME ON!
FSSS
SSSWOOSH
SHUP
SHUP
CH
OMP

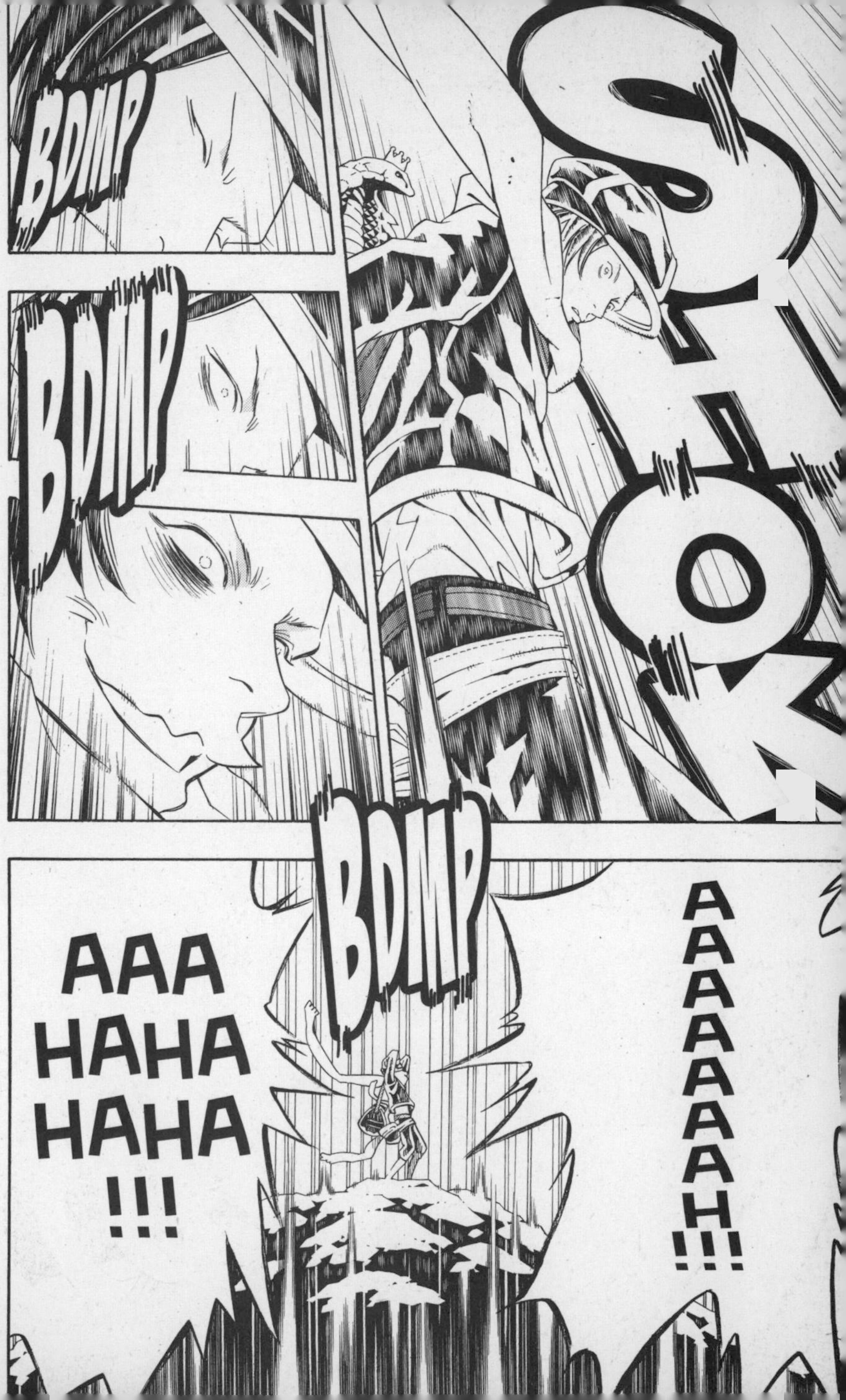
BDMP
BDMP
BDMP
AAAAAAAH!!!
BDMP
AAA HAHA HAHA !!!

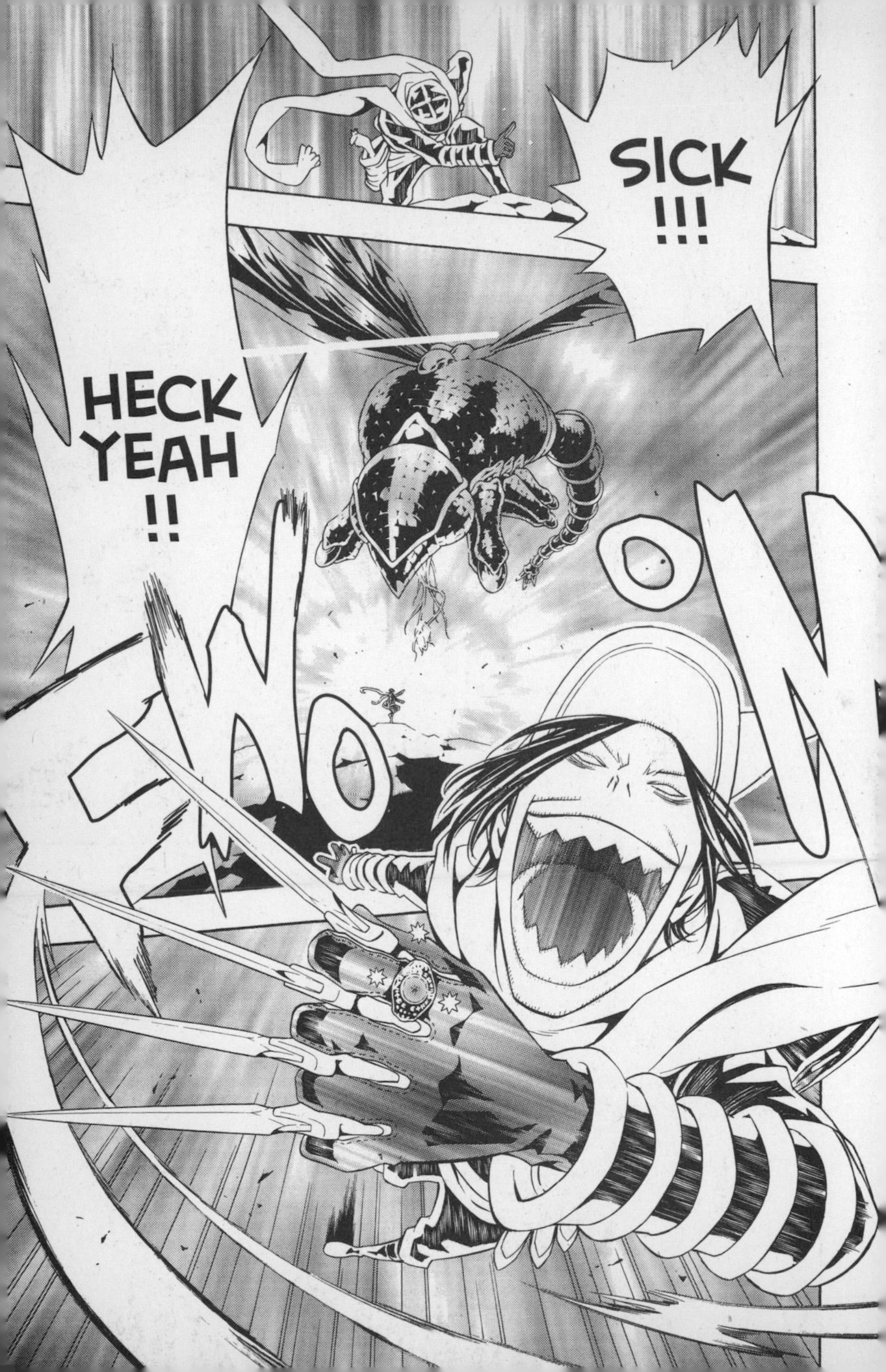
SICK
!!!
HECK
YEAH
!!
WOOOM

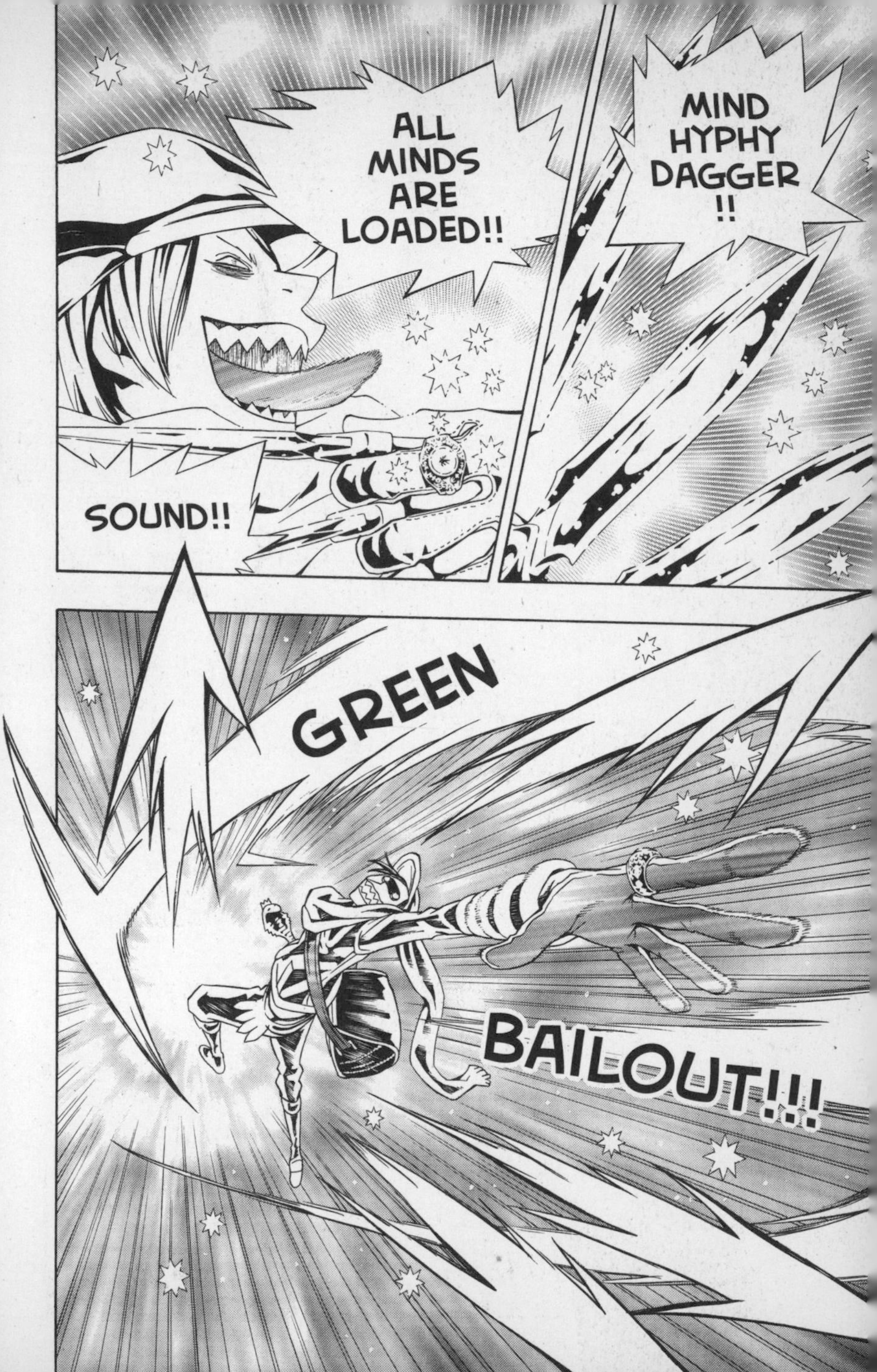
MIND HYPHY DAGGER !!
ALL MINDS ARE LOADED!!
SOUND!!
GREEN
BAILOUT!!!

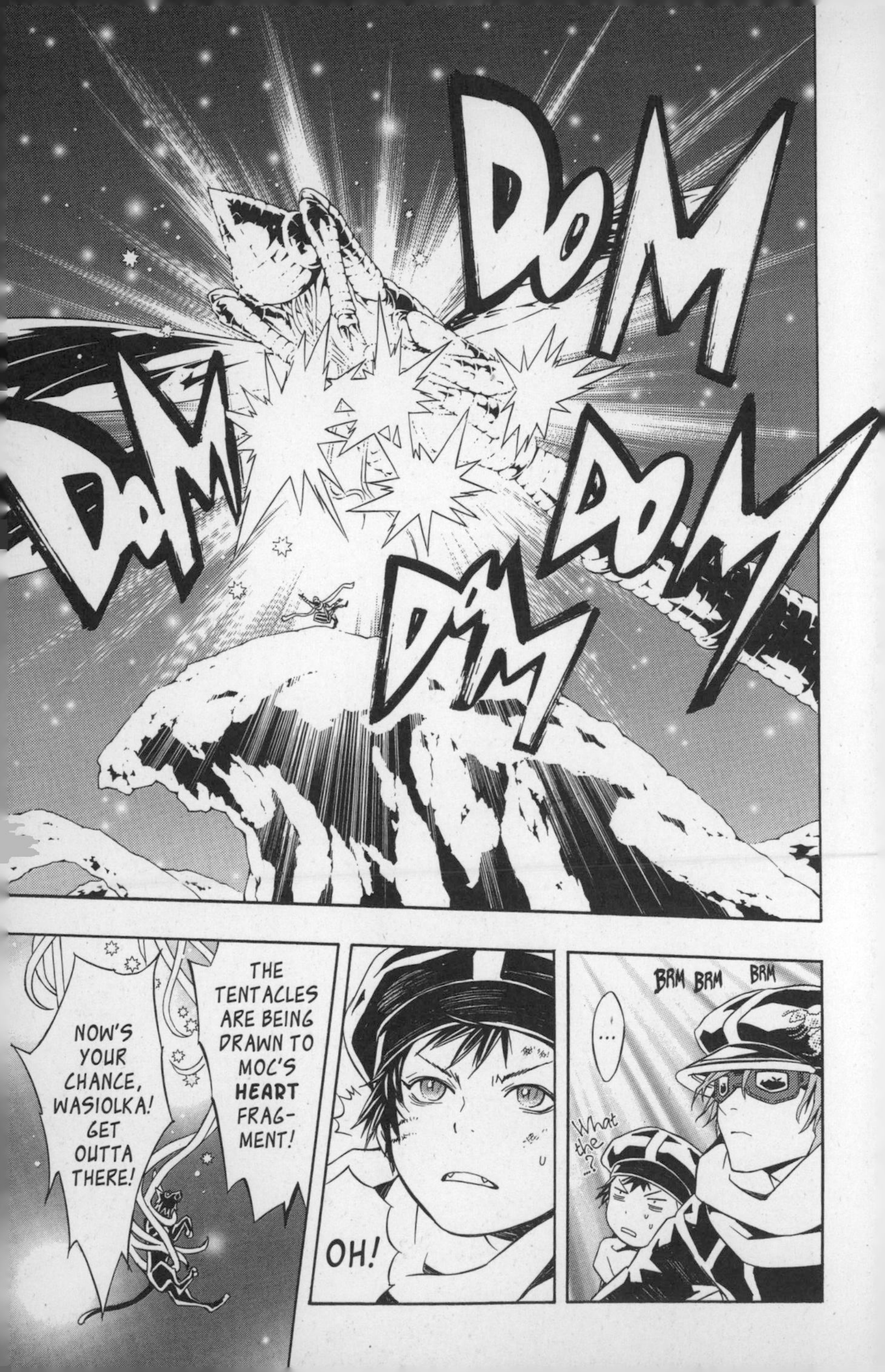
DOM
DOM
DAM
BRM BRM BRM
...!
What the...?
OH!
THE TENTACLES ARE BEING DRAWN TO MOC'S HEART FRAG-MENT!
NOW'S YOUR CHANCE, WASIOLKA! GET OUTTA THERE!

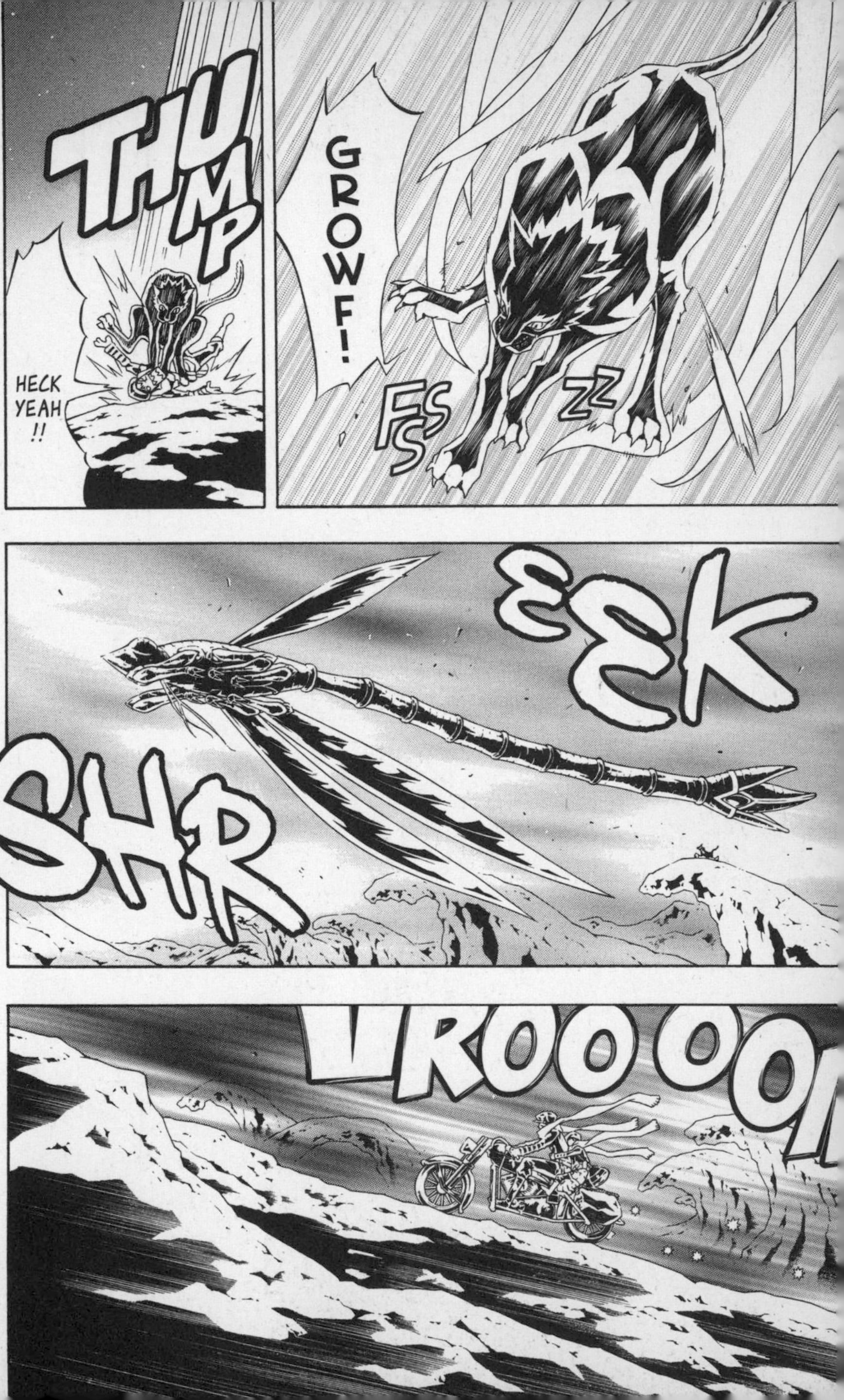
GROWF!
FSS
ZZ
THUMP
HECK YEAH!!
EEK
SHR
VROO OO

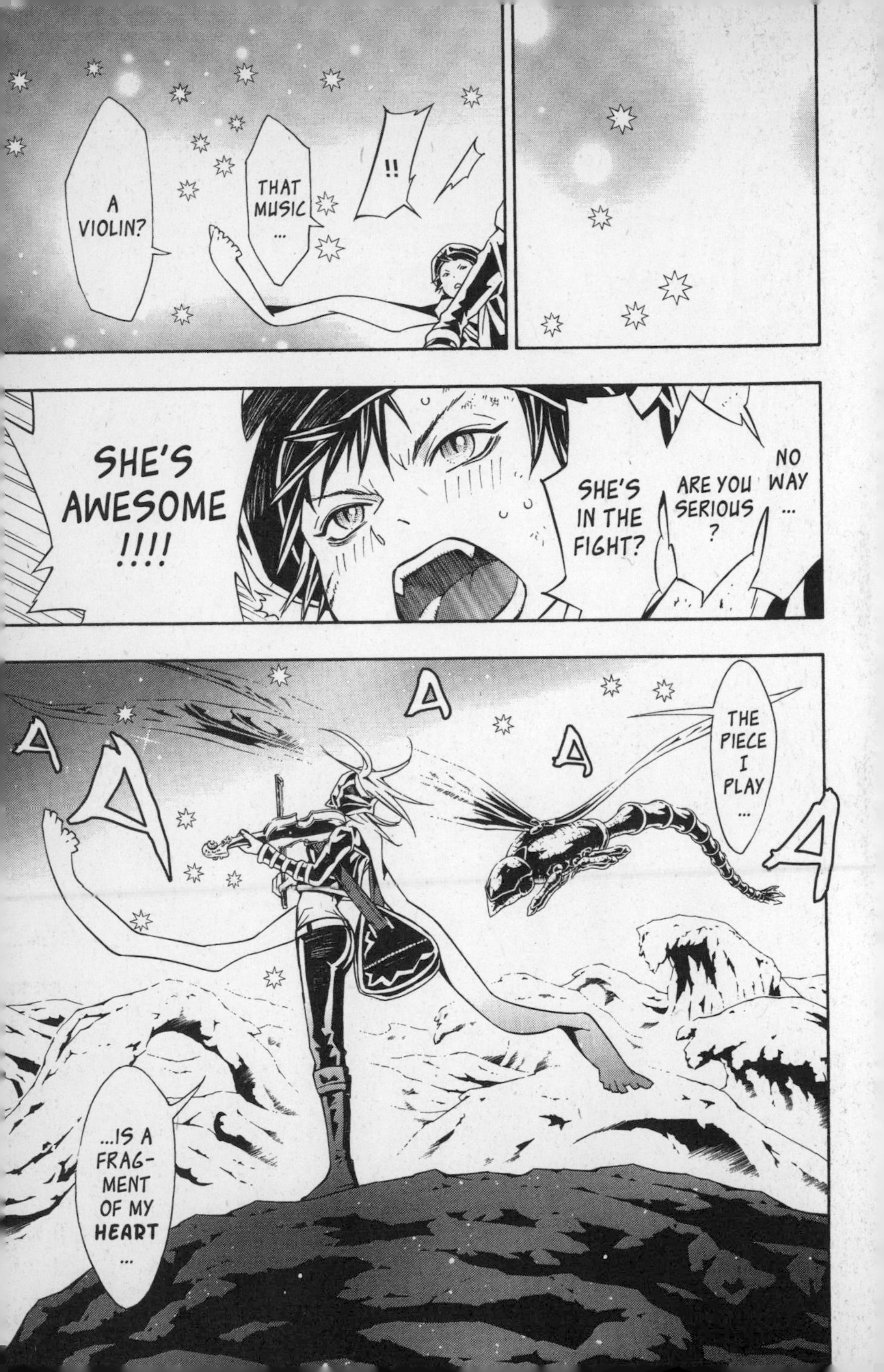
!!
THAT MUSIC ...
A VIOLIN?
NO WAY ...
ARE YOU SERIOUS ?
SHE'S IN THE FIGHT?
SHE'S AWESOME !!!!
THE PIECE I PLAY ...
...IS A FRAG-MENT OF MY HEART ...

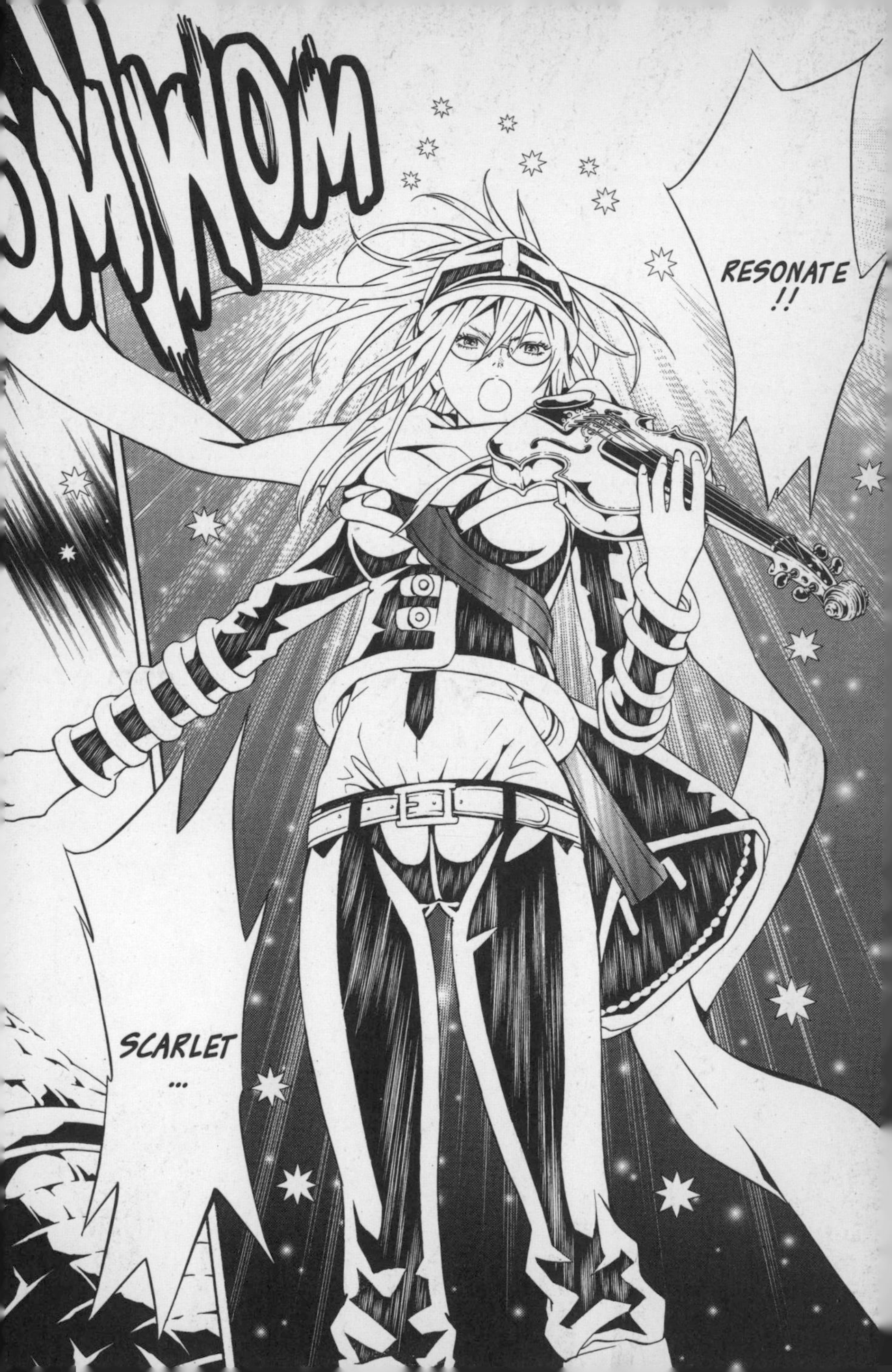
RESONATE !!
SCARLET ...

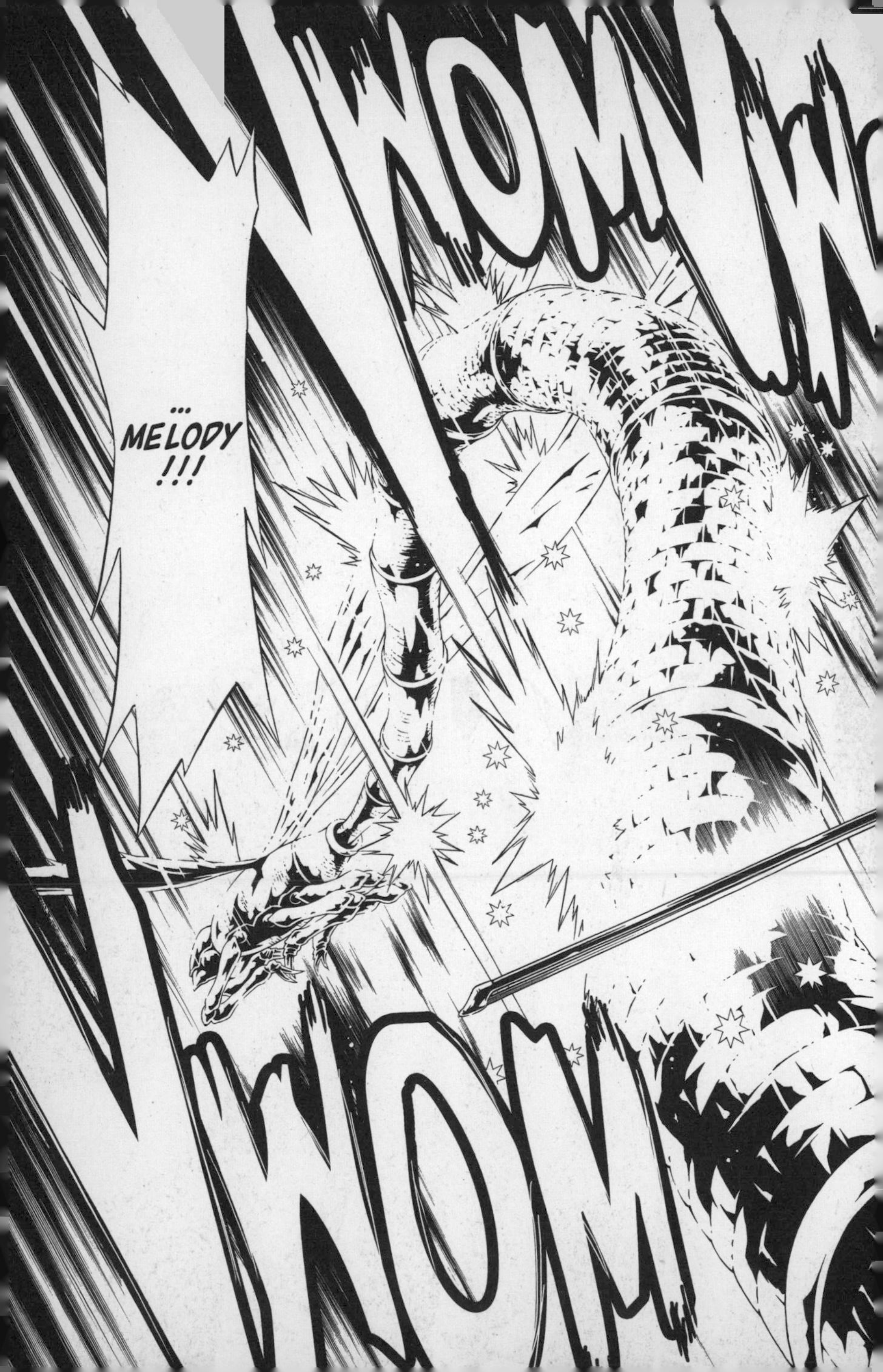
... MELODY !!!

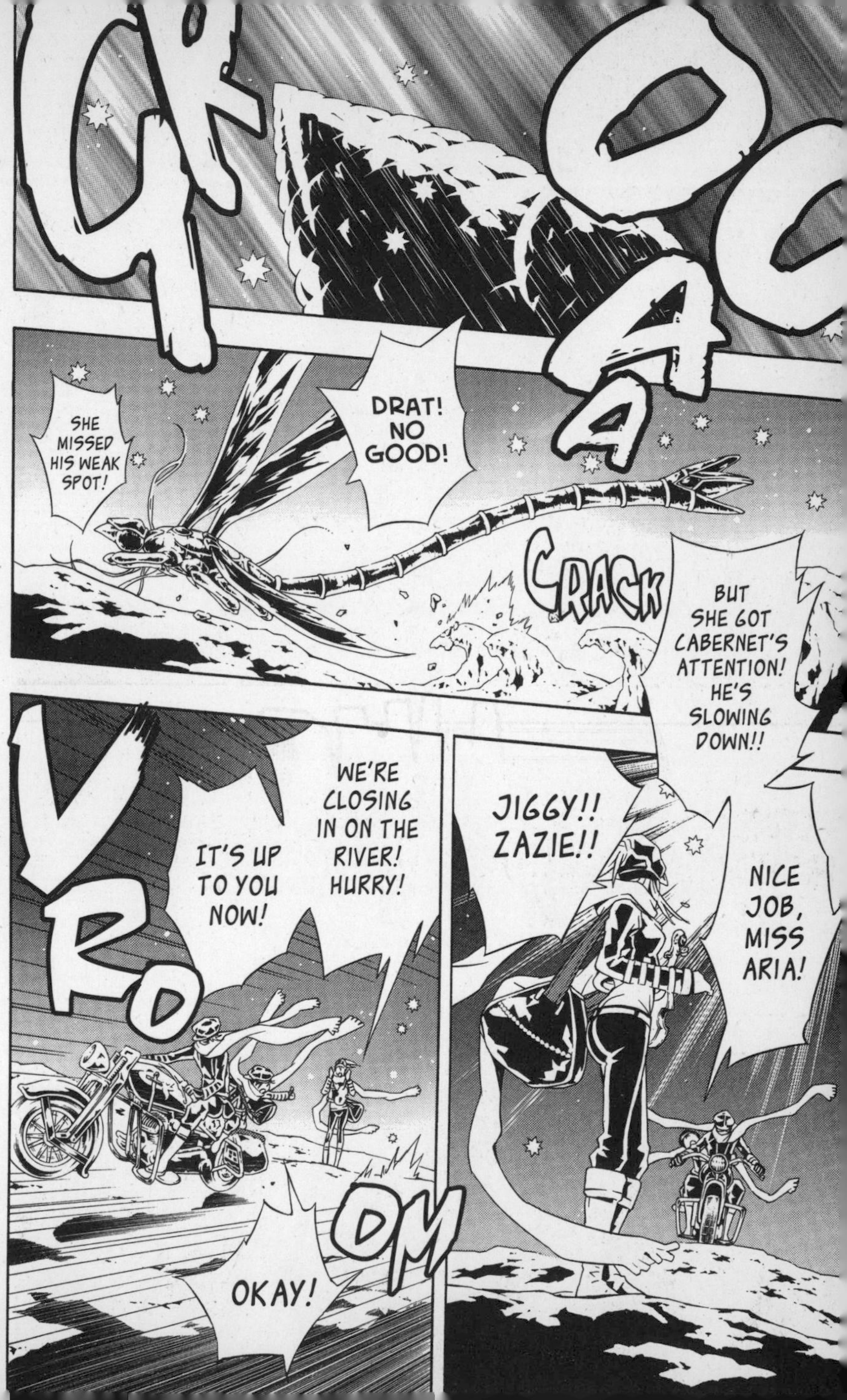
DRAT! NO GOOD!
SHE MISSED HIS WEAK SPOT!
CRACK
BUT SHE GOT CABERNET'S ATTENTION! HE'S SLOWING DOWN!!
NICE JOB, MISS ARIA!
JIGGY!! ZAZIE!!
WE'RE CLOSING IN ON THE RIVER! HURRY!
IT'S UP TO YOU NOW!
VROOM
OKAY!

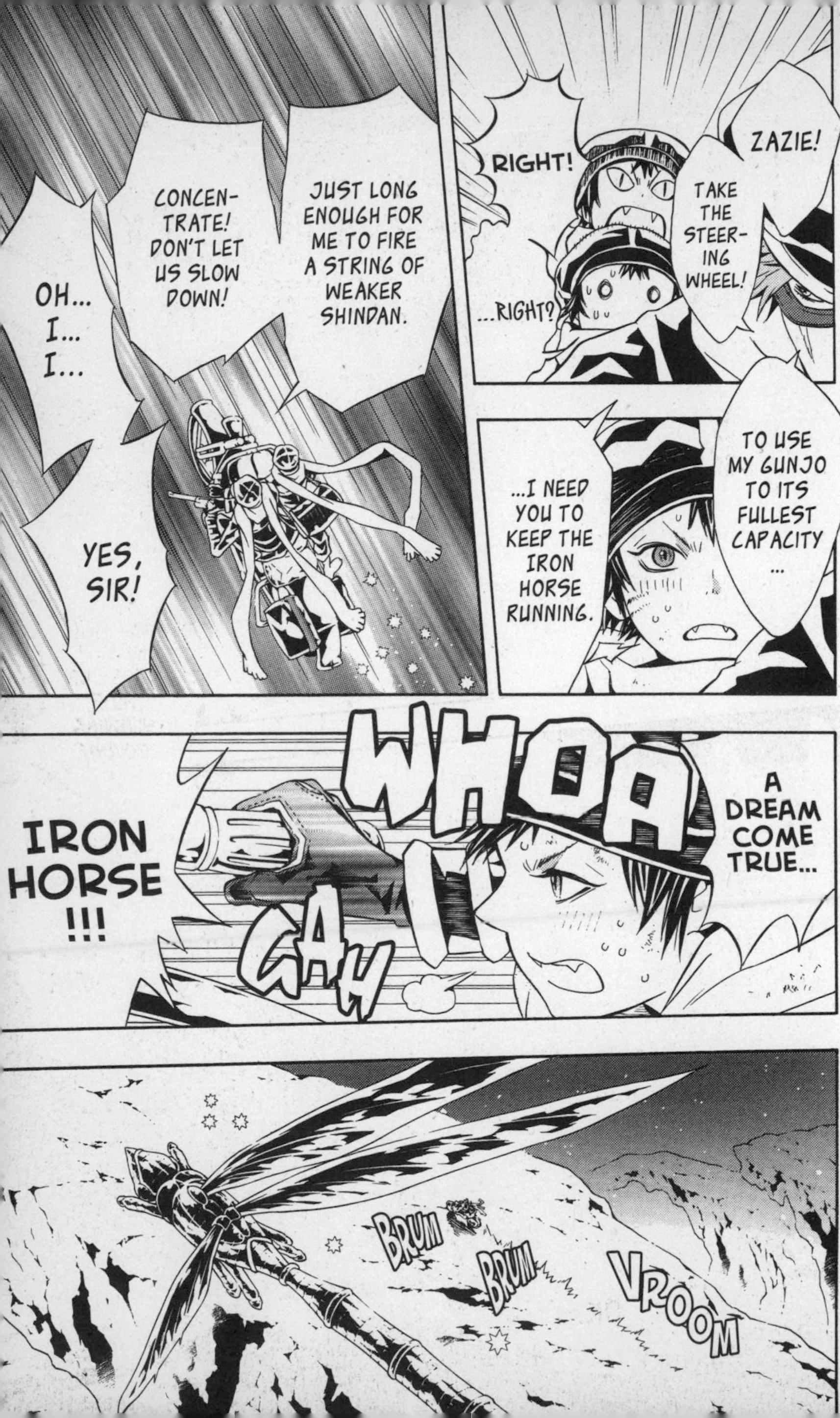
ZAZIE!
TAKE THE STEERING WHEEL!
RIGHT!
...RIGHT?
JUST LONG ENOUGH FOR ME TO FIRE A STRING OF WEAKER SHINDAN.
CONCENTRATE! DON'T LET US SLOW DOWN!
OH... I... I...
YES, SIR!
TO USE MY GUNJO TO ITS FULLEST CAPACITY...
...I NEED YOU TO KEEP THE IRON HORSE RUNNING.
A DREAM COME TRUE...
WHOA
GAH
IRON HORSE !!!
BRUM
BRUM
VROOM

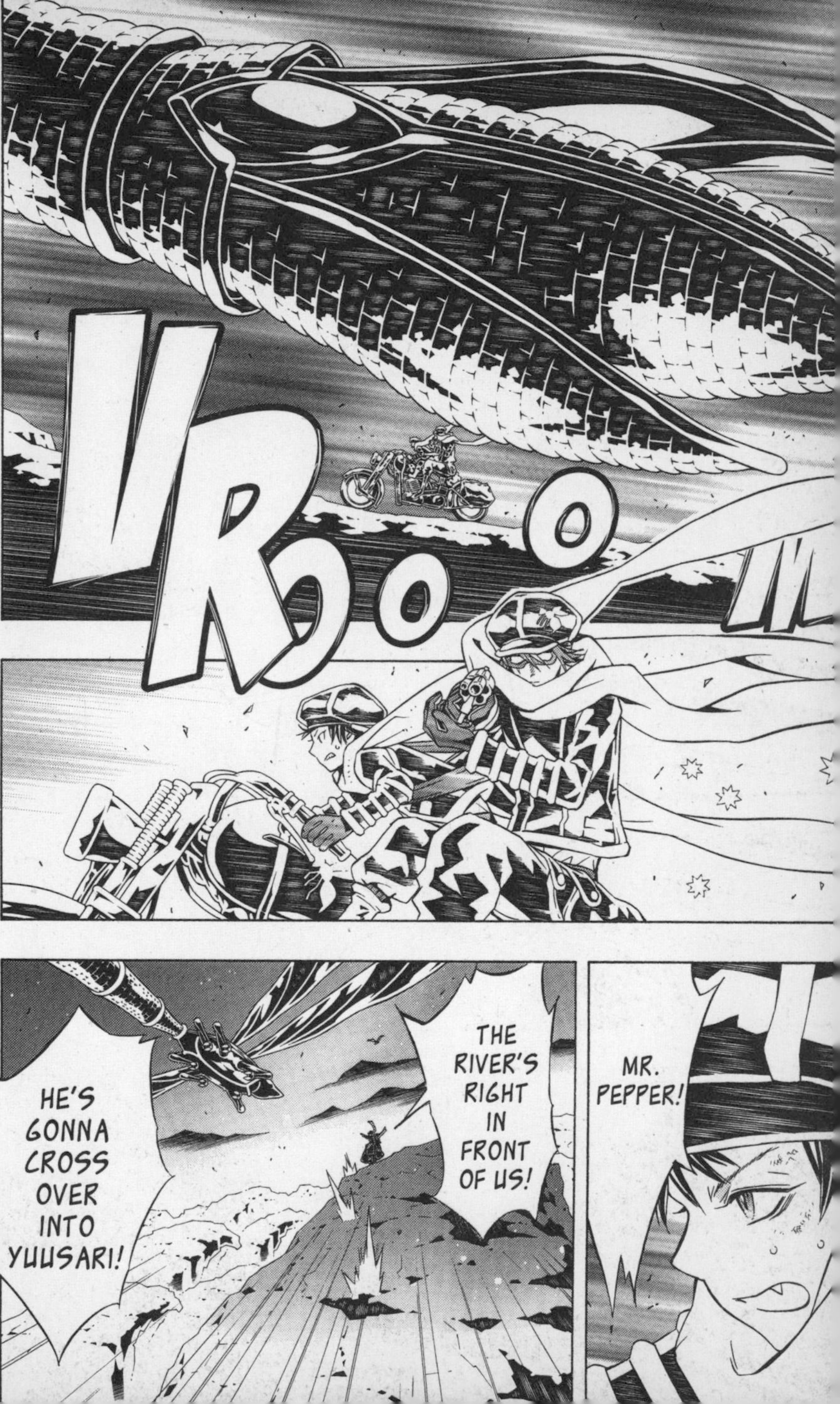
VROOOM
MR. PEPPER!
THE RIVER'S RIGHT IN FRONT OF US!
HE'S GONNA CROSS OVER INTO YUUSARI!

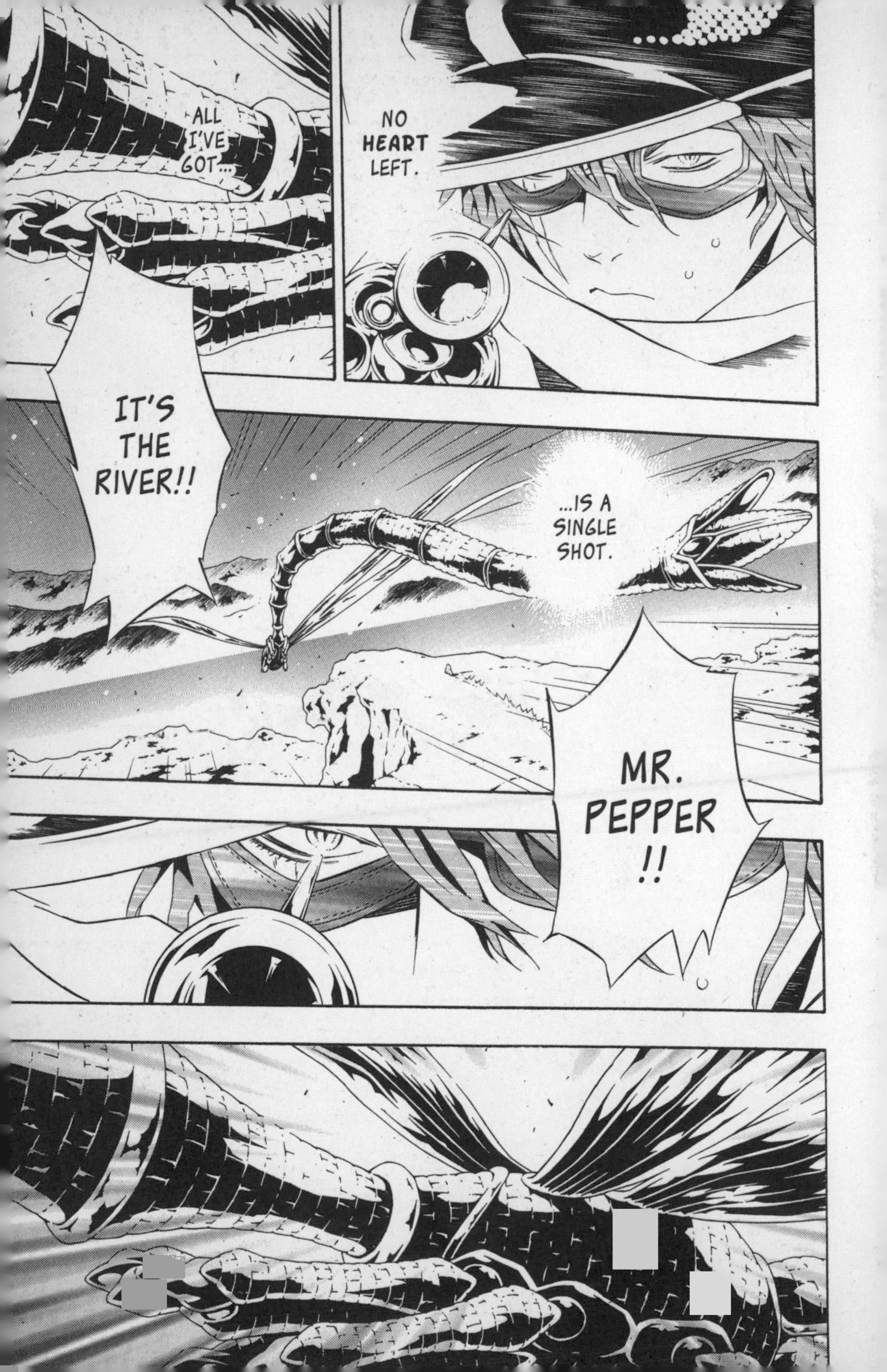
...
NO HEART LEFT.
ALL I'VE GOT...
...IS A SINGLE SHOT.
IT'S THE RIVER!!
MR. PEPPER !!

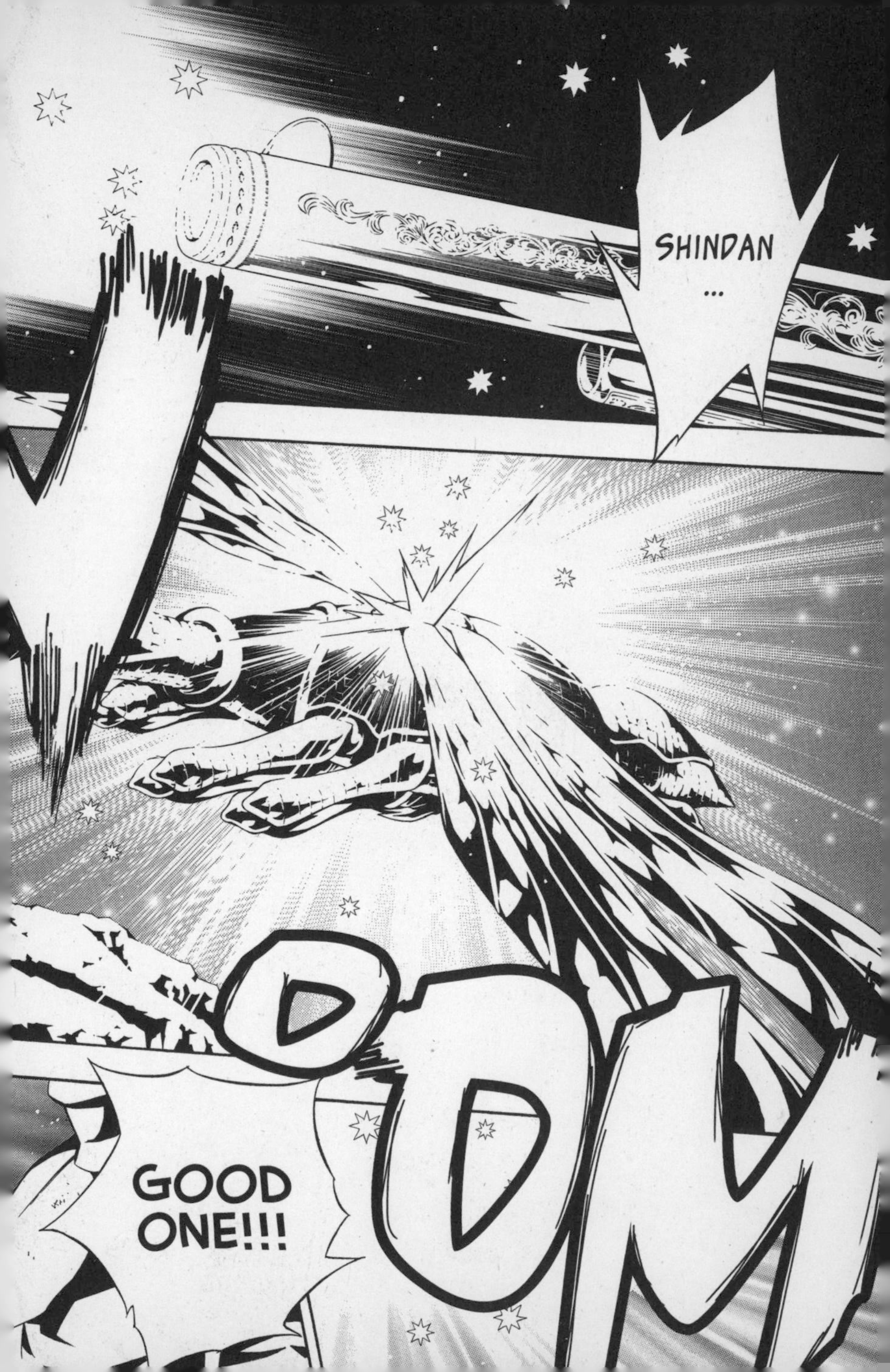
SHINDAN ...
GOOD ONE!!!

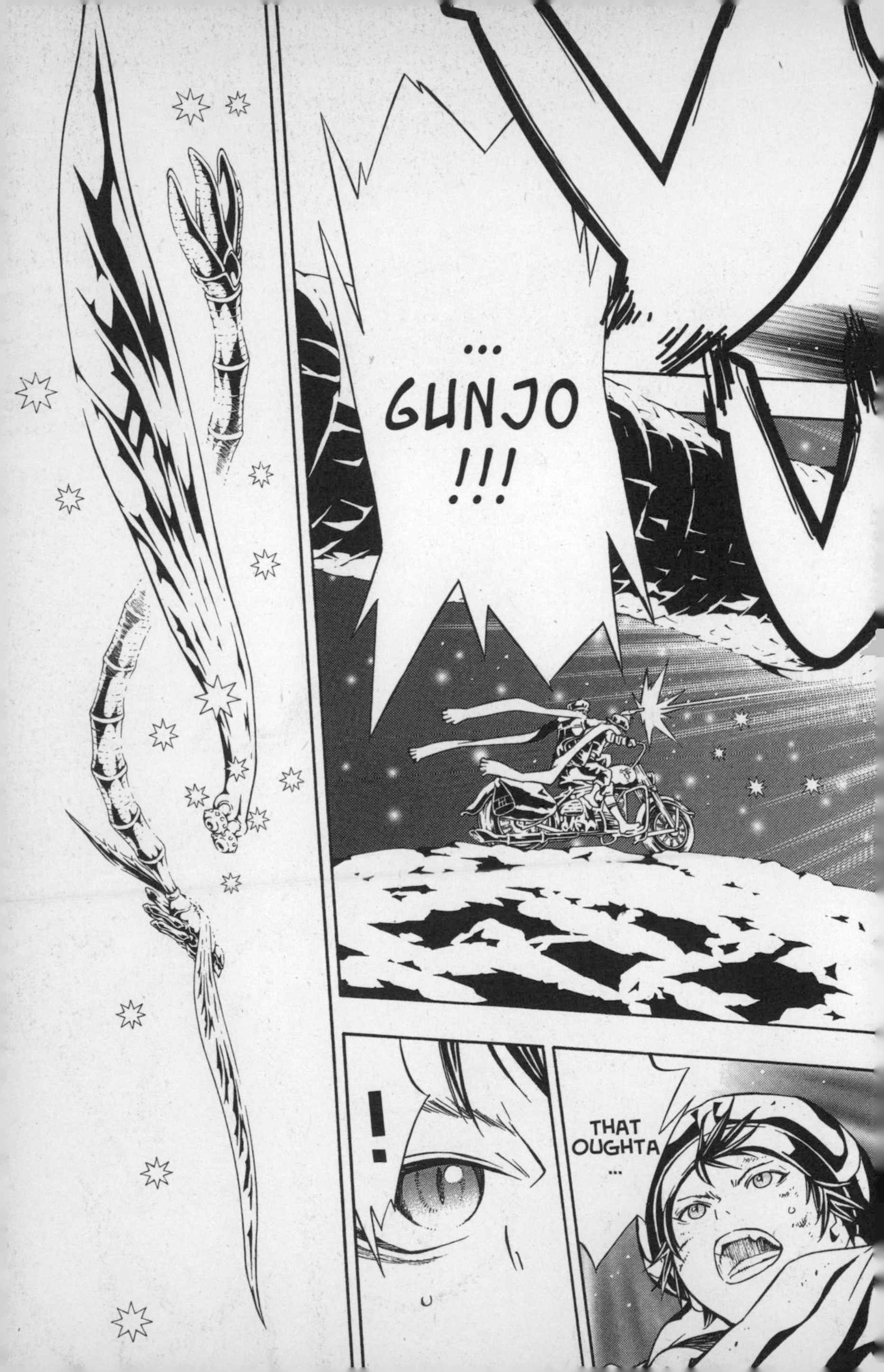
...
GUNJO
!!!
!
THAT
OUGHTA
...

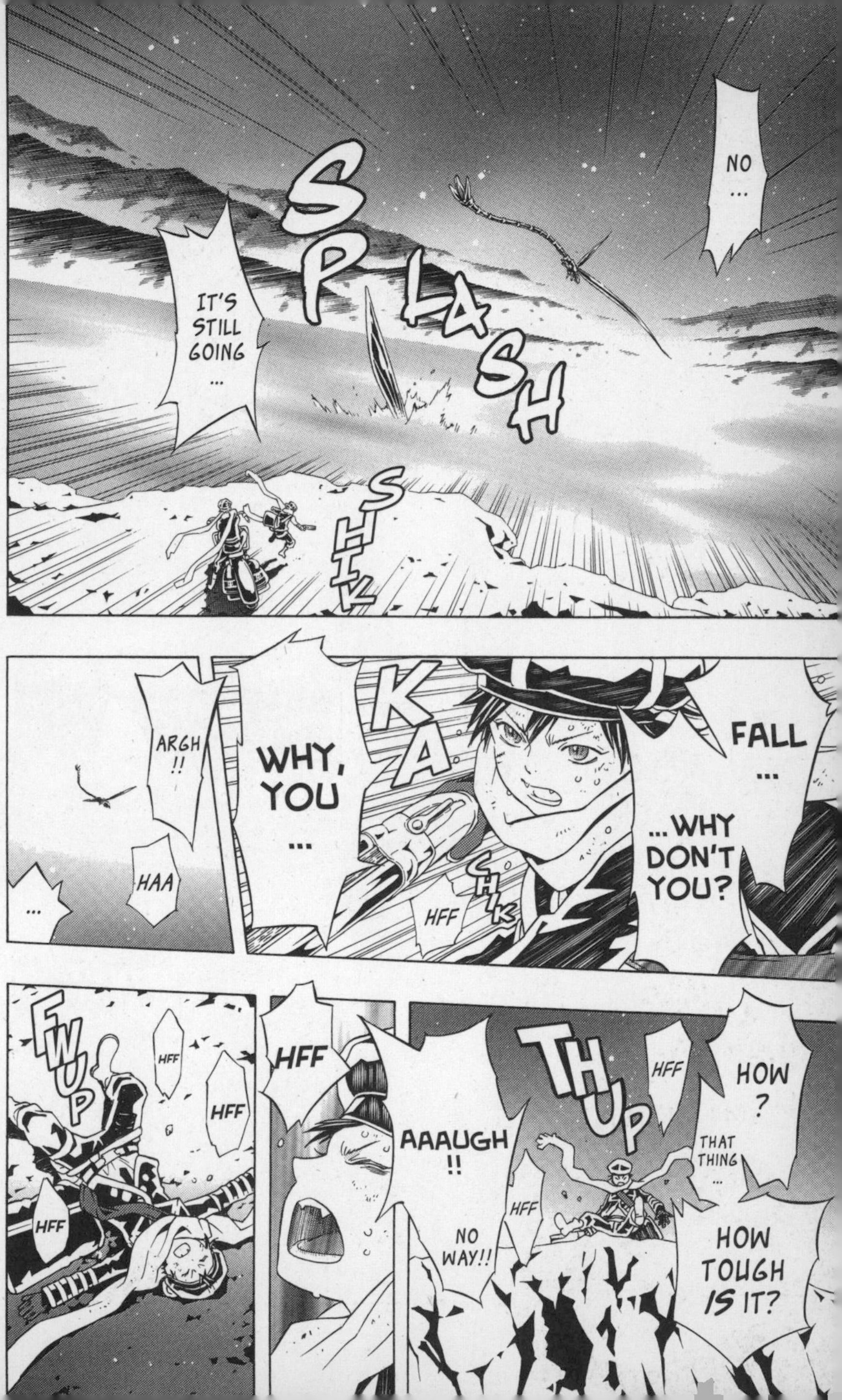
NO ...
SPLASH
IT'S STILL GOING ...
SHIK
FALL ...
... WHY DON'T YOU?
KA
CHIK
HFF
WHY, YOU ...
ARGH !!
HAA
...
HOW ?
THAT THING ...
HOW TOUGH IS IT?
HFF
THUP
HFF
NO WAY!!
AAAUGH !!
HFF
HFF
HFF
FWUP
HFF

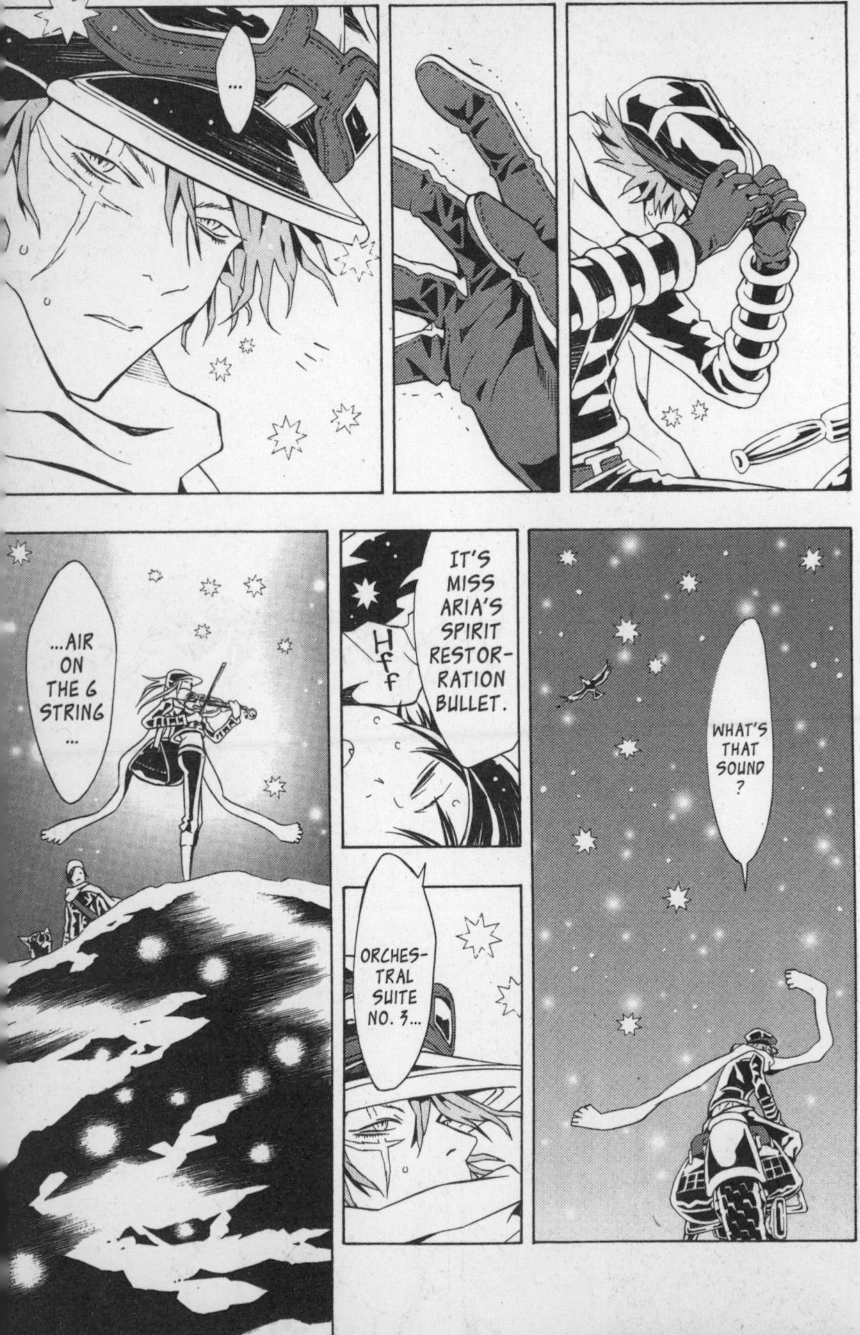
...
WHAT'S THAT SOUND?
Hff
IT'S MISS ARIA'S SPIRIT RESTOR-RATION BULLET.
ORCHES-TRAL SUITE NO. 3...
...AIR ON THE G STRING ...

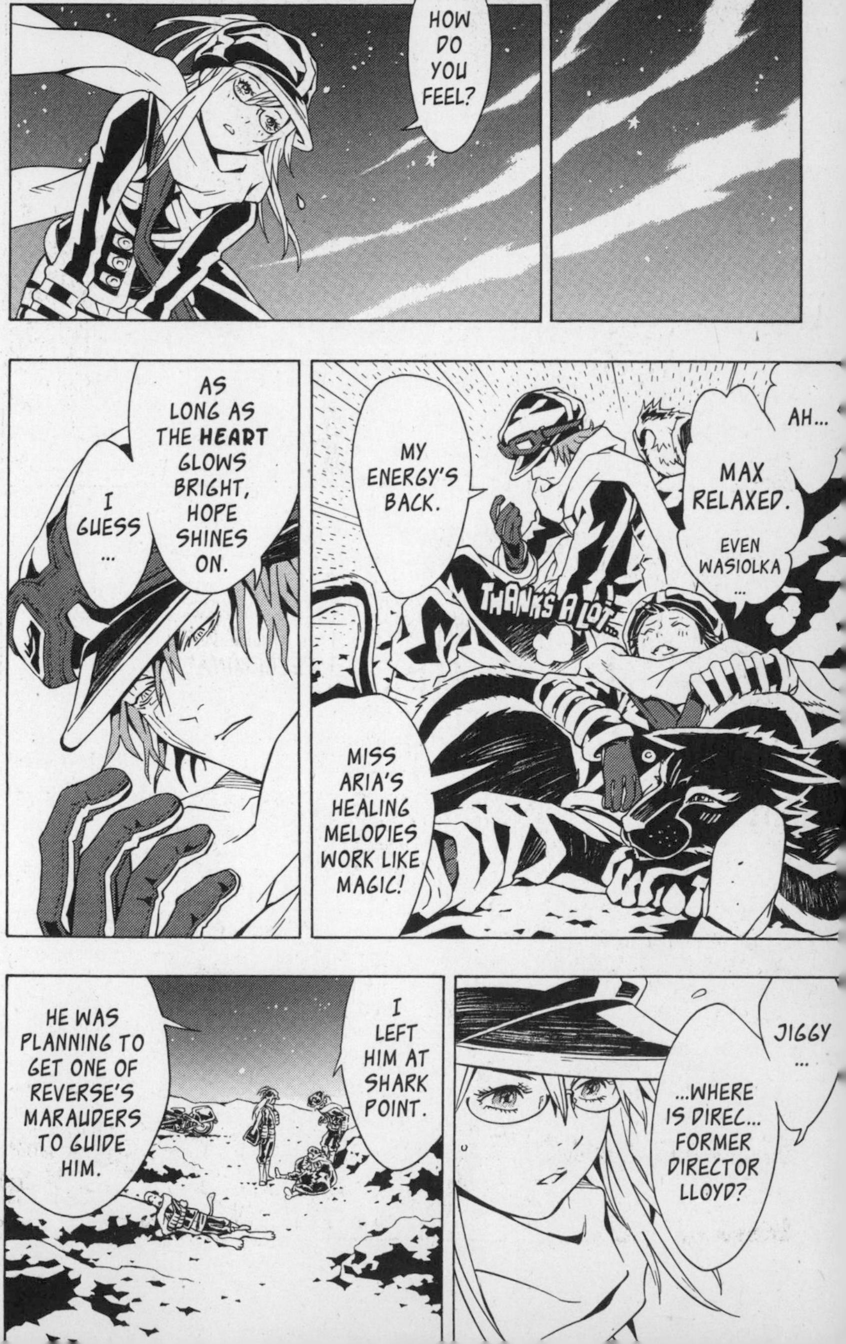
HOW DO YOU FEEL?
AH... MAX RELAXED.
EVEN WASIOLKA...
MY ENERGY'S BACK.
THANKS A LOT...
MISS ARIA'S HEALING MELODIES WORK LIKE MAGIC!
AS LONG AS THE HEART GLOWS BRIGHT, HOPE SHINES ON.
I GUESS...
JIGGY...
...WHERE IS DIREC... FORMER DIRECTOR LLOYD?
I LEFT HIM AT SHARK POINT.
HE WAS PLANNING TO GET ONE OF REVERSE'S MARAUDERS TO GUIDE HIM.

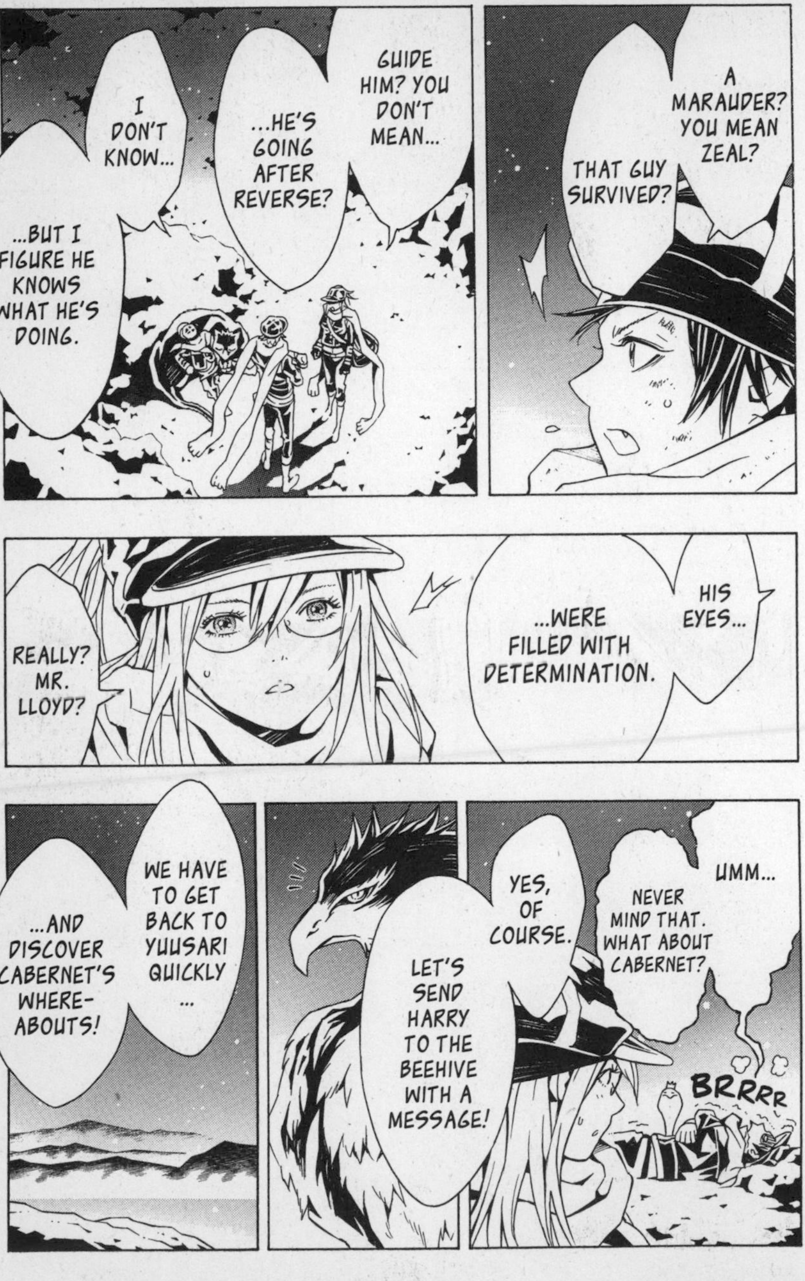
A MARAUDER? YOU MEAN ZEAL?
THAT GUY SURVIVED?
GUIDE HIM? YOU DON'T MEAN...
...HE'S GOING AFTER REVERSE?
I DON'T KNOW...
...BUT I FIGURE HE KNOWS WHAT HE'S DOING.
HIS EYES...
...WERE FILLED WITH DETERMINATION.
REALLY? MR. LLOYD?
UMM...
NEVER MIND THAT. WHAT ABOUT CABERNET?
BRRRRR
YES, OF COURSE.
LET'S SEND HARRY TO THE BEEHIVE WITH A MESSAGE!
WE HAVE TO GET BACK TO YUUSARI QUICKLY...
...AND DISCOVER CABERNET'S WHERE-ABOUTS!

KREE

MUMBLE MUMBLE MUMBLE

SHNUK

NUN! NUNO!

LAG!

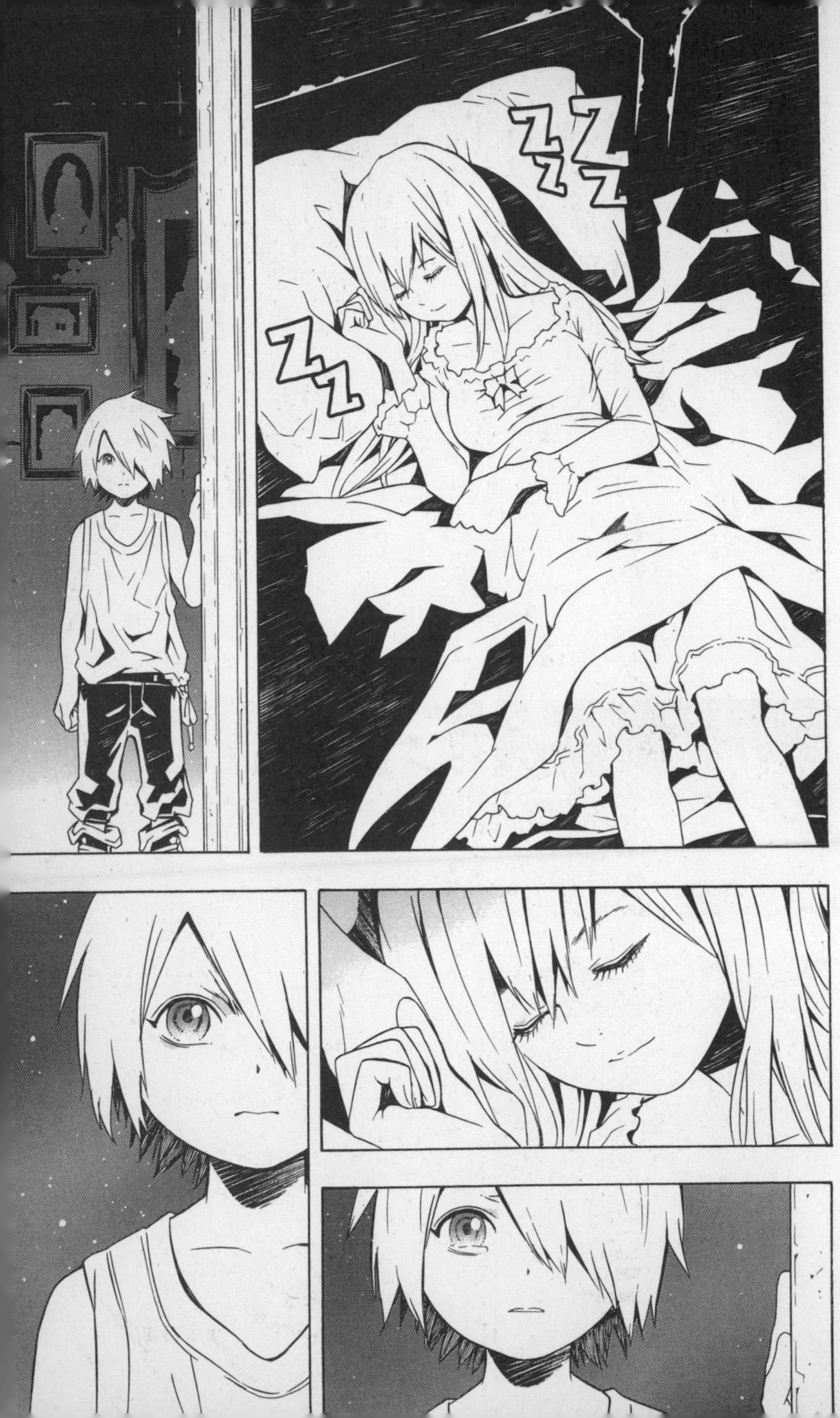
ZZZZ
ZZ

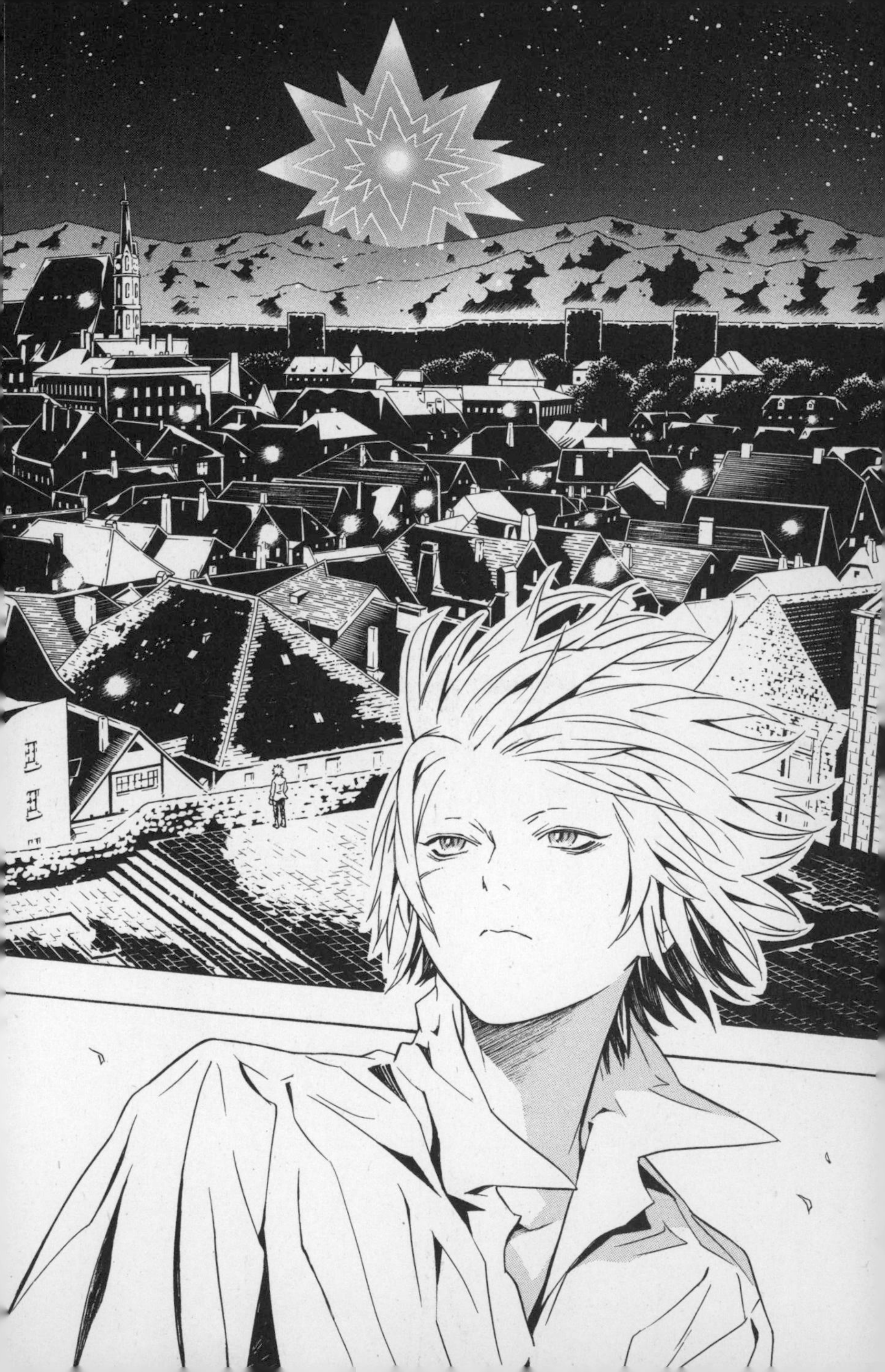

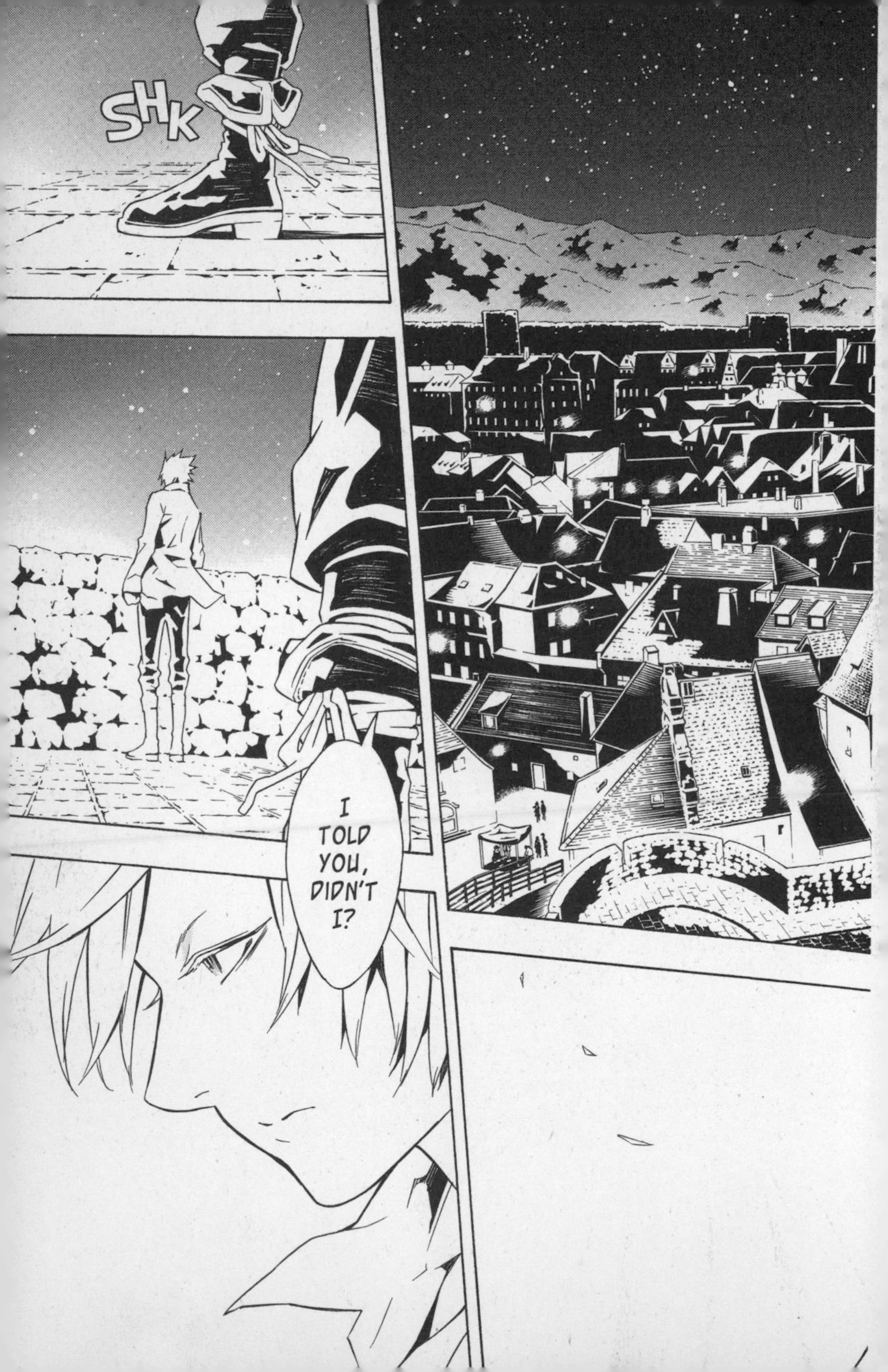
SHK
I TOLD YOU, DIDN'T I?

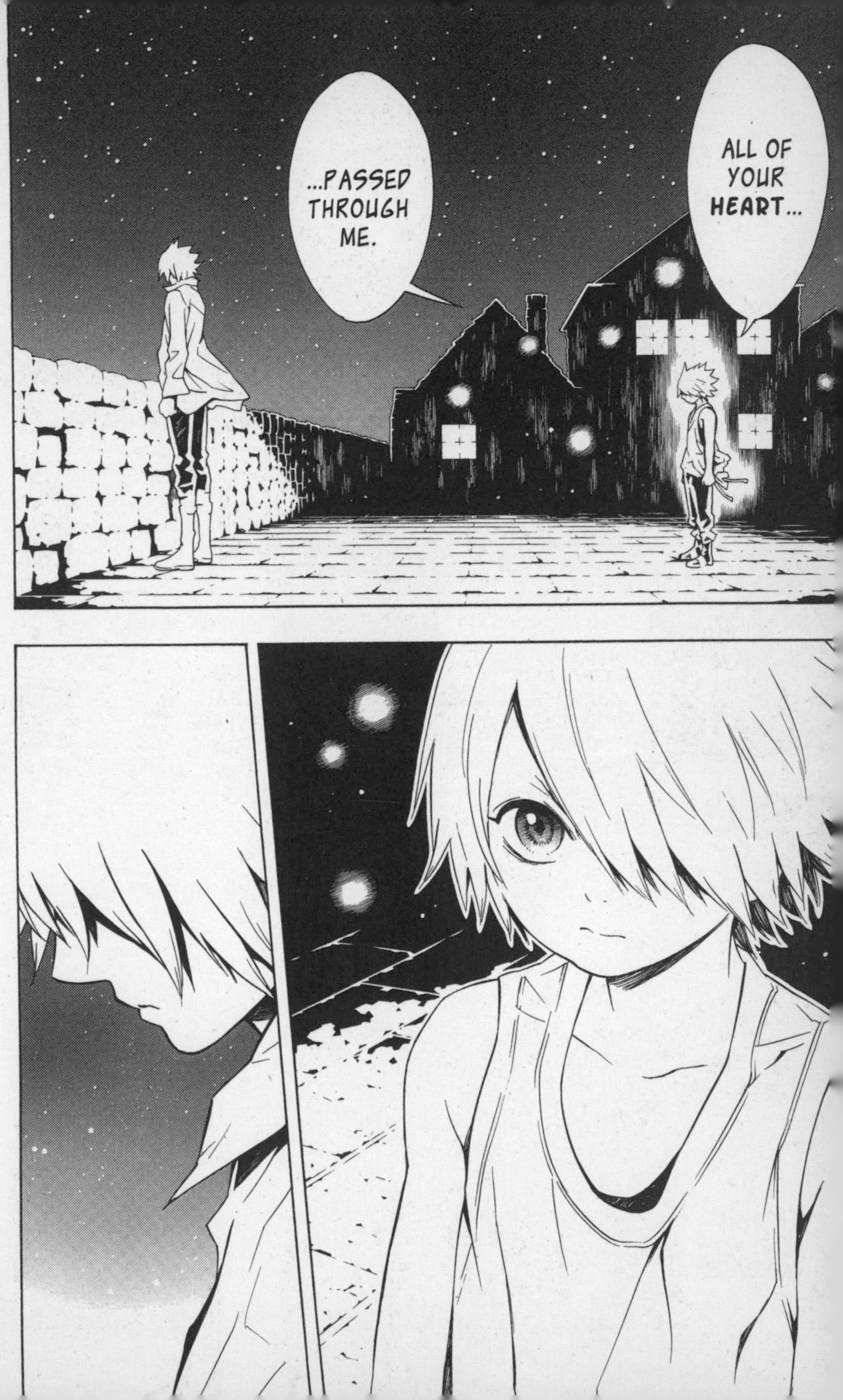
ALL OF YOUR HEART...
...PASSED THROUGH ME.

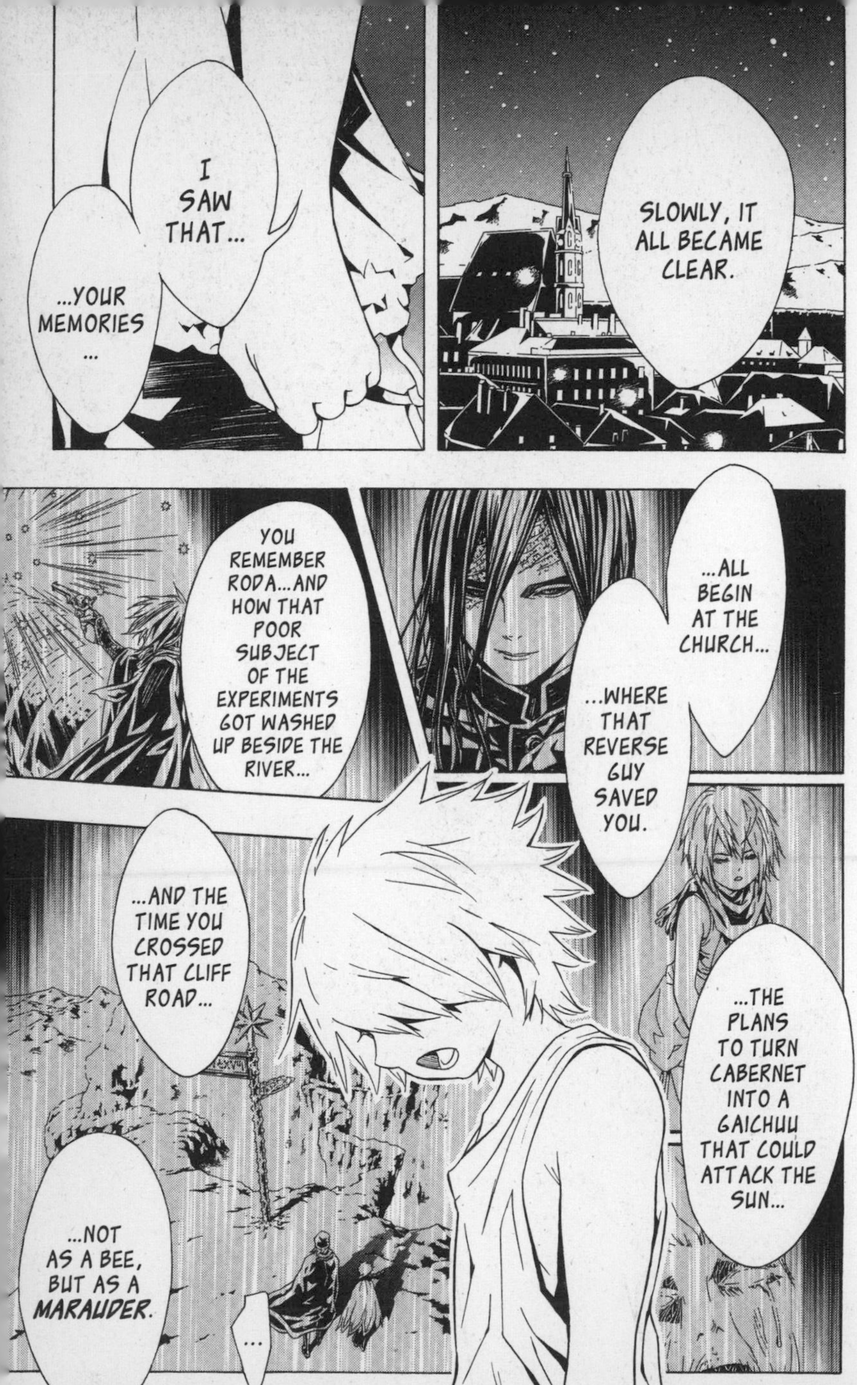
SLOWLY, IT ALL BECAME CLEAR.
I SAW THAT...
...YOUR MEMORIES...
...ALL BEGIN AT THE CHURCH...
...WHERE THAT REVERSE GUY SAVED YOU.
YOU REMEMBER RODA...AND HOW THAT POOR SUBJECT OF THE EXPERIMENTS GOT WASHED UP BESIDE THE RIVER...
...THE PLANS TO TURN CABERNET INTO A GAICHUU THAT COULD ATTACK THE SUN...
...AND THE TIME YOU CROSSED THAT CLIFF ROAD...
...NOT AS A BEE, BUT AS A *MARAUDER*.
...

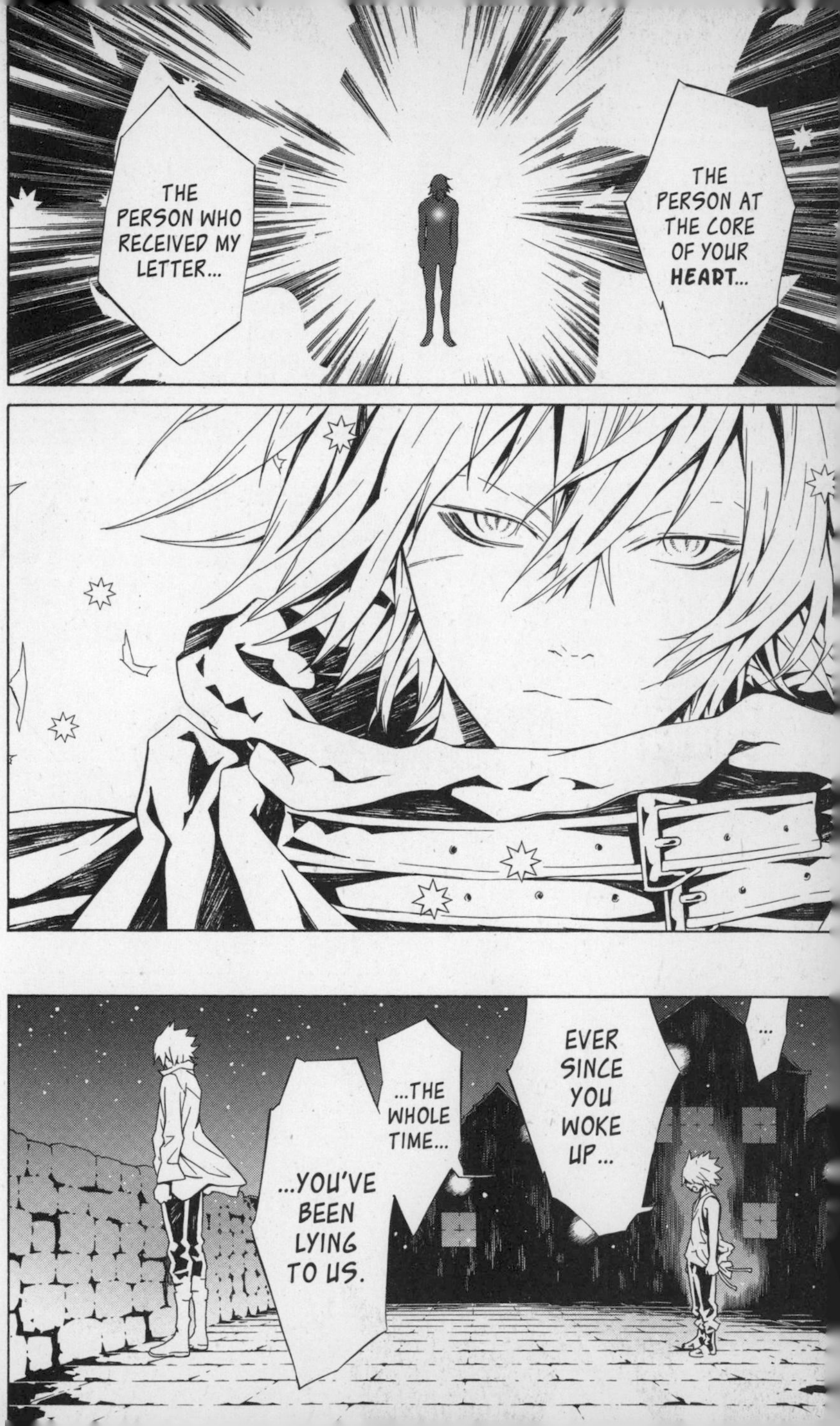
THE PERSON AT THE CORE OF YOUR **HEART**...
THE PERSON WHO RECEIVED MY LETTER...
...
EVER SINCE YOU WOKE UP...
...THE WHOLE TIME...
...YOU'VE BEEN LYING TO US.

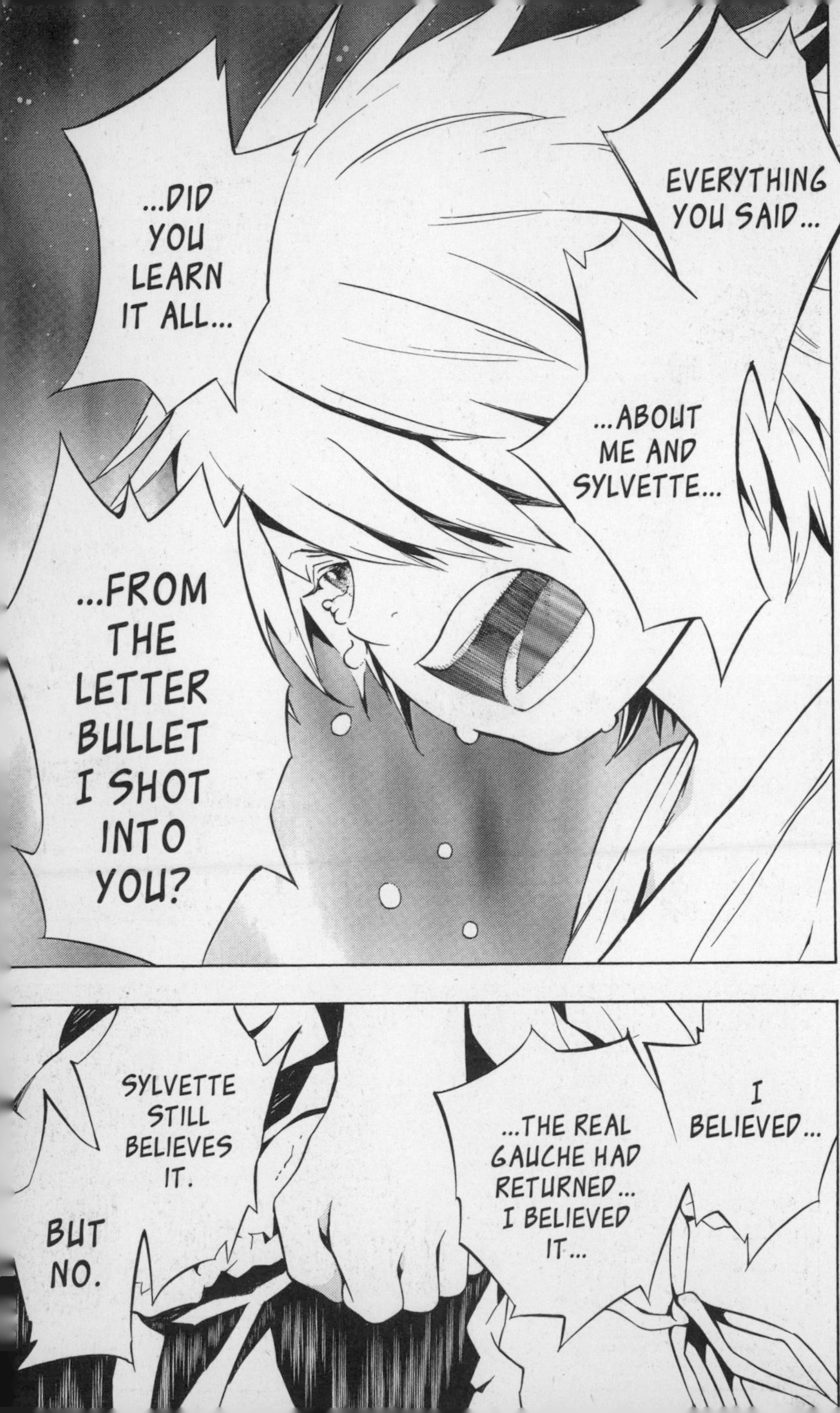
EVERYTHING YOU SAID...
...ABOUT ME AND SYLVETTE...
...DID YOU LEARN IT ALL...
...FROM THE LETTER BULLET I SHOT INTO YOU?
I BELIEVED...
...THE REAL GAUCHE HAD RETURNED... I BELIEVED IT...
SYLVETTE STILL BELIEVES IT.
BUT NO.

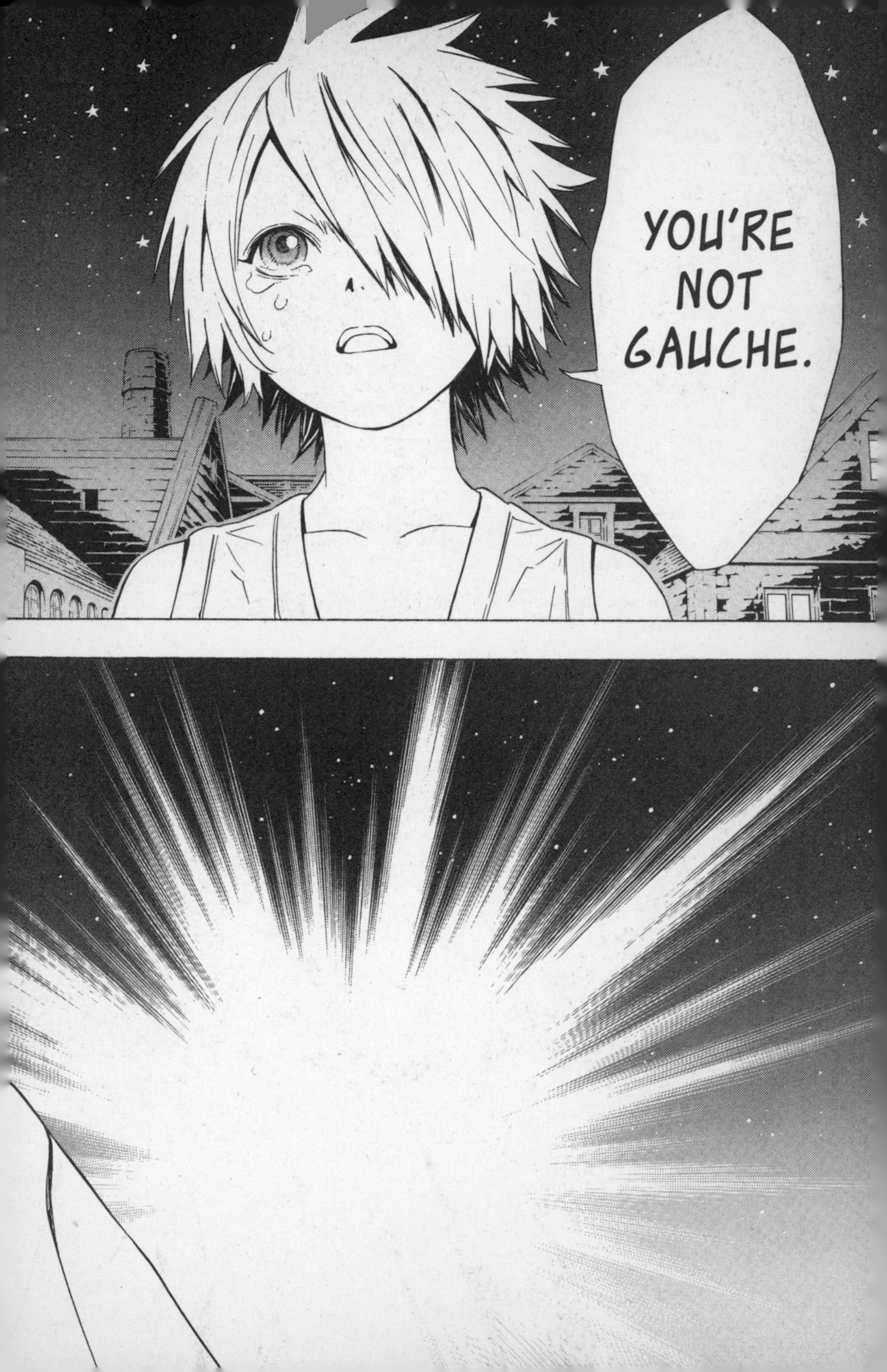
YOU'RE NOT GAUCHE.

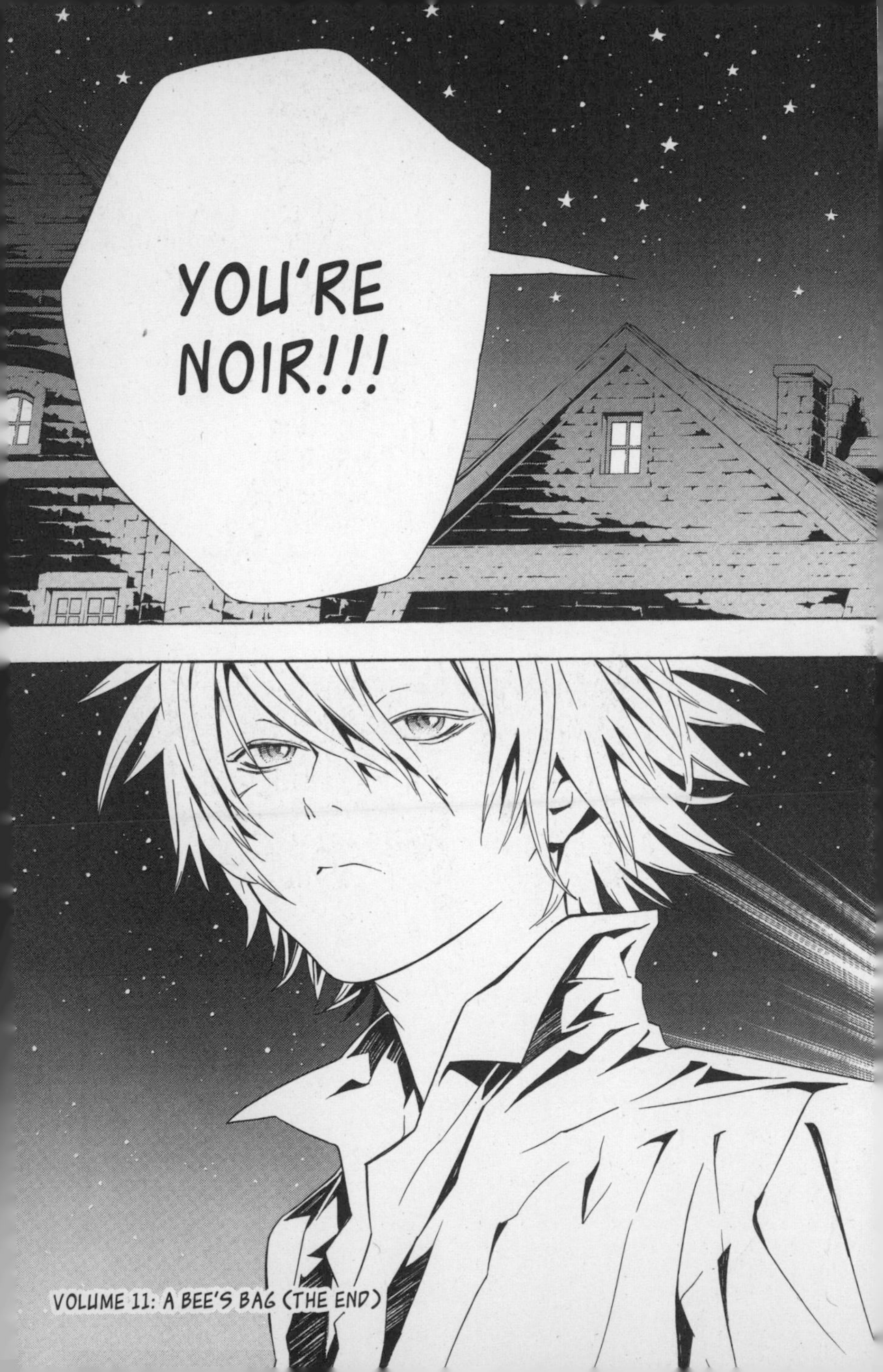
YOU'RE NOIR!!!
VOLUME 11: A BEE'S BAG (THE END)

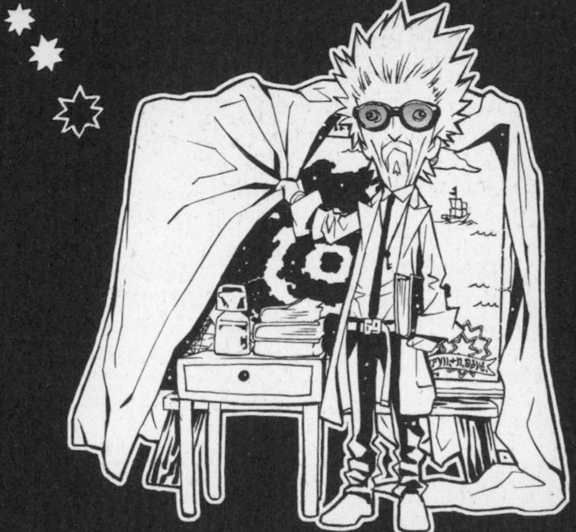

Dr. Thunderland's Reference Desk

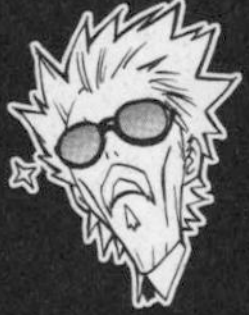

I am Dr. Thunderland.

Time has passed me by…and what with this and that, I've reached a point where I feel I shouldn't be forever railing against the injustice perpetrated against me. Do you follow me? That's right: I've given up on any hope of ever appearing in this manga.

My lab is thick with the air of lonely resignation. My life and lab are adrift from this book, a Beehive in another dimension, perhaps. I study and learn in a hazy mist. As I float through the void, allow me to address some of the matters introduced in this volume. And then I will get back to floating. I quite like the floating, yes. It makes me feel like I'm swimming. Swimming in a sea of not-being-in-this-manga.

■ WATERWAY OF DEATH

Whoa! Zeal's memory of the waterway is exactly as Lawrence described it. It's a dump for the test subjects of experiments at Akatsuki, our beloved capital. Clearly, the government's experiments have merged all sorts of things in an effort to create artificial spirits and spirit amber. Take that poor tree woman. Was she merged with a tree or a rock? I am a man of science, but I stick to the realms of theory. What could the government be thinking? Is this experimentation for its own sake? Or is there a purpose behind it? They seem pressed for time. Roda said that Gauche came not from the waterway, but from the light. What could this mean? Was he not dumped? Did he run away? I must study this.

■ MARAUDERS OF REVERSE

I wonder if Reverse has more people like Zeal. I guess those survivors with the strength to escape become Marauders. I feel pity for those who became test subjects, but using Cabernet to destroy the sun and plunge the world into darkness? It's the height of foolishness!

I wonder what Director...I mean, *former* Director Lloyd is planning. He certainly doesn't share much, but perhaps he will soon. How delightful for him. If only I had such an opportunity—but no!

nb: The Resentments / American roots band from Austin, Texas. Resoundingly called America's number one bar band.

■ A BEE'S BAG

It's not often we see a Bee without his bag when he's on a delivery. Lag remembered Gauche's words well. He has no doubt thought of them again and again from the days when he lived in Cambel, before he became a Bee. I can only imagine how happy it must have made him to hear Gauche say that he had become a real Letter Bee. Why, it makes me cry to see the two of them in their uniforms! I've followed this series from the very start, after all!

Even though I'm not in it… (That makes me cry too.) And yet… Hey, wait a minute! Gauche! What's this? You were actually Noir? Everything was a lie? How could you? How could you say those honeyed words? What…what… And Roda's still keeping an eye on things? That's it! I'll interview her for the next volume! And sneak snippets of my background into the interview! Pretty smart, huh? *Ahem!*

nb: shepherd's pie / English meat pie made with a mashed potato crust filled with lamb or beef.

■ MOC'S SHINDAN

Ew, gross! He uses the venom from his dingo, a king cobra, as a stimulant…and then he says frankly incomprehensible things. I'll bet the aftereffects of this technique are quite rough. This being Moc, I thought he'd say something like, "My shindan is filled with fragments of my sarcasm." *Hmph!* I don't know if you'd call it a Shindan or a Shindagger. The way he throws letters through doors looks like dagger-throwing, as I recall. What? You don't remember that? Go grab volume 4! It's on sale now! *Sigh*…I remember those days, back when I still had hope…

Try to remember me, folks! Where there's a will, there's a way! We must pursue Cabernet into the next volume! And it looks like a big one. They're sure to need some serious science by their side. And you all know my battle cry! (You don't? I've never told you?)

For SCIIIIIIIIENCE!!!

nb: Kick ass / Slang.
nb: Hell yeah! / Slang.

ALL MINDS ARE LOADED!!
SOUND!!
GREEN
BAILOUT!!!

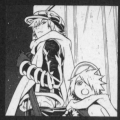

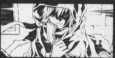

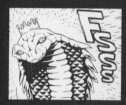

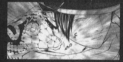

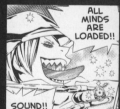

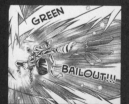

Route Map

Finally, I am including a map, indicating the route followed by Aria and the places Cabernet appeared in this volume, created at Lonely Goatherd Map Station of Central Yuusari.

A: Akatsuki B: Yuusari C: Yodaka

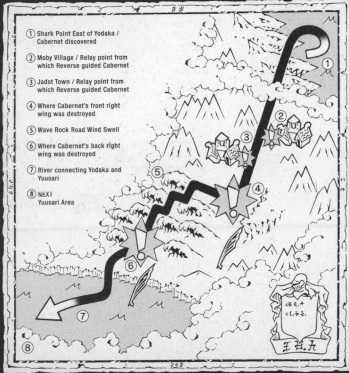

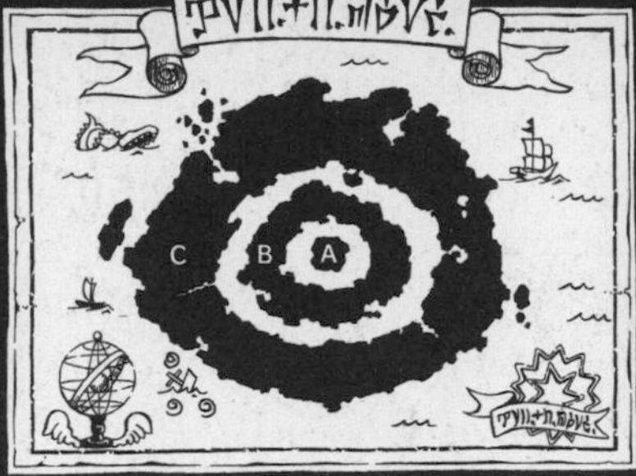
C
B
A

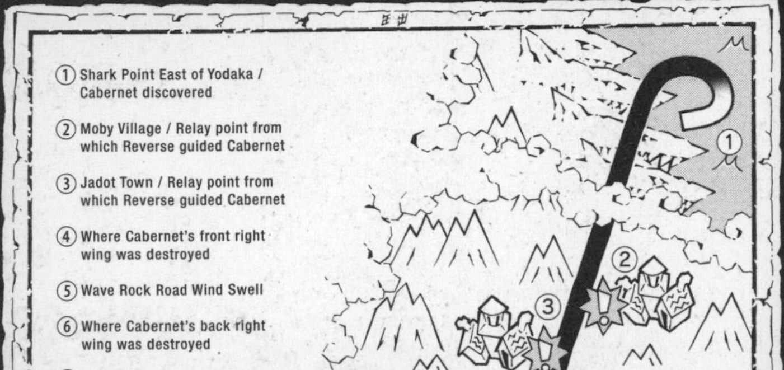
① Shark Point East of Yodaka / Cabernet discovered
② Moby Village / Relay point from which Reverse guided Cabernet
③ Jadot Town / Relay point from which Reverse guided Cabernet
④ Where Cabernet's front right wing was destroyed
⑤ Wave Rock Road Wind Swell
⑥ Where Cabernet's back right wing was destroyed
⑦ River connecting Yodaka and Yuusari
⑧ NEXT Yuusari Area
①
②
③
④
⑤
⑥
⑦
⑧

Not even I could steal the cover from Gauche and Lag this time. Hmm…I'll give them this one. But I'm not sure about volume 12… Heh heh heh! Be prepared!

My mysterious drifting lab may land on Yuusari out of the blue!

In the next volume...

Child of Light

Heartbroken by the revelation of Gauche's true identity, Lag finds that his troubles have only begun. Cabernet is about to attack Yuusari, and the Bees are called into duty to defend the city. Joining the battle, Lag discovers that his fellow Bees have started calling him the "Child of Light"...

Available February 2013!

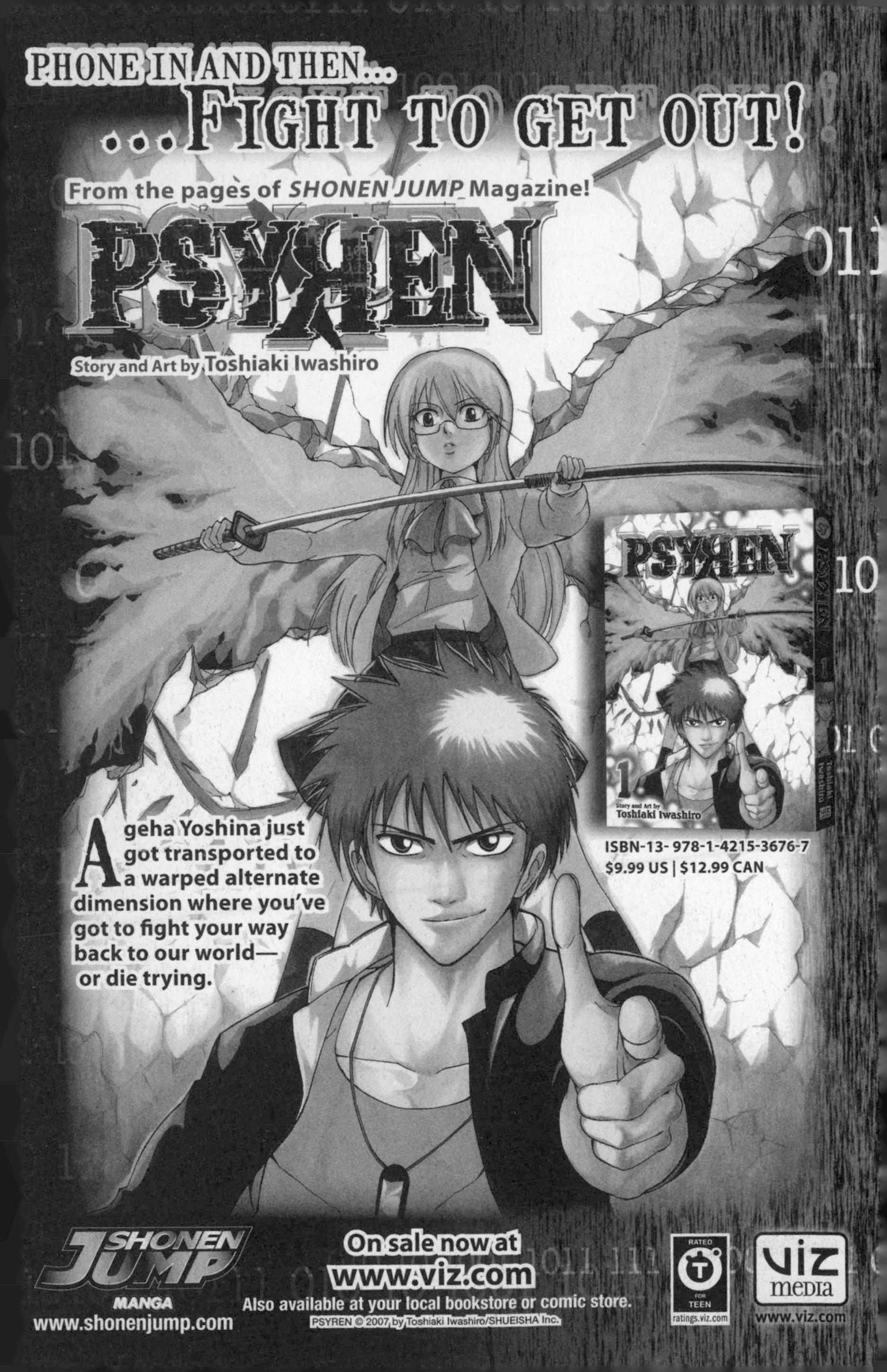
PHONE IN AND THEN...
...FIGHT TO GET OUT!
From the pages of SHONEN JUMP Magazine!
PSYREN
Story and Art by Toshiaki Iwashiro
Ageha Yoshina just got transported to a warped alternate dimension where you've got to fight your way back to our world—or die trying.
PSYREN
1
Story and Art by Toshiaki Iwashiro
ISBN-13- 978-1-4215-3676-7
$9.99 US | $12.99 CAN
SHONEN JUMP MANGA
www.shonenjump.com
On sale now at
www.viz.com
Also available at your local bookstore or comic store.
PSYREN © 2007 by Toshiaki Iwashiro/SHUEISHA Inc.
RATED T FOR TEEN
ratings.viz.com
VIZ media
www.viz.com

On my left arm I have a silver bangle with a skull on it;
I've worn it for about ten years now. It was made by a man
named Gabor, who looked a bit like Gobeni from the arms
shop and bakery called Sinners.

It is always with me and knows everything about me.

Just because something is of good quality doesn't mean
that you will use it for long or that it can be used for long.

However, if you use it for a long time a quality item will
turn into something simply precious.

—Hiroyuki Asada, 2010

Hiroyuki Asada made his debut in *Monthly Shonen Jump* in
1986. He's best known for his basketball manga *I'll*.
He's a contributor to artist Range Murata's quarterly manga
anthology *Robot*. *Tegami Bachi: Letter Bee*
is his most recent series.

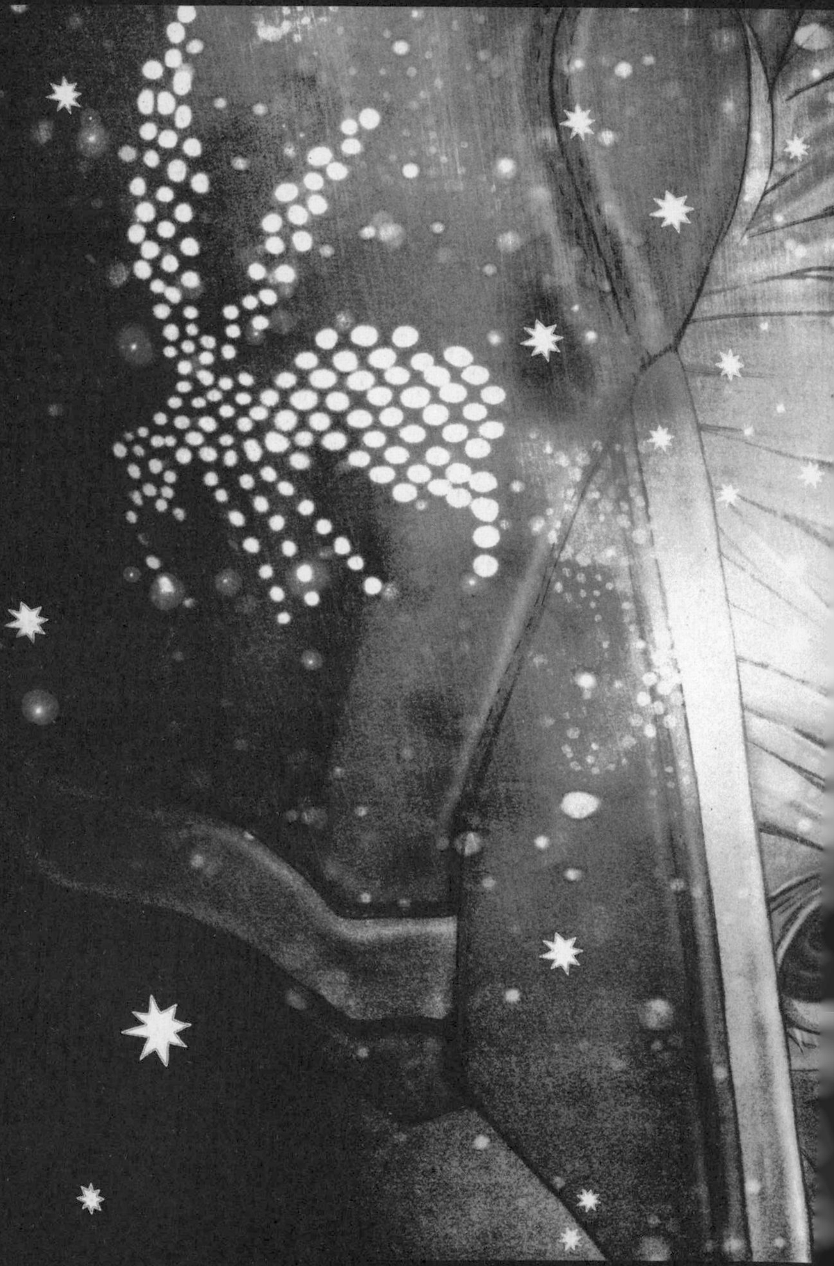